Reduce Warehouse Expenses

Over 700 Ideas, Concepts and Touchpoints
To Improve Your
Direct-to-Consumer, Catalog, Or
Wholesale Warehouse Productivity
&
Reduce Your Operating Expenses

David E. Mulcahy
with
Steven D. Ritchey

Published By: Logistic Planning Service, Inc
Published Via: CreateSpace
ISBN: 1449592937
LCCN: Pending

© 2009 David E. Mulcahy and Steven D. Ritchey. All Rights Reserved.

First Printing November 2009

YOU MAY NOT MODIFY, COPY, REPRODUCE, REPUBLISH, UPLOAD, POST, TRANSMIT, STORE INTO ANY RETRIEVAL SYSTEM OR DISTRIBUTE, IN ANY MANNER, IN WHOLE OR IN PORTION ANY TEXT, IDEAS, IMAGES OR OTHER MATERIAL IN THIS BOOK, WITHOUT SPECIFIC WRITTEN PERMISSION FROM THE COPYRIGHT HOLDERS.

Table of Contents

INTRODUCTION	i
THE OBJECTIVE OF THIS BOOK	i
HOW TO USE THE BOOK	i
THE AUTHORS' INTENTION	i
HOW THE BOOK IS ORGANIZED	ii
THE AUTHORS' OTHER REFERENCE BOOKS	ii
CHAPTER 1	1
SITE, BUILDING, MANAGEMENT TEAM CONSIDERATIONS	1
and COST REDUCTION IDEAS	1
CHAPTER 2	19
TRUCK YARD AREA & RECEIVING ACTIVITY COST SAVING IDEAS	19
CHAPTER 3	36
IN-HOUSE TRANSPORT, STORAGE & INVENTORY CONTROL COST SAVING IDEAS	36
CHAPTER 4	77
SET-UP OR REPLENISHMENT ACTIVITY COST REDUCTION IDEAS	77
CHAPTER 5	95
PICK ACTIVITY COST REDUCTION IDEAS	95
CHAPTER 6	134
PICKED SKU CHECK & PACK ACTIVITY & SHIP SUPPLY ITEM	134
EXPENSE REDUCTION IDEAS	134
CHAPTER 7	163
MANIFEST, SHIP SORT, STAGE & LOAD ACTIVITY EXPENSE REDUCTION IDEAS	163
CHAPTER 8	171
CUSTOMER RETURNS ACTIVITY EXPENSE REDUCTION IDEAS	171
CHAPTER 9	184
OFF-SITE STORAGE EXPENSE REDUCTIONS IDEAS	184
CHAPTER 10	191
VALUE-ADDED & PRE-PACK ACTIVITY EXPENSE REDUCTION IDEAS	191
GLOSSARY OF ABREVIATIONS USED	194
INDEX	195
About the Authors	205
David E. Mulcahy	205
Steven D. Ritchey	206
NOTES	207

INTRODUCTION

THE OBJECTIVE OF THIS BOOK

Using this book, you will learn about numerous ideas for expense savings, employee productivity improvement, enhanced space utilization and other ideas that, if applied, will justify the book purchase many times over. Our main objective is to provide a book that contains a wide range of methods and strategies for expense reduction, for increasing completed Customer Orders (COs), for improving employee productivity & space utilization, as well as insights & tips for a warehouse manager to make his warehouse more efficient with a higher throughput & more cost effective with a lower cost per unit (CPU). With ideas to reduce expenses, increase employee productivity, increase completed CO numbers & improve space utilization, a warehouse manager can convert his operation into a lean operation with minimal operational expenses.

Implementing the book's ideas, a warehouse manager can (1) reduce expenses & make budget, (2) can get a cost reduction incentive bonus, (3) can handle volume increases with lowest expenses & higher levels of complete COs and customer return process in the shortest time, (4) can make your operation lean with minimal operational expenses and (5) can change from a pick cartons operation to a pick eaches/pieces operation.

While, looking at any one expense reduction idea for a specific warehouse activity may only have a minimal impact on a your warehouse budget detail line or individual activity expense, when you add several warehouse activities with expense reduction ideas together, there is a significant impact on your total warehouse expenses that brings your total operation expenses back within or below budget.

HOW TO USE THE BOOK

Many of the book's expense reduction, throughput improvement, space utilization or employee productivity improvement ideas require a minimal cost. Each chapter covers a general area of warehouse activity and associated expense reduction ideas, insights or tips that are considered for implementation in your operation whether your warehouse is large, medium or small and regardless of whether your operation handles carton, GOH or small eaches/pieces. The book contains ideas that assist you in turning your warehouse into a lean operation by (1) reducing operating expenses, improving profits & lowering handling costs, (2) increasing completed orders, employee productivity and units per hour (UPH), (3) improving customer service, (4) enhancing sku, and return sku flows, (5) improving space utilization, (6) maintaining on-schedule shipments & deliveries, (7) reducing sku damage (8) improving employee safety and (9) assuring asset protection.

THE AUTHORS' INTENTION

The Author's write this book for people involved in the industry. As such it contains numerous abbreviations, terms and even slang used by managers, journeymen and vendors to the industry. A number of these, but certainly not all, are defined in the Glossary. In writing this book, The Authors' intention is to help develop the reader's skill and knowledge with specific application of ideas and concepts to reduce expenses and lower costs, increase completed orders processing, increase employee productivity and/or improve space utilization. Since the warehouse profession is constantly changing, the book may not include the very latest changes in the 'state of the art' and references to all the newest warehouse ideas, equipment applications & technologies. It is also necessary to recognize that a book can not cover all ideas, equipment & technologies in the warehouse field. The book can however, assist in staff training and in quickly obtaining the benefits of years of practical experience that has no substitute. It is important for a reader to use the collection of ideas and touch points as a guide. Prior to implementing any idea, insight and tip in your existing or new warehouse activity, if you want to be able to document the improvements, it is essential that you first measure or develop & project accurate activity expenses, sku, customer returns & CO transactions data, equipment layout, sku, CO & customer returns flows, employee & customer acceptance & design factors. Due to the actuality that the factors are the design bases for your proposed warehouse operation expense reduction idea, it is prudent for you to gather & review your existing and proposed change to a warehouse activity with your staff & employees, read vendor literature and visit existing facilities that utilize the suggested idea, insight or tip. The research permits you, your staff and employees to become familiar with operational characteristics of a proposed change or improvement idea that is under consideration for implementation in your facility. Any warehouse activity performance specifications, physical design and installation characteristics are subject to redesign, improvement, modification & are required to meet vendor, local governmental standards & specifications.

HOW THE BOOK IS ORGANIZED

Each chapter in the book deals with a key warehouse activity and the associated expense reduction ideas. The book chapters are sequenced to mirror a vendor delivered sku as it flows through the various potential warehouse activities, from stocking, to picking, to shipping, to return. To assist you in more easily achieving your warehouse objectives, each book chapter is focused on one warehouse activity & associated expense reduction ideas. This permits a manager & his staff to locate and focus on the most relevant or appropriate ideas, tips & insights for each warehouse. Each idea has a title, which allows readers to focus their attention on the specific warehouse activity over which they have budget expense & operational responsibility. If a reader is assigned to reduce expenses, improve customer service or increase the number of completed Customer Orders (CO), the book with its expense reduction, completed CO number increase, customer service improvement, employee productivity increase and space utilization enhancement ideas for each warehouse activity does assist a reader to develop ideas to achieve an expense reduction or lower CPU, customer service or increase CO & UPH objectives. Some expense reduction ideas are directed to warehouse equipment layout, sku, order, customer returns flows, employee productivity, when to use the 80/20 rule, where to locate your power 'A' moving skus, how to route your CO pickers, how to organize employee work for the best productivity & that your most important opportunities are the activities with the highest warehouse employee count and budget expense numbers.

Warehouse expense reductions, completed order increases, space utilization or employee productivity improvement ideas also impact the operations to increase accurate and on-time COs & improve profits. By implementing multiple expense reductions, throughput increases, space utilization or employee productivity improvement ideas, as outlined in the book, you can dramatically lower existing or new warehouse cost, increase productivity and minimizes new construction cost per sq. ft.. Regardless to the quality of any combination of warehouse operation improvements, in order to achieve major operations expense reductions, dramatic space utilization improvements or employee productivity improvements, may require capital investments in new equipment, new construction or changing from a manual operation to a mechanized or automated operation.

THE AUTHORS' OTHER REFERENCE BOOKS

The authors' other reference books include
    Warehouse Distribution & Operations Handbook
    Materials Handling Management
    Order Fulfillment And Across The Dock Operations Concepts, Designs And Operations Handbook
    Eaches And Pieces Order Fulfillment Design And Operations Handbook
    A Supply Chain Logistics Program For Warehouse Management

The authors would like to express thanks to all the warehouse, distribution, logistics, plant and IT or WMS program professionals with whom they have had an association with at various companies, as fellow managers, as clients, as a speakers at seminars and as publishers.

CHAPTER 1

SITE, BUILDING, MANAGEMENT TEAM CONSIDERATIONS

and COST REDUCTION IDEAS

ACROSS-THE-DOCK OR STORE & HOLD
    CUSTOMER SERVICE WITH MINIMAL OPERATION COSTS
Across-the-dock or store & hold strategies are a company's alternative warehouse strategy options. A store & hold strategy is a *demand pull* Customer Order (CO) Shelf Keeping Unit (sku) strategy. It generally requires or involves: a larger sq ft area, fewer dock doors, a square or rectangle shaped building, a greater employee number, a large warehouse activity number & largest sku inventory & sku numbers. An *across-the-dock* (a.k.a. Just-In-Time (JIT) replenishment) strategy is a *push* CO sku strategy associated with: smaller sq ft area requirements, a larger number of dock doors, an over-sized rectangle shaped building, fewer employees & smaller sku inventory & numbers.

CARETAKER OR PRO-ACTIVE WAREHOUSE PHILOSOPHY
    LOWER OPERATION COSTS
Warehouse philosophy options are (1) *caretaker management style* with a warehouse staff & employees use the same activity work methods & equipment that was used to start-up a warehouse. Another term to describe a caretaker philosophy is a rut theory or things do not change & it is difficult to lower a cost per unit/CPU. With an approach there are opportunities for manager & employees to test and decide to implement a new idea to lower your CPU & increase your units per hour/ UPH or (2) *pro-active management style* with a warehouse staff & employee's test & implement new process or activity work methods & equipment in a warehouse.

ALL YOUR EGGS IN ONE BASKET
    LOWER RISK MANAGEMENT & CONTINOUS CUSTOMER SERVICE
All your eggs in one basket is a warehouse growth strategy that considers your additional costs for buildings, employees, I T, warehouse, storage/pick equipment & over-the-road transport costs. A company's basic warehouse strategy options are one (1) warehouse that is expanded with I T, warehouse, storage & pick equipment, employees & transport vehicles to provide customer service from a single facility. A *not all your eggs in one basket* or a multi-facility (2 or more) strategy requires some additional I T, warehouse, storage/pick equipment, some additional employee activities & transport vehicles. The Multi warehouse strategy requires a larger building, additional I T, warehouse, storage & pick equipment & large employee number. In the single facility strategy, if there is an uncontrolled disaster or facility shut down, there is very high potential business loss with little or no customer service as a risk component. With two (2) or more facilities, one of your existing warehouses remains operational with I T, storage/pick equipment, employees & transport vehicles to provide service for the business once handled by both facilities. In the multi facility strategy, with an uncontrolled disaster or a facility shut down, with over-time or additional employees/vehicles the remaining facility provides services that minimize your business loss risk.

HOW DOES IT IMPACT YOUR WAREHOUSE
    MINIMIZE IMPLEMENTATION DELAYS OR COSTLY MODIFICATIONS
How does it impact your total warehouse is a reference to a change in one warehouse activity & its impact on other warehouse activities. During your idea or design phase, you determine your warehouse activity savings & impact on your sku & CO flows. As part of your warehouse project justification & evaluation, you determine your proposed sku & CO flow change impact on upstream & downstream warehouse activities. If you do not consider a

warehouse activity change impact on other warehouse activities, there is potential to have uncontrolled sku & CO surges, employee down time or travel path jams that reduce your warehouse activity benefits & return on cost.

WHERE TO CANCEL CUSTOMER ORDERS
MIMIMIZE I T COMPUTER PROBLEMS, CONTROL LABOR EXPENSE & ADDITIONAL SKU HANDLING

In a warehouse, there is potential for a canceled CO. If a CO is canceled in your host computer, your warehouse does not incur CO process labor and ship supply expenses. If a CO is canceled after release to your warehouse & canceled at a pack or manifest station, your warehouse incurs CO I T department process expense, CO sku replenishment, pick, check and pack labor expense & WMS identified sku re-stock expenses.

BIGGEST BANG FOR YOUR BUCK
LOWER OPERATIONAL COSTS

Most warehouses have a limited capital investment budget to purchase new material handling equipment or to change employee work methods. With limited available capital funds and prior to purchase, most companies require a capital project economic justification; a warehouse manager completes an annual warehouse budget, potential labor costs with associated expense savings, space savings & CO volume increase as capital justification factors. A warehouse manager ranks his potential projects based on each capital project lowest cost & economic justifications for highest labor & expense savings, space utilization improvement or CO increase. With a ranking concept, a warehouse manager places a capital project with lowest cost & highest economic justification in a first position due to a warehouse manager gets *a biggest bang* for his bucks.

WHERE DOES IT COUNT THE MOST & WHERE CAN YOU HAVE EXTRA TIME
CUSTOMER SERVICE

Where does it count the most & where can you have extra time statement is that your warehouse has a fixed employee number for your warehouse activities & your manager allocates labor and equipment to your most important warehouse activities. Most warehouse activities are (1) non-time flexible. In a warehouse, most critical & non-time flexible activities are your CO pick & pack activities that allows your warehouse to maintain your company customer service standard, more complex & completed within a short time period. In most warehouses, a CO/delivery cycle time period is typically 24 hours after CO receipt in a warehouse or (2) time flexible. Other warehouse activities are time flexible & include receiving, storage, customer returns & inventory control. The warehouse activities have a lesser critical time completion requirement & some activities are completed over an extended time period or schedule for completion on another day such as truck delivery schedule to have your receiving activity occur on a day with low COs.

WHO IS FIRST RECEIVING ACTIVITY OR PICK/PACK ACTIVITIES
CUSTOMER SERVICE

In your warehouse, on high CO volume days to have labor flexibility or ability to have employees perform different warehouse activities (another warehouse activity than an employee's regular activity and employee receives a higher wage p/hr) allows an opportunity for on-time customer service. During a normal workday, your warehouse activity sequence has vendor delivered sku activity to occur first and CO pick/pack activities occur second. Your warehouse activities are in response to a vendor delivery schedule or company sales, to some degree your warehouse does have some control over vendor deliveries & limited control over sales. Vendor delivery control is achieved by scheduling vendor deliveries to occur on anticipated CO low volume days & to have minimal vendor deliveries on high volume CO days. In most companies high sales occur on a specific week day & repeat or result from a sales promotion. With on-time customer service as a key to a going warehouse business criteria, your CO pick/pack activities have a higher priority than your vendor delivery/receiving activity. If your warehouse has scheduled a small vendor delivery number on an anticipated high COs or sales day, some receiving, in-house transport & storage put-away employees & equipment have potential for assignment to pick/pack activities such as fast pack.

PEBBLE IN A POND
BEST FACILITY & EQUIPMENT LAYOUT DESIGN

A *pebble in a pond* or a change made to one or several design parameters, a change impacts each warehouse or storage/pick activity with a WMS program and to have complete understanding you calculate a change impact on your storage/pick activities and building design parameters. Some specific design parameters that are (1) vendor sku delivery that includes pallets, master cartons or GOH, (2) CO number, lines per CO & associated pieces per peak day, (3) CO cube & CO/delivery cycle time, weight & sku mix, (4) warehouse storage/pick position bar code or RF tag label location & required line of sight or a radio frequency tag within a transmission range & (5) WMS program to completely understand WMS supported transaction locations and WMS identified sku & CO flows.

PICK THEIR MINDS
IMPROVE YOUR WAREHOUSE

Pick their minds is a phrase that describes what is done on a visit to another company's warehouse. Ideas gathered from your visit provide opportunities to improve your employee productivity, sku & CO flows, customer service & warehouse costs. During most warehouse visits or tours, you are guided through various activities. Most often activities follow a vendor sku or CO flow through process areas. As your spend time at various process activities or locations, your look at a work station design & employee movements. If possible you take pictures or obtain documents. Questions asked help to understand each process & work station unique characteristics. An important aspect is look for details such as bar code scanner/RF tag reader type & location, routing sequences, filler material & location, ship box type, position label features & elevations above a floor.

CUSTOMER ORDER/DELIVERY CYCLE TIME OR IN AND OUT WITHIN X HOURS
CUSTOMER SERVICE STANDARD

A company warehouse customer service standard is the time that a customer anticipates to receive a CO from a warehouse. When a company service standard is maintained by a warehouse, it means that a company has greatest potential for satisfied customers. A company warehouse CO order/delivery cycle time or in & out time is established by a company. Options are (1) hour or day number that a CO is received by a host computer and sent from a warehouse to a CO delivery address or (2) hour or day number that a CO is received by a warehouse and sent from a warehouse to a CO delivery address.

SIS OR SHORT INTERVAL SCHEDULE
IMPROVE PICKER/PACKER & OTHER LABOR PRODUCTIVITY

SIS or short interval schedule is your warehouse supervisor method to track employee activity performance for a manual and repetitive activity such as in-house transport, replenishment & pick activity. After an employee is given a task/sku volume & based on your budgeted productivity rate, your supervisor estimates an employee completion time or time to return for another task/new sku volume. An estimated completion time is noted onto a paper document or entered into a PC & when an employee completes a task/sku volume, an actual time is noted on a paper document or PC & your supervisor determines low productive employees.

OVER-TIME IN THE MORNING OR AFTERNOON
LOWER OPERATIONAL COST & IMPROVE CUSTOMER SERVICE

When a company's sales plan has scheduled a promotion sku or actual sku sales exceeds budgeted/projected sales & to maintain a company customer service standard, a warehouse requires additional employee hours to complete COs. A warehouse manager employee over-time options are (1) in the morning before a warehouse standard start-up time. With a full or skeleton employee number, a warehouse has a warm start-up and greater opportunity to have a larger CO number arrive at a freight company terminal for CO delivery or COs out the door & (2) in the afternoon after a standard work day end. With a full or partial employee number, a warehouse has an opportunity to have COs out the door but arrive late at a freight terminal for CO delivery that means COs are held at a terminal & your company has off-standard customer service. With few delivery trucks loaded at a warehouse, first option has a greater impact on a greater number of customers receiving a company's customer service standard.

LOOK AT YOUR NUMBERS & EMPLOYEES
LOWER OPERATIONAL COSTS

When reviewing your warehouse for expense reduction or customer service improvement opportunities, you look at your warehouse numbers or employees. Critical warehouse numbers are (1) activities that have greatest employee number. An improvement in activities or units per hour (UPH) reduces an employee number & wage expense & (2) activities that have a re-occurrence of errors such as overages (overs), shortages (shorts), damaged goods (damages) or late delivery. Improvement activity has greatest impact on an operation labor expense or customer service standard. Suggested activities are pick/pack activities.

LOOK AT TODAY BUT PREPARE FOR TOMORROW
LOWER OPERATION COST

To design your warehouse sku & CO flows, equipment layout and activity stations, your warehouse design team attains a balance to satisfy today's warehouse sku & CO requirements but prepares for your warehouse future volumes. With a flexible design, your existing warehouse design is modified to satisfy today's volumes & tomorrow sku & CO volumes with minimal interruption to your existing warehouse sku & CO flows.

MINIMIZE PEAKS & VALLEYS BUT SMOOTH WORK LEVEL
IMPROVE EMPLOYEE PRODUCTIVITY & EQUIPMENT UTILIZATION

To assure a constant sku & CO flow, high employee productivity & on-time customer service, your warehouse manager minimizes vendor delivered sku & CO peaks and valleys. Minimize peaks or valleys assures a smooth sku & CO flow more evenly over a work week that enhances your warehouse to obtain budgeted employee productivity & equipment utilization. Opportunities are to (1) change from a 5 day work week to a 6 day work week or (2) shift work between week days to have a more even work volume for each work day. If you schedule your receiving activity, vendor delivery truck assignment is more easily realized or your vendor truck deliveries becomes even over your workweek. With your CO pick/pack activities, a potential opportunity is to pre-pack high single sku volume on low volume days. This permits high pick/pack productivity on high volume days.

HAVE ENOUGH WORK
IMPROVE EMPLOYEE PRODUCTIVITY & EQUIPMENT UTILIZATION

To have an efficient & cost effective warehouse that achieves your budgeted CPU for each employee activity, your warehouse manager schedules sufficient productive work, sku & COs. If there is insufficient work, your warehouse manager schedules employees to other productive warehouse activities, participate in non-productive activity, complete pre-pack activity or grant employees non-paid time off.

REPETITIVE ACTIVITES
LOWER OPERATIONAL COST

Your warehouse repetitive activities are employee activities that are repeated by an employee to complete a sku or CO transaction. Looking at your warehouse repetitive activities & understanding how, what, where & why an employee performs an activity leads to potential labor productivity improvement. By eliminating an activity or reducing an employee physical effort means an increase in skus & COs per hour. Examples are (1) bar code scanning a sku & CO. For a CO single sku quantity activity, to complete bar code scan or RF tag read transaction a pick/pack employee enters 1 sku into a scanner device. To have a bar code scanner defaulted to 1 quantity, eliminates an employee physical activity to enter a transaction into a scanner device. Your labor savings is pick & pack CO single scan transaction entries that are used to offset a scanner modification, (2) folding a CO pack slip to nicely fit onto a sku top in a ship carton. For medium to large CO ship cartons, to place a CO pack slip flat onto a sku top saves an employee pack slip folding effort or employee time to fold a pack slip, (3) using sheet paper filler material concept on an elevated shelf within your employee's reach & above your highest volume carton height, savings result from an employee not moving a carton to reach a filler paper that is a simple pull from a shelf activity, (4) using pre-bagged filler material (peanuts/shredded paper) rather than loose peanut filler material, reduces an employee physical effort to transfer filler material into a ship carton & eliminates a messy work station at a pack station, at a customer returns process station and at a CO delivery location & (5) at a check, pack or CO returns process station, an elevated fixed position bar code scanner (removable and set at an elevation for your sku majority) reduces an employee physical effort reach & turn-on a bar code scanner.

EMPLOYEE TEAM
LOWER OPERATION COSTS & MINIMIZE CHANGE PROBLEMS

When considering making a change to an employee activity with an activity new work method or equipment and with an employee team concept, your warehouse manager explains to an employee group an activity new work method or equipment prior to implementation in an employee group or work area. A warehouse manager knowing an informal employee team leader & selling an activity new work method or equipment to a team leader improves an opportunity for a quick & simple implementation. The practice helps to lessen an employee learning curve (become more productive in a shorter time period) & enhances employee acceptance.

LISTEN, WATCH & WORK WITH YOUR EMPLOYEES
LOWER OPERATION COSTS & INCREASE EMPLOYEE PRODUCTIVITY

Listen, watch and work with your employees at their work stations such as pick, pack, check & customer returns process gives a your manager insights. Some insights are (1) realize an activity work method, (2) become familiar with an activity, (3) assure that an employee is following an activity training or suggested activity work method, (4) realize an opportunity to improve an employee productivity & (5) determine actual employee productivity rate.

EMPLOYEES ARE THE KEY
LOWER OPERATION COST

In a warehouse with manual, mechanized or automated activities, the employees who handle your sku & COs are a key to an efficient & cost effective warehouse. If your warehouse has automatic pick machines, AS/RS cranes, carousel pick machines or manual activities, an employee or an employee controlled machine handles a warehouse inbound skus & completed COs. When employees understand their work activity, work activity requirements and importance for an accurate and on-time activity, there is higher employee productivity with minimal damage.

SET GOALS & DEFINE OBJECTIVES
EMPLOYEE RELATIONS

To achieve an efficient and cost effective warehouse, your warehouse manager sets goals & defines objectives. Your warehouse goals are high UPH for each warehouse activity. Each warehouse department understanding your UPH goal or objective & daily skus p/hr & COs, employee work hours and impact on their department goal, it increases an opportunity for your warehouse departments & total warehouse to achieve the goals. If a department has a low vendor delivered skus & COs, your manager implements a pre-pack activity in anticipation of a high volume day, re-assign employees to another department with a high volume or perform another warehouse activity that does not impact a department CPU or UPH or grant employee non-paid time off.

USE PART TIME EMPLOYEES & MAKE YOUR SCHEDULE FIT THEIR TIME
LOWER OPERATIONAL COST

If your warehouse has an opportunity to use part-time employees, your warehouse has potential to lower your CPU. Since most part-time employees are available at specific hours for work and hours in most cases do not match a warehouse's normal hours (8 hour day). The situation means that part-time employees cannot work in your warehouse for normal work hours or for a complete work day. With a complete knowledge of available skus for pre-pack activity & CO types such as slapper label or fast pack activities, your warehouse manager assures that sku & CO volume is available and activity is set-up (warm start) for part-time employee hours, assures a sufficient work for your part-time employee hours, training or skills & makes your work schedule fit your part-time employee schedule.

SCAN OR RF DO NOT READ
HIGH EMPLOYEE PRODUCTIVITY & FEWER TRANSACTION ERRORS

If your warehouse activity requires an employee to read or verify a warehouse activity transaction, options are to (1) read. To complete a transaction, read option requires your warehouse to have a human readable symbology that is printed onto a label or paper document & to verify completion an employee places a mark onto a paper document.

Features are (a) requires an employee to read, (b) time to verify & handle a paper document, (c) another employee or clerk to complete (enter) a transaction into a computer & (d) paper document, ink & paper trash expenses & (2) scan. To complete an activity transaction, a scan transaction has a human/machine readable symbology that is printed onto a label, paper document or sku. To complete a scan transaction, an employee directs a scanner light beam onto a bar code or bar code passes a scanner light beam, enters a sku quantity into a scanner and presses a scanner send button for scan transaction transfer to a computer. Features are (1) high accuracy, (2) faster transfer, (3) higher employee productivity, (4) no reading requirement, (5) direct computer entry & (6) minimal expenses.

COLD OR WARM START
HIGHER EMPLOYEE PRODUCTIVITY & INCREASED COMPLETED CUSTOMER ORDER NUMBER

A warehouse that has CO pick, sort & pack activities, a daily warehouse pick/pack employee start work options are (1) cold start that has a warehouse pick & pack activities start-up with no completed CO transactions. With a pick, sort and pack operation, a cold start has your pick start with your other employees and sort & pack employees wait for your pick activity to transfer completed COs or (2) warm start-up that assures higher employee productivity and increased completed CO number. With a warm start, your pick activity starts prior to your sort and pack employee activities. Your warm start options are (a) if your pick, sort and pack employees start work at one time, your sort/pack employees are assigned to start as a picker or complete another warehouse activity & at a specific time move to sort & pack activities. Feature is some low employee productivity due to non-productive walk time to complete activity changes and shut-down old activity and start-up new activity or (2) your pick activity employees start prior to your sort & pack activity employees start time. COs flow is from your pick area to your sort & pack work stations and on your travel path COs queue prior to your sort & pack stations. It is noted that a pick/pass or all skus in an automatic pick concept are considered pick/pack warehouse that has all employees start at the same time and to assure a pick/pass or automatic pick concept warm start your pick position set-up or replenishment employees to start before your other pickers & packers.

CALL-IN LIST
LOWER OPERATION COSTS

A call-in list has a warehouse manager complete a list for part-time employees who are available to work for a day or with a short notice. When a call-in employee is not scheduled to work but your manager determines a requirement (based on a projected sku or CO volume) for part-time employees, your warehouse calls-in part time employees. For best results, your staff assures sufficient work for part-time employees who have a lower wage rate.

WHAT HAS TO BE DONE FIRST OR CUSTOMER ORDER IS KING
CUSTOMER SERVICE

What has to be done first is a phrase that looks at your warehouse activities and ranks each activity. In most warehouses, most important activities are (1) receiving & storage & (2) pick, pack & ship. In most companies, a warehouse operation has a budget that is based on COs & is graded on a CPU standard. A CPU is based on a warehouse total cost & completed COs. The criteria has CO pick, pack & ship activities as the activities to be done first with new sku receiving & storage activities completed second. Your customer is king phrase means that your warehouse is designed to completed accurate & on-time COs. Satisfied CO delivery means repeat customers; your warehouse remains in business & has resources to justify new construction or storage/pick equipment costs.

WHAT IS TIME CRITICAL
CUSTOMER SERVICE

What is time critical is a phrase that describes a warehouse's most critical activities. Important warehouse activities are (1) receiving, (2) storage, (3) pick, pack and ship & (4) customer returns. In most warehouses, receiving & storage activities are handling new skus that have a 13 week lead time before COs or sales and most warehouse customer returns department has 7 days to complete a customer return process activity. Most warehouses have a customer service standard that is to complete a CO in the shortest time period. After CO receipt in a warehouse computer, a customer service standard is out the door within 24 hour minimum time. Feature means that CO pick, pack & ship activities are more time critical.

SECONDS & MINUTES COUNT
EMPLOYEE PRODUCTIVITY & COMPLETE CUSTOMER ORDER NUMBER INCREASE

Seconds & minutes count is a reference to insights for employee productivity improvements that reduce labor costs, increases completed CO number or ability to handle a larger CO volume. In many warehouse activities that handle a high CO number, a small employee productivity improvement means a labor expense reduction. An employee productivity increase over a time period (frequency) and times an employee number calculates into a large labor group & labor expense reduction and completed CO increase number. For Example: In a warehouse that handles 8,000 COs per day with 25 pack stations for 7 hour day. Pack rate is 8000/7 X 25 = 45 COs p/hr. Same warehouse with a 10% packer productivity improvement (8000/(6.3 X 25 = 50). The completed CO number increases per hr.

NO DOUBLE FINGERPRINTS
EMPLOYEE PRODUCTIVITY & COMPLETED CUSTOMER ORDER NUMBER INCREASE

No double finger prints is a phrase that refers to a vendor delivered skus or CO skus being handled by employees at least 2 times or at 2 activity/work stations before it is located in a storage/pick position or as a completed CO sent out your door. By reducing an employee activity/work station by 1 means improved employee productivity and completed CO number increase. A vendor delivered sku or CO sku handled at 2 activity/work activity stations requires additional facility space, equipment investment, additional labor & increases potential for sku damage. After observing your vendor delivered sku or CO sku flow through your warehouse, you identify potential activities that have a vendor delivered sku or CO sku handled at a minimum of 2 separate activity/work stations. Whenever possible at your first activity/work station you have your warehouse activity completes preparation for a vendor delivered sku for a CO. Example is at a receiving detail count station, very small loose skus with a pre-determined sku count are placed into a re-seal able bag (count IDed on a bag exterior or paper slip inside a bag) or per your sales history for a similar sku, jewelry sku quantity is placed into a sales presentation cases. The activities reduce another employee handling a sku such as bulk CO picker or sku inventory count person.

DAILY LABOR PRODUCTIVITY DETAIL OR TOTAL MAN-HOURS
LOWER LABOR EXPENSE & ON-TIME CUSTOMER SERVICE

Daily labor warehouse productivity is bases for a warehouse manager to allocate his available or call-in labor to match an actual or I T department CO volume. With your actual CO pieces & labor productivity rates, a warehouse manager improves his control labor allocation to work/activity stations & daily labor expenses & assures CO service matches a company standard. Labor allocation approaches are (1) detail or budgeted labor activity productivity. With an actual warehouse CO volume & budgeted productivity rates, a warehouse staff determines an employee number that is required for each work/activity station. With an insight and before your warehouse start-up, your warehouse manager allocates employee numbers to each activity without non-productive employee change work/activity station time and to call in part-time employees & (2) total man-hour or total operation productivity. A total man-hour or total operation productivity has your daily CO volume divided by your budgeted total operation productivity rate. The approach provides you with required total employee to complete work, but does not consider different volumes for each activity station. For a day's volume, if one activity station has a low volume, an employee has insufficient work to match your budgeted productivity rate and if another activity has a high volume an employee hours are insufficient to handle your actual volume. During a workday, your supervisor detects a situation & allocates labor to another work/activity station with some non-productive employee change activity station time.

WAREHOUSE EXPENSE BUDGET TIED TO PRODUCTIVITY
LOWER OPERATIONAL COSTS

To plan and control a warehouse operation requires a man-hour and operational item expense budget that is based on a company's sku sale forecast and warehouse anticipated employee productivity rate for each activity. Each warehouse expense budget activity line has an expense. Labor expense is related to a forecasted skus that is divided by anticipated employee productivity rate. Management staff & other operational item expenses are based on last year's management staff & item expense with a percent increase for volume & inflation. The approach helps a warehouse manager plan employee number, explain an actual expense that is over or under a budgeted expense occurrence & allows a company to account for new equipment or a change in an activity performance.

WHAT IS MORE IMPORTANT YOUR FIXED OR VARIABLE OPERATIONAL EXPENSES
CONTROL YOUR OPERATIONAL EXPENSES

Your operation has both fixed and variable expenses that impact your annual operation budget. A fixed cost is an operational cost that does not fluctuate with your business volume and costs are not within your warehouse staff control. Some fixed costs are building & equipment depreciation, labor contract wage rate that varies with employee number and over-time and federal/state/local taxes that varies with employee number and over-time. Your variable cost is an operational cost that varies with your business volume and to some degree is controlled by your staff to minimize an impact on your expenses. Some variable costs are employee number, over-time, work method such pick concept and ability to pre-pack or use a slapper envelop, available work volume and productivity, ship supply items such as tape, filler material and box type and utility usage.

KNOW YOUR NEW CATALOG, TV PROGRAM, DIRECT MARKETING OR PROMOTIONAL SKUS & GROUP
IMPROVE PICKER PRODUCTIVITY AND INCREASE COMPLETED CUSTOMER ORDER NUMBER

Know your new catalog, TV program, direct marketing or promotional skus & group is a very important factor to establish a Golden Highway or Power Zone that improves picker productivity and increase completed CO number. You determine your new catalog, TV program, direct marketing or promotional skus or 'A'/fast moving skus by your merchandising department direction (purchase volume), special item or advertisement. If you believe Pareto's Law is true that 80% of your sales are from 20% of your skus, you profile skus into prime real estate positions that are in 1 pick zone, 1 aisle or close as possible to your pack area. The increases your picker hit concentration & density & has the shortest walk distance between two picks & between your pick area and pack area that means increased picker productivity. In most companies, after a sku sales promotion there is a minimal residual sku inventory that is relocated to another pick position.

BEFORE SKUS SALES HOW TO IDENTIFY OR TELL YOUR 'A'FAST MOVING SKUS
IMPROVE PICKER PRODUCTIVITY AND INCREASED COMPLETED CUSTOMER ORDER NUMBER

Before skus sales how to identify or tell your 'A'/fast moving skus is a key factor to assure good hit concentration and density & picker productivity. You sku ID options are (1) advise from your merchandising department, (2) reviewing your TV programmed skus, (3) advertisement copy that show your skus, (4) if special offer is mailed or enclosed in a CO package and (5) seasonal or holiday sku.

CONVERT TO VENDOR READY TO SHIP
IMPROVE PACKER PRODUCTIVITY, INCREASE CO NUMBER & LOWER SHIPPING SUPPLY EXPENSES

Convert to vendor ready to ship is a warehouse idea that has a large single line sku CO number and increases completed CO number, improves packer productivity and lower ship supply expenses. With your purchase, I T, customer service & warehouse, you review each single line sku that is available for COs. A review process determines (1) single line sku number & sku quantity that had single line COs & structural cardboard strength, quality, interior filler material to protect a sku & exterior surface to quality for a vendor ready to ship sku & (2) single line sku number & quantity that has had single line COs but a cardboard carton does not have structural cardboard strength, quality, interior filler material to protect a sku & exterior surface to quality for a vendor ready to ship sku. If a sku qualifies for a vendor ready to ship carton, your I T, warehouse, purchase & customer service team prepares a slapper label (See Pack Chapter) & to introduce vendor ready to ship cartons. If a sku requires a vendor to modify a carton cardboard quality, structural strength, interior filler material or exterior surface, your team meets with a vendor to improve a sku to become a vendor ready to ship carton. For best results or vendor participation, you share some of your savings with a vendor. When a vendor ready to ship carton is compared to a carton repack process, your potential benefits are (1) pack labor savings with a slapper label, (2) no ship supply expenses (tape, carton and filler material), (3) lower CO returns open expense & trash handling (carton and filler material) &

(4) opportunity to avoid regular pack stations or divert a volume to a pick activity or mechanize or automatic the activity.

YOUR VENDOR WRAPS YOUR VENDOR READY TO SHIP CARTON DELIVERIES
IMPROVE PRODUCTIVITY, INCREASE CO HANDLING NUMBER & LOWER TRASH HANDLING EXPENSE

Your vendor wraps your vendor ready to ship carton deliveries is a warehouse option for a single line sku in a vendor ready to ship carton that involves your purchase & warehouse departments. If your warehouse is receiving vendor ready to ship cartons in a master carton (encased in another large cardboard carton) & a sku is sold as a single line sku, your warehouse has an opportunity to improve picker & packer productivity, increase CO handling volume a lower trash handling expenses. Since a sku is packaged in a vendor ready to ship carton & your warehouse sends it customers as a vendor ready to ship carton, a sku carton has structural cardboard strength, quality, interior filler material to protect a sku & exterior surface to meet your customer deliver quality standards. Your opportunity is to have your vendor wrap same sku quantity in plastic wrap, paper or plastic bands that during vendor delivery is a secure method to hold skus on a pallet & a vendor ready to ship carton protects a sku quality. With a plastic wrap concept, during a small pick quantity or fast pack activity, to remove a smaller carton from a plastic wrap is less labor tense than cutting open a large & bulky cardboard carton or trying to pull a smaller carton from a large master carton. After a plastic wrap sku quantity depletion, plastic wrap is easier for an employee to place into a recycle bin & requires less space than a large cardboard carton that reduces your trash expenses.

SMALLER IS SOMETIMES BETTER
IMPROVE PICKER & PACKER PRODUCTIVITY & IMPROVED CUSTOMER SERVICE

Smaller is sometimes better is a phrase that means when a warehouse offers a same item as a master carton sku & as an individual piece sku, a smaller piece quantity per master carton is a warehouse strategy to have your purchase department, I T, customer service & warehouse review each skus sales to determine a best sku quantity per master carton. In many industries, a smaller sku quantity per master carton has a master carton that is picked for a CO improves picker & packer employee productivity with fewer replenishment activities for broken master cartons, less sku damage & where a master carton is opened less trash handling. If your review shows a sku number for a master carton & there is positive customer response, your team reviews a new master carton sku quantity with your vendor to determine any economic impact on a sku cost. Your team considers potential for a sku with a smaller master carton quantity to become a vendor ready to ship sku, I T department to have a WMS computer program for COs to separate skus as single sku or master carton & receive associated employee productivity improvements.

KNOW YOUR SKU & CUSTOMER ORDER FLOWS
LOW OPERATIONAL COST & GOOD CUSTOMER SERVICE

After your warehouse sku inventory & number storage requirements, to develop a new facility or remodel an existing facility, your skus & CO flows are very important design factors. Understanding your sku & CO flows makes a warehouse design or layout cost effective, efficient & enhances on-time customer service. With an across-the-dock operation, sku or CO flow is a straight flow through your warehouse. With a 1 floor level pallet or master carton hold and store (conventional) warehouse, your sku or CO flow is a 'U' or 'W' flow through your warehouse. With a GOH or small item store and hold (conventional) warehouse with a multi-level building, in addition to a 'U' or 'W' flows, with in-house transport concepts that move a large WMS IDed sku quantity in one carrier, vertical up & down sku or CO flows between multiple floors are considerations.

KNOW YOUR SKU RECEIVING, CUSTOMER ORDER & I T DEPARTMENT SURGES
IMPROVE CUSTOMER SERVICE & LOWER OPERATION COST

Know your sku receiving, CO and I T department paper document surges have a warehouse manager aware of the transactions that occur in a warehouse activity. With vendor delivered skus & CO surges, a warehouse material handling concept has potential to create vendor delivered sku & CO flow problems that creates sku & CO flow back-up. A sku & CO flow problem or I T department paper document print problem has potential to create employee downtime. With a problem pre-knowledge or re-occurrence situation, your warehouse manager options are (1) add labor or equipment, (2) for your receiving activity to reschedule vendor deliveries, (3) with COs (a) pre-pack skus, (b) increase vendor ready to ship cartons, (c) increase over-time & (d) CO carry-over. To minimize an IT department paper document preparation surge to (1) print at an early time, (2) increase pre-print lines on receiving documents & customer order pack slips/invoices & delivery labels, (3) add printers & (4) adjust CO wave or print requirement.

WAREHOUSE MANAGEMENT SYSTEM (WMS) IN A WAREHOUSE
IMPROVE INVENTORY CONTROL & ACCURATE TRANSACTIONS

A WMS program in a warehouse has each warehouse activity with a WMS IDed sku or CO entered into a WMS computer program. When a WMS program is matched to warehouse activities, results are improved sku inventory & CO control & flow, on time & accurate transactions, enhanced employee productivity & improved customer service. With a WMS program, each sku & CO has a discreet WMS ID. As a WMS IDed sku & CO flows through a warehouse, each transaction has an employee hand held or fixed position scanner complete a WMS ID scan/read. Each WMS ID scan/read transaction is sent on time or delayed through a warehouse computer to a WMS computer that updates each WMS ID sku & CO status & location. After WMS ID CO completion, a WMS computer sends a WMS ID sku depletion & CO status message to your host computer for update.

WHO IS FIRST (WAREHOUSE CONCEPT OR WMS PROGRAM)
ASSURE YOUR SKU & CUSTOMER ORDER FLOWS MATCH YOUR WMS PROGRAM

Who is first is a situation that you determine when your company considers a WMS program for the warehouse. Two key components are (1) warehouse concept & (2) WMS program. A basic question for a design team is what component (warehouse concept or WMS program) is the most important & is considered first. Best answer to a question is based on your project type, cost, time and other factors. Project types are (1) remodel an existing warehouse that has warehouse concept first due to on-time & accurate customer service (2) new construction with a new warehouse that has first due to old warehouse is maintaining your customer service.

TIE THE WAREHOUSE & WMS PROGRAM KNOT
ASSURE YOUR SKU & CUSTOMER ORDER FLOWS & TRANSACTIONS MATCH YOUR WMS PROGRAM

To have a successful WMS program integrated into a warehouse, your project is like tying a knot. A knot is made from a string that has two ends/strands. One strand is your warehouse concept with its sku and CO flows and transactions and other strand is your WMS program with transaction updates that tracks and accounts for your skus and COs. A project design team leader & team members understand an objective (knot), how a knot will look & how to move two strands to make a knot.

EXCHANGE PALLETS
IMPROVE RECEIVING DOCK TURNS, EMPLOYEE PRODUCTIVITY & DOCK SPACE UTILIZATION

Exchange pallet concept is a warehouse (purchasing and receiving departments) arrangement with a vendor to deliver skus palletized on pallets that match your warehouse pallet quality standards. With a pallet exchange concept, at your warehouse a vendor empty delivery truck picks-up good quality pallets or your backhaul truck takes good quality pallets to a vendor location. To assure pallet accounting, records are maintained to track pallet delivery & receipt. A warehouse delivery options are floor stack or palletized delivery, a pallet exchange program improves employee productivity by a lower receiving department unload time by at least 5 hours for a full 40 ft long trailer & labor expense, improves your receiving dock turns & improves dock space utilization.

BACKHAUL
LOWER OVER-THE-ROAD TRANSPORT COST

Backhaul concept is a warehouse concept that has your company purchase and trucking departments arrange with a vendor for your company or contracted empty truck to pick-up your company purchase order at a vendor location & deliver vendor skus to your warehouse. For a vendor sku pick-up & delivery activity your company receives compensation. In some companies, a backhaul occurs after your truck completes a delivery at a customer location and is empty. With an empty truck, a truck travels from your warehouse to a vendor location, picks-up your purchase order & with purchase order returns to your warehouse. If your CO delivery location is within a short travel distance to a vendor location, your warehouse realizes good cost savings due to a large mile percentage was incurred as your delivery miles to your CO location. A backhaul compensation or freight charge lowers your warehouse delivery costs.

WHAT IS THE BEST TIME TO CHANGE
CUSTOMER SERVICE & MAINTAIN SCHEDULE

When is the best time to change from an old warehouse or material handling concept to a new warehouse or material handling concept is a determined by your warehouse management team. Your management team has your architect, building construction company, storage/pick equipment vendors, I T department and your staff & estimates a best time for a warehouse remodel or new construction project to start-up. To satisfy a company objective for best customer service at a lowest possible cost, your warehouse maintains customer service during a project construction/installation & start-up. With both project types, your new warehouse best time for a start-up is after your warehouse peak sales volume. For a year, the time period has lowest CO volume & sku inventory quantity at lowest levels. In most remodel projects, a remodel project impact is on your warehouse activities that are affected by remodel work. With minimal impact to sku inventory & I T processes, a remodel project detail plans & lays out an expansion into a vacate building area with storage or pick/pack/ship activities. This Feature allows your existing warehouse activities to operate in parallel to a warehouse remodel. With a new construction project, a project has an impact on all your warehouse activities, vendor deliveries & I T processes. A new construction project requires sku inventory relocation, new material handling activities & I T department equipment start-up & debug. Whenever possible, your existing warehouse runs parallel until your new warehouse is 100% operational. During this low sales period, your new warehouse transfer plan considers at a new facility to (1) assure I T processes are de-bugged and ready, (2) handle single line COs, (3) receive all vendor new sku deliveries, (4) transfer all new sku or A movers that still have a sales lead time & (5) progressively transfer other skus that are B & C sku movers and handle combination customer orders & transfer D sku movers last. As part of a start-up plan, you assign a team to assure that your vendors, inbound freight companies, office/ship supply vendors, CO delivery companies and other companies are notified with your new warehouse address and communication numbers.

MINIMUM BUILDING COLUMNS
LOWER BUILDING CONSTRUCTION, IMPROVE SPACE UTILIZATION & EMPLOYEE PRODUCTIVITY

When designing a new multi-floor warehouse or adding a mezzanine level to an existing warehouse, you should keep your building structural support columns to a minimum number as possible. When developing a material handling layout or remodel your existing warehouse with an elevated floor, a minimum building column number permits on a ground floor maximum material handling equipment layout & flexibility, longer storage & pick aisles, maximum space utilization (building columns can occupy 5% of your sq ft area & in a high seismic zone up to 10%), greater storage & pick position number, fewer conveyor travel path curves & forklift truck turns. On an elevated floor, building columns are used to support roof loads that have lower load weight that means possible increase roof steel cost but fewer building columns (steel cost).

WHERE ARE YOUR BUILDING COLUMNS
SPACE UTILIZATION, EMPLOYEE PRODUCTIVITY & STORAGE POSITION NUMBER INCREASE

Where your buildings columns are located is a conventional building design factor that impacts your space utilization, available storage/pick position number & employee productivity. Building columns are not preferred in a storage or pick aisle due to the fact that it creates low employee productivity & potential accident with building, sku & equipment damage. Options are (1) in back-to-back rack flue space that is 3 to 6 in clear space that is allowed between a building column & rack structural member per seismic location varies from a building 12 in up to 3 ft column. For a rack row length, a flue space is not utilized for sku storage. In a conventional forklift warehouse, loss space is (6 in space + 12 in column + 6 in space X 150 ft long row = 300 sq ft & with 25 ft high building = 7500 cubic ft), (2) with a building column in a conventional forklift truck storage rack bay & your storage rack row and your operation requires hand stacked cartons or trash container on a decked rack, loss space is (3 in space + 12 in column + 3 in space X 6 columns = 9 sq ft & with 25 ft high building = 225 cubic ft) & (3) building column in a rack position option is to void a storage position (50 in storage position X 6 columns = 25 sq ft & with 25 ft high building = 625 cubic ft).

MINIMAL WALLS
LOWER BUILDING CONSTRUCTION & MATERIAL HANDLING EQUIPMENT COST

When designing a new or remodeling your existing warehouse, you minimize load bearing walls or firewalls to minimize your building construction costs and material handling equipment costs. If you have a wall in your warehouse, you add building construction costs, your passageway dimensions match your vehicle, sku or CO travel path through wall, firewalls increase conveyor travel path cost due to wall penetration protection & additional powered mobile vehicle turning aisles.

HAVE SUFFICIENT ELECTRICITY
LOWER BUILDING CONSTRUCTION COST & ASSURE EQUIPMENT OPERATES

When designing your new warehouse or remodeling your existing warehouse, you know your electrical factors to assure lower building construction costs and your material handling equipment operates. Your first electrical factor is your warehouse's total electric KVA demand requirement for all electric powered building (lighting, etc), IT, office, material handling equipment and a safety factor for expansion or equipment additions. A warehouse electric power demands are (1) your average electric power demand or normal operating condition with not all your electric powered equipment having a demand or (2) your peak electric power demand that occurs when you start-up or turn on all your electric powered equipment on or all your electric powered equipment is drawing power. Your second electrical factor is what is available at your existing or new warehouse or from a local electric power company.

FIT AROUND OR FIT IN
LOWER BUILDING CONSTRUCTION AND MATERIAL HANDLING EQUIPMENT INVESTMENT

When designing a new warehouse, your design options are (1) fit building columns, shell & roof around your material handling concept that has fewer building columns, other constraints & means lower material handling equipment cost & (2) fit your material handling concept into a building columns, shell & roof that has your material handling concept use curves and turns to avoid building obstacles means low space utilization. When designing your layout for a lease or existing facility, you fit your material-handling concept into a building.

NEW OR EXISTING FACILITY
LOW BUILDING COST & CUSTOMER SERVICE EXPANSION

After your company has concluded that a second warehouse is required to handle your CO volume & to maintain customer service standard, your warehouse expansion strategy options are to (1) purchase land and build a new facility option has a company design a new building with I T, warehouse, & storage/pick/pack equipment layout. A build to suit means that your building construction matches your warehouse requirements and requires time to design and obtain code approval, landscape & site/land preparation & longest time for a facility to be operational, (2) expand your existing warehouse approach has your company design a new building with warehouse, storage & pick equipment layout on your existing site. Your new warehouse is adjacent or remote to your existing warehouse & is finalized by local building codes & risk management. An expansion option has a medium lead-time & medium/high warehouse & storage/pick/pack equipment cost due to land was a previous company cost or (3) remodel another existing warehouse. A remodel an existing warehouse has your company purchase an existing warehouse that matches your warehouse requirements, requires some design & code approval, requires an architect/engineer assure that a building structure & utilities handles your loads, some additional I T, warehouse, storage/pick/pack equipment costs but a shorter time for your warehouse to be operational.

FENCE ME IN
LOWER RISK MANAGEMENT COSTS

Fence me in is a site security consideration that has your warehouse facility & land area engulfed with a fence & berm. In addition to a security fence & berm, an entrance guard controls non-authorized personnel & vehicle entry to your property & most local codes require a 6 ft open space between your property line & building wall.

WHERE ARE YOUR IN & OUT LOCATIONS
LOWER OPERATION COST

To position your warehouse on a new site, both the receiving dock & ship dock locations are critical factors. Your sku & CO type are factors that determine flow patterns, process activities within your warehouse, site & facility size and shape, delivery truck & rail car access & egress between a highway/main rail line & building. Various inbound (delivery) & outbound (ship) location options are (1) all trucks on 1 side & rail on a back side, (2) trucks at both building ends on 1 side & rail on a back side & (3) on opposite sides or adjacent sides with rail on another side.

KNOW YOUR SIZE
LOWER BUILDING CONSTRUCTION & MATERIAL HANDLING EQUIPMENT COST

Know your building size is a key factor plus roadway and parking that determines your required land area. Your building size is determined by your warehouse type & associated processes (across-the-dock or store & hold), design year customer number & sku inventory with an allowance for expansion. An across-the-dock warehouse is a fluid warehouse that does not have a large sku store & hold warehouse, requires a large dock number & performs few warehouse processes and it requires a smaller sized facility with a large truck dock number on both facility sides. A conventional store & hold warehouse has a large storage area & as required pick/pack & other warehouse activities/processes areas. Truck docks are located to assure cost effective and efficient sku & CO flows. With dense storage concepts or tall rack (VNA or AS/RS) storage concept, your warehouse area that is allocated to a storage activity has a smaller sq. ft area but a conventional warehouse storage area has a large sq ft area.

BUILD OR LEASE
LOWER OPERATION COST & REDUCE CASH FLOW

After your company determines a new warehouse total sq. ft. requirement, next major warehouse decision is to lease or build a building. A leased building option has your company design a warehouse, storage and pick concept to fit into an existing building. Leased options are to (1) lease an existing facility that has a short start-up time & low cost for your warehouse operation & (2) 'build to lease' a new facility that has a leasing company constructs a building to your company specifications. The approach has a longer start-up time with a medium cost. Your company construct a new building has your company purchase a site & with an architect & construction company to obtain local authority approval and build a facility. During & after building construction, your warehouse, storage & pick concept is installed in the facility. The own land & build approach has a longer start-up time & higher cost.

NO SKUS OR CUSTOMER ORDERS IS A POWERED CONVEYOR SHUT-DOWN SITUATION
ENERGY SAVINGS

No skus or COs (after a pre-determined time period) on a powered conveyor travel path provides an opportunity for your powered conveyor travel path shutdown. If your warehouse has a powered conveyor travel path, electric powered motors that use electricity move a conveyor travel path. Powered conveyor travels paths are used in several activities such as in-house transport, pick, pack, ship & customer returns activities. Since electricity is a warehouse expense, a warehouse objective is to control or minimize warehouse expenses and to incur an expense as employees or equipment handle a sku or CO. A powered conveyor travel path turn on or turn off options are (1) at a warehouse open or work day start time, to turn all powered conveyor travel path sections on and leave electric drive motors on all day. With an 8 to 12 hour workday, the feature has high electric power usage & associated expense. During a warehouse workday, there are time periods (nothing available, breaks or lunches) or occasions with no sku or COs moving on a conveyor travel path. The situation means that a warehouse has an expense with no sku or CO being handled that incurs an expense with no sku or CO to account for an expense or (2) when skus or COs are scheduled for movement over a powered conveyor travel path, your warehouse turns on a powered conveyor travel path. If no sku or CO (after a pre-determined time period) is on a powered conveyor travel path, powered conveyor travel path sensing devices and controls turn off electric drive motors for a powered conveyor travel path and with a sku or customer order on a powered conveyor travel path, sensing devices and controls turn on electric drive motors for a powered conveyor travel path. The situation means that your warehouse only incurs an expense when skus or COs are being handled that means a CPU with skus or COs to account for an expense. Your powered conveyor manufacturer or electric company projects your electric expense savings that are based on your electric cost & hours not being used. Per your warehouse type, powered conveyor sensing device/control options are (1) a supervisor who turns on/off a switch with no cost or (2) electric/micro-computer type with a cost.

LIGHTS ON & OFF IN YOUR ACTIVITY AREAS
ENERGY SAVINGS

Lights on/off (after a pre-determined time period) in a warehouse activity section or workstation are an idea to save electric power expense. Each warehouse activity requires lights to illuminate an aisle or work station area that allows an employee complete an activity or transaction, powered vehicle travel over a travel path or an employee to walk through an aisle or area. Local codes & company policy set illumination standards for each warehouse activity aisle, work area or work station such as minimal light fixtures on, safety lights or single-phase lights. Some warehouse areas are (1) receiving dock area that includes dock lights, (2) storage vehicle aisles & best opportunity is with carton or pallet AS/RS crane concept, (2) single item, master carton, GOH or pallet pick sections or aisles, (3) check & sort/pack stations, (4) manifest, sort & loading dock areas that includes dock lights & (5) customer returns dock area that includes light and process areas. Since electricity is a warehouse expense, a warehouse objective is to control or minimize expenses and to incur an expense that is associated with the handling for a sku or CO. Light turn on or turn off options are (1) at a warehouse open time, to turn all warehouse sections lights on & leave lights on all day. With an 8 to 12 hour workday, the feature has high electric power usage & associated expense. During a warehouse workday, there are time periods (nothing available, breaks or lunches) occasions with no employees or powered vehicles in an aisle or work area. The situation means that a warehouse has an expense with no employee handling a sku or CO. This means a CPU with no sku or CO to account for an expense or (2) when a warehouse activity is scheduled for area or a vehicle or employee moves into an area, your warehouse turns on aisle or work area lights and lights remain on for a pre-determined time period or as an employee or powered vehicle remains in motion or creates a noise that has lights remain on. If powered vehicle or employee (after a pre-determined time period) is working in an area, area motion sensing devices/controls turn off lights & as required turning on lights. The situation means that your warehouse has an expense with skus or COs being handled that means a cost per unit with skus or COs to account for an expense. Your electric contractor or electric company projects your electric expense savings that are based on your electric cost & hours not being used as a percentage for total work day hours. Example: You Work day is 9 hours with 30 minute lunch and 2 each 15 minute breaks. This means that 60 minutes in a work day or 11% of your total work day where you have no employees in a work area & by turning lights off you could realize an 11% savings on your electric expense that is associated with lights. It is noted that best quick turn on lights are fluorescent tube. As of this writing the purchase cost of highly efficient LED lights in an intensity suitable for warehouse use is prohibitive in most instances. Per your warehouse type, area lighting on/off sensing devices/controls options are (a) supervisor who turns on/off a light switch that has no cost or (2) motion or noise electric/micro-computer type that has a cost.

LIGHTS ON & OFF IN YOUR CAFETERIA & BREAK ROOM AREAS
ENERGY SAVINGS

Lights on/off (after a pre-determined time period) in a warehouse cafeteria or break rooms is an idea to save electric power expense. Each warehouse activity requires lights to illuminate a cafeteria, break room or restroom that allows an employee use or enjoy the area. Local codes & company policy set illumination standards for each warehouse area such as minimal light fixtures on, safety lights or single-phase lights. It is noted that best quick turn on lights are fluorescent tube. If your warehouse leaves a cafeteria, break room or restroom lights remain on for an entire workday; your warehouse incurs an expense with no return or benefit to an employee or operation. Per your warehouse type, cafeteria or break room light turn on/off sensing devices & controls are (a) a supervisor who turns on/off a light switch that has no cost or (2) with a restroom area motion or noise electric/micro-computer type that has a cost. The situation means that your warehouse has an expense with an employee is using or enjoying the area and accounts for an expense. Your electric contractor or electric company can project your electric expense savings that are based on your electric cost & hours not being used as a percentage for total work day hours.

FANS MOVE AIR
ENERGY SAVINGS & IMPROVE EMPLOYEE PRODUCTIVITY
Fans move air is a warehouse idea that creates energy savings & improves employee productivity. In your warehouse, ceiling fans above aisles, workstations and dock staging areas provide opportunities to use ceiling fans to move air. During summer months with warm & humid weather, ceiling fans rotate & move air in a work area or aisle below that improves an employee work area environment. If your warehouse is located in a high humid area, moisture build-up on a floor surface creates a slippery floor with potential powered vehicle accidents & in cardboard cartons that reduce carton support strength & creates damaged skus. Ceiling fans moving air in storage aisles reduces moisture build up on a floor & minimizes moisture build up in cardboard cartons. During winter months with cold weather, ceiling fans rotate & move warm air from a ceiling to a work area below that improves your employee work area environment & has potential to turn off your heating thermostat & lower your heating fuel expense.

DO YOUR DOCK DOORS NEED CURTAINS
ENERGY SAVINGS & HOUSE KEEPING EXPENSE SAVINGS
Do your warehouse dock doors need curtains is an energy savings idea that are dock curtains along your receiving & ship open dock edge to block an enclosed open dock. A sliding dock curtain is a bi-parting rubberized/treated fabric curtain that is installed at an open dock edge and spans a truck dock position. When a truck is not at a dock position, a closed sliding dock curtain minimizes outside cold/warm air & dust from entering a dock position & staging area that improves internal temperature control & improves housekeeping. When a truck is parked at a dock position, a sliding dock curtain is pulled to each side & secured at a side that creates a passageway for a pallet truck or forklift truck to enter/exit a delivery truck.

MATS FOR THE FEET
IMPROVE EMPLOYEE PRODUCTIVITY
Mats for your employee feet or mats on a workstation or pick line floor is a workstation or pick line idea that reduce employee fatigue & improves employee productivity. A warehouse work stations requires an employee to stand at detail receiving, check station, pick/pass line, fast pack, regular pack or customer returns activity or to walk along a pick/pass line. When an employee stands on a cement floor in 1 position or walks in a pick line aisle, a cold floor or just standing on a hard cement floor over time will tire employees, reducing their effectiveness. A rubber mat on a pick line or workstation floor provides employee feet a cushion that creates insulation from a cold or hard floor. If a sku is dropped onto a rubber mat instead of onto a cement floor, rubber is a cushion that minimizes sku damage.

LIGHTS WHERE
IMPROVE EMPLOYEE PRODUCTIVITY & REDUCE ERRORS
Lights where is a new construction or facility remodel idea that improves employee productivity & accurate transaction completion. **Lights where** means that your warehouse light fixtures are located to illuminate an aisle or area for an employee to accurately & quickly complete a transaction or read/complete a document. A warehouse has many areas or aisles that require light fixtures and your building construction company attach light fixtures to a 20 to 25 ft high ceiling. Preferred options are (1) in a pick aisle with a manual pick concept to have light fixtures that are attached to a shelf/rack overhead tie or adjustable chain hung from a ceiling & (2) at a pack, check or customer returns work station overhead supported from a workstation structural support member or adjustable chain hung from a ceiling. When lights are hung over a rack/shelf, aisle illumination is minimal with most light on cartons.

ASSURE SUFFICIENT & GOOD EMPLOYEE CAFETERIA
EMPLOYEE MOTIVATION

Assure sufficient & good quality employee cafeteria and break areas that are clean and well equipped is an idea that motivates employees. A cafeteria with sufficient microwave ovens, refrigerators or hot meal service allows employees to eat quickly, rest, relax & get prepared for the next work session. With local no smoking codes that prohibit smoking in a facility, provide sheltered outside smoking areas.

HOW LONG DOES IT TAKE
CASH FLOW MANAGEMENT

How long does it take refers to a new or remodel facility construction/material handling equipment installation & start-up time period. After a warehouse management team decides to build or remodel a facility, construction & installation time period by month is very important to your warehouse financial department. Important factors are (1) time period that your existing warehouse continues with business activities that determines existing lease extension, additional build lease or multiple shift operation at your existing warehouse, (2) when a new warehouse is available to receive vendor deliveries that requires your purchase department to notify vendors & receiving department to notify truck & rail companies, (3) to obtain necessary local & official documents to have a warehouse that includes a building occupancy permit, (4) what is required for cash outflows to support building construction & material handling vendor contract payments & (5) when to terminate existing leases & sell existing warehouse equipment or building.

BUILDING CONSTRUCTION & MATERIAL HANDLING LAYOUT COSTS ARE FIXED COMPARED TO YOUR FUTURE VARIABLE LABOR COSTS
BUILDING CONSTRUCTION COSTS & FUTURE EMPLOYEE PRODUCTIVITY IMPROVEMENT

When you are designing a new or remodeling a warehouse, your major cost factors are building construction & warehouse, storage, pick & process equipment/layout. In a project, the costs are budgeted 1-time fixed costs that are depreciated over a period of time. Your major costs savings or economic justification components are your variable labor cost factor & your ability to handle additional COs & sku volumes. You assure that your building & warehouse, storage, pick/pack & process equipment & layout are designed to match your requirements. When we compared a building item to a warehouse, storage, pick/pack & process equipment item has tremendous influence or direct relationship on your future employee productivity & variable warehouse costs.

WHERE IS YOUR ELECTRICAL BACK-UP
CUSTOMER SERVICE

Where is electric power back-up is a new construction or remodel warehouse option when a brown occurs to assure a constant electric power supply to your warehouse. During an electric power company power failure, an electric power supply back-up concept provides electric power to your warehouse. Your back-up power supply options are (1) re-chargeable battery to provide power for a short run or time period & for a few items & (2) diesel powered generator to provide power for a long run or time period and for several items. Prior to your back-up power selection, you determine how much power is required for your warehouse. Your options are (1) key activities or items such as I T and PC equipment & (2) key activities are previously mentioned plus specific or all your warehouse activities. It is good practice to have your electric power supply protected from spikes or surges.

JUST A WAREHOUSE OPERATIONAL FACTS
BUILDING SIZE & COST

Just a warehouse operational facts are a warehouse phrase that refers to gathering your warehouse costs, expense & volume facts. In a remodel or new warehouse construction, the facts are used to economic and operational justify your new idea purchase & implementation. Important facts are (1) storage units, projected sku inventory volume and sku number that determines your building storage area space/size & equipment, (2) projected vendor sku deliveries and CO package number & pieces that determines your process space/size, employee number and equipment & (3) present warehouse vendor deliveries, CO number & pieces, operational costs, employee number & facility size that become your bases to justify a new project.

WHAT IS YOUR CLEAR HEIGHT
MINIMIZE EQUIPMENT, SKU & BUILDING DAMAGE & REPAIR EXPENSE

What is your clear height is a warehouse feature that determines your sku, CO & forklift truck overall height. In a warehouse your clear height considerations are (1) in a storage area your clear ceiling height between a floor surface & lowest ceiling structural member is a major design factor that determines your sku stack height, (2) in a warehouse, your passage way/door frame height determines a forklift truck overall mast or overhead guard height & (3) in your warehouse, your wall or elevated floor penetration determines your sku & CO overall height. Knowing the information, you have opportunities to have efficient sku & CO flows is greatly enhanced & you (1) avoid additional costly building or equipment modifications, (2) limit on your sku & CO height & (3) limit on your forklift truck ability to complete transactions in other facility locations.

VERIFY FLOOR CRACKS
MINIMIZE YOUR REPAIR EXPENSES

When your review a building for purchase or lease and a proposed building has floor cracks and cracks around a building column, your verify that cracks will not impact your vehicle travel and your vehicle travel with no expand cracks. You take pictures and date and include an architect's statement in your lease or purchase contract.

LIGHTS CAMERA
IMPROVE SAFETY & SECURITY

Lights and camera is a truck yard safety and security concept that improves a truck yard safety and security. A well-illuminated truck yard and roadway improves a truck driver's vision that helps to improve safety. At key locations & along a building exterior wall (such as emergency doors) lights & cameras focused at key locations. Each camera has a communication network to a guard shed that allows a guard to be aware of a potential security problem.

ALARM YOUR 'E' DOOR
IMPROVE SAFETY & SECURITY

Alarm your 'E' door is a building security concept. The concept has your building emergency doors that are equipped with a breakaway alarm device. When an employee presses against an alarm door breakaway bar, it disconnects a light beam or electric component that activates an alarm, door location appears on a guard station monitor & an emergency door is open that allows employees to exist a facility.

ADEQUATE AISLES & AISLE WIDTH
LOWER EMPLOYEE PRODUCTIVITY & IMPROVED SPACE UTILIZATION

When designing a warehouse, you allow sufficient aisle number & aisle width in various powered mobile equipment activity areas to assure good forklift truck productivity and improved space utilization. Sufficient aisle number permits employees or powered mobile vehicles to easily & quickly transfer between aisles or complete a right angle turn storage, pick or in-house transport transaction. In a conventional forklift truck operation with a wide aisle (WA) or narrow aisle (NA) forklift truck, to a vehicle manufacturer's recommended aisle width you add 6 to 12 ins. In a guided high rise order picker truck (HROS), very narrow aisle (VNA) vehicle or AS/RS crane aisle you use your vehicle manufacturer's recommended aisle between 2 rack rows.

NUMBER SYSTEM TIES VEHICLE, BATTERY & CHARGER TOGETHER
REDUCE ELECTRIC POWER EXPENSES

The best equipment number system ties your vehicle, battery & charger together that assures all vehicles/batteries are placed on a charger. If you have an electrical problem with a vehicle, battery or charger, it is easier to identify problem equipment. Example is forklift truck vehicle = 301FT, battery = 301B and charge 301C.

WHEN TO CHARGE YOUR BATTERIES
REDUCE ELECTRIC POWER EXPENSES

When to charge your batteries is determined by two factors. Factors are (1) when is a full charged battery is required in your operation, (2) for a two-shift operation, do you have a battery rotation program (3) does your electric power provides have a different electric rate for specific hours. Whenever possible your operation charges batteries in a time period that provides you with lowest electrical rate.

WHAT IS SCRAP & WHERE TO PLACE IT
   IMPROVE SPACE UTILIZATION & IMPROVE SANTIATION

In a warehouse there is a possibility to have obsolete or not used material handling equipment in a warehouse. Non-used equipment occupies positions or space in your warehouse that is considered expensive real estate. If your warehouse has a requirement for storage space, relocate obsolete equipment to another area. Relocation is an opportunity to increase available space for good skus. To create space for good skus, scrap equipment is placed in a storage position with a longest travel distance from a pick & pack area, in off-set storage, under a cover & elevated on pallets that are outside in a truck yard or sold.

CHAPTER 2
TRUCK YARD AREA & RECEIVING ACTIVITY COST SAVING IDEAS

VENDOR MAKE A DELIVERY TRUCK ARRIVAL DATE
 IMPROVE RECEIVING EMPOLYEE PRODUCTIVITY & DOCK UTILIZATION
Make a date is a receiving truck dock scheduling idea that is designed to improve your receiving department productivity, improve your dock & dock equipment utilization. Dock scheduling is based on your company's purchase order sku delivery date. After your receiving department receives a purchase order, a receiving clerk with a vendor or freight company verifies or confirms a delivery vehicle date & delivery type (floor stack, pallets, slip sheets or containers), estimates unload & document sign times and assigns a truck dock to a vendor delivery. Truck delivery assignment to a truck dock is completed on a manual or PC spread sheet that blocks for a receiving dock for entire unload & document sign time. On a paper or PC sheet, a dock block activity prevents another vendor from delivery being assigned to a dock. For each warehouse work day, a dock schedule spread sheet has across a spread sheet top a series of column with each column as a dock door & down a spread sheet side a series of rows that represents a work day time periods. Breaks & lunch each have a row on a spread sheet. Changes to a dock assignment are reviewed & approved by a receiving manager vendor/freight company & made to a manual or PC spread sheet & e-mail/fax confirms a vendor delivery truck change.

GATED FACILITY
 IMPROVE SECURITY
Gated facility is idea to improve security and is a reference to a warehouse that has a security fence & entrance/exit gates that engulfs your warehouse center property. For a vendor or CO delivery truck to enter a truck yard area, at an entrance gate, each delivery truck is required to travel past a guardhouse. With a dock schedule program as a delivery truck arrives at an entrance gate, a security gate guard communicates a vendor or CO delivery truck arrival at your operation. Per your dock schedule program or management, a dock manager advises a gate guard to indicate to a vendor or CO delivery truck driver to an assigned dock position or truck yard parking location & is allowed to enter your warehouse truck yard.

YARD SET-BACK WITH BERM & FENCE
 IMPROVE SECUIRTY & SAFETY
Yard setback with a berm & fence is a yard security & safety idea. A warehouse yard setback with berm & fence engulfs your warehouse & most specifically a truck yard. A setback is X feet wide & is required by a local code to assure emergency vehicle travel between a property line & building. A berm is a dirt pile with a grass cover that minimizes unauthorized person entry, delivery truck yard view from an outside & reduces truck yard noises from traveling to an outside. A fence along a property line assures unauthorized person entry onto your warehouse land.

TRUCK YARD TRAFFIC LINES
 IMPROVE SAFETY
Traffic line on a truck yard roadway is a safety idea. Like a government highway traffic lines, truck yard traffic lines separate a truck yard roadway that directs a truck in the proper direction & minimizes truck yard accidents.

BUMPERS ALONG A BUILDING WALL OR FENCE
 PROTECT BUILDING AND FENCE ASSESTS
Bumpers along a building wall or security fence are an idea to protect a building or security fence from damage. Each bumper is secured to your truck yard/ground and bumper distance from a building wall or security fence is determined by a delivery truck rear wheel location from a delivery truck rear. A rear wheel setback is the distance from a delivery truck rear side and to a delivery truck rear wheel ear side. As a delivery truck is backed into a

parking location, a delivery truck rear wheel strikes a bumper and prevents a delivery truck rear side from striking & damaging a building wall or security fence.

ONE-WAY OR TWO-WAY TRUCK YARD TRAFFIC
MINIMIZE ACCIDENTS
One-way or two-way truck travel in a truck yard is a truck yard vehicle direction of travel pattern through a truck yard that controls a delivery truck flow to minimize accidents. With most warehouses, a truck yard truck flow pattern is determined by (1) site size, (2) operation type (a) conventional store and hold or (b) across-the-dock & (3) receiving and ship door arrangement and locations. A two-way truck yard flow has all delivery trucks enter through one combined gate that is an entrance and exit gate/guard station. A two-way truck travel concept requires a wider truck yard roadway that is along a dock front or building one side. One-way truck yard flow has all vendor delivery or ship trucks enter an entrance gate and exist through a separate exist gate. A one-way concept requires a narrow truck yard roadway that is along the dock front and engulfs a building.

KNOW YOUR DELIVERY TRUCKS & OCEAN GOING CONTAINER DIMENSIONS
LOWER BUILDING CONSTRUCTION COSTS
Know your delivery truck & ocean going container dimensions is an important feature to assure that a new facility or leased building has a proper dock height, width & height to match your delivery truck doors. A truck or container height determines your canopy or elevated floor elevation above ground. When designing a new facility dock number per building column span or a platform dock, distance between 2 truck mirrors determines a truck dock number. A truck (tractor & trailer) or container length determines a truck yard depth in a dock front or parking location length. A truck rear wheels determine truck yard drain location & parking space rear wheel bumper location. A truck or container bed elevation above the ground determines a truck dock height or dock leveler extension or length into a facility dock area.

NO DELIVERY TRUCK BLIND SIDE
IMPROVE SAFETY
No blind side is a truck yard safety idea that refers to a delivery truck backing-up direction to your dock. With a warehouse located on a property with a delivery truck road and maneuvering area to assure as a delivery truck is backed-up to a dock position that a truck driver uses side mirrors to have a vision of a truck body as a delivery truck is being turned & backed to a dock.

CAN YOU TURN DELIVERY TRUCK & TRAILER
IMPROVE SAFETY
Can you turn is a safety idea that truck yard has sufficient open space from a warehouse wall to a property line for your longest delivery truck or ocean going container to complete a turn & is properly aligned for reverse travel to a delivery truck dock.

GET YOUR DELIVERY TRUCKS OFF THE ROAD
IMPROVE SAFETY
Get off the road is a safety idea that provides a delivery truck access road from a government highway to your warehouse entrance gate. An entrance road has sufficient length for your longest delivery truck or ocean going container to clear a government roadway & adjacent to your guard station/entrance gate. If additional delivery truck parking space is required for early arrival delivery trucks, a truck yard road between a guard station & your first truck dock has sufficient width for truck parking or there is remote truck parking area within your truck yard area. In most communities, police officials desire to have no truck queue on a government highway due to high potential for accidents or traffic congestion.

GET YOUR DELIVERY TRUCKS ON THE ROAD
IMPROVE SAFETY
Get on the road is a safety idea that provides an exit road from your warehouse guard station to a government roadway. An exit road has sufficient length for your longest delivery truck or ocean going container to clear a guard

station/exit gate and government highway. In most communities, police officials desire a truck driver completed view of a government highway prior to entry onto a highway. Feature reduces potential for accidents or traffic congestion.

SLOPE YOUR TRUCK DOCK FRONT TO A DRAIN
   IMPROVE SAFETY

Slope to a drain at a delivery truck maneuvering area and warehouse wall is a safety idea. A drain is set at pre-determine ft number from your warehouse wall. Open space between a building wall and drain is for a delivery truck rear wheels. A delivery truck-maneuvering slope is gradual toward a drain that assures melting snow & water flow to a drain. A gradual & maximum allowed slope direction toward your warehouse helps prevent a truck rollaway.

YOUR TRUCK YARD HAS DIRECTION MAP, NUMBER IDENTIFICATION ON DOORS & LIGHT DOCK DOORS
   IMPROVE SAFETY

Truck yard directional maps, number ID on each dock door and light for each dock door are ideas that improve delivery truck driver & truck yard safety. A directional map options are (1) a paper document that is given by a gate guard to a truck driver or (2) signs that are placed in key truck yard or roadway locations. A directional map provides a truck driver with a proper direction to travel from a gate station (parking area) to an assigned dock location. Number ID on each dock door is large & discreetly identifies each dock door. Door ID is clearly visible by a delivery truck driver in a day or at night a light shines on each dock ID & dock door.

HOLD EARLY ARRIVALS OR HOLD THE EARLY DELIVERY TRUCKS OFF THE STREET
   IMPROVE SAFETY

Hold early arrivals is a safety idea to provide a truck parking area for early arrival vendor delivery trucks. If an early arrival vendor delivery trucks exceed your receiving dock positions and warehouse roadway parking positions, your warehouse provides additional remote parking locations with a tractor that remain under a trailer. Various early arrival vendor delivery truck parking options are (1) back to back with two roadways, (2) straight line along a perimeter with one roadway & (3) angled along a perimeter with one roadway.

BACK-UP LINES OR GUIDE RAILS IN YOUR TRUCK DOCK FRONT
   IMPROVE SAFETY & IMPROVE TRUCK DRIVER PRODUCTIVITY

Back-up lines or guide rails in each truck dock front or maneuvering area or parking area are ideas that improve truck yard safety and truck driver productivity. To assist a truck driver in a delivery truck back-up activity, options are (1) back-up lines that are painted on to a truck yard surface and onto a dock wall front & (2) delivery truck guide rails are metal tubes secured to a truck yard. Width between 2 lines or guide rails assist a truck driver to direct a delivery truck reverse travel into an assigned truck yard location and properly position at a truck dock spot or parking location. Feature minimizes truck back up time, building damage & adjacent delivery truck damage.

DOCKS ON A BUILDING ONE SIDE OR TWO SIDES
   IMPROVE SKU ACROSS-THE-DOCK CUSTOMER ORDER FLOW

Truck docks on one building side or two building sides are building design options for truck dock locations on a building wall. With a low volume store & hold warehouse, a warehouse has docks along one building side. Features are has low construction costs, one roadway along one building side and maneuvering area requires less land and two-way truck traffic. With a high volume store & hold or across-the-dock warehouse, a warehouse has docks on both building sides. Features are higher construction costs, one roadway that engulfs a warehouse facility with 2 maneuvering areas, requires additional lane & truck traffic is one-way or two-way.

STOP THE RAIN
   IMPROVE DOCK SAFETY & IMPROVE DELIVERY TRUCK UNLOADING & LOADING PRODUCTIVITY

Stop the rain is a truck dock safety and employee unload/load productivity improvement idea. Stop the rain idea has a 6 ft long & truck door width canopy that is attached to each building wall and extends outward from a building wall above each truck dock door. Some building canopies are installed on an entire building front that covers all dock doors & open space between 2 dock doors. A canopy elevation assures that delivery trucks travel unobstructed under a canopy & properly nest against a truck dock. A canopy outward extension & solid surface directs rain or water from a building wall side onto a truck body top & away from a dock leveler. A canopy provides a dry dock leveler that improves dock safety & improves employee unload/load productivity. If a truck dock front or maneuvering area is under an elevated building floor, an elevated floor stops the rain but consideration is given to additional lighting, fire safety & fire sprinkler protection & building column protection.

OPEN DOCKS OR DOCK NUMBER PER BUILDING COLUMN SPAN
LOWER BUILDING CONSTRUCTION COST, DOCK SAFETY & EMPLOYEE PRODUCTIVITY

Open docks or dock number per building column span is a building construction cost, dock safety & employee productivity idea. An open dock is basically a cement platform that extends a minimum of 6 ft from a building wall and is set at an elevation above a ground to match your delivery truck bed height. A 6 ft width permits powered or non-powered vehicles to unload/load a delivery truck & building doors along a building wall permit vehicle transfer between a dock & building. An open dock is very flexible and has low construction cost but has minimal dock safety, difficult to control door opening that allows external temperature to enter a building interior (air curtains reduces air transfer), requires a roof over a platform dock area and limits employee activity to one delivery truck. A dock door in a building wall has a building floor basically at the same delivery truck bed elevation that permits a dock leveler to facilitate an employee with a non-powered or powered vehicle to unload/load a delivery truck. A dock door in a building wall with a dock shelter or seal minimizes the outside air transfer to a building interior, improved safety & good employee productivity with controlled sku placement onto the receiving staging area.

ONE TRUCK ONE DOOR
IMPROVE SECURITY & CONTROL ENERGY CONSERVATION

One truck one door is a common warehouse receiving/shipping dock design. When compared to an open dock design, one truck one dock concept with a delivery truck that is backed up to a dock shelter/seal improves security and energy conversation.

SIDE UNLOAD A DELIVERY TRUCK WITH A FORKLIFT TRUCK IN THE TRUCK YARD
IMPROVE SAFETY, ADDS UNLOAD POSITIONS & IMPROVE EMPLOYEE PRODUCTIVITY

Do it (side unload) with a forklift truck in your truck yard is receiving safety, employee productivity & space utilization idea. If your warehouse has a vendor truck delivery on a side load/unload vehicle that does not occur frequently, you unload a vendor delivery vehicle in your truck yard with a forklift truck is unload option. With a counterbalanced forklift truck with normal forks, one pallet is handled per trip between a delivery truck and dock. With long forks or double wide forks on a heavy counterbalanced forklift truck 2 pallets are handled per trip that unloads a delivery truck in half the time. After a pallet is removed from a delivery truck, a forklift truck travels from a delivery truck to a dock & places a pallet in an assigned dock door. Inside your facility another pallet truck transfers a pallet to an assigned staging lane. To handle a random but scheduled side unload vendor truck delivery, the approach increases a receiving dock capacity with minimal equipment & building cost. When compared to a manual master carton unload activity, there is employee productivity increase. Truck yard safety factors are (1) that your truck yard is extended beyond the first or last dock location to accommodate a delivery truck and allow a forklift truck to complete a unload turn and transaction and (2) first or last dock door is assigned to the delivery vehicle that minimizes a potential forklift truck and delivery truck accidents.

HOW TO BRIDGE THE GAP BETWEEN YOUR BUILDING EDGE & DELIVERY TRUCK REAR
IMPROVE SAFETY & IMPROVE EMPLOYEE PRODUCTIVITY

How to bridge a building edge and delivery truck rear gap is a receiving dock idea that improves dock safety & receiving employee productivity. For each vendor delivery truck, a portable dock board or a dock leveler is used to bridge a gap between a receiving dock edge & delivery truck rear bed. After a gap is bridged, a portable dock board or in-floor dock leveler is a bridge that permits a non-powered or powered vehicle to enter and exit a delivery truck.

USE TWO LONG OR TWO WIDE FORKS TO SIDE UNLOAD DELIVERY TRUCKS
IMPROVE UNLOADING PRODUCTIVITY & RECEIVING DOCK TURNS

Two long or 2 wide forks is a counterbalanced forklift truck pallet-unload concept for side loaded delivery trucks when compared to employee unload master cartons improves unload productivity & receiving dock turns. The concept allows a receiving activity to unload a side loaded delivery truck in less time & increases receiving dock turns. A properly designed counterbalanced forklift truck that has counterweight and is equipped with a set of 2 long forks or two sets of short forks that handles 2 pallets per unload transaction. After removing 2 pallets from a delivery truck, a forklift truck travels over a truck yard to an assigned delivery door and places 2 pallets into an open receiving dock door. From an open receiving dock door, a mobile receiving dock pallet vehicle moves a pallet into a staging lane. When compared to a conventional forklift truck handling 1 pallet per transaction, a set of 2 long forks or a set of 2 wide forks improves employee productivity & increases receiving dock turns with an additional one time cost for a heavy counterweight forklift truck, additional hydraulics to lift two pallets with 2 wide or 2 long forks.

SIDE-BY-SIDE RECEIVING DOCK STAGING LANES
REDUCE SKU DAMAGE & IMPROVE EMPLOYEE PRODUCTIVITY

One delivery truck side by side dock receiving staging lanes is a receiving activity idea that reduces sku damage & improves employee productivity. After a receiving dock is assigned to a vendor delivery, 2 staging lanes directly behind an assigned dock door are assigned for a vendor delivered sku staging. With each pallet opening facing a dock door & other pallet opening facing a main traffic aisle & 2 pallets wide on a nominal wide receiving dock of 60 ft depth, there is (1) sufficient space for 2 wide pallet lanes and 10 pallets deep & sufficient space between pallets for a receiving clerk to complete a count, (2) verify no sku damage, (3) verify a pallet is per a company quality standard, (4) WMS identify each sku & (5) minimize employee injury.

CAN YOU TURN TRUCK YOUR FORKLIFT TRUCK IN YOUR RECEIVING STAGING AREA
IMPROVE EMPLOYEE PRODUCTIVITY & REDUCE SKU DAMAGE

Can you turn refers in a receiving dock area that all aisles have sufficient width to permit your powered dock vehicle to complete a right angle transaction or turn from one aisle to another aisle. Feature reduces possible sku damage & improves employee productivity.

AISLES AT A STAGING LANE BOTH ENDS
REDUCE SKU DAMAGE & IMPROVE EMPLOYEE PRODUCTIVITY

Aisles at a staging lane both ends is an idea that has mobile vehicle turning aisles at both receiving staging lanes ends. A front aisle is between a dock leveler edge & staging lane end width that permits a receiving or mobile vehicle to travel between a dock leveler edge & staging area. A rear aisle is between a staging lane end & a warehouse wall or rack that permits a transport vehicle to turn, pick-up a sku & travel from your receiving area to your storage area.

GET FROM YOUR DOCK TO YOUR TRUCK YARD
IMPROVE SAFETY & IMPROVE EMPLOYEE PRODUCTIVITY

Get from your dock to your truck yard/ground is a receiving dock idea that improves receiving dock safety & employee productivity. Get to the ground idea has a vertical dock lift or constructed ramp that moves a forklift truck or permits a counterbalanced forklift truck to travel from a receiving dock to a truck yard. With a dock ramp assure that your dock to ramp transfer location does not have forklift truck undercarriage hang-up, ramp to ground does not have a forklift fork tips strike the ground and ramp slope allows a controlled forklift truck travel. If your warehouse has side unload activity, equipment storage in the yard or other reason, a forklift truck requires access to the ground.

LET THERE BE LIGHT
IMPROVE EMPLOYEE PRODUCTIVITY & IMPROVE SAFETY

Let there be light or lights action on a dock is an idea to improve your dock area safety, minimize sku & equipment damage and increase employee productivity. To assure that a delivery truck at your receiving or ship dock is unloaded/loaded with fewest sku, equipment damage & good employee productivity, a truck interior is illuminated by a dock light. A dock light is attached to a dock interior wall & has an arm that extends to a truck upper left or right rear side. In a position, a dock light assures sufficient light inside a truck for an employee to complete a load or unload activity. At many warehouses, a dock light is properly located between 2 docks to provide service to both docks. With a dock door open switch, dock lights are designed to turn on with an open door & off with a closed door that has your warehouse conserve electric expense & extends a light life.

LIGHTS ACTION
IMPROVE SAFETY

At a receiving or ship truck dock, lights action is phrase for an idea to improve dock safety. A dock safety light device is located on your interior dock wall. When a dock safety device comes in contact with a delivery truck at a truck dock, a proper light is activated. Dock safety lights are (1) red light that means do not enter a delivery truck from a dock, (2) yellow light that means no delivery truck at a dock & (3) green light that means a delivery truck is at a dock and is ready for dock activity.

RECEIVING DOOR WINDOW TO VIEW YOUR TRUCK YARD
ENERGY CONSERVATION, IMPROVE SAFETY & EMPLOYEE PRODUCTIVITY

Windows to a truck yard refers to a receiving door with a window that views your truck yard to improve safety, improve employee productivity and enhance energy conservation. From inside a warehouse with a closed truck dock door, a truck door window permits a receiving clerk to verify an immediate dock area and determined that a delivery truck is at a dock. With a truck rear door frame is engulfed by a dock seal/shelter, a receiving clerk sees a delivery truck rear & opens a dock door. With the situation, opening a dock door improves dock area safety and security, minimizes controlled air to escape thereby energy conservation, minimizes dust entry into a facility & minimizes bird entry into a facility.

CONTROL YOUR RECEIVING DOCK TEMPERATURE
SKU PROTECTION

Control inside receiving dock temperature is a receiving activity idea that requires a temperature controlled receiving area to maintain a sku quality. To assure temperature control, travel from a temperature controlled receiving dock area through a passage way assures minimal temperature loss, each receiving dock door has a dock seal/shelter & door way to a storage area has a fast acting door, air curtain or plastic strips. In some warehouses, a receiving area is a temperature-controlled vestibule between a truck yard & dock area.

YOUR DOCK DOOR HAS A SEAL OR SHELTER
IMPROVES SECURITY & ENERGY CONSERVATION

Dock door seals or shelters are receiving dock idea that improves your warehouse security & energy conservation. Dock seals & shelters are attached to a building exterior wall & from a dock doorframe extend outward on both sides & top. After a delivery truck is parked at a dock, a seal or shelter engulfs a truck opened rear door. A tight delivery vehicle and dock seal/shelter fit has no opening between a truck rear doorframe & a seal/shelter that reduces temperature loss & improves security.

BLOCK OR ICC BAR HOLD YOUR DELIVERY TRUCK
IMPROVES SAFETY

Block or ICC bar hold is a receiving dock idea that improves dock area safety and minimizes a delivery truck rollaway. A truck wheel block is a rubber or metal triangle shaped device that is attached to a warehouse exterior wall. When a delivery truck is parked at a dock, a delivery truck driver places a block under a rear wheel that restricts a truck forward movement. An ICC bar is a hook shaped dock leveler component. After a delivery truck is parked at a dock, a hook device extends outward & upward to hook a truck ICC bar that secures a delivery truck at a dock.

PROTECT YOUR RECEIVING DOCK DOOR
MINIMIZES DAMAGE & ASSURES DOCK TURNS

Protect a dock door frame is a receiving area exterior & interior dock door frame idea to minimize dock door frame damage. At exterior dock door frame, cement filled pipe is secured to the ground to minimize dock door frame damage from a delivery truck accidental striking a dock door frame. At an interior dock door frame, cement filled pipes are secured to a floor in a dock door frame front to minimize dock door fame damage from a pallet or forklift truck hitting a door frame.

PAINTED LINES ON THE RECEIVING DOCK FLOOR
REDUCE SKU DAMAGE & IMPROVE EMPLOYEE PRODUCTIVITY

Painted lines on a receiving dock floor is idea that reduces sku damage & improves employee productivity. Line control on a receiving dock has 6 in wide painted lines on a receiving dock floor surface. Parallel white painted lines on your floor start at each staging lane start that is opposite a dock turning aisle & extend to a staging lane end or main traffic aisle side. For each sku staging lane there are two 6 in wide lines that means 2 staging lanes has 3 painted lines. Space between 2 parallel painted lines has the width for a pallet and is consider a sku staging lane.

WHAT TO DO WITH A VENDOR DELIVERY OVERS, SHORTS, DAMAGE & WRONG SKU
IMPROVE INVENTORY CONTROL & RECEIVING EMPLOYEE PRODUCTIVITY

What to do with a vendor delivered overs, shorts, damage or wrong sku is a receiving procedure to improve sku inventory control & receiving employee productivity. During a bulk (pallet, slip sheet, GOH or master carton) receiving activity, a receiving clerk completes a receiving activity by comparing an actual vendor delivered sku quantity to a company purchase order sku quantity. Part of the receiving activity is to separate a sku quantity that is over a purchase order quantity, identify a sku shortage to a purchase order quantity, separate damage & wrong skus. After over, short, damage & wrong skus are IDed and counted, a receiving clerk notifies the merchandising department for proper instruction to handle and account for over, short, damage & wrong skus.

WHAT IS ABOVE YOUR DOCK STAGING LANE
IMPROVE SPACE UTILIZATION

What is above your dock staging lane has potential space for your employee support activities expansion. If your existing building floor surface to ceiling bottom clearance allows an additional floor for office, IT department or employee support activities, you have an opportunity to add a free standing mezzanine. The idea requires local code approval, additional light fixtures, sprinklers and air circulation (HVAC). During your low business period, you plan your expansion. This results with a lower cost sq ft.

BRIDGE YOUR DOCK AND PASSAGE-WAY DOORS
IMPROVE SPACE UTILIZATION

Bridge your receiving/ship dock and passage-way doors and if you require storage space, a rack bridge is an opportunity to provide additional single deep pallet rack storage positions. If your floor to ceiling clearance and door open travel path does not interfere with a rack bridge (single deep rack bay upright posts and load beams) is installed in a door bay. The posts are anchored to the floor and protected with guards and load beams have front to rear members with a clear space between your floor surface and load beam bottom for a forklift truck entry/exit between your dock and vendor truck. If you desire a wider aisle than your standard load beam, with your pallet weight and aisle width specifications, your rack manufacturer calculates the preferred standard load beam. The storage positions are used for empty pallets, ship supply items or obsolete skus. If potential skus falling to the floor is a potential problem, plastic wrap pallets or add a removable barrier to a pallet position front.

WHERE YOUR WAREHOUSE SKU FLOW STARTS
ACCURATE SKU INVENTORY

At a receiving dock, your warehouse starts with delivered sku unloaded onto a dock, vendor delivered sku & piece quantity match a company purchase order, purchase order is closed & a sent to updated your WMS program. With a WMS or inventory control program, each sku receives a WMS license plate that is associated with a piece quantity. With a WMS IDed sku, a WMS IDed sku is tracked through a warehouse.

TAG EACH SKU
IMPROVE INVENTORY CONTROL

Tag each sku is a receiving activity procedure that improves inventory control & inventory tracking as a sku flows through a warehouse. To tag each sku, a receiving clerk places a human written readable or machine printed human/machine readable discreet ID on each sku. A hand or machine written tag with colored borders is a method for human readable date ID on each sku. Each color border represents one month within a 6 or 12 month time period. Per your warehouse, a discreet ID is a human or human/machine readable symobology. After a receiving clerk separates a QA sample, each sku receives a special QA ID in addition to a sku or WMS ID. A tagged sku discreetly IDs each sku, serves as a signal to start an in-house transport activity from a receiving dock & permits a sku tracked as it flows through your warehouse.

WAREHOUSE OPERATION WITH A WMS PROGRAM
IMPROVE INVENTORY CONTROL

A warehouse with a WMS program, each vendor delivered sku, customer return sku & CO receives a WMS ID. A WMS program ID uniquely or discreetly identifies a sku or CO. Feature allows each WMS ID sku or CO bar code scanned or RF tag read, transferred to a WMS program & updated in a WMS program computer as a WMS IDed sku or CO flows through your warehouse.

HOW TO DATE IT (RANDOM OR JULIAN)
SKU INVENTORY CONTROL

How to date it (random or Julian) is a receiving idea to ID each sku received date that improves inventory control. After your receiving clerk attaches a WMS ID to each sku that has an expiry or expiration date or requires a FIFO rotation, each WMS ID is associated with a received date. Received date options are (1) random ID date that requires a WMS program computer to track each WMS IDed sku date or (2) Julian date as part of a WMS ID that accounts for a date received. A Julian date with 5 digits accounts for 10 years with 265 days per year. With a human/machine readable symbology, it permits both a human/machine to recognize a date. Example: Julian date, for June 10, 2005 is 05161. 05 as a year & 161 as June 10 in a Julian calendar (accumulated date from Jan 1.)

ONE IDENTIFICATION FOR ALL YOUR VENDOR DELIVERED SKUS/PIECES
IMPROVE SKU INVENTORY CONTROL

One for All is a sku WMS ID concept that is used in a warehouse to ID a sku. A warehouse receiving clerk attaches one WMS ID for an entire vendor delivered skus (pallets, master cartons or GOH) & piece quantity. The One for All WMS ID concept requires all skus continuously moved from a receiving department to a storage area. In a storage area for best inventory control all skus are placed into adjacent floor stack storage positions and a sku with a WMS ID is a last sku withdrawn. One WMS ID for all skus is very difficult to manage, relies on employee to control sku flow & in a dynamic warehouse there are potential inventory control & FIFO rotation problems.

ONE IDENTIFICATION FOR ONE YOUR VENDOR DELIVERED SKU/PIECE
IMPROVE SKU INVENTORY CONTROL

One for one is a sku or WMS ID concept that is used in a warehouse to ID each sku. A warehouse receiving clerk attaches one WMS ID to each vendor delivered sku (pallet, master carton or GOH) & piece quantity. One for one WMS ID concept has each sku moved from a receiving department to a storage area. In a storage area with by any storage position concept, each sku is placed into single deep or dense storage position & per a WMS program a WMS ID sku is suggest for withdrawal. One WMS ID for each sku is easy to manage, enhances sku flow control & assures a FIFO rotation and used in a dynamic warehouse.

SPECIAL SKU IDENTIFICATION TAG
IMPROVE SKU INVENTORY CONTROL
A special tag is a receiving idea that in addition to a WMS ID is used to ID each sku or serves as an in-house transport instruction. A WMS ID sku with a special ID indicates to a warehouse in-house transport activity that is to receive a sku and ready for transport to an assigned area. An example is a special tag that is used to ID QA skus.

CLEAR YOUR RECEIVING DOCK STAGING LANES
IMPROVE EMPLOYEE PRODUCTIVITY, DOCK TURNS & SPACE UTILIZATION
Clear the Docks is a receiving department WMS ID sku flow idea that has a continuous sku flow from a receiving area to an in-house transport concept that improves employee productivity, space utilization & dock turns. Clear the docks concept has a receiving clerk count, verify piece quantity, verify carton/pallet quality and WMS ID each sku. After a sku receives a WMS ID, it is a signal for an in-house transport concept to move a WMS ID sku from a dock area. In a WMS ID storage position, a WMS ID sku is placed in 'not available for sale' status until your QA department inspection approves or rejects a vendor sku delivery. A QA department approval allows your receiving department to change a sku status as available for sale and a rejection has your company hold a sku in 'not available for sale' status for vendor pick-up. A continuous WMS ID sku flow opens a dock staging area, increases dock turn number, improves employee productivity and creates a constant sku flow rather than a surge.

COUNT BY NUMBERS (PALLETS, MASTER CARTONS AND GOH) & DETAIL OR PIECE COUNT
ACCURATE SKU INVENTORY, IMPROVE INVENTORY CONTROL & IMPROVED DOCK TURNS
Count by the numbers is used for small items or GOH that require a detail or piece count and a receiving idea to clear the docks, enhance dock turns, create an accurate sku inventory count and improve inventory control. The idea has your receiving department count a bulk vendor delivered small sku or GOH quantity & if required to send a vendor delivered and bulk received sku quantity to a detail or piece count receiving activity. First receiving activity assures that a vendor delivered small item or GOH total quantity matches a company purchase order quantity. When a bulk delivery has mixed skus on a vendor delivery (such style, color and size), a bulk-received quantity receives a warehouse tracking ID & is sent to a detail or piece receiving/count activity. At a detail count receiving activity, each WMS ID sku (style, color and size) is counted, receives a WMS ID & entered into a WMS program.

SKU QUANTITY HANDLED ON A PALLET OR AS INDIVIIDUAL MASTER CARTONS
EMPLOYEE PRODUCTIVITY & IMPROVE SKU INVENTORY CONTROL
Pallet or master carton quantity refers to a receiving department idea for ID and handling a less than one pallet WMS ID sku quantity. Receiving options are with a WMS ID on each master carton or master carton quantity on a WMS ID pallet. To assist a receiving department with a decision to handle a vendor delivered sku quantity as one pallet with several master cartons or individual master cartons, a warehouse manager establishes a standard or procedure to handle (1) X master carton number or less as individual master cartons and each master carton receives a WMS identification. The concept is used for a warehouse that has a carton storage area to improve employee productivity, inventory tracking and space utilization. Feature is true for a warehouse with a carton AS/RS storage concept or (2) several master cartons on one WMS ID pallet. The concept is used in a warehouse with only pallet storage. A storage area has ½ high pallet positions to handle a small master carton quantity. As a master carton quantity becomes depleted in a pallet position, it creates poor position/space utilization.

WHERE DO YOUR RECEIVED SKUS GO
IMPROVE SKU INVENTORY CONTROL
Where do your received skus go is phrase that describes an idea that has a WMS human/machine readable ID included as a warehouse section or environmental condition for a WMS ID sku. In addition to a human readable location ID, a colored ink for human readable section or a colored border helps to identify a WMS ID sku destination. After a WMS ID with a colored border is placed onto a sku, an in-house transport and storage area employee has a clear and understandable instruction for a sku preferred warehouse storage/pick location. Examples are high value sku/security section, refrigerated section, freezer section, GOH section, low rack position, high rack position, bonded warehouse and humidity controlled section.

ONE GOH OR 3 TO 5 BUNDLED GOH
IMPROVE EMPLOYEE PRODUCTIVITY & IMPROVE SKU INVENTORY CONTROL

One GOH or bundled GOH is a GOH receiving idea that improves employee productivity & inventory control. As GOH is moved through a warehouse, 1 GOH per WMS ID storage or pick transaction requires 1 WMS scan & employee movement transaction. After a detail receiving activity, a receiving employee with a rubber band or twister creates 3 to 5 GOH per bundle as a bundled GOH moves through your storage/pick activities, an employee increases GOH per transaction. As a bundled GOH is placed into a WMS ID storage or a picker completes a pick transaction, there is an increase GOH number per scan & employee movement transaction that increases productivity. If your GOH operation is for retail stores, your GOH pieces per bundle is based on your historical retail store first time sku CO quantity. If your GOH warehouse has a bulk pick activity, your GOH pieces per bundle is based on your first time sku bulk pick quantities. With a 3 or 5 bundle concept, an individual GOH piece transaction is completed by entry on a scanner device.

KNOW YOUR MASTER CARTON & SKU CUBE (L, W, H & WT)
IMPROVE SPACE UTILIZATION & IMPROVE EMPLOYEE PRODUCTIVITY

Know your master carton & sku cube (length, width and height) & weight are important ideas that impact both a carton warehouse's storage space utilization and replenishment as well as pick employee productivity. Accurate master carton & sku data in a WMS program files assures maximum a master carton number to fit into a storage/pick position and accurate sku master carton dimensions assures maximum master carton number replenished to a pick position. In a carton AS/RS storage area, a master carton dimensions determine a master carton number on a tray or wide in a rack bay. To assure accurate sku information, as a new sku enters to your warehouse or a computer flags sku on a receiving or QA document that indicates to a receiving or QA clerk that an employee is responsible to take a master carton or sku cube data & WMS computer data transfer. Cube data collected options are manual measure and scale, 3-dimensional cube platform that has 3 separate colored lines for each carton size & scale & cube machine.

HOW IS YOUR SKU DELIVERED (PALLET, SLIP SHEET, FLOOR STACK)
EMPLOYEE PRODUCTIVITY, DOCK TURNS & SPACE UTILIZATION

How is your sku delivered (pallet, slip sheet or floor stack) is important information to your receiving department that assures your receiving department has proper employee number, proper dock equipment, good employee productivity & increases dock turns. In most warehouses, as a receiving clerk is developing a vendor delivery schedule, with a vendor or from a purchase order a receiving clerk verifies a sku type & vendor delivery method. Sku type indicates a sku storage conditions or warehouse section. The delivery method determines the required dock time & dock equipment that is required to complete a unload activity such as floor stacked vendor delivered master cartons has a long unload time & unitized (pallets or slip sheets) has a shorter unload time.

GET TO KNOW YOUR SKUS (PIECES) PER MASTER CARTON OR PALLET (PACK KEY)
ACCURATE INVENTORY & IMPROVE EMPLOYEE PRODUCTIVITY

Get to know your skus (pieces) per master carton or pallet is referred to as a pack key or sku piece number that is important to a WMS program to allocate a sku quantity to complete a replenishment or pick transaction with high employee productivity. A sku or piece quantity per master carton & quantity per pallet (pallet TI or master cartons per layer & pallet HI or master carton layer high) is printed on an advance ship notice & is verified by a receiving clerk. When your WMS program allocates a WMS ID sku number for transfer from a storage position to a pick position, from a sku or piece number per master carton & master cartons per pallet a WMS program determines a master carton or pallet number that is required to complete a WMS ID pick position set-up or replenishment transaction. If your WMS program rounds-up your master carton replenishment activity to your fast moving sku pick section, a sku number per master carton is very important to assure that a proper master carton number is allocated/replenished to your fast moving sku pick section & 1 master carton is allocated to your other pick section.

WMS IDENTIFICATION ON A SKU FRONT OR SIDE
ACCURATE SKU INVENTORY, COMPLETE SCAN TRANSACTIONS & IMPROVE EMPLOYEE PRODUCTIVITY

WMS ID on a master carton or pallet front or side is determined by your in-house & storage transaction requirements and assures sku good scan transaction, accurate sku tracking and good employee productivity. In most warehouses, as a sku enters a warehouse, each sku receives a WMS ID. For each storage (deposit) or replenishment transaction and each sku on a powered conveyor in-house transport concept, each sku WMS identification is read by a bar code scanner device that sends an update message to your WMS computer. For maximum good reads with good employee productivity a bar code scanner requires line of sight to a sku bar code. In most storage and replenishment transactions, a front WMS ID is a preferred location due to the fact that a bar code faces an employee and an employee does not have non-productive time to orient a master carton for a scan transaction and re-orient a master carton to complete a replenishment transaction. With a front sku WMS ID to a match an in-house transport side scanner requirements, a powered conveyor travel path has a device to turn a sku or pulls a gap between 2 skus for a scanner line of sight. On most in-house transport concepts (except a pallet on forklift truck), a side WMS ID is a preferred location due to line of sight and short depth of field (bar code distance from a scanner). Prior to an in-house transport concept discharge station, a sku turning device turns a pallet to have a WMS ID face a forklift truck driver. To minimize material handling equipment cost & assure a storage/replenishment & in-house transport concept bar code line of sight, a warehouse bar code label options are to use (1) 2 identical WMS IDs on a sku. With 1 ID on a sku front & other ID on a sku side, 2 bar code location satisfies all your warehouse activity bar code line of sight requirements; but this represent additional print time, 2 labels & potential label control problems or (2) 1 wrap around WMS ID label. A wrap around ID is 1 long label with 1 WMS ID that faces a sku front & same (other) WMS ID that faces a sku side. Wrap around label configuration satisfies all your warehouse activity bar code line of sight requirements, slightly less label print time, one label & minimizes label control problems. It is mentioned that a RF symbology reader to a recognize a WMS ID does not require line of sight but at most warehouse sku transfer or replenishment station a human requires line of sight to a RF tag human readable symbology.

WHY DO YOU WANT PALLETS OR SLIP SHEET DELIVERIES
IMPROVE EMPLOYEE PRODUCTIVITY & INCREASE DOCK TURNS

To achieve good master carton receiving productivity & increase dock turns, a warehouse idea is to have vendor sku delivered unitized & wrapped onto a good quality pallet or slip-sheet. A good quality pallet matches your warehouse standards. A slip-sheet is corrugated sheet with a lip that permits a slip-sheet equipped forklift truck to unload & on a receiving dock transfer a slip-sheet onto your warehouse pallet. When compared to a master carton floor stack vendor delivery, a pallet or slip-sheet delivery requires less unloading time.

VENDOR LOAD	COST	UNLOAD TIME	DOCK TURNS
FLOOR STACK	$ 0	2 EMPLOYEES 6 TO 8 HRS	1
PALLET	$15	1 EMPLOYEE 1 TO 2 HRS	3
SLIP SHEET	$2.50 (*)	1 EMPLOYEE 1 TO 2 HRS	3

(*) For maximum efficiency requires a forklift truck slip-sheet device $15,000 & dock slip sheet back board $2,500 that is depreciated or expensed per your accounting department.

SLIP SHEET BACK STOP
IMPROVE EMPLOYEE PRODUCTIVITY & LOWER COSTS

Slip-sheet backstop is a receiving dock device that is used in a slip-sheet unload activity to improve forklift truck driver productivity and lower slip sheet handling costs. A vendor slip-sheet delivery has at a vendor facility master cartons that are placed onto a kraft corrugated or plastic slip-sheet. Each slip-sheet has a 6 in lip that extends outward and is clamped by a forklift truck slip-sheet device. In a vendor delivery truck, a forklift truck pulls a slip-sheet onto slip-sheet device and exits a vendor delivery truck. With a slip sheet back stop, as a forklift truck with a slip sheet load exists a vendor deliver truck & arrives onto a receiving dock, a forklift truck with a slip sheet travels to a slip sheet back stop for slip sheet transfer onto a pallet. At a slip sheet back stop is a pallet stack on a two sided 90 degree metal device that is secured to a warehouse floor & building column. Above a pallet top, a forklift truck places a slip-sheet load & pushes a slip-sheet load forward from a slip-sheet device onto a pallet top. A 2-sided metal backstop device assures proper slip-sheet alignment on a pallet & permits a forklift truck with chisel forks to transfer a slip sheet onto a pallet.

SIGNAL WHEN A SKU IS READY FOR IN-HOUSE TRANSPORT
IMPROVE EMPLOYEE PRODUCTIVITY, SPACE UTILIZATION & CONTROLLED SKU FLOW
Signal when ready for in-house transport is a receiving activity idea that improves employee productivity, enhances space utilization & controlled sku flow. After unloaded skus are properly staged on a receiving dock, each pallet sku has a fork opening side & WMS ID face a warehouse main aisle. each master carton has a direction of travel & WMS ID face a warehouse main aisle/conveyor travel path & GOH lead piece & WMS ID face a direction of travel/conveyor travel path. After a sku & a WMS ID is placed in a proper staging location, a sku WMS ID that faces a main vehicle aisle or in-house transport travel path serves as a signal to an in-house transport employee that a sku is ready for transport or a receiving activity has released sku to an in-house transport activity. A sku with no WMS ID means that the receiving process in not complete and a sku remains in a receiving staging area.

BAR CODE OR RF TRANSACTION RECORD
IMPROVE EMPLOYEE PRODUCTIVITY & ACCURATE INVENTORTY TRACKING
To use a bar code (BC) or RF tag (RF) as a sku WMS ID is an idea that improves employee productivity & enhances accurate inventory tracking as a sku flows through a warehouse. When compared to a human readable symbology and manual record keeping transaction, a bar code & RF tag (machine readable) symbology improves employee productivity, assures an accurate transaction with verification & on-time data transfer to warehouse or WMS computer. When we compare a human/machine readable bar code & RF tag symbology, major differences are that a bar code requires a line of sight & presently has a lower cost & a RF tag does not require a line of sight & presently has a higher cost.

HUMAN/MACHINE READABLE SYMBOLOY RATHER A HUMAN READABLE SYMBOLOGY
IMPROVE EMPLOYEE PRODUCTIVITY, FLEXIBILITY & ACCURATE INVENTORTY TRACKING
To use a sku WMS human/machine readable symbology is an idea that improves employee productivity, provides operation activity flexibility and enhances accurate sku ID reads and on time date transfer. When we compare human readable symbology to a human/machine readable symbology, a machine readable section is added to a human readable label face. A human readable symbology read and data transfer activity has potential for transposition or writing errors, warehouse employee & office clerk time to read and write onto a form & delayed data transfer. A human/machine readable symbology read activity has minimal transposition error potential due to complete a transaction, a scanner requires a line of sight to a machine readable symbology that increases an employee sku data collection and transaction productivity & accurate & on-time data transfer.

HUMAN READABLE SYMBOLOGY ON TOP OR BOTTOM OF MACHINE READBLE SYMBOLOGY
IMPROVE EMPLOYEE PRODUCTIVITY, FLEXIBILITY & ACCURATE INVENTORTY TRACKING
WMS sku human readable alpha characters/digits or machine readable symbology label locations are best placed on a label bottom or top. In a warehouse, a human/machine readable symbology can then be included as part of a storage employee or picker instruction. At a receiving dock, an in-house transport employee reads a sku WMS ID on a GOH, master carton or pallet that directs an employee to move a WMS ID sku to a storage position. A sku WMS ID purpose is to assure quick & readable employee line of sight. Human/machine readable ID label locations are a label on the bottom or on the top. Human readable alpha characters/digits on a sku WMS label bottom means that human readable alpha characters/digits are above your bar code symbology. Features are (1) assures employee/scanner line of sight & at a lower elevation of a nominal 2 ins above a conveyor or cart surface. To read

a sku WMS, it requires an employee to lift a carton or bend to read a pallet ID that means non-productive time & physical effort, (2) same label print cost & (3) no impact on bar code line of sight. Human readable alpha characters/digits on a sku WMS ID top means that a bar code symbology is below your human readable characters/digits. Features are (1) assures an employee or scanner line of sight, at a higher elevation of a nominal 8 ins. above a conveyor or cart surface. To read a sku WMS ID, it does not require an employee to lift a carton or deep bend to read a pallet ID that means less physical effort with minimal non-productive time, (2) same label print cost & (3) no impact on bar code line of sight.

HOW MUCH SKU QUANTITY TO HOLD IN YOUR STAGING AREA
IMPROVES SPACE UTILIZATION, SMOOTH SKU FLOW & TRUCK DOCK TURNS
How much to hold on a receiving dock staging area is a receiving activity idea that improves a receiving dock space utilization, truck dock turns & smooth sku flow from a receiving dock area to a storage area. After a sku is placed into a receiving dock lane or position, a receiving clerk verifies receipt, sku & pallet quantity & quality & places a WMS ID onto a pallet. A receiving dock side by side lanes and pallet positions permit sufficient receiving work area to unload vehicle & deposit a sku for an in-house transport vehicle WMS ID sku pick-up. With a WMS ID on a sku, an in-house transport vehicle moves a WMS ID sku from a receiving area to a storage area/drop location. In most warehouses with a WMS program, as a WMS ID sku is moved to a storage area, each sku is placed on hold (not available for sale) until QA approval or receiving department authorization & a sku is change to available for sale.

HOW TO HOLD YOUR SKUS OR STAGE SKUS
IMPROVES SPACE UTILIZATION, TRUCK DOCK TURNS & INVENTORY CONTROL
How to hold or stage it (vendor delivered sku) is an idea to improve receiving dock space utilization, truck dock turns and inventory control. Your receiving dock staging options are (1) basic receiving dock staging concept is a floor stack concept that has pallets in side-by-side rows from a dock turn aisle to a warehouse turn aisle. The concept requires a large floor area with poor space utilization. With stable, uniform & high strength skus, floor stack pallets are stacked 2 high. The concept increases space utilization but requires a forklift truck to complete all elevated transactions, (2) standard rack staging concept permits 3 to 4 pallets high that requires all skus received and WMS ID before transfer to a rack position, increases space utilization, additional rack cost requires a wider turn aisle & forklift truck to complete elevated transactions, (3) push back rack staging concept has 3 high & 3 deep pallets that requires all skus received & WMS ID before transfer to a rack position, increases space utilization, requires a wider turn aisle, additional rack cost & forklift truck to complete elevated transactions & (4) gravity flow rack concept has 3 to 4 pallets high and 5 to 6 pallets deep requires all skus received & WMS ID before transfer to a rack position, increases space utilization, a higher rack cost and requires 2 aisles. One aisle on a receiving dock is used for a forklift truck to complete deposit transactions & a second aisle on the storage area side is used to complete withdrawal transactions. Per local code, all rack concepts require fire sprinklers, back-to-back ties, floor anchors, rack post protectors & overhead ties.

HOW TO HANDLE VENDOR DELIVERED REJECTED SKUS
INVENTORY CONTROL
How to handle rejection is a receiving dock and storage area activities that control location & movement of a vendor delivered & rejected sku delivery. In a warehouse sku rejection situation, a vendor delivery truck has departed a warehouse & WMS ID skus are placed into a WMS ID storage position with a not available for sale status. With a WMS program tracking WMS ID skus, rejected WMS ID skus are held in WMS ID storage positions as not available for sale. On a scheduled rejected sku return to vendor date, rejected skus are withdrawn from WMS ID positions & assembled for loading onto a delivery truck & deleted from inventory.

QA SKU SAMPLE QUANTITY
INVENTORY CONTROL & INVENTORY TRACKING
QA sampler is a receiving clerk activity that separates a vendor delivered sku quantity as a sample for quality inspection. From a large sku delivery, random selected full master cartons permit a receiving clerk to assure sufficient QA sku quantity. Full master cartons as a QA sample assure improved inventory control & allow pallet

WMS ID. If a vendor delivery has a master carton with a different sku piece count, a master carton is preferred for a QA sample. Each QA sample full master carton with a WMS ID & QA tag improves inventory control and transfer. If a vendor delivery has several pallets or master cartons, for best inventory control each opened master carton receives a WMS ID that allows a WMS program to track a sku & assure accurate replenishment & pick activities.

KNOW YOUR PALLET TI & HI, POSITION HEIGHT & EMPLOYEE REACH HEIGHT
IMPROVE SPACE UTILIZATION & EMPLOYEE PRODUCTIVITY

Know your pallet TI & HI, your storage position height or employee reach height is a purchase and receiving department idea in a warehouse that optimizes a pallet load handling, improves space utilization and improve employee productivity and helps to secure master cartons onto a pallet. Ti is a master carton number on a layer & in most occurrences there is no master carton overhang of a pallet dimensions. Hi is a master carton layer high on a pallet that assures maximum master carton number on a pallet, a pallet fits into your storage position & height allows your forklift truck to handle maximum master carton number on a pallet. A pallet height is at a height that allows an employee to easily complete a carton pick transaction from a pallet top that assures good picker productivity.

HANDLE A VENDOR SKU QUANTITY AS MASTER CARTONS OR PALLET
SPACE UTILIZATION, IMPROVE EMPLOYEE PRODUCTIVITY & IMPROVE INVENTORY CONTROL

Handle as master cartons, half-high pallet or full pallet is a receiving activity idea that starts at a receiving dock & improves in-house transport & storage area employee productivity, space utilization & inventory control. After a vendor sku delivery is unloaded onto a dock, a sku master carton number & characteristics influence how to handle a sku as an in-house transport & storage area WMS ID sku. A full pallet is handled with one WMS ID that is placed into a full pallet WMS ID position. Each full pallet is handled as 1 WMS ID transaction. Less than a full pallet options are to handle as (1) a full pallet with one WMS ID and placed into a ½ high WMS ID storage position. When compared to a ½ high pallet in a full pallet position, a ½ high pallet position improves space utilization. Each ½ high pallet is handled as one WMS ID transaction or (2) as individual WMS ID master cartons. In a receiving area each master carton receives a WMS ID & is handled a 1 WMS identified sku. With a carton storage concept, an individual WMS ID master carton is placed into a carton AS/RS or decked rack WMS ID position that permits access to each WMS ID master carton, assures good space utilization and good employee productivity.

HOW TO UNLOAD PALLETS, SLIP SHEETS, MASTER CARTONS & GOH
IMPROVE EMPLOYEE PRODUCTIVITY & INCREASE DOCK TURNS

How to unload pallets, slip-sheets, master cartons or GOH is a receiving idea that improves employee productivity & increases receiving dock turns. When a receiving activity uses a manual (company employee or truck driver) unload concept, the result is low employee productivity & fewer receiving dock turns. To have a company purchase department have a vendor unitized master cartons onto pallets or slip-sheets improves unload productivity & dock turns. If you allow vendor truck drivers to use manual powered pallet truck or your employee to use powered pallet or forklift truck to transfer a pallet from a delivery truck onto a dock increases employee productivity & truck dock turns. With a floor stack vendor delivery to minimize sku or master carton double handling, as a vendor loads a delivery vehicle a vendor separates each sku that permits your employee to easily identify and palletize master cartons. Feature means higher employee productivity & increased dock turns.

WHAT IS THE SIZE & WHERE TO SEND A SKU
IMPROVES EMPLOYEE PRODUCTIVITY & SPACE UTILIZATION

What is the size and where to send it is a receiving activity idea that increases storage space utilization & forklift truck productivity. If a warehouse has a wide sku size mix & a WMS program that flags in a sku WMS ID a sku specific storage area, a WMS ID on a sku directs an in-house transport & storage activities to move & store a specific WMS ID skus in a specific storage area. Such as (1) large skus are allocated to a floor stacked or stacking frame storage area and are handled by conventional forklift trucks & (2) regular sized skus are sent to a standard rack storage area and are handled by very narrow aisle forklift trucks or AS/RS cranes.

EMPTY PALLETS HOW MANY & WHERE TO LOCATE EMPTY PALLETS
IMPROVES EMPLOYEE PRODUCTIVITY & DOCK TURNS

Empty pallets how many and where to locate is a receiving activity to assure that there is a sufficient empty pallet quantity at a dock location to handle a vendor delivery. With a floor stack staging concept, slip sheet load or pallet exchange program, a receiving department requires an empty pallet large number to handle a vendor delivery sku pallet number. When a receiving department completes a dock schedule appointment with a vendor or freight company, a receiving clerk reviews a vendor delivery type such as floor stack, slip sheet or palletized load. With the information, for each dock position, a receiving department knows a required empty pallet number. For good receiving productivity & truck dock turns, no empty vendor delivery truck departure delays, an empty pallet quantity is readily available to the receiving clerk. Empty pallet location options are (1) floor stack pallets between two dock doors. To minimize building damage, protection posts are located in-front of dock door frames and wall, (2) floor stacked in one empty staging lane, (3) with standard rack staging to use elevated rack positions, (4) with push back rack staging concept to use elevated rack positions & (5) with gravity flow rack concept, use pre-determined reverse flow lanes that flow pallets from a storage area to a receiving dock.

SMALL SKU OR GOH DETAIL COUNT & PACK
IMPROVE EMPLOYEE PRODUCTIVITY & INVENTORY CONTROL

Detail count & pack is a receiving activity idea to improve storage & pick employee productivity & enhance inventory control. Detail count receiving activity has a receiving clerk exactly count a vendor delivery by each sku size, color and style. In a warehouse, a detail count occurs with jewelry, GOH, spare parts or very small skus. Detail count options are (1) manual count activity that has an employee physically handle each sku or (2) a scale count activity that has an employee use a scale to weigh a pre-determines sku quantity. After an entire sku quantity is placed onto a scale, a sample weigh count determines a total count. After a detail count activity, a receiving employee transfers a sku quantity into a bag or container. To optimize future storage or pick employee activity, a detail receiving employee places a pre-determined sku number into a re-sealable and re-useable bag or container & writes a sku quantity onto a tag. A tag is placed inside or onto a container with a sku quantity facing the outside. In a conventional GOH warehouse after GOH detail receiving activity, with a rubber band or twister a receiving clerk bundles GOH into quantities of 3 or 5. Feature improves storage & picker future productivity.

RECEIVING OFFICE WITH DRIVER FACILITIES
IMPROVE EMPLOYEE PRODUCTIVITY & SECURITY

A receiving office with driver facilities is a receiving idea that improves security, space utilization & employee productivity. A receiving office with driver facilities is located for an office to have a view of most dock doors & dock staging lanes & minimize receiving clerk walk time & distance between an office & dock location and controls/restricts drivers from entering a warehouse area. In a small size warehouse with few docks, a receiving office is best located on one side of a receiving area. In a large warehouse with a large dock number, a receiving office is often best located in the middle along a main aisle or dock staging rear area. With adequate ceiling height, to optimize space utilization, an office can also be elevated above the floor. Note local codes and requirements,

PRE-INSPECT VENDOR SKUS
IMPROVE EMPLOYEE PRODUCTIVITY & INCREASE DOCK TURNS

Pre-inspect your vendor manufactured skus at a vendor facility is a receiving & QA idea that increases your receiving dock productivity & receiving dock turns. Pre-inspect at a vendor manufacturing facility concept has a company or third party inspector who your company has qualified to complete your company sku inspection prior to a vendor loading your company purchased skus onto a vendor delivery vehicle. Your vendor site sku inspection assures that a vendor-manufactured skus are per your company purchase order, company standards & government codes. After vendor-site inspector sku approval, a vendor loads skus onto a delivery vehicle for delivery to your warehouse. At a warehouse, your receiving department unloads and receives a vendor sku delivery onto your receiving dock. Per your company receiving & QA policy, as a vendor delivery is unloaded at your warehouse, an on-site QA inspector completes a random sample sku QA quality inspection or check. With a vendor sku delivery that a pre-inspection status, a vendor sku is unloaded, received and placed into a WMS identified storage position with a not available for sale status until QA approval.

SKU PIECE COUNT IS IMPORTANT
ACCURATE SKU INVENTORY, INVENTORY CONTROL & IMPROVE EMPLOYEE PRODUCTIVITY

Sku piece count per WMS ID pallet or master carton is very important to assure an accurate sku inventory, inventory control & high employee productivity. During a sku flow through a warehouse, an accurate sku pallet & master carton piece count that is attached to a WMS ID permits a WMS program to match a WMS ID sku master carton to pallet replenishment activity or CO pick transaction. When there is piece count variance for each WMS ID pallet or master carton for an employee to match a WMS ID sku transaction quantity requires an employee to handle each pallet or master carton & count each master carton or pallet WMS ID sku quantity withdrawn instead of counting or handling a WMS ID pallet or master carton quantity.

SCALE COUNT SMALL SKUS
IMPROVE EMPLOYEE RECEIVING, PUT-AWAY & INVENTORY COUNT PRODUCTIVITY

Scale count is a detail receiving activity that improves receiving, put-away and inventory count employee productivity. When your warehouse receives loose very small or small items that are at a receiving dock bulk or master carton received, to verify an actual vendor delivered sku quantity, your receiving department completes a detail or specific sku receive or count activity that is entered into your WMS program or inventory program files. If your detail receiving activity uses a scale count concept, when compared to a manual count activity there is a reduction in time to complete a sku count.

COUNT SMALL SKUS INTO IDENTIFIED BAGS
IMPROVE EMPLOYEE RECEIVING, PUT-AWAY & INVENTORY COUNT PRODUCTIVITY

During your detail receiving activity, your receiving clerk counts each sku quantity. For maximum receiving efficiency your receiving clerk can count small sizes into manageable quantities such as 25 or 50 pieces. After your receiving clerk count activity, your options are (1) consolidate total sku quantity into one container. Features are (a) for inventory count or return to vendor, low count productivity and preparation, (b) skus are loose in a container that means no additional picker open activity and (c) skus are not protected and (2) each sku count quantity is placed into a bag with count quantity placed into a bag. Features are for inventory count or return to vendor minimal employee effort, (b) additional picker activity to open a bag and (c) skus are protected in a bag.

VENDOR DELIVERED SKUS ARE AVAILABLE FOR SALE OR NOT AVAILABLE FOR SALE
IMPROVES RECEIVING & IN-HOUSE TRANSPORT PRODUCTIVITY & INCREASES DOCK TURNS

When a not available for sale concept is compared to available for sale concept, not available for sale concept has a vendor delivered sku unloaded, received and put-away in a constant flow that improves receiving & in-house transport employee productivity & increases receiving dock turns. An available for sale concept has a vendor delivered skus unloaded, received and held in a receiving dock staging lane for QA approval. After QA approval, WMS identified skus are in-house transported from a receiving dock for put-away to a WMS ID storage position. Waiting for the QA approval, available for sale concept requires additional receiving dock staging area & decreases a receiving dock turns. A not available for sale concept has a vendor delivered skus unloaded, received, WMS ID & in-house transported to a WMS ID storage position. During your QA department inspection activity, your receiving docks are cleared & your receiving & QA department places WMS ID skus into a QA hold or not available for sale inventory status. After your QA department sku approval, your QA department notifies your receiving department & with an entry into a WMS or inventory control program your receiving department changes a vendor delivered sku status from not available for sale to available for sale status. The procedure assures that quality skus are available for sale & your in-house transport/put-away activities have a constant sku flow to a WMS ID storage positions.

DAMAGED/WRONG PALLET DO NOT DOUBLE STACK A PROBLEM PALLET ONTO A GOOD PALLET
IMPROVE EMPLOYEE PRODUCTIVITY & MINIMIZE SKU DAMAGE

Damaged or wrong pallet do not double stack onto a good pallet means your receiving department has skus on a pallet that is not acceptable to your warehouse. A not acceptable pallet has a broken stringer or deck board or has dimensions that do not your storage area specifications. With close clearances (open space) in storage rack positions, there is a potential problem for a manual forklift truck or AS/RS crane complete a storage transaction to a rack storage position. In your warehouse a picker has additional non-productive time to handle pallets. For skus entry into your storage concept, your options are (1) manual re-palletize skus that increases your cost per unit & occupies dock space, (2) mechanical transfer or invert a problem pallet skus onto your captive good pallet that requires equipment cost & some labor cost & (3) stack a problem pallet onto your captive good pallet that has minimal receiving labor cost, with an unstable load, potential problems & if your warehouse is a master carton or pieces operation, at pick position a picker has increased non-productive time to remove pallets that has potential to create a pick line back-up.

UNDER-SIZE OR OVER-SIZE VENDOR CARTON
IMPROVE SPACE UTILIZATION, GOOD INVENTORY CONTROL & ACCURATE REPLENISHMENTS

When your receiving department unloads a vendor delivery with under-sized or over-sized master cartons, your receiving department contacts your purchasing department and advises your purchasing department that a vendor sku delivery requires re-packaging into your standard size cartons. Per a purchasing department direction and after a vendor or your operation re-packages a sku, a vendor sku is received and each package receives a WMS ID. A sku re-packaged into a standard size carton assures accurate replenishment activity and good inventory tracking. To assure vendor compliance with your standard size carton, your purchasing department advises new vendor and periodically e-mails/advises exiting vendors as to your standard carton size.

HOLD FOR IN-HOUSE RE-WORK OR SEND TO OUT-SIDE RE-WORK
IMPROVE SPACE UTILIZATION & GOOD INVENTORY CONTROL

After your receiving department has unloaded and received a vendor delivery and your QA department has ID a sku quality or sku carton size problem (not per your company standard, your receiving department notifies your purchasing department about a problem. If your purchasing department is not available, your receiving department WMS IDs a problem sku and in your WMS computer program enters a sku status as 'not available for sale'. With 'not available for sale' status, a sku is placed into your 'D' sku section or remote storage position. After your purchasing department determines a problem sku disposition (re-work in-house with company or vendor labor or send to an out-side re-work company, your storage activity transfers a problem sku to an assigned re-turn to vendor or re-work station.

CHAPTER 3
IN-HOUSE TRANSPORT, STORAGE & INVENTORY CONTROL COST SAVING IDEAS

WHEN A SKU IS READY TO LEAVE YOUR RECEIVING DOCK
   IMPROVE EMPLOYEE PRODUCTIVITY & SMOOTH SKU FLOW

When a sku is ready to leave your receiving dock is an-house transport concept that improves employee productivity and assures a smooth sku flow. When a sku is ready to leave your receiving dock, a tag (signal) is attached to an unloaded and received sku that is a signal (label) that a sku is ready to leave a receiving dock staging lane. In a receiving dock staging lane, a receiving clerk places a WMS ID onto a pallet, master carton, GOH or container side or front that faces a storage or main travel path aisle. In a position, a sku ID is clearly visible to an in-house transport employee or powered conveyor travel path scanner/reader.

BAR CODE OR RF TAG SKU IDENTIFICATION
   MAXIMUM READ CAPACITY

Bar code and RF tag sku IDs are an in-house transport sku symbology options. A bar code or RF tag both are machine readable symbologies that uniquely or discreetly identify one sku from another sku & IDs a sku destination or travel path drop location. In most warehouses, a bar code or RF tag label face have a human readable ID. With a bar code symbology, as a bar coded sku travels over a travel path, a bar code scanner along a travel path requires bar code line of sight. A line of sight requirement in some warehouses requires a bar code as a wrap around or two section label with the same bar code printed on two sections of a label. When a wrap around label is properly placed onto a sku, it permits bar code scanner line of sight from two directions (sku side or front). On sku travel path, a RF tag sends a signal or transmission that is received or read by receiver or reader that is along the travel path. Feature means that a RF tag does not require line of sight that means a simple reader or receiver & travel path design. At present a RF tag has a slightly higher cost & is not used in all warehouses/supply chains that is another reason for a human readable symbology on a tag/label face.

SKU TAGGED WITH A WMS IDENTIFICATION TELLS WHERE A SKU GOES
   IMPROVES EMPLOYEE PRODUCTIVITY & ASSURES CORRECT STORAGE AREA

Sku tagged with a WMS ID tells where a sku goes is an in-house transport concept idea that improves employee productivity & assures compliance with your sku storage strategy. In a receiving area, each sku receives a human/machine readable WMS ID or is pre-tagged with the ID. After reading a tag with a hand held scanner that sends a sku WMS ID to a computer program, a computer program sends a message back to a hand held scanner display scan. A display scan shows or directs an in-house transport concept employee, AGV or powered conveyor travel path to deliver a sku to a specific storage area or aisle. ID options are (1) human/machine readable symbology, (2) colored border or (3) hybrid that is both.

SKU IDENTIFICATION HAS ONE FACE, WRAP AROUND OR HYBRID
   ASSURE LINE OF SIGHT & MAXIMUM GOOD READS

Sku ID has one face, wrap-around or hybrid bar code label are label design options to assure line of sight for a sku bar code reader or employee that increases maximum good read number. Bar code label line of sight assures good employee or scanner productivity by reducing your bad read number or scan attempts. A one face label on a paper has one bar code per label. A one face label on a sku (pallet, master carton, tote or GOH) faces one direction that is a sku side, top or front. Features are low label paper & ink expense & with some applications to complete a scan transaction requires additional employee time or a mechanical device to turn a sku. A wrap-around label has 2 bar codes that face 2 directions and on a sku a wrap-around label faces a sku front and side. Features are minimizes additional employee time or mechanical equipment to turn a sku for a scan transaction, has a higher paper & ink expense. An example has a wrap around label placed onto a sku with 1 bar face a front & second bar code face a side. A sku hybrid label has one bar code in two different orientations on one label/face. A hybrid label faces one direction (side, front or top) but your bar code print format has a picket fence orientation &

has a ladder orientation. A hybrid label has the same features as a 1 bar code label, but with the same bar code in two different orientations permits scanner light beam flexibility and higher paper & ink expense.

ONE IDENTIFICATION FOR ALL VENDOR DELIVERED SKUS (MASTER CARTONS OR PALLETS)
EMPLOYEE PRODUCTIVITY, SPACE UTILIZATION & INVENTORY CONTROL

One identification for all your vendor delivered skus (master cartons or pallets) is a sku ID concept. With 1 for all concept, an entire vendor received sku quantity has 1 sku WMS ID & has an entire sku quantity attached to 1 sku WMS ID. After a sku is received 1 WMS ID is placed onto 1 sku & all skus (X carton or pallet number) are transferred to a storage area. In a storage area all skus are placed into adjacent position or positions behind a sku with a WMS ID and WMS scanned to 1 WMS ID storage position. WMS scan transactions are sent to a WMS computer. As skus are withdrawn a WMS program indicates a WMS ID storage position & sku quantity. After a withdrawal transaction, a sku with a WMS ID remains in a WMS ID storage position or a sku WMS ID is transferred to another sku. Features are (1) most pallet applications use a dense floor stack storage concept that has a 66% utilization factor with low space utilization & small master carton situations use a standard pallet or decked rack storage concept, (2) potential for a sku WMS ID to become lost or damaged, (3) difficult to assure good inventory tracking & (4) to assure accurate withdrawal transaction requires an employee to count & add, (5) difficult to use with a WMS program, (6) requires non-productive employee time, (7) as a sku inventory becomes depleted, there is limited flexibility and ability to move a sku with multiple pallets into standard rack positions & (8) limited to use in an employee hand stack or manual controlled forklift truck storage operation.

ONE IDENTIFICATION FOR EACH SKU (MASTER CARTON OR PALLET)
EMPLOYEE PRODUCTIVITY, SPACE UTILIZATION & INVENTORY CONTROL

One ID for each sku (master carton or pallet) is a sku ID concept. With 1 for 1 concept, a vendor received sku quantity is handled as 1 sku (master carton or pallet) & each sku receives 1 WMS ID. After a sku receives a WMS ID, each sku is transferred to a storage area. In a storage area, each WMS ID sku is placed into a WMS ID storage position & WMS scan transactions are sent to a WMS computer. As skus are withdrawn, a WMS program indicates each WMS ID storage position & sku quantity to complete a withdrawal transaction. Features are (1) used in a single deep storage concept that has a 85% utilization factor with good space utilization & small master carton situations use a standard pallet or decked rack storage concept, (2) WMS ID remains on a master carton or pallet, (3) assures good inventory tracking & with a WMS computer suggesting a WMS ID pallet or master carton, accurate withdrawal transaction with good productivity, (4) use with a WMS program, (5) as a WMS ID sku inventory becomes depleted, flexibility & ability to move a sku with multiple pallets into standard rack positions or few master cartons to a decked position & (6) used in an employee hand stack, manual controlled forklift truck or AS/RS crane warehouse.

SKU IDENTIFICATION IS ON YOUR MASTER CARTON OR PALLET FRONT RIGHT SIDE
IMPROVES EMPLOYEE PRODUCTIVITY

Sku ID is on your master carton or pallet front right side is a master carton or pallet storage area idea that improves employee or forklift truck driver WMS ID scan and put-away productivity. This concept works on the basis that most forklift truck drivers are right hand employees, thus reducing movement to complete WMS scan transactions. To complete a WMS ID sku deposit, WMS IDs are (1) carton or pallet wrap around WMS ID on a pallet right hand stringer or block front and side or on a carton right front and side and (2) carton or pallet WMS ID on a lower right front & (3) storage rack pallet position WMS IDs on a storage position load beam right side. In locations, both sku & storage position WMS IDs face an aisle & assure line of sight for an employee hand held scanner device light beam. With both sku & storage position WMS IDs on a sku & storage position right side, you can minimize employee time to locate WMS Ids & minimize time to move & complete sku ID and position WMS scan transactions. It should be noted that most forklift truck drivers are right hand employees that reduces movement to complete WMS scan transactions.

HUMAN, MACHINE OR HUMAN/MACHINE READABLE IDENTIFICATION
ASSURE ACCURATE & ON-LINE INFORMATION &EMPLOYEE PRODUCTIVITY

Human, machine or human/machine readable ID are options that discreetly identify your sku & storage position from other skus & storage positions. In a manual warehouse operation with a paper document, a storage transaction has a forklift truck driver read & write a sku & position human readable IDs onto a paper document that is sent to an office. In the office a clerk enters a data into an inventory control computer. Features are requires an employee to read, write & key data with potential errors, restricted to use in a low volume operation with few skus, delayed data transfer, computer update & requires a smaller label. In a warehouse that has a WMS/inventory control computer program, each storage concept sku & position has a human/machine readable ID. To complete a storage transaction, an employee or handling device requires a bar code scanner that completes a delayed or on-line WMS sku and position ID scans that are sent wireless to a WMS computer for update. Features are restricted to use in a warehouse with a high volume and large sku number, requires a label, requires a mechanical device to read an ID & accurate data transfer to a WMS computer program. In most operations, a bar code scanner (it is noted that a paper document is possible) is used to ID skus & positions & communicate a storage transaction completion to a WMS computer program. Features are requires a larger label, used in other warehouses, requires a mechanical device to read an ID & accurate data transfer & with a scanner transfer improved accuracy.

RECHARGEABLE BATTERY/ELECTRIC BATTERY POWERED HAND HELD SCAN DEVICE
IMPROVES LOW EMPLOYEE PRODUCTIVITY

Rechargeable battery or electric battery powered hand held scan/read device are a bar code scanner power options. A rechargeable battery powered scanner receives its power from a rechargeable battery. If a battery is not full charged, there is a possibility for low employee productivity due to extra scan transaction attempts or a no read means a round trip travel time to battery replacement location & time to transfer batteries. An electric powered vehicle battery powered scanner has a scanner obtain its power source from a vehicle's battery. In most warehouses, an electric rechargeable battery has an electric charge that lasts for one shift that assures power to a scanner & minimizes employee non-productive time.

YOUR FORKLIFT TRUCK SCANNER HAS A SHORT OR LONG CORD
IMPROVES EMPLOYEE PRODUCTIVITY

Your forklift truck scanner short or long cord are options for an employee hand held bar code scanner device cord connection to a storage vehicle battery that allows a forklift truck driver to have a mobile scanner device for good bar code line of sight. With WA or NA forklift trucks, a scanner with a short cord restricts an employee mobility to complete a WMS ID sku & WMS ID position scan transactions. If a powered vehicle is not in proper location, there is a possible to have no scan transaction that means low employee productivity due to no scan transaction & time to relocate a forklift truck. Scanner devices with a re-tractable long cord assure maximum employee mobility to complete a scan transaction from a forklift truck operator's platform or seat & minimize cord damage.

YOUR FORKLIFT TRUCK SCANNER DEPTH OF FIELD
IMPROVES EMPLOYEE PRODUCTIVITY

Your forklift truck scanner depth of field is a bar code scanner feature that determines distance between a bar code scanner & a WMS ID to complete a good scan transaction. A WMS ID and scanner with good depth field assures maximum good read number or a scanner device light beam crosses all bar codes within sufficient time to complete a read. A WA forklift truck depth of field is from a forklift truck driver seat to a sku or position WMS ID. A NA or VNA forklift truck depth of field is from a forklift truck driver's platform to a sku or position WMS ID. Minimum depth of field is longest distance between an employee hand held scanner to a sku or position WMS ID. Hand held scanner device tests determine a scanner device that gives your forklift truck drivers a maximum good read number that improves employee productivity.

YOUR FORKLIFT TRUCK SCANNER HAS A DEFAULT AS ONE
IMPROVES EMPLOYEE PRODUCTIVITY

Your forklift truck scanner has a default as one is a warehouse storage area idea to improve employee hand held scanning a WMS ID scan productivity. In a storage area with a WMS program, each sku (master carton, pallet or

GOH) has one WMS ID and each storage/pick position has one WMS ID. This means that each storage area WMS scan transaction has an entry for a quantity of one WMS ID. To complete a WMS ID hand held scan transaction, after a good read an employee enters (presses) one button to complete a WMS ID scan transaction. If a scanner device is programmed to default as one, there is an employee scan productivity increase. Productivity increase results from an employee not looking for & pressing a one button due to the fact that a hand held scanner is programmed with a good scan transaction recognizes it as one.

DEFAULT YOUR HAND HELD SCANNER TO ONE (See Customer Returns Chapter)

DELAYED OR ON-LINE STORAGE TRANSACTION UPDATE
   MINIMIZE COMPUTER COST & IMPROVE EMPLOYEE PRODUCTIVITY

Delayed or on-line storage transaction update are options for a storage activity employee, employee controlled forklift truck or AS/RS crane storage transaction completion or data transfer from a storage area to WMS or inventory control computer to update an ID sku & ID storage position status in the files. Both concepts assure accurate sku & position transaction transfer and improve employee productivity. A delayed storage deposit or withdrawal transaction completion transfer concepts are (1) an employee to register transactions on a paper document and requires clerk to enter data into a WMS or inventory control computer or (2) a bar code scanner or AS/RS crane computer that sends storage transaction data to a warehouse micro-computer for later at a pre-determined time (established by your IT & warehouse departments) to transfer data to a WMS or inventory control computer. An employee document & clerk transfer concept is not preferred due to potential errors. A delayed transfer to a micro-computer features requires a warehouse micro-computer that has capacity to handle all data and send message (receive, store and send) activities that means improve employee productivity due to no waiting time to verify data transfer, IT & warehouse departments determine transfer data times, less costly WMS or inventory control computer, some potential extra storage positions, WMS computer to complete other programs & inventory is updated to reflect sku quantity & position status. On-line storage transaction transfer completion concept after a deposit or withdrawal transaction completion has a bar code scanner/RF tag reader or AS/RS crane computer that sends data to a WMS or inventory control computer program. Features are a larger capacity WMS or inventory computer & cost, some situations have slow verification message sent to an employee or AS/RS crane that creates low productivity & fewer extra positions.

AISLE IDENTIFICATION LOCATION
   IMPROVE EMPLOYEE PRODUCTIVITY & INVENTORY CONTROL

Aisle ID location is a manual storage concept that has an ID at an aisle entrance. Proper aisle ID improves employee productivity & enhances inventory control. With a suggested sku deposit or withdrawal transaction concept, an aisle ID indicates to an employee or employee controlled forklift truck a sku assigned aisle. An aisle ID has each aisle discreet ID in a location for an employee or employee controlled forklift truck clear view. In an employee or employee controlled forklift truck storage operation, an aisle ID is a nominal 6 ft above a floor surface or at height that minimizes any forklift truck damage. In an AS/RS crane storage area, aisle IDs are attached to each rack row front & are used by trouble shooting employees. An aisle ID has alpha characters or digits that have contrast colors between alpha characters/digits and background surface, have sufficient height & width for clear view & understanding from a main traffic aisle middle & 6 ft above a floor surface and at an aisle entrance extends outward from a rack row end into a main aisle. Aisle ID options are (1) one surface that is attached flat against a rack frame & adjacent to an aisle entrance that is preferred for an AS/RS storage concept, (2) two surfaces that are attached to both rack row end rack posts, extend outward into a main traffic aisle & adjacent to an aisle entrance that is used for an employee controlled forklift truck operation & (3) three surfaces in a triangle shaped format that is ceiling hung slightly higher than a WA or NA highest component in a main aisle & above an aisle entrance and is used for a WA aisle or NA aisle forklift truck operation with floor stack & rack storage operations.

STORAGE POSITION IDENTIFICATION ON A RACK UPRIGHT POST
   IMPROVE EMPLOYEE PRODUCTIVITY & INVENTORY CONTROL

Storage position ID placed on a rack upright post has a storage position ID that is placed onto a rack post that improves employee productivity and enhance inventory control. To be effective a storage position ID, an ID width matches or fits onto a rack post width and faces an aisle. With a 1 pallet or 2 pallets wide rack bay, there is consistent association of a post ID to a storage position. To help with the post ID to a storage position, directional arrows or colored labels (borders) assist a forklift truck driver. Feature is used when a load beam front or aisle face does not have sufficient space for an ID label or with a man-down forklift truck to complete elevated storage & bar code scan transactions to assure good inventory tracking. In a very narrow aisle (VNA) forklift truck or high rise order picker truck (HROS), additional storage position IDs are attached to a rack post side at a higher elevation than a sku in a storage position. As a VNA or HROS truck travels in an aisle, a position ID location above a normal pallet height allows an operator clear view.

STORAGE POSITION NUMBER SEQUENCE IS VERTICAL
   IMPROVE EMPLOYEE PRODUCTIVITY & ENHANCE INVENTORY CONTROL

Storage position number sequence is vertical in a storage aisle. A storage position sequence concept is required with WA, NA, VNA forklift trucks & AS/RS crane and in all storage types (floor stack, standard racks, gravity flow racks, drive-in/drive-thru racks or mobile racks). A storage position number sequence discreetly identifies one sku storage position from another sku storage position & for a storage transaction completion IDs a storage position for a sku storage transaction. This feature assures good employee productivity & accurate storage transaction completion for better inventory control. A vertical number sequence has each sku storage position number sequence progress from a bottom/floor level sku storage position to a top sku storage position. A vertical number sequence has an aisle first storage position number in a rack bay at a bottom that progressively moves up to a top storage position. An example is in a rack bay, the first/bottom storage position number is 01001A, second level is 01002A, third level 01003A & so to a highest storage position number on next rack bay, a first/bottom storage position number is 02001B, second level is 02002B, third level is 02003B & so to a highest storage position number & progresses for each rack bay and storage position in an aisle. Features are uses a 5 digit number with first two digits as a rack bay, next three digits as pallet position in a rack bay and alpha character IDs level and with an alpha character that means it is used for a storage concept with 26 vertical positions.

WITH TWO IDENTIFICATIONS ON ONE LOAD BEAM USE DIRECTIONAL ARROWS & COLORS
   IMPROVE EMPLOYEE PRODUCTIVITY & ENHANCE INVENTORY CONTROL

With two IDs on one load beam use directional arrows and colors on your storage position ID label to identify a storage position. Two storage position ID on a load beam are used in a WA, NA, VNA forklift truck operations with bottom pallets on the floor to improve employee productivity & enhance inventory control. In most employee controlled forklift truck warehouses, bottom pallet storage positions are supported by the floor and all elevated storage positions are supported with a pair of load beams. With a standard 1 in high and normal width human/machine readable storage position ID, most storage operations use a load beam front for storage position ID attachment. A pallet position front load beam surface faces an aisle with sufficient space for 1 or several storage positions/IDs attachment & each storage position label is placed onto a load beam in a consistent & repeated configuration. With 1 storage position label on a load beam, a position ID label refers to a pallet position above a storage position label. With 2 storage position labels on one load beam, a bottom ID label refers to a pallet position below a storage position ID label & a top ID label refers to a pallet position above a storage position ID label. If a man-down warehouse has 3 to 4 storage positions in a pallet rack design, required ID labels are placed onto a load beam in a step configuration that is consistent. With a multiple ID label concept, as you travel down aisle in an arithmetic progression, multiple storage position ID label configuration has (1) first position ID label adjacent to a first rack post & is a bottom ID label that refers to a bottom storage position, (2) second position ID label is slightly forward of & above a first position ID label that refers to a first elevated or second high (next) storage position, (3) third position ID label is slightly forward & above a second position ID label that refers to a second elevated or third (next) high storage position & (4) fourth position ID label is slightly forward & above a third position ID label & refers to a third elevated or fourth (next) storage position. To assist a man-down forklift truck driver to determine each pallet position, with a multiple position ID label configuration on one load beam, for each elevated position, each position ID label has a colored border that is consistent on all load beams. An example is (1) blue for a first position & bottom ID label, (2) yellow for a second position & second ID label, (3) green for a third position & third ID label & (4) brown for a fourth position or fourth ID label. In addition with a 2 or 3 high pallet storage position rack, directional arrows are attached to each ID label & refer to an ID label & pallet storage position location. An example is (1) a first ID label directional arrow points down for a first position, (2) in a two high pallet configuration, second ID label directional arrow points up for second a first position (3) in a three high pallet configuration, second ID label directional arrow is level or parallel to the floor & (4) in a three high pallet configuration, third ID label directional arrow points up for a third position. If your rack storage concept has two pallets per bay & you attach position ID labels to a rack position, your position ID labels are placed onto a rack post in a stacked configuration. The configuration has bottom position ID label refer to a bottom position, second ID label in a stack refers to a first elevated or second position & so on. Since a rack post is between 2 bays & each bay has 2 unique pallet positions, an aisle first rack post has one from rack bay or an aisle first pallet & bottom position ID label 01001. To assure proper forklift truck instruction, a position ID label directional arrow point to an adjacent position. An aisle second rack post has 2 bottom pallet position ID labels (this configuration occurs for each rack bay to an aisle end) that are (1) 01001 or second pallet from rack bay one with a position ID label directional arrow point to an adjacent position & (2) 02001 or first pallet from rack bay two with a position ID label directional arrow point to an adjacent position. If a rack configuration has multiple elevated storage positions, then you use a color code & arrow combination & on a rack post have each rack bay in a separate group that is identified.

SKU & STORAGE POSITION IDENTIFICATION LARGE OR SMALL LABEL
IMPROVE EMPLOYEE PRODUCTIVITY & ENHANCE INVENTORY CONTROL

Sku & position ID large or small label is a warehouse position label size options. In most employee or employee controlled forklift truck operations with a WMS computer program, a sku position label is a human/machine readable label to assure good inventory control, good employee productivity & accurate transaction completion. Each sku & position label has a human readable storage position identification (alpha characters & digits) & machine readable bar code or RF tag symbology. As an employee or employee controlled forklift truck travels in an aisle, storage position labels are an employee instruction that assures an employee arrives at the suggest storage position & a sku label assures accurate sku tracking. In most aisles, an employee is 2 to 3 ft from a position label face & moving at a good travel speed, thereby a position label human readable alpha characters & digits have sufficient size for an employee to easily & quickly read position number. To assure good employee label read or productivity, most sku & storage position label human readable alpha characters & digits are 1 to 2 ins high and have sufficient width. In most storage operations with a WMS computer program, for each storage transaction, an employee with a gun or hand held scanner completes a storage position & sku machine readable symbology scan transaction. A scan transaction or laser light beam crossing all bar codes is completed from an aisle location that has a range from 2 to 3 ft and has to assure a good read. To have a fast good read, an over squared bar code (total bars and white spaces equals tallest bars) assures increase opportunity for an employee direct laser light beam to cross all bar codes for improve employee productivity.

USE A GUN OR HAND CONTACT SCANNER
EMPLOYEE PRODUCTIVITY & CONSTANT GOH FLOW

Using a scan gun or hand contact scanner are a forklift truck driver bar code scanner options. With a gun bar code scanner and from a forklift truck operator's platform, a gun is a device that directs a laser light beam onto a storage position bar code that completes a scan transaction. Features are (1) slightly higher cost, (2) longer depth of field and (3) improved employee productivity. With a hand contact bar code scanner, a forklift truck operator leaves a forklift truck and walks to a storage position bar code and completes a scan transaction. Features are (1) close to a bar code depth of field, (2) slightly lower cost and (3) lower employee productivity.

FLAT OR INDENTED LOAD BEAM
EMPLOYEE PRODUCTIVITY & SCANNER GOOD READS

Flat or indented standard pallet rack load beam are hand stack or standard pallet rack load beam options. A flat load beam has the entire face/front surface for storage position ID. When you require two storage positions on a load beam, you use a standard storage ID and with a man-down vehicle minimal difficulty to complete an elevated storage position scan transaction. An indented load beam has interior section is set-back from top/bottom load beam section that restricts the front/face surface for storage position ID. When you require two ID storage positions on a load beam, you could use a narrower storage ID and with a man-down vehicle potential difficulty to complete an elevated storage position ID scan transaction.

STORAGE POSITION LABEL ATTACHMENT
EMPLOYEE PRODUCTIVITY & SCANNER GOOD READS

Storage position label attachment is your storage position ID placement onto a storage position load beam or upright post. For maximum employee scan transaction productivity and maximum good read number, your label placement is consistent and assures employee or hand held scanner line sight.

PLAIN OR COATED POSITION IDENTIFICATION
ASSURE GOOD EMPLOYEE PRODIVITY

Plain or coated storage/pick position ID are a warehouse bar code label options. A plain bar code label is black bar codes that is printed onto a paper surface and placed onto a storage/pick position. Features are potential black bar code damage from equipment or sku and less expense. A coated bar code label is plain bar code label that a coated surface that covers all black bars and is placed onto a storage/pick position. Features are slight cost increase with reduced black bar code damage.

QUIET ZONES, OVER-SQUARED AND BAR EDGES
IMPROVE EMPLOYEE PRODUCTIVITY

Quiet zones, over-squared and bar code edges are bar code label characteristics that improve good read number and employee productivity. Bar code quiet zones are on a bar code label both sides and is space between a paper edge and first black bar code and a last black bar code and paper edge. This Feature assures a clean break between a metal structure and black bar code. An over-squared bar code label has a total bar code and white space width equal to a black bar code length. Feature allows a laser beam to cross all bar codes and white spaces. Bar edges is a sharp contrast between a white space and black bar code. Feature assures a laser beam reads a bar code proper width.

FLOOR STACK STORAGE POSITION IDENTIFICATION LOCATION
EMPLOYEE PRODUCTIVITY AND INVENTORY CONTROL

Floor stack storage position ID location is in a location to assure employee or WMS scanner line of sight and to assure proper floor stack lane ID. Proper floor stack storage position ID location assures employee productivity, accurate storage transaction and good inventory control. Floor stack position ID locations are (1) ceiling hung placard that is chain hung from the ceiling and extends downward. The extension permits pallet storage transactions but the height is difficult to complete a WMS storage position scan transaction, (2) floor embedded is tape, glued or plastic cover that is in each floor stack position from. An ID cover permits a WMS scan transaction and there is potential for position ID damage. Some additional cost and (3) upright post is located at a floor stack front side that is located at a lane clearance space. Directional arrows point to a floor stack lane and assures line of sight. Some potential damage and upright post cost.

SKU WMS IDENTIFICATION DIRECTORY OR SUBSTITUTION FOR YOUR WMS PROGRAM TO TRACK SKUS IN A FLOOR STACK OR DENSE STORAGE POSITIONS
EMPLOYEE PRODUCTIVITY AND INVENTORY CONTROL

Dense storage concepts are floor stack, two-deep, drive-in rack, push-back rack. With the dense storage concepts, your WMS program suggests the first sku WMS ID that was WMS scanned and physically deposited to a WMS ID dense storage position. A first sku WMS ID scanned and deposited to a dense storage concept is not available for a withdrawal transaction due the last or other sku WMS IDs are at a dense storage position withdrawal position. Sku WMS ID directory or substitution for your WMS program are options for you to track skus in a floor stack or dense storage concept positions. A directory concept has at your dense storage concept deposit position a directory that has a WMS ID for each deposit transaction, for each dense storage lane your WMS program suggests the lowest WMS ID position number, for each storage transaction your forklift truck driver WMS scans the appropriate storage WMS position and your WMS computer program considers a WMS ID storage position is occupied and does not accept another sku WMS ID in a position. Example your first position transaction has your dense storage position highest number and your last position transaction has your highest storage position number. With a sku WMS ID approach, your WMS program accepts all sku WMS IDs scanned to a storage WMS ID. When required to withdraw a sku WMS ID, a WMS computer program suggests a WMS ID and at a dense storage concept, forklift truck driver withdraws a sku and scans a sku WMS ID and storage position WMS ID. As a sku WMS ID scan transaction is sent to a WMS computer program that reviews a storage position sku WMS IDs. After a review and match of a sku WMS IDs, a WMS computer program approves a withdrawal transaction and reduces sku WMS ID from a dense storage lane sku WMS IDs.

WHAT IS YOUR SKU TRAVEL PATH WINDOW
MINIMIZES SKU & RACK DAMAGE

What is your travel path window is an in-house transport concept design criteria that determines your travel path space and minimizes your sku or equipment damage. Your in-house transport concept travel path window is determined by your carrier or conveyor structural support member dimension & your sku dimension. If your in-house transport concept travel path is a closed loop concept with potential for a sku to move over an entire travel path, your travel path window has a constant window dimension. If your in-house transport concept travel path a closed loop concept travel path with a sensing device, run-out or divert station to assure an empty carrier or conveyor travel path has no sku, a return travel path window shrinks to a carrier or conveyor travel path structural support members. With a master carton, pallet or GOH return travel path, the feature minimized your return travel path window required space (especially GOH) that is shorter due to no sku dimension.

HUMAN CONTROLLED VEHICLE OR POWERED CONVEYOR IN-HOUSE TRANSPORT
IMPROVE EMPLOYEE PRODUCTIVITY & LOW COST PER SKU

Human controlled vehicle or powered conveyors are in-house transport options that impact your employee productivity & cost per unit. It is understood that a human controlled vehicle transport concept has an employee control a vehicle to complete an in-house transport activity. A human controlled vehicle transport concept is best for a low volume operation, uses a variable travel path, delivers skus to different warehouse locations, has a low one-time equipment cost & has a low labor CPU. A manual transport concept is a flexible concept that allows an employee and vehicle allocated to other warehouse activities. A powered conveyor transport concept is best for a high volume operation, has a high fixed one-time cost, has a fixed travel path, low labor CPU due to most concepts require an employee or employee controlled equipment to transfer a sku onto or from a conveyor travel path and requires your sku to meet a concept design specifications.

IN-HOUSE TRANSPORT CONCEPT - IN-FLOOR, FLOOR LEVEL OR OVERHEAD TRAVEL PATH
IMPROVE FLOOR UTILIZATION

In-floor, floor level or overhead in-house transport concepts are your warehouse in-house transport options. Your in-house transport travel path concept is determined by your sku type, sku characteristics & volume, facility ceiling structural member & floor structural characteristics, operation type & desire to use your floor space. An in-floor transport concept is a micro-computer controlled carrier to move over a fixed travel path that requires a smooth, even with some grade change, debris and crack free, high travel path surface & ability to hold an electric motor driven chain or cart pulling chain travel path. An in-floor travel path concept does not allow other warehouse activities performed in a travel path. An across-the-floor or floor level in-house transport concept has the same characteristics and features as the in-floor concept except that has a manual or controller/computer controlled vehicle, fixed or variable travel path & most transport vehicles are used in other warehouse activities. An overhead transport concept is a manual or controller/computer controlled carrier to move over a fixed travel path that requires a facility ceiling structural members to support new static & dynamic loads per your facility seismic location and sku decline/incline travel paths. With safety netting under a travel path, warehouse activities are completed in the area.

WHAT ARE YOUR IN-HOUSE TRANSPORT CONCEPT DESIGN PARAMETERS
ASSURE CONSTANT SKU FLOW

What are your in-house transport concept design parameters or what are your operational factors that impact your in-house transport concept objectives to assure a constant sku flow and on-time sku delivery to a correct address. Your projected in-house transport concept design parameters are (1) sku average, most frequent & peak volume, (2) sku flow as a constant or surge flow, (3) sku physical size, length, height and weight, (4) WMS ID symbololgy characteristics and presentation direction, (5) proposed route, (6) each pick-up & delivery station characteristics as an assisted or unassisted activity and (7) safety and risk management design. In addition you have to assure that your proposed in-house transport concept carrier (1) travel path window has sufficient space, (2) travel speed & (3) number to match your projected volume. Your design factor understanding assures a constant sku flow over an in-house transport concept for on-time and accurate deliveries, no surges & minimal carrier down time & a low CPU.

HOW LONG DOES IT TAKE TO COMPLETE AN IN-HOUSE TRANSPORT TRIP
ASSURE CONSTANT SKU FLOW & IDENTIFY COST SAVING ACTIVITY

How long does it take to complete an in-house transport trip is a warehouse in-house transport phrase that refers to the time that is required for an in-house transport carrier to complete a one-way to round trip activity. One-way trip activity includes a sku pick-up, dispatch, carrier travel time, delivery activities & carrier return travel time. A round trip activity includes all one-way trip activities plus additional pick-up, travel & delivery activities. To understand your in-house transport concept cost saving opportunities, you obtain an actual time for each activity completion that provides you with an idea where to improve your existing in-house transport concept or with a proposed in-house transport concept your estimate each activity completion. Your estimates are based on other company experiences with your proposed in-house transport concept or vendor data. Your in-house transport carrier trip number per hour is an operational factor that has impact on an in-house transport concept selection. An increase in a trip number per hour increases your employee productivity, lowers CPU & assures a constant sku flow.

PUSH 'E' BUTTON OR PULL 'E' CORD
IMPROVE SAFETY & RISK MANAGEMENT

Push 'E' button or 'E' pull a cord are safety & risk management idea that has an employee to turn-off or stop a n in-house transport powered conveyor or carrier concept. Push a button or pull a cord are emergency or 'E' stop devices when activated stop a powered conveyor travel path or carrier forward movement to prevent sku, building or equipment damage and employee injury. An 'E' stop button is a red colored mushroom shaped button that has a specific location and usually located on a floor within sight of your overhead transport concept. If an employee is adjacent to a push button, to activate requires an employee to a push button that does quickly stop an in-house transport concept & if an employee is not adjacent to a button, an employee walks to a push button location and activates a button that stops an in-house transport concept. An 'E' stop pull cord is a red colored spring activated cord that is connected between 2 locations and usually used on a powered conveyor travel path and along a floor conveyor travel path with work/pick stations adjacent. When an 'E' cord is pulled by an employee, an 'E' cord stops an in-house transport concept. An 'E' stop pull cord concept minimizes an employee walk distance. In most operations, an activated 'E' push button or pull cord has a red illuminated in the area and to re-start your transport concept, requires your employee to access your transport control panel.

EMERGENCY STOP FOR LINE OF SIGHT OR SPECIFIC AREA
IMPROVE SAFETY & RISK MANAGEMENT

Emergency stop for line of sight or specific area are emergency are 'E' stop concept option for a powered conveyor travel path stop that minimizes potential sku, building or equipment damage & employee injury. 'E' stop control options are (1) specific conveyor travel path concept has an 'E' stop device that is designed to stop a specific conveyor travel path. When a problem exists, there is potential for an employee not to be adjacent to an 'E' stop and not immediately activate an appropriate 'E' stop device. Features are potential increase damage, potential injury increase & additional 'E' stop devices & controls or (2) line of sight from an 'E' stop concept has one 'E' stop control all conveyor travel paths within an employee sight from an 'E' stop device. When a problem exists on a conveyor travel path, an employee who has line of sight to a problem activates the nearest located 'E' stop device to a stop conveyor travel path. Features are greater opportunity to minimize damage or injury, fewer 'E' stop devices, controls & simple employee training. Your selected 'E' stop control option is approved by your conveyor manufacturer, insurance company & local code authority. To re-activate an 'E' stopped conveyor, an employee activates a conveyor travel path at a control station.

FEWER TRAVEL PATH ELEVATION CHANGES & HORIZONTAL CURVES
   LOWER TRANSPORT COST, MINIMIZES SKU JAMS & LOWER ELECTRIC EXPENSE

Fewer travel path elevation changes & horizontal curves on an in-transport concept means a lower transport concept one-time cost, minimizes sku jams & lower electric cost. For a powered carrier or conveyor travel path to service a work/activity station on a different elevation an in-house transport concept travel path makes an elevation change. When a travel path makes an elevation change, your sku travel path requires (1) at both charge & discharge ends a horizontal run-out, (2) sloped travel path with side guards, (3) underside protection and penetration through a floor with employee & fire barrier protection and (4) additional electric drive motors. To avoid a building or work station an in-house transport concept horizontal travel path makes a turn/curve. When a sku travel path makes a turn/curve, for minimal sku damage & continuous flow and to have proper travel dimension, skus can be separated in single file order or singulated on a straight conveyor that is prior to a curve and a curve has a faster travel speed. Many curves have tapered rollers or special rollers that require an additional electric motor. When a powered conveyor travel paths make an elevation change or curve, in most applications a sku powered travel path requires an additional drive motor & controls that increases the electrical expense.

IN-HOUSE TRANSPORT CONCEPT: CLOSED LOOP/ROUND TRIP OR ONE-WAY TRIP
   ASSURES ON-TIME & ACCURATE DELIVERIES & ENHANCE DUAL CYCLES TO IMPROVE PRODUCTIVITY

In-house transport concept as a closed loop/round trip or one-way trip are your in-house transport concept options. Your selected option impacts your warehouse smooth & constant sku flow, assures on-time and accurate deliveries and enhances dual cycles (handles an in-bound pallet and handles an outbound pallet) to improve productivity. One-way sku in-house transport concept is used in a large warehouse that has a powered conveyor transport concept for sku delivery to an AS/RS crane or GOH storage concept. During a WMS identified sku travel on an in-house one-way travel path, a WMS ID scanner devices & in-house transport concept computer and diverters assure that a WMS ID sku is diverted to an assigned aisle for a storage put-away transaction. If a sku divert transaction is not completed, an in-house transport along a GOH or AS/RS storage area front has a re-circulation travel path or a did-not-divert sku travel path that is a descending travel path to the floor. A closed loop/round trip sku in-house transport concept is used in a warehouse that handles master cartons, pallets or GOH. With a very narrow aisle, carton or pallet AS/RS or GOH concept, an in-house transport concept travel path is a closed loop travel path that has a transport concept pick-up a pallet from a receiving area for transport to a storage area and in the storage area pick-up an outbound sku for transport to a pick area or ship area. With a human controlled powered sku carrying vehicle, an employee follows a fixed or variable travel path to a storage/delivery aisle & returns over a fixed or variable travel path to a receiving/pick area. Per a warehouse type, a sku transport vehicle moves an outbound sku from a storage area to a pick area, ship or receiving area. With ability to pick-up & transport an outbound sku, an in-house transport concept has an opportunity to complete dual cycles that improves employee productivity & lower sku cost. A conveyor closed loop travel path has additional conveyor, I T 1 time cost and requires your inbound transport transactions to equal (occur in the same time period) your outbound transactions. If a sku divert transaction is not completed, an in-house transport path handles a did-not-divert sku with a re-circulation conveyor that has a did-not-divert sku re-introduced to a scanner/reader or diverts a did-not-divert sku to the floor.

AN IN-HOUSE TRANSPORT CONCEPT TWO PALLETS PER TRIP IS BETTER THAN ONE PALLET
   IMPROVE EMPLOYEE PRODUCTIVITY

An in-house transport concept two pallet per trip is better than one pallet is a pallet in-house transport idea that improves employee productivity. A storage area with a conventional wide aisle (WA) or narrow aisle (NA) forklift truck requires a wide turning traffic aisle, back to back rack row design and random sku placement into a storage position. Per trip a 2 pallet truck moves 2 pallets from a receiving area to a storage area. When a two-pallet truck drops 2 pallets at a back-to-back flush storage rack row or floor stack row end, each pallet WMS ID faces 1 forklift truck storage aisle that permits a forklift truck driver to complete a sku WMS ID scan transaction. If another aisle forklift truck driver from another storage aisle desires to put-away a pallet in its aisle, to complete a sku WMS ID scan transaction a forklift truck driver is required to complete a forklift truck 360 turn that has lower productivity. If a cart train is used to transport skus, at a delivery station, after carts are dropped-off at an aisle end, an employee arranges a cart at an aisle end to have each pallet WMS ID face a storage aisle or an in-house transport forklift transfers pallets from a cart onto an aisle end position.

WHAT IS YOUR FORKLIFT TRUCK STORAGE & TURNING AISLE WIDTH
MINIMIZES DAMAGE & IMPROVES EMPLOYEE PRODUCTIVITY

What is your forklift truck storage & turning aisle width is a wide aisle (WA) or narrow aisle (NA) forklift truck right angle/stacking turn requirement to complete a storage transaction that improves employee productivity & minimizes sku & rack damage. With most WA counterbalanced or NA forklift trucks, rack to rack plus 12 in is a manufacturer's recommended stacking aisle width. If a storage stacking or turning aisle width is narrower than a manufacturer's stated dimension, there is potential sku & rack post damage. If a storage stacking or turning aisle width is wider than a manufacturer's stated dimension, your storage area has wide aisle that has low space utilization.

IN-HOUSE TRANSPORT TRAVEL PATH IS FIXED OR VARIABLE PATH
ASSURES CONTINUOUS SKU FLOW & ON-TIME ACTIVITY COMPLETION

Fixed or variable travel path are a warehouse in-house transport concept travel path options to assure continuous sku flow and on-time activity completion. A fixed in-house transport travel path concept is common with a controller/computer controlled powered in-house transport concept. With a fixed travel path carrier or conveyor, a sku is moved with a constant travel speed over one travel that assures a constant & scheduled flow. The concept handles a high volume, high 1-time fixed costs with minimal on-going labor costs, requires a free & clear travel path & at a delivery or pick-up station, sku transfers are an unassisted or assisted activity and an assisted activity has a higher cost per unit (CPU). A variable in-house travel path concept is most common in a low sku warehouse that uses an employee controlled vehicle. With a variable travel path concept, an employee controls a vehicle travel speed over an employee selected travel path between 2 locations & at a pick-up or delivery location, an employee controlled vehicle completes an unassisted sku transfer & has a lower CPU.

YOUR IN-HOUSE TRANSPORT STRAIGHT AISLE & TURNING AISLE WIDTH DIMENSIONS
IMPROVE SPACE UTILIZATION & MINIMIZE DAMAGE EXPENSE

Your in-house transport carrier straight aisle width and turning aisle width allows a transport carrier to move over a travel path & to travel from one aisle to another aisle. A straight aisle width has sufficient clearance between a carrier & sku or rack to improve space utilization and minimize sku, building or equipment damage. A turning aisle width is used at an aisle end or in a cross/middle aisle that allows a carrier to transfer from one aisle to another aisle. If a travel path straight or turning aisle width is narrower than a transport concept manufacturer allowance, there is potential sku, building or equipment damage. If a travel path aisle width is wider than a manufacturer's allowance, there is poor space utilization with potential for re-design or adjustment.

EMPLOYEE POWERED PALLET TRUCK IS BETTER PULLED THAN PUSHED
IMPROVE EMPLOYEE PRODUCTIVITY, MINIMIZE POTENTIAL DAMAGE & SAFETY

Employee powered pallet truck is better pulled than pushed are a manual powered pallet truck direction of travel options. A pallet truck push concept has an employee push a manual pallet truck forward over a floor. As a pallet truck moves over a travel path when a pallet truck makes a right turn, a pallet truck handle is turned to the left that is no automotive steering. Other features are (1) to start moving a loaded pallet truck, it requires additional physical effort, (2) employee had limited travel path view due to a pallet blocks an employee view that potential for a pallet truck wheel hang-up in a crack or on debris & (3) when to make a quick stop there is potential sku damage from a sku falls to the floor & non-productive clean-up time due to no protection from a back-rest. A pallet truck pull option has an employee pull on a pallet truck over a floor. When required to make a right turn, an employee turns a pallet truck handle to the right (automatic steering). Other features are (1) to start moving a full pallet truck requires less physical effort, (2) employee has complete travel path view that minimizes a pallet truck wheel hang-up in a crack or on debris & (33) when to make a quick stop with a back-rest on a pallet truck, there is lower potential sku damage from falling to a floor & non-productive clean-up time due to back-rest restricting sku movement.

PALLET IN FRONT OR BEHIND A FORKLIFT TRUCK DRIVER
IMPROVE SAFETY

Pallet in front or behind a forklift truck driver are forklift truck pallet carrying or direction of travel options. When a counterbalanced (WA) or narrow aisle (NA) forklift truck carries a pallet over a travel path with a pallet in the front, a pallet on a set of forks is in the lead. Features are (1) forklift truck driver has limited travel path view due to mast & pallet obstruction & (2) with a standard WA or NA forklift truck, a forklift truck steering method is automotive that is common to most forklift truck drivers. Automotive steering means as a driver turns a steering wheel to the right a vehicle turns right. When a forklift truck travels with a counterbalanced (WA) forklift truck driver faces rear (chassis end) or narrow aisle (NA) forklift truck driver faces a lead direction of travel (chassis end), a pallet or set of forks is in a trail. Features are a driver has complete travel path view but with a standard forklift truck, a forklift steering is non-automotive that means as a driver turns a steering wheel to the right & a vehicle turns left.

USE A TUGGER/WA FORKLIFT TRUCK WITH A CART TRAIN OR DOUBLE PALLET TRUCK
INCREASE TRANSPORT UNITS PER TRIP & IMPROVE EMPLOYEE PRODUCTIVITY

Use a tugger/WA forklift truck with a cart train or a double pallet truck are manual controlled sku in-house transport options. Both concepts with skus for one destination, you improve employee productivity for each trip over a long travel distance. A powered tugger or WA forklift truck with a cart train or double pallet truck are transport concepts that require at a delivery location, a forklift truck to complete a storage put-away transaction. When compared to a single pallet truck concept, an electric powered double pallet truck increases capacity and improves employee productivity by 1 pallet with a slightly higher equipment costs & wider turning aisles. A powered tugger/WA forklift truck with cart train has up to 4 carts in a train. To assure good cart trailing characteristics, each 4-wheel cart has proper steering & hitch/coupler concept. With a tugger and cart concept, at both pick-up and delivery locations, a forklift truck is required to transfer a pallet on to a cart & requires a cart train to return carts and empty/outbound pallets to a pick-up location. With a WA forklift truck and cart concept, a forklift that pulls a cart train completes a pallet transfer transaction. To assure maximum employee productivity, on a return trip to a dispatch station, an in-house transport concept backhauls skus or empty pallets.

ONE-WAY WIDE OR TWO-WAY WIDE VEHICLE TRAVEL PATH
ASSURE MAXIMUM SPACE UTILIZATION

One-way or two-way wide vehicle travel path are in-house carrier travel path design options. One-way travel path design has all carriers move skus in a forward direction. Forward direction is from a dispatch/pick-up station, over a travel path and to a destination/delivery station. A 1-way travel path design has a narrower travel path window width due one carrier is on your travel path. A 2-way travel path design has all carriers move sku in a (1) forward direction from a dispatch/pick-up station, over a travel path and to a destination/delivery station and (2) after sku discharge at a delivery station, a carrier return travel is from a delivery station over a travel path and to a dispatch/pick-up station. In a travel path window, your outbound carrier travel path is parallel and in the same window as your return carrier travel path. A 2-way travel path has carriers traveling in different directions and requires additional clearances that create a wider travel path window. In most applications, a 2-way travel path design has better space utilization & potential equipment savings.

PEOPLE PATH
IMPROVED SPACE UTILIZATION & SAFETY

People path is a floor or in-floor in-house transport concept travel path option that permits an employee to walk parallel to a powered in-house carrier or conveyor travel path entire length from a dispatch/pick-up station to a destination/delivery station. People path colored floor markings are easily identified and used in most applications.

PEOPLE PATH & VEHICLE TRAVEL PATH COLORS
IMPROVE SAFETY

People path & vehicle travel path colors are important in-house transport concept design features. When a people path is adjacent to a manual or powered vehicle/carrier travel path & to assure minimum potential for employee injury, a people travel path is painted with parallel and diagonal lines in a local approved safety color & a vehicle or carrier travel path is painted with parallel & diagonal lines in the a local approved safety color. To assure maximum awareness, human readable & symbol signs are posted at key locations & along both travel paths.

POWERED VEHICLE BACKREST IS A MUST
DECREASE SKU DAMAGE & INCREASE EMPLOYEE PRODUCTIVITY

Backrest why is a manual or powered vehicle or carrier option that reduces potential for sku damage from falling to the floor and non-productive employee clean-up & re-palletize time. A backrest has hardened metal members that are welded together & attached to a vehicle or carrier base & extend upward. After pallet pick-up, a pallet front or rear rests against a backrest. During travel across a floor & when a vehicle or carrier sudden stop occurs, a backrest prevents one side of a pallet from moving & thereby reducing sku damage from falling to the floor.

PALLET TRUCK DRIVER LEADS OR FOLLOWS A PALLET
IMPROVE EMPLOYEE PRODUCTIVITY, REDUCE DAMAGE & IMPROVE SAFETY

Pallet truck driver leads or follows a pallet are a powered walker or rider pallet truck an in-house transport concept direction of travel options. Proper pallet truck direction of travel improves employee productivity, minimizes sku, equipment & building damage and improves safety. A pallet truck driver lead option has a pallet truck forks in a lead direction of travel & driver on a truck front (ahead a pallet). When your pallet truck driver turns a pallet truck control handle to the right, a pallet truck turns to the right left. Driver lead features are (1) similar to automotive steering method that results with faster travel speed & low potential damage due to maximum travel path view that has potential for pallet truck wheel to avoid hung-up on cracks or debris & (2) if a pallet truck has a back-rest & with a quick stop, a backrest is protection for a sku to fall onto a floor that creates non-productive clean-up & re-palletize time. A pallet truck driver follow option has a pallet forks/pallet first and a driver follows. With a driver follow option, your driver is behind a pallet/forks and a pallet is in front as a pallet truck moves over travel path. When your driver turns a pallet truck handle to the right, a pallet truck turns to the left. A pallet truck steering method is not similar to driving an automobile (not automotive steering). Driver follow are (1) slower travel speeds & with limited travel path view that increases potential for pallet truck wheel hang-up on cracks or debris & if a pallet truck makes a quick stop back-rest, there is no sku protection that increases potential for a sku falling to a floor.

WALK WITH OR RIDE ON A POWERED PALLET TRUCK
IMPROVE EMPLOYEE PRODUCTIVITY

Walk with or ride on a powered pallet truck is a basic in-house transport concept option to move a pallet from a receiving area to a storage area. Walk with an electric battery powered pallet truck concept has an employee walks with a pallet truck across a travel path. A walkie electric powered pallet truck moves a pallet over a travel path that minimizes an employee physical effort, a higher cost, human paced concept & with a slower travel speed slightly improves employee productivity. A rider electric powered pallet truck is a machine paced concept that moves a pallet & employee across a travel path. Features are (1) carries a heavier load, (2) higher cost, (3) travels over a long travel path at faster travel speeds and up slight grades and (4) good employee productivity.

POWERED PALLET TRUCK OR FORKLIFT TRUCK AS A MANUAL CONTROLLED TRANSPORT VEHICLE
IMPROVE EMPLOYEE PRODUCTIVIT, LOWER UNIT COST & ONE-TIME COST

Pallet truck or forklift truck are a manual controlled in-house pallet truck concepts that move pallets from receiving to a storage area & have a one-time cost difference improving employee productivity & unit cost. A pallet truck concept has a pallet truck move a pallet from a receiving dock floor position to a storage floor level delivery position that is at a rack row end but requires a forklift truck to complete a storage transaction. A powered pallet truck concept features are a lower wage rate employee completes an in-house transport activity with a lower cost vehicle and a high cost forklift truck driver on a high cost vehicle remains in a storage area completing storage transactions. A forklift truck concept has a forklift truck move a pallet from a receiving dock floor position area direct to a conventional storage concept storage position that completes a storage transaction or to a VNA P/D station. If a forklift truck completes an in-house transport activity, there are increased forklift travel distances that decreases forklift truck productivity that requires additional forklift trucks & drivers that have a higher unit cost.

AT INTERESTING AISLE USE SAFETY MIRRORS
IMPROVE SAFETY

Safety mirrors are a powered mobile manual controlled vehicle in-house transport concept option that improves your operation safety. At blind or right angle turns with high employee & vehicle 2-way traffic, a safety mirror at a proper location shows on-coming traffic. With proper employee training, an employee walking or driving a vehicle approaching a turn or intersection looks into a mirror & assures an on-ward travel path is clear.

USE AN OVERHEAD/HEAD ACKE BAR, HIGHWAY GUARD RAIL/ POST & WHEEL-STOP
MINIMIZE DAMAGE & IMPROVE EMPLOYEE PRODUCTIVITY

Overhead/head ache bar, highway guard rail/post & wheel-stop are manual controlled powered pallet truck & forklift truck options to minimize equipment & building damage and improve driver productivity. An overhead or head ache bar is a ceiling hung chain with a bar that extends downward or rack bay that is located prior to a facility wall passage way or door frame bottom. If a forklift truck with an elevated sku strikes a head ache bar or rack bay, it is noticed that your forklift driver who should stop a vehicle forward movement & lower an elevated sku & avoid door damage. Highway guard rails are floor anchored & used in a powered pallet truck or forklift truck in-house transport concept along walls, stationary equipment or people paths to prevent a moving vehicle from striking & damaging a wall, equipment or employee injury. Per a sku elevation above a floor, a guard rail bottom, middle or top members are set above a floor. The elevation protects guard rail support post from damage & sku hang-up on a guard member. Guard posts are cement filled floor anchor or sunk post that is placed in front of a door frame. A guard post prevents a moving pallet or forklift truck from striking & damaging a door frame. Wheel stop is an inverted and flatten 'V' shaped harden metal members that is floor anchored in front of a forklift truck transfer location for sku transfer to or from a P/D station, flow rack conveyor lane or conveyor travel path. A wheel stop is set at a distance from a material handling equipment to restrict a forklift truck front wheels forward movement that prevents a forklift truck from striking & damaging equipment but permits a forklift truck to complete a sku transfer transaction and assure good employee productivity.

MASTER CARTON INCLINE TRAVEL PATH
CONSTANT SKU FLOW & LOW COST PER UNIT

Master carton movement over an incline travel path is used in a warehouse as a powered belt conveyor or vertical lift to assure a constant sku flow at a low CPU. An incline travel path moves closed master cartons or totes from a lower level horizontal conveyor to an elevated level horizontal conveyor. A powered belt conveyor travel path has a sloped that is determined by your master carton length, carton/tote width and height characteristics, building area and elevated floor depth & a powered tail & nose over. As a master carton travels over a belt conveyor travel path, there is controlled flow & with a faster speed between 2 belt conveyor sections, a gap is build between 2 master cartons. Feature assures a constant master carton flow with a wide carton mix with a carton length that determines a carton quantity that moves over an inclined travel path, a 'Z' master carton movement characteristic, handles a high volume and minimal jams. If an incline conveyor travel path penetrates an elevated floor, the concept requires underside & side guards, personnel & fire protection. A vertical lift is a series of moving slats evenly spaced on a dual chain travel path that are moved over a fixed travel path. As a master carton is moved forward on a horizontal conveyor, a conveyor pulls a fixed gap between 2 cartons. A gap length is determined by your longest & tallest carton. At a vertical lift in-feed station, revolving slats pull a master carton forward onto a vertical travel path. With a master carton on a vertical lift slats, slat travel is in a vertical direction to a discharge station. At a discharge station, revolving slats move a master carton forward onto an elevated horizontal conveyor travel path. If a vertical lift does not penetrate an elevated floor, four sides have employee safety screen. If a vertical lift penetrates an elevated floor, most local codes require four solid sides fire protection. A vertical lift travel path configuration options are (1) 'C' shaped that on an elevated floor moves a master carton in a different travel direction than a lower floor travel direction & (2) 'Z' shaped that on an elevated floor moves a master carton in same travel direction as a lower floor travel direction. Features are a small floor space, constant travel speed, handles a fixed master carton volume, high one-time cost & master carton length & height are fixed characteristics.

MASTER CARTON DECLINE WITH GRAVITY OR POWER CONVEYOR
CONSTANT SKU FLOW & LOW COST PER UNIT

Master carton decline with gravity or powered conveyor travel path options are to move master cartons/totes from an elevated horizontal travel path to a lower level horizontal travel path. With both gravity & powered decline travel path options, master carton length, width, height and weight, available space & elevation change are important design factors. An open or closed master carton with fragile/crushable skus travels over a powered decline belt conveyor travel path due to increased master carton control as it moves over a decline travel path. If a warehouse has limited decline conveyor travel path run-out space, a powered conveyor travel path is preferred. A powered belt conveyor travel path has a 20 degree of slope, requires less run-out space, and requires electric motors & therefore has a higher ongoing cost. Closed master cartons & non-fragile/non-crushable skus travel over a gravity travel path due to increased sku protection. A gravity travel path requires a travel path top and end curves/transition locations to handle your longest carton and a long run-out length. Travel path options are (1) solid slide, (2) strand slide, (3) skate-wheel conveyor & (4) roller conveyor. If master cartons/totes travel speed is too fast, potential solutions are (1) tilt a decline travel path to one side that has a master carton/tote side rub/ride along a guard rail, (2) restrict specific skate wheels or rollers from turning or (3) from an elevated bar above a decline travel path add plastic stripes that come in contact with a master carton/tote and slows master carton/tote travel speed. To assure proper master carton flow, a gravity travel path has a charge-end nose over end with a proper designed curve for transfer onto a lower level travel path & decline travel path control devices that stop/start a charge-end belt conveyor. A gravity decline travel path features are low cost, no electric motors & low maintenance.

MASTER CARTON DIRECTION OF TRAVEL ON A CONVEYOR TRAVEL PATH
ASSURE CONTROLLED TRAVEL, MINIMIZE JAMS & SKU DAMAGE

Master carton direction of travel on a conveyor travel path or how your master carton travels on a conveyor travel are bottom flaps options that are (1) in a direction of travel or (2) cross to a direction of travel. Most master cartons have top and bottom flaps & a rectangle shape with a top & bottom flaps on a long rectangle shaped sides. When a bottom sealed master carton is placed onto a conveyor in the direction of travel, a rectangle shaped master carton long dimensions are in the direction of travel. With a master carton long dimension in a direction of travel, there is a greater roller or skate wheel number under a master carton & direction of travel has a master carton bottom surface in roller or skate wheel contact that provides better tracking & smooth travel. Bottom flaps cross to a direction of travel has potential for carton trailing problem due to a short dimension.

WHAT IS THE BEST BELT CONVEYOR TRAVEL PATH
IMPROVE SAFETY & ASSURE CONTROLLED TRAVEL

What is the best belt conveyor travel path surface is determined by your master carton incline or decline degree of slope or required controlled carton travel on a travel path. When your conveyor travel path makes an incline or decline or travels past an activity station such a label print & apply machine, you require controlled master carton movement on a travel path. With a standard master carton (length & height) with travel direction in a long dimension, a decline or incline travel path degree of slope or angle has an influence on your selected conveyor travel path belt surface. A belt surface options are (a) smooth belt conveyor surface that has a solid and smooth surface & is used for a nominal degree of slope, has minimal co-efficient of friction and low cost per in. ft., (2) rough top belt conveyor surface that has a cushion like surface, used for a steeper degree of slope, has medium co-efficient of friction & medium cost per inch. ft. and (3) cleated belt conveyor surface that has a series of ½ to 1 in high cleats or extensions evenly spaced for your longest master carton & full belt surface width, used on a steep degree of slope, has a high co-efficient of friction & has a high cost per inch. ft.

KNOW YOUR SKU TRAVEL PATH CHARACTERISTICS
MINIMIZE COST & ASSURE BEST TRAVEL

Know your sku (master carton) travel path characteristics are important features that determine your conveyor travel path design, cost & sku travel. Your sku important characteristics are height, length, width & weight. A sku length has an impact on your conveyor roller or skate wheel number per inch ft. With a standard 3 rollers or skate wheels under a master carton, a long master carton requires fewer rollers or skate wheels and has a lower conveyor cost per inch. ft. With 3 rollers or skate wheels under a master carton and a master carton in the long dimension on a travel path means good tracking, smooth carton travel & less potential to turn & create jams. A sku width determines a conveyor travel path window width. A narrow master carton width requires a narrow conveyor travel window that means a slightly shorter roller or skate wheel width with some small impact on cost with good carton travel over a conveyor. A sku height determines a travel path window height that determines a passage way height and has no impact on a conveyor cost but has an impact on a stable sku travel. A sku weight determines a conveyor travel path support member number per inch. ft. A heavier sku requires support members on close centers and heavy duty rollers, skate wheels & frames that increase a conveyor cost per inch. ft.

USE ALARM LIGHTS & SIGNALS TO INDICATE A CONVEYOR TRAVEL PATH DOWNTIME
   MINIMIZE POWERED CONVEYOR TRAVEL PATH DOWN TIME

Alarm lights & signal is a powered conveyor travel path concept option when an emergency stop is activated then it minimizes time to locate an activated 'E' stop & re-start a powered conveyor travel path. After an 'E' stop is activated by an employee or jam control sensing device, it and conveyor controls stop a powered conveyor travel path forward movement. To re-start a powered conveyor travel path, it requires a logistics operation staff to identify & correct the problem. An activated 'E' stop mast light or alarm signal permits quick problem location ID.

FOR A SKU CONVEYOR TRANSPORT TRAVEL PATH RE-CIRCULATION IS A MUST
   IMPROVE EMPOYEE PRODUCTIVITY, CONSTANT SKU FLOW & LESS DOWN TIME

Re-circulation is a must for a pallet, carton or GOH warehouse powered in-house transport concept & is a feature to assure a constant sku flow between 2 transaction locations such as between receiving and storage activities & storage & process activities. Re-circulation section on a powered in-house transport concept is a powered carrier or conveyor travel path with no divert locations & has ability to queue skus prior to re-entry to a main sku travel path. A re-circulation powered travel path requires additional conveyor controls & travel path cost, but with a sku available for an employee, forklift truck or AS/RS crane pick-up or delivery assures good employee productivity, constant sku flow & less down time for all associated warehouse activities.

NO QUEUE ON YOUR CONVEYOR TRAVEL PATH THEN LOOK-OUT
   IMPROVE EMPOYEE PRODUCTIVITY, CONSTANT SKU FLOW & LESS DOWN TIME

No queue look-out is a warehouse in-house powered transport travel path philosophy that states your in-house powered transport travel path requires some sku queue to assure smooth & constant sku flow from receiving to a storage area or next warehouse activity station. An in-house powered transport concept with a queue travel path prior to a discharge or delivery station assures skus are ready & available for forklift truck or AS/RS crane pick-up/put-away transaction. Skus ready for pick-up or put-away transaction increases forklift truck or AS/RS crane productivity & assures that an in-house transport is moving a designed sku number. An in-house transport concept with no queue increases potential for powered in-house transport travel path down-time, decrease in-feed, unload and put-away productivity & sku damage.

WITH WIDE AISLE (WA) OR NARROW AISLE (NA) FORKLIFT TRUCK TAKE A PALLET INTO A STORAGE AISLE OR LEAVE A PALLET AT AN AISLE END
   IMPROVES EMPLOYEE PRODUCTIVITY & IMPROVES EQUIPMENT UTILIZATION

With a wide aisle (WA) or narrow aisle (NA) forklift truck storage activity your in-house transport vehicle pallet drop-off options are (1) take a pallet into a storage aisle. A warehouse with a small storage area, a low forklift truck storage transactions & aisles that perpendicular to a receiving dock, take a pallet into a storage aisle concept has good equipment utilization & good employee productivity. In a warehouse with a wide storage area & aisle that are parallel to a receiving dock and a high forklift truck storage transactions, take a pallet into a storage aisle represents poor forklift truck utilization & low employee productivity. To transport a sku with a high wage rate forklift truck driver and a high equipment cost, it represents a high CPU or (2) leave a pallet an aisle end. An option is to have an in-house transport vehicle deposit a pallet at an aisle end. Leave or deposit a pallet at an aisle end with a single or double pallet truck as an in-house transport vehicle has a lower equipment cost, lower truck driver wage rate & lower cost per unit. With a pallet truck in-house transport concept, a storage area main travel aisle requires a wider aisle that permits storage pallet placement at an aisle end floor level drop station & proper pallet placement at an aisle end to have a sku WMS ID face a forklift truck driver.

WITH A VERY NARROW AISLE (VNA) FORKLIFT TRUCK STORAGE TAKE A PALLET INTO A STORAGE AISLE OR LEAVE A PALLET AT AN AISLE END P/D STATION
IMPROVE EMPLOYEE PRODUCTIVITY & IMPROVE EQUIPMENT UTILIZATION

With a very narrow aisle (VNA) forklift truck storage activity your in-house pallet transport vehicle pallet drop-off options are (1) take a pallet into a storage aisle or (2) leave a pallet an aisle end P/D station. Options impact your in-house transport employee productivity, VNA forklift truck driver put-away productivity, potential rack post damage & potential sku WMS scan low productivity. Take a pallet into a storage aisle option has an in-house transport vehicle travel into a VNA aisle, deposit a sku in an aisle & exist from a VNA aisle. Features are (1) to complete a take a pallet into a storage aisle concept, an in-house transport vehicle travels in a very narrow aisle with a pallet truck travel in both lead and driver trail directions that has potential for low pallet truck driver travel speed & potential rack post damage, (2) if a VNA forklift truck is in an aisle, a sku WMS ID has potential to face a wrong direction for a WMS scan transaction. In many operations, when an employee is in an aisle, for safety reasons an alarm or yellow chain is drawn and hooked across an aisle entrance that is considered a safe activity and (3) if a VNA forklift truck is not in an aisle, a sku WMS ID faces a proper direction for a WMS scan transaction, but a forklift truck driver has to wait for a pallet truck to clear an aisle that is low forklift truck driver productivity. Leave a pallet at an aisle end P/D station has an in-house transport pallet or forklift truck deposit a sku at an aisle end pick-up & delivery (P/D) station. With leave a pallet at an aisle end P/D station, a saw-tooth P/D station design assures adequate in-house transport vehicle turning aisle to have a sku placed into a P/D station with a sku WMS ID facing an aisle.

VERY NARROW AISLE FORKLIFT TRUCK (VNA) P/D STATION AISLE WIDTH
IMPROVE EMPLOYEE PRODUCTIVITY & REDUCE DAMAGE

Very narrow aisle forklift truck (VNA) pick-up and delivery (P/D) station aisle width options are determined by your VNA P/D station design. A VNA forklift truck P/D station design assures an in-house transport vehicle & VNA forklift truck sku drop or queue location, easy sku pick-up & delivery location and assures WMS ID has proper orientation. In most 'turn a load' in an aisle VNA forklift truck applications, a rack to rack aisle width is 6'-6" wide. With a 'do not turn' a load in an aisle VNA forklift truck application, a rack to rack aisle width is 6'-0" wide. If we consider a 2 in pallet overhang of each rack load beam, isle widths shrink to 6'-2" and 5'-8" wide aisle. Your VNA P/D station design affects your in-house transport vehicle selection, VNA forklift truck driver productivity and sku/rack damage. VNA P/D station options are (1) flush VNA forklift truck P/D station design has both rack rows end even and between 2 rack rows an aisle width is too narrow for an in-house transport vehicle truck to complete a right angle turn for a P/D transaction or (2) saw-tooth drop or delivery VNA forklift truck P/D station aisle width includes at both ends, 2 exterior rack rows that extend by one rack bay toward a main aisle, 2 VNA forklift truck aisles & 2 interior rack rows that one bay less than 2 exterior rack rows. An aisle width is more than sufficient for an in-house transport vehicle to complete a right angle turn for a P/D transaction. Also, with saw-tooth P/D station design, you have storage positions above the P/D stations that increases your pallet position number.

VNA P/D STATION FLUSH, JAGGERED SAW-TOOTH OR SAW-TOOTH
IMPROVE EMPLOYEE PRODUCTIVITY & REDUCE DAMAGE

Flush, jiggered saw-tooth or saw-tooth very narrow aisle forklift truck pick-up & delivery (P/D) station design assures that a sku is available for an in-house transport vehicle sku drop-off (delivery) or pick-up (outbound) & a sku is properly oriented for VNA forklift truck pick-up with a sku WMS ID line of sight. A flush P/D station design has an in-house pallet truck complete a right angle turn for a pick-up or delivery transaction. Aisle width is an aisle width that is between 2 rack rows. In most VNA applications with a flush P/D station design, a P/D station aisle width has a narrow width that limits good in-house pallet transport productivity, creates potential sku and equipment damage & no additional storage positions above P/D stations. But does provide a sku in proper orientation for a good VNA deposit & pick-up productivity. A jagged saw-tooth P/D station is a modified flush or saw-tooth P/D station that has a VNA aisle & 1 rack row (not 2 rack rows) that creates a P/D station aisle width has a nominal 10'-6" aisle width between 2 jiggered P/D station rack rows. Aisle width has sufficient aisle width for a pallet truck & most counterbalanced forklift truck to complete a right angle turn for a pallet pick-up or delivery transaction with good employee productivity & minimal sku & equipment damage. With 1 P/D station side there is limited sku queue, fewer storage positions above a P/D station & with 2 pallets in a P/D station, potential confusion as to what pallet is outbound or inbound but can be minimized with each P/D station pallet position properly ID for inbound or outbound. A saw-tooth P/D stations design has 2 VNA forklift truck aisles & 4 rack rows. 2 interior rack rows are flush & 2 exterior rack rows extend 1 rack bay beyond the flush rack rows. A saw-tooth P/D station provides a P/D station aisle width with sufficient aisle width for a pallet truck & most counterbalanced forklift trucks to complete a right angle turn for a pick-up or delivery transaction with good employee productivity & minimal sku and equipment damage. With 1 P/D station side there is limited sku queue, fewer storage positions above a P/D station & with 2 pallets in a P/D station, potential confusion as to what pallet is outbound or inbound but can be minimized with each P/D station pallet position properly IDed.

ABOVE YOUR SAW-TOOTH P/D STATION USE FOR STORAGE POSITIONS
   INCREASE STORAGE POSITION NUMBER & IMPROVES STORAGE TRANSACTION PRODUCTIVITY

Above your saw-tooth P/D station use run-out space for storage positions is a very narrow aisle forklift truck end front aisle rack options that increase your pallet storage position number & storage transaction productivity. With a VNA forklift truck rack P/D station concept, a VNA forklift truck has to complete a pallet P/D station transaction to each P/D station pallet position. With pallet rack storage positions above a P/D station pallet position a VNA forklift truck is able to complete a storage transaction to positions. The concept requires a P/D station upright posts to extend up above a P/D station & increases pallet position number that are considered prime pallet storage positions. To complete a storage position to pallet positions above a P/D station does not require down aisle forklift travel that represents an employee productivity increase. The concept increases a pallet position number by positions above each P/D station on an aisle both sides.

VNA P/D STATION RUB BAR & BACK STOP
   IMPROVE EMPLOYEE PRODUCTIVITY & REDUCE DAMAGE

A very narrow aisle forklift truck (VNA) pick-up & delivery (P/D) station rub bas and back stop are P/D station design options that minimize rack damage & assure proper pallet orientation for good VNA truck pick-up productivity. A rub bar is a hardened metal member that is attached full length between a P/D station rack posts depth. If a P/D station rack has a side anchor bolt, a rub bar coverage includes a rack post side anchor bolt. A rub bar height assures that a deposit pallet will not become hung-up on a rub bar. As a pallet truck or counterbalanced forklift truck completes a P/D station deposit or pick-up transaction, a rub bar assures that a pallet does become hung-up on a rack post. A back stop is a harden metal right angle member that is anchored to a P/D station floor rear with an angle iron flush side facing a P/D station aisle. A back stop height assures that a pallet deposit does not become hung-up on a back stop. Most powered pallet trucks & forklift trucks do not have fork tips extend beyond a pallet deck board. As a pallet truck for forklift truck completes a pallet deposit into a P/D station, pallet deck board comes in contact with a back stop flush front. Feature assures that a sku is in a proper orientation with a WMS ID facing an employee and alignment for exact pallet pick-up. Exact pallet placement on a VNA set of forks means proper placement into a storage rack position with minimal pallet put-away problems and exact placement onto load beams.

WIDE AISLE (WA) OR NARROW AISLE (NA) FORKLIFT TRUCK DEPOSITS A PALLET OR HAS AN IN-HOUSE TRANSPORT VEHICLE DROP PALLETS AT AN AISLE END
   IMPROVE EMPLOYEE PRODUCTIVITY & IMPROVE EQUIPMENT UTILIZATION (see in-house transport)

Do it all the way is an in-house transport & storage activity that has a wide aisle or narrow aisle forklift truck complete a sku pick-up at receiving & put-away to a WMS storage position. A warehouse with a small storage area and aisles that face a receiving dock & a low sku volume, do-it-all-the-way concept has good equipment utilization & good employee productivity. A warehouse with a wide storage area & aisle that do not face a receiving dock & a high sku volume, do it all the way concept represents poor forklift truck utilization & low employee productivity. To transport a sku with a high wage rate forklift truck driver & a high equipment cost, it represents a high CPU. An option is to give away. A give-away concept uses a single or double pallet truck as an in-house transport vehicle that has a lower equipment cost, lower wage rate & lower CPU. With a pallet truck in-house transport concept, a storage area requires a wider aisle for a pallet placement at an aisle end & proper pallet placement at an aisle end to have a sku WMS ID face a forklift truck driver.

VERY NARROW AISLE (VNA) FORKLIFT TRUCK TRANSPORTS & DEPOSITS A PALLET OR PICKS A PALLET FROM AN AISLE END P/D STATION
GOOD EMPLOYEE PRODUCTIVITY & GOOD EQUIPMENT UTILIZATION (see in-house transport)

Do it all the way or give it away are very narrow storage are in-house transport vehicle pallet delivery to a storage area options. Options impact your in-house transport employee productivity, VNA forklift truck driver put-away productivity, rack post damage & potential sku WMS scan low productivity. Do-it-all-the-way option has an in-house transport vehicle travel into a VNA aisle, deposit a sku in an aisle & travel from a VNA aisle. To complete a give-it-away transaction, an in-house transport vehicle travels in both a driver lead & driver trail directions that has potential for low driver travel speed & potential rack post damage. If a VNA forklift truck is in an aisle, a sku WMS ID has potential to face a wrong direction for a scan transaction. If a VNA forklift truck is not in an aisle, WMS ID faces a proper direction for a WMS scan transaction, but a forklift truck driver must wait for a pallet truck to clear an aisle. Give it away option has an in-house transport pallet or forklift truck deposit a sku at an aisle end pick-up & delivery (P/D) station. With a give it away option, a saw-tooth P/D station design assures adequate turning aisle to have a sku placed into a P/D station with a WMS identification facing an aisle.

VNA DELIVERY STATION (P/D STATION) AISLE WIDTH
EMPLOYEE PRODUCTIVITY & REDUCE DAMAGE)

A very narrow aisle forklift truck drop aisle width is a warehouse VNA flush or saw-tooth drop or delivery station design that affects your in-house transport & VNA forklift truck driver productivity & sku rack damage. A VNA delivery station design assures an in-house transport & VNA truck sku drop location or queue location, easy sku pick-up & delivery location, assure WMS ID proper orientation. In most turn a load in an aisle VNA application, a rack to rack aisle width is 6'-6" wide. With a do not turn a load in an aisle has a rack to rack aisle width is 6'-0" wide. If we consider a 2 in pallet overhang of each rack load beam, aisle widths shrink to 6'-2" & 5'-8" wide aisle. In a flush VNA delivery station design that has all rack rows end evenly & an aisle between 2 rack rows, an aisle width is too narrow for an in-house transport forklift truck to complete a right angle turn for a pick-up or delivery transaction. A saw-tooth pick-up & delivery station has a width that includes 2 rack rows & 2 aisles & has a width that is more than sufficient for an in-house transport forklift truck to complete a right angle turn for a pick-up or delivery transaction.

VERY NARROW AISLE FORKLIFT TRUCK FLUSH, JAGGERED SAW-TOOTH OR SAW-TOOTH P/D STATION
EMPLOYEE PRODUCTIVITY & REDUCE DAMAGE (see in-house transport)

Very narrow aisle (VNA) forklift truck pick-up & delivery (P/D) station design assures that a sku is available for an in-house transport vehicle sku drop-off (delivery) or pick-up (outbound) & a sku is properly oriented for VNA forklift truck pick-up with a sku WMS ID line of sight. Your P/D station options are (1) Flush P/D station design has an in-house pallet vehicle complete a right angle turn for a P/D transaction. Aisle width is an aisle width that is between 2 rack rows. In most VNA applications with a flush P/D station design, a P/D station aisle width has a narrow width that limits good in-house pallet transport productivity, creates potential sku & equipment damage & additional storage positions above P/D stations. But does provide a sku in proper orientation for a good VNA forklift truck deposit & pick-up productivity, (2) Jagged saw-tooth P/D station is a modified flush or saw-tooth P/D station that has a VNA forklift truck aisle & 1 rack row (not 2 rack rows) that creates a P/D station aisle width has a nominal 10'-6" aisle width between 2 jaggered P/D station rack rows. An aisle width has sufficient aisle width for a pallet truck & most counterbalanced (WS) forklift truck to complete a right angle turn for a P/D transaction with good employee productivity & minimal sku & equipment damage. With 1 P/D station side there is limited sku queue, fewer storage positions above a P/D station & with 2 pallets in a P/D station, potential confusion as to what pallet is outbound or inbound but is minimized with each P/D station pallet position identified in-bound and out-bound & (3) Saw-tooth P/D stations design has 2 VNA forklift truck aisles & 4 rack rows. Two interior rack rows are flush & 2 exterior rack rows extend 1 rack bay beyond flush rack rows. A saw-tooth P/D station provides a P/D station aisle width that has sufficient width for a pallet truck & most counterbalanced (WA) forklift truck to complete a right angle turn for a P/D station transaction with good employee productivity & minimal sku & equipment damage. With 1 P/D station side there is limited sku queue, storage positions above a P/D station & with 2 pallets in a P/D station, potential confusion as to what pallet is outbound or inbound but is minimized with each P/D station pallet position properly IDed.

VNA FORKLIFT TRUCK P/D STATION RUB BAR & BACK STOP
EMPLOYEE PRODUCTIVITY & REDUCE DAMAGE (see in-house transport)

A very narrow aisle forklift truck (VNA) pick-up & delivery (P/D) station rub bar & back stop are P/D station design options that minimize rack damage & assure proper pallet orientation for good VNA truck pick-up productivity. A rub bar is a hardened metal member that is attached full length for a P/D station rack posts depth. If a P/D station rack has a side anchor bolt, a rub bar coverage includes a rack post side anchor bolt. A rub bar height assures that a pallet deposit does not become hung-up on a rub bar. As a pallet truck or counterbalanced (WA) forklift truck completes a P/D station transaction, a rub bar assures that a pallet does become hung-up on a rack post. A P/D station back stop is a harden metal right angle member that is anchored to a P/D station floor rear with an angle iron flush side facing a P/D station aisle. A back stop height assures that a pallet deposit does not become hung-up on a back stop. Most powered pallet trucks & WA forklift trucks fork tips do not extend 3 ins beyond a pallet deck board. As a pallet truck for WAS forklift truck completes a pallet P/D station transaction, pallet deck board comes in contact with a back stop flush front that assures a pallet is at the proper depth and orientation. Feature assures that a sku is in a proper orientation with a WMS ID facing an employee & alignment for exact pallet pick-up. Exact pallet placement on a VNA forklift truck set of forks means proper placement into a storage rack position with minimal pallet put-away problems & exact placement onto load beams.

SKU LIFE CYCLE
DETERMINES BEST POSITION, IMPROVES PRODUCTIVITY & ENHANCES SPACE UTILIZATION

Sku life cycle is a chart or percentage presentation that shows a sku's historical movement over a time period that is 1 week, month or season. A sku life cycle shows after a sku has a sales promotion or advertisement that a sku sales are very high or 'A' or 'B' moving sku. Each additional day, week or month, a sku sales volume declines until a sku becomes a 'C' or 'D' mover with very few sales. A sku life cycle indicates a time period that a sku remains in a prime storage position as an 'A' or 'B' moving sku and the time that a sku is relocated from an 'A' or 'B' moving sku storage position to a 'C' or 'D' moving sku storage position. Features are improved employee productivity & enhance storage utilization. If a sku life cycle is considered for a sku with similar characteristics, it indicates the date that a sku has low sales and is a candidate for transfer from a prime storage position. Feature is that your sku moves can be completed on low volume days or on an off-shift.

AVERAGE INVENTORY OR MOVING AVERAGE INVENTORY
PROPERLY DESIGN YOUR STORAGE SQ. FT. AREA, RACK & VEHICLE REQUIREMENTS

Average inventory projection or X month moving average inventory projection are a warehouse manager's options to project a design year sku/pallet inventory. Your design year sku/pallet inventory projection has a direct impact on your proposed facility sq. ft. or cubic ft. area, storage rack type, forklift truck or AS/RS crane type and required cost. An average inventory project is calculated by dividing 12 (months) into your annual sku/pallet inventory & the result is multiplied by your required months of inventory on-hand such as annual pallet inventory/12 months = average inventory. A moving average inventory projection has several steps. First your determined your company's each months sku/pallet inventory. Next, you determined a number of months (time period such as 3 months) for your proposed operation on-hand inventory & you calculate each 3 months inventory such as (1) Jan, Feb & Mar, (2) Feb, Mar & Apr, (3) Mar, Apr & May, (4) Apr, May & June, (5) May, June & July, (6) June, July & Aug, (7) July, Aug & Sept, (8) Aug, Sept & Oct, (9) Sept, Oct & Nov, (10) Oct, Nov & Dec & (11) Nov, Dec & Jan. A time period (3 month period) with a highest sku inventory is used to project your design year sku/pallet inventory. Using a moving average projection method provides you with a more accurate inventory for your peak business season & if you use an average inventory, it could be understated.

WHAT IS YOUR TOTAL STORAGE AREA OCCUPANCY RATE
IMPROVES SPACE UTILIZATION & DEVELOP YOUR STORAGE AREA PLANS

What is your total storage area occupancy rate is an existing warehouse total storage area study that indicates an opportunity to improve your storage space utilization. To calculate your total storage area occupancy rate is a multiple step process. First step, you determine your total storage positions. Second step is to count your occupied storage positions. Your total storage area occupancy rate is calculated by dividing your total storage position number into your occupied storage position number. Your total storage area occupancy rate helps you to develop plans for improved storage area occupancy.

WHAT IS YOUR STORAGE POSITION OCCUPANCY RATE
IMPROVES SPACE UTILIZATION & IMPROVE EMPLOYEE PRODUCTIVITY

What is your storage position occupancy rate is your existing warehouse storage position survey. Your storage position occupancy rate indicates how full are your storage positions that provides you with an opportunity to improve your space utilization and employee productivity. To calculate your storage position occupancy rate is a multiple step process. First step, you establish your storage position occupancy factor. Factors are full, ¾ full, ½ full, ¼ full and 1 master carton layer or less. Second, you inventory your storage positions and identify each position by its factor that determines your total position number and each factor storage position number. To calculate your total storage area occupancy rate, you divide each storage position factor position number by your total storage position number. If your results show that your storage area has a high percentage for ¼ full or less occupied storage positions, you have an opportunity to improve your space utilization. If your storage rack posts are capable to support additional load beam levels, your ¼ full storage positions have load beams added to create two ¼ storage positions and vacate storage position is full height storage position. When designing a new storage area or remodeling an existing storage area, you match your storage position heights to match your storage position occupancy rate that has a sku height match a storage position height. The results are you increase your sku and skus per sq. ft due to less unused open space in full height pallet positions with less than full high pallets & improves your employee productivity due to hit concentration and hit density per aisle.

HOW TO HANDLE YOUR AVERAGE SKU STORAGE
IMPROVE EMPLOYEE PRODUCTIVITY, ENHANCE SPACE UTILIZATION & POSITION OCCUPANCY

How to handle your average sku storage is a storage concept to handle 80% of your skus & 20% of your volume. Most average 'B' & 'C'/moving skus have a medium to small sku inventory that has 1 to 2 master cartons, pallets or few GOH inch. ft. A storage concept for an average inventory are (1) master carton quantity is single deep storage position that is a decked pallet rack position, (2) pallet quantity is a single deep, ½ high or normal high standard pallet rack position &(3) GOH is static rail. For best results, sku storage positions are located at an aisle rear or in 1 aisle. The concept improves your storage space utilization, position occupancy & employee productivity.

HOW TO HANDLE YOUR PROMOTIONAL SKU STORAGE
IMPROVE EMPLOYEE PRODUCTIVITY, ENHANCE SPACE UTILIZATION & POSITION OCCUPANCY

How to handle your promotional sku storage is a storage concept to handle 20% of your skus & 80% of your volume. Most promotional or 'A'/fast moving skus have a large sku inventory (many pallets or large GOH inch. ft). A storage concept for a promotional sku inventory is a dense storage position (flow rack, drive-in/drive thru, floor stack or 2 deep) or a VNA forklift truck/AS/RS crane one deep position. For best results, 'A'/fast moving sku storage positions are located near at an aisle exist or located with a short travel distance to your pick area. The concept improves your storage space utilization, position occupancy & employee productivity.

EMPLOYEE REACH HEIGHT OR VENDOR PALLET HEIGHT
IMPROVES PRODUCTIVITY, FEWER STORAGE TRANSACTIONS & ENHANCES SPACE UTILIZATION

Employee reach height or vendor pallet height are storage pallet height options. If a master carton on a pallet bottom layer has sufficient structural strength to support a master carton pallet TI (master cartons per layer) & HI (master carton layers high) & a delivery trailer has weight capacity to handle a heavier pallet, a tall master carton stacked pallet is an option. In most warehouses an employee reach height (easily handle a master carton) has a range from 5 ft 6 ins to 6 ft high. When compared to an average vendor pallet height of 4 ft 6 ins, an employee reach pallet height is 18 ins or above an average vendor pallet height. If an employee reach pallet height is used in a warehouse, results are for same sku inventory quantity are (1) fewer pallets, (2) fewer storage transactions, (3) improved employee productivity, (4) fewer pallet storage positions, (5) less clearance space & (6) improved space utilization. For a new or remodel operation, pallet height & weight are rack structural member, forklift truck/AS/RS crane & building floor design facts.

PROMOTIONAL SKUS LOCATED IN YOUR FRONT POSITIONS
IMPROVES EMPLOYEE PRODUCTIVITY & IMPROVES SPACE UTILIZATION

Promotional or sales skus are located in your front or prime real estate position. A promotional or sale sku has a high sales volume, large sku inventory & have a short sku life cycle. To improve employee productivity & space utilization, with a WA or NA forklift truck operation, skus are assigned to a storage aisle exist end or as close as possible to an exist end & in 1 storage area or aisle. With a VNA forklift truck or AS/RS crane operation, skus are spread over aisles to storage positions that are at a P/D station end or as close as possible to a P/D station. With promotional skus located to storage positions at an aisle exit end approach, there is less travel time to complete VNA forklift truck or AS/RS crane sku put-away & withdrawal transactions. After sku promotion there are vacant positions for new skus, minimizes non-productive forklift truck travel past storage positions with medium 'B' or slow moving 'C'/'D' skus & residual sku inventory is transferred to another storage position.

DAMAGED/WRONG PALLET DO NOT DOUBLE STACK ONTO A GOOD PALLET
IMPROVE EMPLOYEE PRODUCTIVITY & MINIMIZE SKU DAMAGE

When you have a damaged or wrong pallet, do not double stack onto a good pallet. At a warehouse receiving department a pallet with vendor delivered skus is a 'not acceptable' pallet to your warehouse. A 'not acceptable' pallet has a broken stringer or deck board or dimensions that do not your pallet specifications. With close vertical clearance space between a pallet top and above load beam in a storage rack position, there is a potential problem for a manual forklift truck storage transaction to a rack storage position. A standard pallet height is nominal 6 ins and a double stacked pallet has a nominal 12 in height. In most AS/RS operations, a pallet size and weight station rejects a double stacked pallet due to a pallet height is not with your pallet standards. In your warehouse transport activity, there is a potential for an unstable pallet to tip and create an in-house transport concept down-time and in your pick area and when a depleted pallet (double stacked pallet) occurs, a picker has additional non-productive time to handle 2 empty pallets For skus on a damage pallet to enter your storage concept, your options are (1) manual re-palletize skus onto a captive pallet that increases your CPU & occupies dock space or (2) mechanical transfer or invert a problem pallet skus onto your captive good pallet that requires equipment cost & some labor cost.

WHAT IS OLD INVENTORY & HOW TO STORE YOUR OLD INVENTORY
INCREASE SKU FACINGS, IMPROVE SPACE UTILIZATION & EMPLOYEE PRODUCTIVITY

What is the old inventory stored is a term that describes a warehouse dated (old) inventory or skus and how to store your old inventory have several options. With an ABC & D sku inventory classification, old inventory skus have a 'C' & 'D' classification that have few or very few COs and have a receiving date (tag) that is at least several months old. In most warehouses, 'C' & 'D' sku types have a medium sku number & few skus per sku. If you consolidate your 'C' & 'D' skus into 1 aisle or at an aisle remote positions (hand stack onto decked rack bays or with additional load beams create additional short pallet positions) increases sku facings, enhances space utilization and provides a good sku hit density & concentration that improves employee productivity.

YOUR STORAGE PHILOSOPHY
IMPROVE SPACE UTILIZATION & EMPLOYEE PRODUCTIVITY

Your storage philosophy is your selected concept that determines a sku location in a storage aisle. A sku storage philosophy is based on a sku's historical sales, estimated sales such as a promotional sku and is implemented through your WMS computer program with computer program directed storage transactions. A sku storage location has an impact your employee productivity and space utilization. Various storage philosophies are (1) ABC & D philosophy has from your skus historical movement usually 6 to 12 months separated into 4 groups that is based on Pareto's Law. 'A'/fast moving skus that account for 80% of your picks and have few sku number. Preferred storage locations are dense storage or single deep positions that are close as possible to your pick section and has the shortest travel distance to your pick section. 'B' & 'C' slow to medium moving skus that account for an estimated 15 % of your picks and are old 'A' skus that have lower sales. Skus have a large number with typical medium to small inventory and are assigned to standard pallet rack positions that have a medium travel distance to your pick section. 'D'/very slow moving or obsolete sku that account for an estimated 5 % of your picks. Skus have a large number with a small inventory and are assigned to remote ½ high or hand stacked standard pallet positions that have a longest travel distance to your pick section, (2) power allocation that is based on your merchandising department promotional sku and account for 80% of your picks. Your promotional skus are few sku numbers with a large inventory. Preferred storage locations are dense storage or single deep positions that are close as possible to your pick section with a short travel distance to your pick section, (3) seasonal skus that have specific life cycle for a pre-determined number of months. Preferred storage locations are dense storage or single deep positions that are close as possible to your pick section, (4) family sku group or pairs that are skus used to produce one sku, language specific nationality that have a large to medium inventory and are assigned to standard pallet rack positions that have a medium travel distance to your pick section or unique skus that a sale of sku creates sale for another sku such as salt and pepper shakers and toy and electric battery. Skus are assigned to standard pallet rack positions that have a medium travel distance to your pick section, (5) size skus that are separated by a sku overall height. When you have a pallet or carton storage area, your standard pallet rack positions have two heights for your storage positions that are one full high position and one half high position, (6) FIFO sku that requires that your oldest sku is the first withdrawn for replenishment or CO. Standard pallet position and gravity/air flow are preferred positions, (7) flammable skus are required storage in a containment chamber and standard pallet rack is preferred, (8) toxic skus that require storage in a meshed area that during a fire restricts air pressurized can flight & (9) random approach that has an employee select the first available vacate storage position. In most operations, it does not improve employee productivity due to increased travel distances to your pick area.

WHEN TO MOVE & WHERE TO MOVE A SKU
   IMPROVE EMPLOYEE PRODUCTIVITY, ENHANCE SPACE UTILIZATION & POSITION OCCUPANCY
When & where to move a sku are storage activity decisions that focus on when & where to relocate a sku from its present/prime storage position to a less prime storage position. If a sku has low demand (sales), a sku relocation from a prime storage (dense storage or standard pallet near an aisle exist) position to a less prime storage (rail, decked rack, half-high or standard pallet position in an aisle rear) position improves employee withdrawal productivity due to a reduction in travel time and distance to complete a high volume sku storage transaction. When skus are ready for relocation to a less than prime position, in most cases a sku has a small sku inventory. With a small inventory in a less than prime position, it provides storage space improvement & increases storage position utilization. To answer when to move or relocate question, you look at a sku life cycle or a storage computer program print-out that shows each sku present storage position or just skus in prime storage positions, age & historical movement (demand or sales) for a specific time period such as 6 months.

HOW TO IDENTIFY YOUR OLD INVENTORY
   INCREASE SKU FACINGS, ENHANCE SPACE UTILIZATION & IMPROVE EMPLOYEE PRODUCTIVITY
How to identify your old sku inventory is a warehouse activity that has an employee or computer program to identify your out-of-date or 'C' & 'D' skus. An out-of-date sku has a sku life or date that has expired & cannot be sold to customers. 'C' & 'D' inventory class sku is a sku that has very few or no COs due to lack of customer interest or sku inventory quantity is below your company inventory quantity criteria to qualify as a sku for customer sales. In most warehouse operations, 'C' & 'D' skus have few skus/master cartons but some skus could have a pallet quantity on a pallet in a storage position that is consider in a prime real estate or high rent area (near an aisle entrance/exit). If your company has an inventory control or WMS computer program, a warehouse manager has a computer program print a sku list that lists from oldest received sku sequence that shows each sku position and quantity to your latest sku received date. If your company has a sku receiving & inventory tag with a color code or printed receiving date, an employee is assigned to walk warehouse aisles & for each sku with a color code/received printed date to list each sku and sku number, position & quantity. A second old sku ID concept is to notice accumulated dust on a sku exterior surface that indicates an old sku. In a warehouse to consolidate your 'C' & 'D' skus into 1 aisle or remote storage/pick positions, hand stack onto decked rack positions or place in short pallet

positions increases sku facings, provides a good sku 'C' & 'D' hit density & concentration that improves employee productivity & enhances space utilization. If your old skus have a pallet quantity, a few skus/master cartons are placed in an aisle with other old skus & a full /partial pallet quantity is placed in a most remote warehouse position or off-site storage.

'D' SKUS ARE IN AN AISLE REAR OR IN ONE STORAGE AISLE
IMPROVE SPACE UTILIZATION & IMPROVE EMPLOYEE PRODUCTIVITY

'D' skus are consolidated in an aisle rear or in one aisle storage positions is a storage philosophy for your slow moving skus that have very few COs or have 'not available for sale' status. When you consolidate your slow moving 'D' skus in one area, you have increased your sku hit concentration & density & with a small master carton quantity improves your space utilization. Increase in your sku hit concentration & density improves your employee productivity due to (1) in your storage aisle, if your fast ('A') & medium ('B' & 'C') moving skus are adjacent to each other it means less employee travel time & distance to complete a storage transaction & (2) with 'D' skus in one area, if there are several master carton storage transactions there is less travel time & distance to complete storage transactions. Since a 'D' sku has relatively no movement & if a 'D' sku has a large master carton inventory, a small master carton quantity is a hand stacked storage position & large pallet inventory is placed into a very remote or off-site storage position that improves your space utilization.

ONE SKU OR MUTLIPLE SKUS IN A PICK POSITION
EMPLOYEE PRODUCTIVITY & POSITION OCCUPANCY

One sku or multiple skus in a WMS identified storage position are small item 'D' slow moving/obsolete sku options to improve space utilization and position occupancy. When you have one sku per WMS ID storage position, your storage & pick transactions are simple, less opportunity for errors and high storage and pick employee productivity. If you have multiple skus per storage position, your options are (1) no separation that has your WMS ID skus in 1 storage position. Features are (a) improves storage position utilization, (b) simple sku deposit transaction, (c) easy to count and (d) to complete a pick, increase search time that has low picker productivity & (2) separated skus that has each WMS identified sku physically separated with a divider/separator from other skus. Features are (a) slightly lower storage position utilization, (b) simple sku deposit transaction, (c) requires a zero scan transaction, (d) easy to count & (e) to complete a pick, decrease search time that improves picker productivity.

HOW TO SCRAP YOUR OLD INVENTORY
INCREASE SKU FACINGS, ENHANCE SPACE UTILIZATION & IMPROVE EMPLOYEE PRODUCTIVITY

How to scrap your old inventory is a warehouse activity that has old or aged sku inventory removed from a warehouse storage position and donated to charity, sold to another company or disposed in trash. An old inventory scrap program objective to remove old skus from a warehouse storage position & create vacant positions for new sku inventory. After a warehouse manager has received authorization to scrap old or aged sku inventory, you are required to select skus for your scrap inventory activity. With the same age, your sku scrap selection options are (1) by age that scraps oldest sku first, (2) random sku selection that scraps skus, (3) book inventory or sku value that scraps highest valued skus first & (4) SILO or small-in and large-out that scraps skus by size. In conclusion, with a limited dollar inventory scrap amount by scrapping high cube skus first, a SILO scrap program creates greatest vacate position number in a warehouse that increases sku facings, enhances space utilization and with no traveling past positions with old skus improves employee productivity.

SKU OVER-HANG A PALLET
POOR SPACE UTILIZATION, POOR EMPLOYEE PRODUCTIVITY & POTENTIAL SKU DAMAGE

Sku over-hang a pallet is master carton or bag that extends beyond a pallet top deck boards. In most warehouse storage concepts, a pallet floor or rack storage concept design parameter allows for a master carton or bag to extend 2 ins beyond each deck board side. When designing a pallet position for a 40 in wide pallet deck board with an over-hang allowance, it means that a pallet floor stack lane or rack position allowance for a pallet is 44 ins wide. No sku over-hang or an over-hang allowance assures good forklift truck productivity, good space utilization & minimal sku damage. If master carton or bag over-hangs or extends beyond your pallet over-hang allowance, there is potential for low forklift truck productivity, sku damage & with 1 pallet in a position & unable to use an adjacent position, poor space utilization. Prior to your storage area floor stack or rack position design, complete a pallet survey to determine your sku over-hang dimensions.

HOW TO HANDLE YOUR SLIP SHEET LIP
IMPROVES SPACE UTILIZATION, IMPROVES EMPLOYEE PRODUCTIVTY & MINIMIZES SKU DAMAGE

How to handle your slip sheet lip is a warehouse storage concept to remove from or secure a slip sheet lip to a sku side that minimizes sku damage & improves space utilization. If a slip sheet is received at your dock, your slip sheet lip options are (1) slip sheet with a lip requires a wider storage lane or pallet position due to a slip sheet lip is considered pallet over-hang. Features are poor space utilization, lowers employee productivity & increases potential sku damage or (2) for storage, with tape a slip sheet lip is secured to a sku side and after withdrawal for a CO in your ship area, the tape is removed that allows a slip sheet lip to used in a ship activity. If a slip sheet is not used for another warehouse operation transaction, in a receiving lane, an employee with a knife cuts a lip from a slip sheet and disposes a removed lip into the trash. A slip sheet sku with no lip requires a narrower storage position due to minimal over-hang, improving employee productivity and minimizes potential sku damage.

WHERE TO PLACE SKUS WITH SMALL INVENTORY QUANTITY & AGED SKUS
IMPROVES EMPLOYEE PRODUCTIVITY & ENHANCE SPACE UTILIZATION

Where to place skus with a small inventory quantity or aged skus are skus that occupy a storage position, do not have many COs ('C' or 'D' skus) and have a small inventory quantity that does not permit advertisements. Most warehouse operations that have 'C' and 'D' skus mixed with high & medium volume 'A' or 'B' moving skus in 1 aisle storage positions, creates non-productive storage put-away or withdrawal employee travel past your small inventory or aged skus. When skus with a small inventory quantity or aged skus with a 'C' or 'D' classification are grouped in 1 aisle or at an aisle rear positions, the approach improves sku hit concentration & hit density that improves forklift truck driver withdrawal productivity & permits.

WHO DIRECTS A SKU WITHDRAWAL TRANSACTION
EMPLOYEE PRODUCTIVITY & ACCURATE INVENTORY

Who directs a withdrawal transaction options are (1) employee directed or (2) computer suggested. An employee directed withdrawal transaction is used with an employee or employee controlled forklift truck concept & has an employee determine from what storage position to withdraw a sku. Features are (1) transaction position potentially does not match your storage area philosophy or FIFO rotation, (2) in most applications there is a delayed transaction completion data transfer & (3) for good inventory management, requires a forklift truck driver to write each sku ID & storage position onto a paper document & have a clerk complete book entry that increases potential for errors. A computer suggested withdrawal transaction is used in an employee, employee controlled forklift truck or AS/RS crane storage operation that has a WMS program/inventory control program to identify a specific or WMS ID position & associated sku quantity. Features are (1) withdrawal transaction matches your storage area philosophy or FIFO rotation, (2) transaction is delayed or on-line transferred to a computer via paper document or RF device for computer update & (3) with a RF device the transaction data transfer is more accurate and faster.

COMPUTER DIRECTED SKU PUT-AWAY OR DEPOSIT
MAINTAIN YOUR STORAGE PHILOSOPHY & IMPROVES EMPLOYEE PRODUCTIVITY

Computer directed sku put-away or deposit transaction is a WMS ID sku deposit to a WMS ID storage position that was suggested by an inventory control or WMS computer program. With a computer directed deposit an employee, employee controlled forklift truck or AS/RS crane travels in an aisle to a suggested WMS ID position and completes a sku (master carton, pallet or GOH) deposit transaction. To assure accurate inventory, sku & storage position WMS IDs are scanned & sent to a WMS computer that minimizes any sku inventory tracking or position status problems. Features are maintains your storage philosophy & improves productivity.

EMPLOYEE DIRECTED SKU PUT-AWAY OR DEPOSIT
DIFFICULT TO MAINTAIN YOUR STORAGE PHILOSOPHY & LOW EMPLOYEE PRODUCTIVITY

Employee directed sku put-away or deposit transaction is a WMS identified sku deposit to a WMS ID storage position that is determined by an employee or employee controlled forklift truck. After an employee or employee controlled forklift truck enters a storage area, an employee or employee controlled forklift truck places a sku into a vacant WMS ID position. To assure accurate inventory control, sku & storage position WMS IDs are scanned & sent to a WMS computer that minimizes any sku inventory tracking or position status problems. Features are difficult to maintain your storage area philosophy & low employee productivity.

VNA/ASRS FORKLIFT TRUCK OR CARTON SINGLE OR DUAL COMMANDS
INCREASE PRODUCTIVITY

VNA forklift truck single or dual commands are a VNA/ASRS forklift truck activity commands or instructions to complete a storage transaction. A VNA forklift truck single command is a standard command. A VNA forklift truck carrier single command has a vehicle make an aisle trip from a P/D station into a storage aisle. Travel command options are (1) with a sku for deposit to a WMS ID storage position and after deposit for a vehicle return empty to a P/D station and (2) empty to a WMS ID storage position and at a storage position after sku withdrawal to return travel with a sku to a P/D station. In conclusion, a single command has a vehicle complete only 1 inbound or 1 outbound WMS ID sku transaction per aisle trip and does not require a work hour balance for inbound skus at a P/D station and outbound CO withdrawal transactions. A VNA forklift truck concept with a WMS program concept a dual command program requires some additional computer programming, sku deposit & withdrawal communications & aisle end P/D station designed with inbound and outbound queue lanes. A VNA forklift truck in a dual command mode has a vehicle (1) with a sku travel from a P/D station to a WMS identified storage position and complete a sku deposit storage activity, (2) from a storage position travel empty to another WMS ID storage position for sku withdrawal from another storage position and (3) with a sku on board travel to a P/D station and transfer a sku to a P/D station. In conclusion, a dual command mode has a vehicle complete both 1 inbound and 1 outbound WMS ID sku transaction per aisle trip and does require a work hour balance for inbound skus & outbound CO withdrawal transactions and P/D stations have inbound and outbound queue lanes. Per aisle trip a dual command mode per aisle almost doubles skus that are handled per hour, but it is combined in-bound & outbound activities that creates a UPH increase.

WHAT ARE YOUR STORAGE AREA TRANSACTION NUMBERS
ASSURES ON-TIME TRANSACTION COMPLETION

What are your storage area transaction numbers refers to a warehouse storage area design year peak sku deposit and withdrawal transaction number. Your storage concept design year peak deposit & withdrawal transaction number impacts your storage transaction employee or vehicle (employee, WA, NA, VNA forklift or AS/RS crane) number & P/D station number with associated queue capacity, bar code scanners/RF readers and transaction communication network. In an employee or manual controlled WA or NA forklift truck operation each sku deposit transaction is 1 transaction per aisle trip & each sku withdrawal transaction is 1 transaction per aisle trip. An example has 500 deposit transactions & 500 withdrawal transactions that equals 1000 single transactions. If an employee or vehicle completes 20 single transactions per hour, with a 7 hour work day, 7 to 8 vehicles or employees are required for your storage area. In most VNA forklift truck or AS/RS crane operations with P/D station queue positions/lanes, a warehouse attempts to have deposit & withdrawal transactions occur within the same work day time period. When deposits and withdrawal transactions occur within a work day same time period, a VNA forklift truck or AS/RS crane completes dual command transactions. With an aisle trip, a vehicle travels from a P/D station with a sku & completes a deposit transaction, continues empty aisle travel to a storage position and completes a sku withdrawal transaction and travels with a sku to a P/D station. With a balance for deposits and withdrawals per hour, a dual command completes 2 transactions per aisle trip. A storage area P/D station pallet position queue with vendor delivery scheduling & CO sku profile helps to obtain a balance for deposits & withdrawals. It is noted with additional aisle travel time, that a dual command mode increases transactions per trip by an estimated 50% to 80%. An example has 500 deposit transactions & 500 withdrawal transactions that equals 1000 single commands. If an employee or vehicle completes 30 dual commands or transactions per hour, with a 7 hour work day, 5 vehicles or employees are required for your storage operation. Knowing your storage transaction number allows you to determine an accurate vehicle and scanner number.

YOUR VENDOR OR YOU CUT & TIE YOUR GOH BAG BOTTOM
IMPROVES EMPLOYEE PRODUCTIVITY & ENHANCE SPACE UTILIZATION

Your vendor or employee cut or tie your GOH bag bottom has your GOH vendor or an employee assure that a GOH plastic bag extends 1 to 2 ins beyond a GOH length. Most vendors send GOH with a plastic bag that extends 12 to 18 ins beyond a GOH bottom and with multi level GOH storage positions, a lower GOH ID is blocked by the above GOH plastic bag extension. GOH with 1 to 2 in length permits at least 2 GOH rails high and an elevated GOH bag does not block a lower level GOH ID. If your GOH vendor cuts or ties each GOH bag, there is minimal cost added to cost of goods. If your employee cuts or ties a GOH bag, there is a small additional warehouse labor cost. Features are (1) dust barrier, (2) shortens a GOH overall length & (3) in a vertical GOH storage stack assures that there is line of sight to a lower position WMS ID.

SHORT OR TALL GOH STORAGE POSITIONS
IMPROVES SPACE UTILIZATION

Short or tall GOH positions are your two basic GOH storage positions. Each GOH storage position matches a GOH length that means a short length GOH fits into a short storage position or if all short positions are full, a short GOH fits into a tall GOH position. Only tall GOH fits into a tall GOH position. To maximize your GOH storage area utilization, your important storage position design facts are (1) employee reach height, (2) your short & long GOH sku number and inventory quantity, (3) number of summer GOH skus & winter skus & GOH per linear ft, (4) ability to have 2 deep static storage positions & (5) to have unassisted access to (a) 2 or 3 short GOH levels, (b) 1 long and 1 short GOH levels & (c) elevated walkway with GOH hanging below a walkway in a fire and employee protected well.

ONE DEEP OR TWO DEEP GOH STORAGE RAILS
IMPROVE EMPLOYEE PRODUCTIVITY & INCREASE STORAGE DENSITY

one deep or 2 deep GOH storage rails are floor level static rail GOH storage concept options that improves employee productivity and increase storage density. One deep floor level static rail GOH storage concept has 1 rail that is adjacent to an aisle & is full aisle length. After GOH are deposited onto a rail, a GOH storage position WMS identification is fixed or slides over a rail. GOH occupies as many inch. ft. that is required for a vendor delivery. Features are (1) with 1 GOH sku that occupies a large inch. ft length in one aisle, there is additional travel & distance to access other GOH storage positions & to complete a storage transaction, creates low employee productivity, (2) low storage density per aisle inch. ft. & (3) few skus per aisle. A 2 deep floor level static GOH rail concept has a front rail that is adjacent to an aisle & is full aisle length. A second GOH floor level static rail is full aisle length & directly behind the front rail. In a GOH storage module, there is sufficient space for GOH transfer equally onto both front & rear rails. When a new WMS ID GOH is evenly divided between both front and rear static rails, a WMS ID storage position ID is attached to both rails & slides over both rails that allows a storage position WMS ID to match a GOH sku quantity. To assure a GOH quantity is even on both rails & both rails have the same WMS ID GOH sku, after GOH withdrawal transactions have depleted a front GOH rail quantity, an employee notices a large open space on a front rail. Since a WMS ID GOH was WMS scanned to a 1 WMS ID storage position that included both front and rear rails, an employee moves a GOH sku quantity from a rear rail to a front rail & slides a storage WMS ID from a large space to a smaller space. Features are (1) increases sku facings per inch. ft that increases space utilization, (2) increases storage density per aisle, (3) some additional employee effort to consolidate skus from a rear rail to a front rail & move a position identifier and (4) with short employee travel time & distance to complete a storage transaction, increases employee productivity.

GOH HANGS IN A HOLE
INCREASE STORAGE CAPACITY & IMPROVE EMPLOYEE PRODUCTIVITY

GOH hangs in a hole or cavity is a GOH storage concept that improves employee productivity, increases space/cube utilization and enhances storage density per aisle. A GOH hang in a hole/cavity concept options are (1) in a multiple level standard rack or structural pipe storage concept, there are walkways between two static rail rows and GOH rails are set at a pre-determined elevation to a walkway. In relation to a walkway, a GOH rail is above a cavity that allows for GOH to hang into cavity. Rails above a cavity improves employee access to (a) 3 short GOH storage levels or (b) 1 long GOH storage level with 1 short GOH storage level & (2) in a floor level GOH storage area, an elevated walkway is installed between 2 static rail rows and GOH rails are set at a pre-determined elevation to a walkway. A walkway elevates an employee to a GOH rail. With an employee elevated to GOH rails, it improves employee access to (a) 3 short GOH storage levels or (b) 1 long GOH storage level with 1 short GOH storage level. Prior to an in-rack or pipe structure cavity concept or elevated walkway concept, you review your local codes & insurance company for walkway handrails, kick-plates, required steps & cavity material and structural strength to support an employee load and fire barrier & sprinkler requirements.

CONVERT YOUR SHELF OR HAND STACK PALLET RACK STORAGE POSITION TO GOH STORAGE
INCREASE GOH STORAGE & STORAGE AREA FLEXIBILITY

Convert your standard shelf or hand stack pallet rack storage position to GOH storage is a warehouse concept that permits a warehouse manager to convert a master carton hand stack standard pallet rack or shelf storage/pick concept to a GOH rail storage/pick concept. During peak GOH season a standard shelf concept middle 2 to 3 shelves are removed from a shelf bay and top and bottom shelves remain. The 2 to 3 removed shelves are stacked onto the bottom shelf. Below the top shelf by 1 to 2 ins, you add a hang bar support devices to each side post & a hang bar is placed into support members. To convert decked standard pallet rack or angle iron hand stack bay to a GOH storage position, your options are (1) use eyebolts, nuts & washers. After 2 eyebolts are inserted through deck material (wood, wire mesh or sheet metal) adjacent at a rack bay ends or next to load beam cross members and each top is secured with a washer and nut. Through eyebolts an employee inserts a GOH hang bar & (2) in a standard rack bay to add special designed cross or front to rear members to load beams. In a front to rear member middle are two drilled holes for an inverted 'U' shape bolt attachment. Through each inverted 'U' bolt you insert a hang bar and add nuts to the threaded inverted 'U' bolt ends. With secured bolts, your position is ready for GOH. A flipped shelf or rack bay has capacity for (a) 1 long GOH & (b) 2 short GOH. Feature increases your GOH storage capacity with minimal equipment, labor cost & storage flexibility due to a shelf/rack bay is converted to master carton or GOH storage.

GOH SKUS SLIDE TO A STORAGE ROW REAR OR FRONT
IMPROVE EMPLOYEE PRODUCTIVITY, ENHANCE SPACE UTILIZATION & POSITION OCCUPANCY

GOH skus slide to a storage row rear or front is a GOH static rail storage concept for a single side employee routing pattern that increases employee put-away & pick productivity, enhances rail utilization & rail occupancy. With GOH slide to a rear or front concept, at an aisle entrance that is nearest a pack area an employee transfers GOH onto a rail. As GOH is transferred onto a rail, an employee pushes GOH forward over a rail. After a last GOH is transferred onto a rail, an employee places a sliding position WMS ID onto a rail at a GOH lead end. Features are reduces a put-away employee walk distance to complete a put-away transaction and new skus are closest to your pack area. As another GOH is added to a rail, an employee repeats an old GOH push forward & adds a new sliding position WMS ID onto a rail at a GOH lead end and adds a new GOH to a sliding rail. The concept moves GOH closer to an aisle exist to a pack location thereby to complete a pick reduces an employee walk distance to complete a pick transaction, sliding GOH improves rail utilization.

HANG GOH IN A CAVITY
GOOD EMPLOYEE PRODUCTIVITY, SPACE UTILIZATION & POSITION OCCUPANCY

Hang in a cavity is a GOH static storage concept that has GOH hang from an elevated rail into a cavity or below an employee walkway. The concept increases GOH storage capacity by adding another short GOH rail (increase from 2 rails to 3 rails or have 1 long GOH rail below 1 short GOH rail) & improves an employee's productivity due to elevated GOH rail is within an easy reach. Cavity design that allows lowest rail level GOH to hang into a cavity options are created from a rack or pipe structural members to support GOH rails & elevated walkway loads and on a floor to build an elevated walkway to support an employee. Walkway steps, kick-plates & handrails are per your local codes & company policy.

HOW TO HANDLE WINTER, SPRING, SUMMER & FALL OR PROMOTIONAL GOH SKUS
IMPROVES EMPLOYEE PRODUCTIVITY, ENHANCES SPACE UTILIZATION & POSITION OCCUPANCY

Winter, spring, summer and fall are a year four major seasons and promotional GOH skus has an impact on your sku mix. This aspect is especially true for a warehouse that handles GOH. For a particular season, your company purchase department issues POs to bring skus in your warehouse for a season & skus have a sale promotion. In most cases, a season 20% skus account for 80% of your warehouse activities. With this high specific sku volume or high hit concentration & hit density to improve your employee put-away & pick productivity, space utilization & position occupancy, your GOH storage philosophy & layout is planned with 4 sections and each section has skus for each season. Each section is designed to handle your sku peak inventory volume for one season and consideration is given for winter skus that have few GOH skus per inch. ft. & summer skus that have larger GOH per inch. ft. If at the completion of a season, residual GOH sku quantity is allocated to an aisle remote rail area or consolidated into one aisle with the season section.

GOH SCAP HANDLING CONCEPT
IMPROVE EMPLOYEE PRODUCTIVITY

GOH SCAP is a term that describes a warehouse concept to place GOH in a temporary storage position in a GOH SCAP (sort, count & pick area). When compared to a GOH manual transport & transfer to a static rail storage position, a GOH SCAP concept improves employee productivity due to less employee walking distances & lower GOH transfer to a storage position transaction. GOH SCAP equipment options are (1) 4-wheel cart with a hang bar & (2) overhead non-powered trolley with a load bar. With both options, there are 3 cart lanes or trolley travel paths. Two exterior lanes/paths are used for inbound GOH & middle lane/path is for detailed received GOH. GOH SCAP area has two design options. The first is after GOH is bulk received onto a middle lane or path carts/trolleys, GOH remains in lanes/paths, WMS scanned to a temporary storage/pick position and is ready for withdrawal. The second option has carts/trolleys moved from the detail receiving area to another area lanes/paths, WMS scanned to a temporary storage/pick position and is ready for withdrawal. You design your GOH SCAP area on your GOH sku quantity that is sold after a sku sales promotion or historical sku sales data (based on a vendor delivered sku quantity, a sku percentage that was sold). After allocating the pre-determined GOH quantity to a SCAP area, a residual sku quantity is sent to static rail area.

WHAT IS YOUR GOH HANGER TYPE
ASSURE CONSTANT GOH FLOW

What is your GOH hanger type is a very important design factor for your automatic GOH storage/pick concept. Your GOH hanger design and material selection are determined by (1) your customer preference such as your retail sales floor, (2) how your GOH is shipped to your customer such as on delivery truck rope loop, hanger box or GOH on a cardboard fold, (3) hanger cost and (4) automatic machine vendor requirement such as metal, wood or plastic.

WHAT ARE YOUR GOH STATIC STORAGE RAIL TYPES
SKU ACCESS & SPACE UTILIZATION

Your GOH static storage galvanized rail diameter matches your hanger neck, position identifier and provides a GOH storage/pick position. GOH static rail allows hanger material flexibility. GOH static position types are (1) manual concept with 1 deep and 1 high or 2 levels high, (2) with a manual concept two deep and 1 high or 2 levels high, (3) with an employee elevating concept 6 to 8 levels high HROS vehicle, (4) with GOH hanging in a cavity 2 to 3 levels high, (5) manual push back trolley lanes, (6) dynamic or trolley gravity flow lanes and (6) with an elevated employee walkway 2 to 3 levels high.

GOH AISLE DUST BARRIER
MINIMIZE SKU DAMAGE

GOH aisle dust barrier is a solid cardboard or sheet metal barrier that is anchored to the floor and upright posts. As an employee or vehicle travels in an aisle, a solid barrier prevents dust and dirt moving from an aisle onto the floor below your GOH. Feature are (1) reduces dust collection on to GOH and (2) reduce housekeeping time.

GOH STORAGE POSITION IDENTIFICATION
EMPLOYEE PRODUCTIVITY AND INVENTORY CONTROL

GOH storage position ID assure employee or hand held scanner line of sight that provides good employee productivity and inventory control. For an effective GOH ID, above GOH does extend downward and cover a below

GOH ID and each GOH position ID upward extension is above your GOH. GOH ID options are (1) plastic placards, (2) large cardboard doughnuts, (3) rectangle shaped placards, (4) clip on, (5) cardboard triangles and (6) 'Z' shaped holder. The preferred GOH position ID holder is a cardboard holder that has a GOH position ID upward extension or height above GOH on a rail height to assure easy and quick employee or hand held scanner line of sight.

WHAT ARE YOUR GOH MECHANIZED OR AUTOMATIC STORAGE CONCEPTS
FEWER EMPLOYEES & LOW UTILITY EXPENSES

Your GOH mechanized or automatic storage concepts require that your hanger material matches your equipment manufacturer's specifications. A mechanical GOH concept has at a transfer station an employee completed a storage/pick transaction. Mechanized concepts computer controlled are (1) powered horizontal carousel that requires horizontal space. Options are (a) single unit and (b) multiple units in a horse-shoe layout and (2) powered vertical carousel that requires vertical space. Automatic concepts require GOH on a standard hanger that matches your automatic storage/pick machine specifications. Some Automatic machine options at the time of this writing are (1) Promech, (2) 200 GOH trolley-less storage/pick and (3) MTS trolley-less storage/pick.

SINGLE DEEP OR TWO DEEP STORAGE POSITIONS
IMPROVES SPACE UTILIZATION

One or two deep storage positions is a warehouse with GOH, carton or pallet sku depth in the storage area. A 1 deep storage position has one WMS ID sku in a WMS ID storage rack position & is adjacent to an aisle. With a 1 deep concept, at a WMS ID storage position an employee, forklift truck or AS/RS crane completes WMS ID sku deposit or withdrawal transaction. 1 deep storage concept has 85% utilization, direct access to a WMS ID sku, assures FIFO sku rotation & good storage density per aisle. With a 2 deep storage concept, there are 2 deep (cartons, GOH or pallets) storage positions per face/bay. There is 1 storage position in the front & a second storage position in a rear. An employee, NA forklift truck or AS/RS crane completes a sku first storage transaction to an interior position and a sku second storage transaction to an aisle position. With most 2 deep storage operations, skus in a 2 deep concept are the same skus. With a 2 deep storage concept, most WMS programs require modification such as a WMS ID substitution, NA forklift truck or AS/RS crane carrier has a 2 deep carrier with a standard stroke to access an interior position & master carton requires a decked position. In most 2 deep storage applications a rear position has 85% utilization & front position has 66% utilization. When storage transactions are made to an interior position, lower productivity due to additional time for a deep stroke or reach, costly to have a FIFO rotation & has high sq ft or space utilization.

ALL STORAGE RACK OPENINGS HAVE SAME HEIGHT
MAXIMUM STORAGE AREA FLEXIBLITY

All storage rack openings have the same height is a warehouse storage area that has all storage rack pallet position set at the same height and assures maximum storage area position flexibility. All pallet storage positions set at the same height means that an open space between 2 standard rack load beams have same dimension. With a full pallet in & out storage operation, all storage rack positions at same height provide best space utilization, maximum pallets per sq. ft. & maximum flexibility. In a pick operation, all pallet storage rack positions at same elevation has some limitations. The limitations are (1) less than a full pallet in a storage position means low storage position utilization, (2) difficult to store maximum sku number and (3) lower employee productivity. In a GOH warehouse, all storage positions set for a long GOH dimension permits maximum storage position flexibility but with a short GOH in a long position means low storage position utilization and lower employee productivity.

DIFFERENT OPENING HEIGHTS FOR YOUR STORAGE RACKS
MAXIMUM STORAGE AREA & POSITION UTILIZATION & IMPROVE EMPLOYEE PRODUCTIVITY

Different opening height for your storage racks means that a warehouse storage area racks have at least 2 rack opening heights. In a warehouse there is great potential for a storage area to have less than full pallets or to have 'C' or 'D' moving sku with a small master carton quantity. When a less than full pallet occupies a full high pallet rack storage position, there is unused space in a pallet storage position that creates poor storage position and space utilization, low skus per sq. ft. or storage area and low employee productivity. If a storage area has a percentage of rack positions that are less than full or high (based on your storage position occupancy rate), results are improves storage position and space utilization, improved productivity with improved hit density and hit concentration per aisle, increased skus per sq. ft. & additional load beam cost & maybe new upright post to support a heavier new load.

SEPARATE STORAGE & PICK POSITIONS
IMPROVE EMPLOYEE PRODUCTIVITY

Separate storage and pick positions means that a master carton or GOH warehouse has separate sku WMS ID storage positions & pick positions. In most warehouses, all inbound or new skus are assigned to a WMS ID storage or pick position and a storage position is accessed by a forklift truck & a pick position is accessed by an employee. As COs deplete skus from a WMS ID pick position, a WMS computer program advises an employee or forklift truck to complete a WMS ID sku replenishment activity. A replenishment activity has an employee or forklift truck move a WMS ID sku from a storage position to a sku same pick position or different pick position. WMS ID sku quantity & pick position scanned and sent to a WMS computer for update. Features are that it requires a replenishment activity & improves picker productivity.

ALL STORAGE POSITIONS ARE PICK-ABLE
LOW EMPLOYEE PRODUCTIVITY

All storage positions are pick-able means that a master carton or GOH warehouse sku positions are pick-able. A pick position means that an order picker has to access a sku quantity from a WMS ID position to complete a CO. All pick-able position concept means that received and WMS ID skus are placed into any position. Position & sku WMS IDs are scanned and sent to a WMS computer for update. Feature means if a sku quantity becomes depleted in an employee access WMS ID position & to complete a CO for additional skus from an elevated WMS ID position, a picker has non-productive time to locate forklift truck to access skus from an elevated WMS ID position but no replenishment activity.

TALL OR SHORT STORAGE POSITION LOCATION
SPACE UTILIZATION, ACCESS POSITIONS & MATCH EQUIPMENT CAPABILITY

Tall or short pallet storage position location is a storage rack design with 2 sku heights and locates a specific dimensioned storage position at an upright post top or bottom. With a human controlled WA, NA or VNA forklift truck, a set of forks has a load back rest. When handling a short pallet, a back rest height exceeds a pallet height that requires at your top pallet position for your forklift truck backrest, you require a tall pallet position for a clearance to complete a transaction. With an AS/RS crane, a pallet moves vertical on a single mast or dual masts & other crane and rack structural features that require a standard clearance at a top storage position. To assure access to high pallet storage positions, have maximum space utilization & rack structural strength, your rack design has short pallet storage positions that are located at a upright post base (floor level) & tall pallet storage positions are located at a upright post top (highest level). Most tall pallets have a light load weight & most short pallets have heavy load weight, which matches a forklift truck or AS/RS crane load weight reduction at maximum elevation above the floor.

DECKED PALLET RACK ROW DESIGN
INCREASE SKU FACINGS, IMPROVE SPACE UTILIZATION & ACCESS POSITIONS

Decked standard pallet rack or slotted angled rack row is a warehouse master carton storage design for 'C'/'D' sku movers that increases sku facings, space utilization and permits access to all pick positions. Decked standard pallet rack or slotted angled rack designs are similar with upright posts, load beams & deck material (wood, wire mesh, metal sheet, conveyor or particle board) but an exception is that a standard pallet rack height design can exceed an angle iron rack height design. With standard pallet rack, above your human accessible position additional storage positions are designed to handle master cartons or pallets. Rack row design options are (1) single rack row with one master carton with an aisle on both sides. Features are (a) provides maximum sku facings, (b) 85% highest space utilization, (c) easy sku access, (d) easy to have FIFO rotation & (e) mid-deck divider that is wood, pipe or rope restricts master carton moving another master carton into the opposite aisle & (2) back to back rack row with 2 deep master cartons per rack row with an aisle on each rack row side. Features are

(a) provides maximum master carton storage, (b) good utilization with a rear position at 85% utilization & front position at 66% utilization, difficult to access a sku, (c) difficult to have FIFO rotation & (d) to maintain a flue space, it requires rear deck stop.

YOUR HIGHEST STORAGE POSITION GETS WARM
ASSURE SKU QUALITY

Your highest storage position gets warm is a storage area situation that occurs at your highest storage rack positions. In all storage concepts, a storage area warm air rises to a ceiling that causes internal temperature to increase at your highest storage rack positions. Temperature increase occurs in a low warehouse building (20 to 25 ft high ceiling) and is especially true for a VNA forklift truck or AS/RS crane tall rack warehouse facility (40 to at least 80 ft high ceiling). To protect your temperature sensitive skus in your storage area, for your temperature sensitive skus your WMS computer program or inventory control program has a flag that suggests or indicates to a receiving clerk to direct a sku put-away or deposit transaction to a low (floor level) pallet rack storage position. The approach protects your sku quality with minimal cost. An example is chocolate skus.

YOUR HIGHEST STORAGE POSITION IS A SECURED POSITION
ASSURE SKU SECURITY

Your highest storage position is a secured storage position. In all storage concepts, in a storage area your highest storage rack positions increase an employee difficulty to access storage positions. A tall pallet position security feature occurs in a conventional warehouse building and is especially true for a VNA forklift truck or AS/RS crane tall rack warehouse that has at least a 40 ft high ceiling & requires a VNA forklift truck or AS/RS crane to access your highest storage positions. To protect your high value skus in your storage area, for your high value skus your WMS computer program or inventory control program has a flag that suggests for a receiving clerk to direct a sku deposit transaction to a high pallet rack storage position. Features are high value sku security with a minimal cost.

HOW YOUR CARTON OR PALLET FACES IN A STORAGE POSITION
IMPROVE SPACE UTILIZATION & IMPROVE EMPLOYEE PRODUCTIVITY

How your master carton, pallet & GOH faces in a storage position (sku orientation) is a major storage position and storage vehicle design consideration. Most master cartons, pallets & GOH have a rectangle shape with a long & short dimension. When a master carton, GOH or pallet sku is placed in a storage position with a rectangle short side facing an aisle, there is an increase sku storage positions per inch. ft., easy to complete a WMS scan transaction with a wrap around label that faces an aisle, easy to complete a storage transaction that improves employee productivity with a short travel distance & time & with a short load beam length or distance between to support arms, less potential for master carton or pallet bow/deflection that a lower rack cost. When a sku in a storage position has a long dimension face an aisle, the results are longer travel distance & time to complete a storage transaction, fewer storage positions per aisle inch ft & longer load beam length or distance between to support arms, greater potential for master carton or pallet bow/deflection & higher cost.

LOCK YOUR PALLET ONTO A STORAGE POSITION LOAD BEAMS
MINIMIZE SKU DAMAGE & IMPROVE SECURITY

Lock your pallet onto your storage rack load beams concept is a warehouse storage rack & pallet bottom deck board concept that locks a pallet onto a storage rack load beams. If your warehouse is located in a medium or high seismic zone & you desire to secure your pallets in a rack position & permits a forklift truck or AS/RS crane to complete a storage transaction, lock a pallet onto a storage rack load beams concept is consideration. Lock your pallet onto a storage rack load beam concept has your pallet bottom deck board designed at both fork openings (ends) an open space between the first & second deck boards. The open space has sufficient width for a storage rack front load beam to set in a pallet front deck board opening & a storage rack rear load beam to set in a pallet rear deck board opening. Second design factor is your storage rack upright post span is design to have front & rear load beams to fit between in a pallet bottom deck board opening. Since a pallet bottom deck board is a nominal ¼ thick, a 2 pallet bottom deck boards secure a pallet between load beams that restricts a pallet forward or reverse movement & a pallet stringers rest on the load beams. Since a lock pallet stringer rests on your load beams, a lock a pallet onto a storage rack load beams concept does not diminish a pallet fork opening dimensions. This assures a forklift truck or AS/RS crane set of forks complete a storage withdrawal transaction from a pallet position.

TWO TALL PALLET ON THE FLOOR
    INCREASE SPACE UTILIZATION & IMPROVES FORKLIFT TRUCK PRODUCTIVITY
Two tall pallet on the floor is a standard pallet storage rack concept that has a storage bottom (floor level) pallet rack position with height for 2 pallets high (1 pallet stacked on another pallet) & elevated pallet rack positions have an opening for 1 pallet. Two pallets high on a floor rack concept is used in a warehouse with palletized skus that have the structural strength to support another full pallet weight. Two pallets on the floor concept requires 1 less load beam pair and one less forklift truck replenishment transaction. Prior to implementation, your rack manufacturer assures that your upright post design or structural strength supports a 2 tall pallet opening or rack position requires a double upright post design that has an additional cost. Features are increases pallet positions in an aisle, increases storage density, access to all skus, increases space or cube utilization, used with a WA or NA forklift truck, reduces an overall stacking height by a nominal 12 ins & reduces your forklift truck replenishment transaction number.

STACK YOUR NON-STACKABLES
    INCREASE SPACE UTILIZATION & MINIMIZE SKU DAMAGE
Stack your non-stackables is a storage concept that is used to allow your warehouse to contain your fragile, crushable or non-supportable skus in a stackable container. With your non-stackable skus in a stackable container, your storage area has similar operational features as a 3 or 4 high & 3 or 4 deep floor stack storage concept. Your stackable container options are (1) tier rack or metal frames that are connected at the top & set on a pallet. For best results a nail secures each tier rack leg to a pallet (2) four-wall and bottom wire mesh container with fork openings & (3) stacking frames with four upward extending legs connect at a top & fork opening on the bottom that permits your to hand stack cartons onto or to place a full pallet into a stacking frame. Stacking frame options are (a) full length fork sleeves to minimize a metal frame sliding on a metal set of forks, (b) when not being used nestable frames and (c) plastic wrapped or rubber bands to secure skus onto a pallet. Features are improves your space & cube utilization, minimizes sku damage especially with a container wrapped in plastic, increased storage density per aisle, interfaces with a WA or NA forklift truck & difficult to use with a WMS computer program.

PARALLEL OR PERPENDICULAR STORGE RACK ROWS AND AISLES FLOW TO YOUR PICK AREA
    ASSURE SKU FLOW
Parallel or perpendicular storage rack rows and aisles flow to your pick area are storage area rack & forklift truck aisle direction of travel options. In a rectangle shaped building, a parallel rack row and forklift truck aisle direction of travel has storage rack rows & aisles parallel to your next warehouse activity. For a forklift truck to drop pallets at the next warehouse activity, you add a middle aisle or your forklift truck uses end turning aisles. Features are increased in-house transport time, distance & cost. A perpendicular rack row & forklift truck aisle direction of travel has a storage area rear turning aisle adjacent to the next warehouse activity. For best operational results, your end turning aisles have additional width due to one aisle interfaces with your receiving activity and other aisle interfaces with your pick activity.

WHAT IS YOUR STORAGE AISLE ROUTE OR POSITION NUMBER PATTERN
    IMPROVE EMPLOYEE PRODUCTIVITY
What is your storage aisle route or position number pattern is a warehouse storage area position number route, pattern or sequence between 2 rails, shelf or rack rows that directs an employee, employee controlled forklift truck or AS/RS crane to sku storage position for a storage transaction completion. An aisle routing pattern has an arithmetic progression from an aisle first sku position with the lowest possible position number, through an aisle and to an aisle end or last sku position with the highest possible position number. An aisle number sequence options are (1) for a storage & warehouse an aisle that is base on a warehouse routing sequence such as positions with odd numbered last digits on an aisle left side positions (01001, 01003 and so on) & with even numbered last digits on an aisle right side positions (01002, 01004 & so on) & (2) for a storage operation that handles pallets in/out has each rack row positions on an aisle side with a unique prefix that IDs all positions in an aisle on one side &

progresses from an aisle first/lowest number to an aisle last/highest number and on an aisle other side a rack row positions have a unique prefix. An example is aisle 1 with position numbers as 01001, 01002 & so on is number sequence for an aisle right side row positions and aisle 2 with position number 02001, 02022 & so on is number sequence for an aisle left side row positions.

WHERE ARE YOUR REMOTE OR READY RESERVE STORAGE POSITIONS
ON-TIME REPLENISHMENT & MAXIMUM COMPLETED CUSTOMER ORDER NUMBER

Where are your remote or ready reserve storage positions are a warehouse sku storage positions in a WMS or inventory control program that assure on-time replenishment to a pick position for maximum completed customer order number. A remote storage position is in a warehouse main storage area, has a large pallet storage position number and has forklift trucks or AS/RS cranes to complete sku deposit and withdrawal transactions. In a remote storage position, a sku is held until required for a pick position replenishment transaction. In most warehouses and when compared to other main facility ready reserve storage position, a remote storage position holds a sku for a longer period of time. After a sku quantity from a remote reserve position exceeds a pick position sku quantity, your over-flow sku quantity is placed into a pick area ready reserve position. Until required for replenishment to a pick position, a sku is held in a ready reserve storage position. A ready reserve position is above, adjacent or behind a pick position. In some manual master carton or pieces/eaches warehouses, sku remote storage positions are pallet positions above pick positions.

1, 2 OR 3 PALLETS WIDE
SPACE UTILIZATION & OCCUPANCY RATE

1, 2, or 3 pallets wide is a pallet storage option with 3 pallets in a standard pallet rack bay. When you have medium volume skus, an option is to have sku palletized onto 40 long (stringer) by 32 wide (fork opening) and your storage rack bay load beam with sufficient length for 3 pallets. Benefits are increased sku hit concentration and density, improved space utilization and enhanced pallet position occupancy.

FLOOR LEVEL PALLETS ARE 1 OR 2 HIGH
EMPLOYEE PRODUCTIVITY & MIINIMIZE SKU DAMAGE

Floor level pallets in a floor stack or standard pallet rack storage/pick area has your storage activity double stack two pallets in a floor level bottom standard pallet position and in all floor stack positions. Prior to implementation, you assure that your bottom level sku (pallet) has structural strength to support the additional weight and your double high pallet sku in a pick position allows a picker to complete a pick transaction. During a forklift truck deposit transaction to a storage/pick position, the first pallet is set on a floor position and your driver completes a WMS scan transaction (100A) and second pallet is set onto the floor level pallet and your driver completes a WMS scan transaction (100A). Features are (1) one less forklift truck pallet replenishment transaction, (2) standard pallet rack upright post structural strength to support the additional height that could require an additional upright support structural member and anchored and is approved by your rack manufacturer, (3) with one less load beam level, lower pallet rack cost and (4) improved space utilization.

BRIDGE YOUR MIDDLE AISLES, TURNING AISLES AND PASSAGE-WAYS (DOORS)
IMPROVE SPACE UTILIZATION

Bridge your middle aisles, turning aisles and passage-ways (doors) and if you require storage space, bridge is an opportunity to provide additional single deep pallet rack storage positions. If your floor to ceiling clearance and door open travel path does not interfere with the rack, a bridge single deep rack bay upright posts and load beams are installed in a door bay, middle aisles and turning aisles. The posts are anchored to the floor and protected with guards and load beams have front to rear members with a clear space between your floor surface and load beam bottom for a forklift truck travel under. If you desire a wider aisle than your standard load beam, with your pallet weight and aisle width specifications, your rack manufacturer calculates the preferred standard load beam. Storage positions are used normal skus, empty pallets, ship supply items or obsolete skus. If potential skus falling to the floor is a potential problem, plastic wrap pallets or add a removable barrier to a pallet position.

NARROW AISLE FORKLIFT TRUCK BOTTOM LEVEL STORAGE POSITION IS FLOOR LEVEL OR UP & OVER
VERTICAL OR HORIZONTAL SPACE UTILIZATION & IMPROVE EMPLOYEE PRODUCTIVITY

Narrow aisle (NA) forklift truck bottom storage position options are (1) floor level or (2) up & over. Floor level and up & over concept is used with a NA forklift truck that interfaces with single deep or 2 deep storage concept. With a floor level storage concept, bottom storage position pallets are set on a floor. A floor level pallet storage concept with a straddle forklift truck requires 5 to 6 ins open space between 2 pallets & pallet and upright post. An open space permits a forklift truck straddles to enter a bottom level storage position and complete a storage transaction. Features are (1) adds 15 to 18 ins to each storage rack bay horizontal dimension, (2) longer rack load beam length that creates low space utilization and lower employee productivity due to open space in each rack bay and a forklift truck driver assures a truck straddles engulf a floor level pallet & (3) creates a long rack row. Up & over concept has a bottom storage position pallets set on a pair of load beams that have a 6 in open space between a floor & load beam bottom. With the concept, to complete a storage transaction a NA forklift truck straddles go under load beams. An open space & bottom storage position load beam adds 12 ins to a rack vertical stack dimension. Features are (1) short load beam length that improves employee productivity due minimal space in a rack bay, (2) creates a long rack row, (3) additional 12 ins per rack level that creates low vertical space utilization & (4) additional load beam cost.

REGULAR LEVEL FLOOR FOR YOUR WA OR NA FORKLIFT TRUCK STORAGE AREA
ON-TIME CONSTRUCTION & MATCH YOUR FORKLIFT TRUCK SPECIFICATION

Regular level floor for your WA or NA forklift truck storage area is a warehouse storage area floor that is designed for a wide aisle (WA) or narrow aisle (NA) forklift truck storage area floor. A WA or NA forklift truck completes a storage transaction to a rack position height that is 20 ft or less above a floor. A regular or conventional storage area floor is F-25 or industry standard as a level factor. Since a forklift truck set of forks maximum elevation height is 20 ft., there is minimum deflection at a highest pallet position. Floor features are less cost per sq. ft., less time to pour & complete construction & floor matches your rack and forklift truck specifications.

VNA FORKLIFT TRUCK REQUIRES A DEAD LEVEL FLOOR
ON-TIME CONSTRUCTION & MATCH YOUR STORAGE VEHICLE SPECIFICATION

VNA forklift truck requires a dead level floor is a term to describe a floor surface for a tall rack storage area and matches your VNA forklift truck specifications. For a VNA forklift truck storage operation, a dead level floor is a finish spec. of F-50 to F-100 smooth and level floor within a 10 ft area. To minimize a VNA forklift truck set of forks (not parallel to the floor), a storage area floor in aisle & between 2 racks is dead level & has the same flatness. With a dead level floor & when required to complete a tall rack storage transaction, a VNA forklift truck set of forks is on the same plane as a pallet fork openings on a load beam storage position or platen on the same plane as an opening under a pallet on a set arms storage position. If a VNA forklift truck in an aisle does not have a dead level floor to a pallet storage position, there is potential for a set of forks deflection that restricts a VNA forklift truck crane to complete a tall rack elevated storage transaction. To correct a non-level floor situation adds costs and time to your storage facility construction. It is noted that during your building construction and rack installation your rack manufacturer or building company laser beam (shot your floor) your floor to confirm that the levelness is per your specification.

SHOT YOUR VNA OR AS/RS FORKLIFT TRUCK FLOOR
ON-TIME CONSTRUCTION & YOUR FLOOR MATCH SPECIFICATION

Shot your very narrow aisle (VNA) floor is a term that is used to describe a method to verify that your VNA/ASRS forklift truck storage area floor matches your VNA forklift truck & rack vendor levelness specifications. After your storage area floor pour, you have your construction company, VNA forklift truck vendor or rack vendor shot your floor with a laser beam device. Shot your floor assures that your storage area floor levelness permits your VNA forklift truck set of forks or platen to complete a storage transaction at a highest storage position. This means at a highest rack position that there is no VNA fork deflection to a pallet openings. If you do not shot your floor & your floor is not level, to obtain a no VNA forklift truck with no set of fork or platen deflection to a rack position requires additional cost & time to grind a VNA forklift truck aisles to attain no set of fork or platen deflection to a rack position. The situation creates a warehouse start-up delay.

VNA FORKLIFT TRUCK TURN A LOAD IN AN AISLE
SIMPLE FORKLIFT INSTRUCTIONS & GOOD EMPLOYEE PRODUCTIVITY

Very narrow aisle forklift turn a load in an aisle concept is the most common VNA forklift concept. A turn a load in an aisle concept has a VNA forklift truck as it travels in a storage aisle to turn a pallet for proper orientation & deposit in a storage position or P/D station. Proper pallet orientation has a pallet WMS ID face an aisle & permits a WMS scan transaction. Features are a standard VNA aisle width that is 6 in wider than a diagonal pallet or manufacturer's stated rack to rack dimension, assures employee productivity to have proper pallet orientation at a rack or P/D station position & simple forklift truck driver training.

VNA FORKLIFT TRUCK DOES NOT TURN A LOAD IN AN AISLE
LESS STORAGE SQ. FT. AREA & GOOD EMPLOYEE PRODUCTIVITY

Very narrow aisle forklift truck does not turn a pallet in an aisle concept has a VNA forklift truck as it travels in an aisle do not turn a pallet. For half storage or P/D station transactions or transactions to one rack row storage positions, a pallet is properly oriented (WMS ID faces an aisle) for a storage or P/D transaction. For half storage or P/D station transactions or transactions to one rack row storage positions, a pallet is not properly oriented (WMS ID faces an aisle) for a storage or P/D transaction. In a storage position to have a pallet with a proper orientation, at a P/D station & before pallet pick-up a VNA forklift truck driver completes a pallet WMS ID scan transaction. With a pallet & WMS scanner, travels to a WMS ID storage position, deposits a pallet into a WMS ID position & completes a pallet storage position WMS scan transaction. Both WMS sku and WMS position ID scan transaction are sent to a WMS computer for update. At a P/D position to have a pallet with a proper orientation, after pallet withdrawal from a WMS ID storage position, a VNA forklift truck travels to a P/D station & at a P/D station, before pallet delivery to a P/D station a forklift truck driver turns to have a pallet WMS ID face an aisle. Features are (1) VNA forklift driver training for ½ half of rack row positions to complete a WMS ID sku scan transaction at a P/D station and a storage position to complete a WMS ID position scan transaction. This is not a repetitive activity that creates confusion or errors with potential low employee productivity, but confusion is minimized with storage position number pattern that has (a) odd numbered positions on an aisle left & even numbered positions on an aisle right or (b) each rack row has unique number such as between an aisle left rack row is 11 & right rack row is 12, (2) when compared to a turn in an aisle alternative, for each aisle has a 6 in narrower dimension & (3) at a saw-tooth P/D station, some non-productive forklift truck driver time to turn a pallet.

YOUR VNA FORKLIFT TRUCK OR HROS VEHICLE HAS GUIDED OR NON-GUIDED AISLE TRAVEL
MINIMIZE RACK DAMAGE & IMRPOVE EMPLOYEE PRODUCTIVITY

Your VNA forklift truck or HROS vehicle has guided or non-guided aisle travel are your storage vehicle in aisle travel options. A VNA forklift truck & HROS truck travel is in a very narrow aisle between 2 rack rows (an estimated 3 to 6 in clearance between truck & rack) to complete a sku storage deposit or withdrawal transaction at a floor level or elevated storage position. During aisle travel or at a storage position, a VNA forklift truck or HROS truck inclines/declines to have an employee or a set of forks complete a storage transaction at an elevated storage position. To assure maximum travel speed for good employee productivity with minimal vehicle steering & minimal rack, vehicle and sku damage, a VNA forklift truck or HROS truck has an aisle guidance concept to guide truck travel in an aisle. In an elevated travel path, a VNA forklift truck & HROS truck aisle guidance is a must. Aisle guidance permits a VNA forklift truck or HROS truck as it travels in an aisle to travel horizontal & vertical (incline or decline an employee or set of forks) to have proper elevation to complete storage transaction at an elevated storage position or aisle end P/D station. The horizontal & vertical travel feature increases employee productivity. Guidance options are rail or electronic guidance concepts.

WHEN TO USE RAIL OR ELECTRONIC GUIDANCE
MINIMIZE DAMAGE & IMRPOVE EMPLOYEE PRODUCTIVITY

When to use rail or electronic VNA forklift truck or HROS truck guidance concept is a basic question that is determined by your warehouse storage aisle number, vendor equipment & floor features. A rail guidance concept has entry guides & single or double rail (angle iron) with each iron section connection joint ground smooth. Guide rail is secured to an aisle floor surface, built up floor section side or rack bay for full aisle length that allows a VNA forklift truck or HROS truck multiple guide wheel device to ride along or connect onto a guide rail. When your warehouse has few aisles or a captive vehicle to an aisle, rail guidance is a consideration. Electronic guidance options are (1) wire guidance that has (a) a closed loop wire embedded in your floor. An impulse driver sends out an electric impulse, sent through all aisles and sent back to an impulse driver & (b) vehicle underside sensor device that picks-up an electric impulse from a wire. As long as a truck under side sensor receives an electric impulse, a truck travel is guided through an aisle. If a truck under side sensor does not receive an electric impulse, a truck emergency stop concept halts truck travel in an aisle or (2) laser beam guidance that has light beam targets strategically located in an aisle. A light beam is transmitted from a truck & hits a target that reflects a light beam back to a truck receiver. As long as a truck receiver has a light beam, a truck travel is guided through an aisle. If a truck receiver does not receive a light beam, a truck emergency stop concept halts truck travel in an aisle. If your new construction storage area has multiple aisles & at least several trucks, an electronic guidance is a consideration. When you consider to remodel an existing storage operation with high metal content in the floor that has potential to prevent an electric impulse transmission or an uneven floor surface that can break a truck sensor connection to an impulse transmission, before a wire guidance concept selection you have your truck manufacturer warranty a wire guidance concept & if no warranty consider rail or laser beam guidance.

HOW TO SLOW DOWN A VNA FORKLIFT TRUCK OR HROS VEHICLE AISLE END TRAVEL SPEED
ENHANCE SAFETY & MINIMIZE VEHICLE DAMAGE

How to slow down a VNA forklift truck or HROS vehicle aisle end travel speed truck is a manual or electro-magnetic concept to slow down a vehicle travel speed prior to main aisle entry or to halt a vehicle travel at a dead end aisle end. When a VNA forklift truck or HROS truck enters a main aisle at slow travel speed or to stop at a dead end aisle end, it enhances safety and minimizes potential vehicle damage & employee injury. Manual slow down concept options are (1) for entry to a main aisle, painted rack upright posts & load beams such as yellow & red colors & (2) at a dead end aisle, colored racks and a floor anchored bumper full aisle width at a distance from your last storage position to allow storage transaction at a rack row last position. A manual slow down concept is most frequently used with a rail guidance concept, requires employee training & is low cost. An electro-magnetic slow down concept has a sensor device on a truck underside & magnetic devices embedded in an aisle floor. Magnetic devices are set at pre-determined distances from an aisle end. As a vehicle travels over magnetic devices, a signal is picked-up by a vehicle sensor that sends a command to automatically slow down a vehicle travel speed.

VNA FORKLIFT TRUCK MAN-DOWN OR MAN-UP VEHICLE TYPE
IMPROVE EMPLOYEE PRODUCTIVITY & MINIMZE SKU DAMAGE

Very narrow aisle (VNA) forklift truck man-down or man-up are to complete a storage transaction a VNA forklift truck operator location options. To complete a storage transaction, a man-down VNA forklift truck has an operator platform remain stationary at the floor level. To complete an elevated storage transaction, an operator eye-balls or uses a range/position level finder to assure that a VNA forklift truck set of forks are at the proper elevation. When storage area pallet rack storage positions are in a low bay building, if a man-down VNA forklift truck has a lower cost combined with low operator productivity & potential sku/rack damage are important considerations. With a man-up VNA forklift truck to complete a storage transaction, an operator platform moves up with a set of forks to an elevated level that permits an operator to have view of a storage transaction. In a low building or a 40 ft high building with tall racks, a man-up VNA forklift truck has the same cost as a man-down VNA forklift truck, your increased employee productivity & low sku/rack damage are important considerations.

TO IMPROVE PALLET PICK-UP, PAINT STRIPS ON YOUR VNA FORKLIFT TRUCK SET OF FORKS
IMPROVE EMPLOYEE PRODUCTIVITY & REDUCE SKU DAMAGE

To improve pallet pick-up, paint stripes on your VNA forklift truck set of forks is a warehouse option to improve employee productivity. During a pallet pick-up transaction at a P/D station, painted stripes on a set of forks helps an operator to assure that a pallet is properly aligned on a set of forks for exact put-away or deposit onto a storage rack position load beams. At a P/D station & after a pallet is on a set of forks, an operator moves a pallet carrier to a position for an operator to view a set of fork painted stripes. With paint stripes in view, it means that a pallet is in a proper location for exact pallet storage position deposit. An exact pallet storage position deposit has a pallet 2 bottom deck boards evenly placed on a storage rack position front & rear load beams. With a proper position pallet in a storage position, it reduces potential for sku damage from a misaligned pallet & assures good employee productivity for pallet withdrawal from a storage position & deposit at a P/D station.

FOR IMPROVED PALLET DEPOSIT IN A TALL RACK STORAGE POSTION, PAINT STRIPS ON YOUR TALL RACK STORAGE RACK LOAD BEAMS
IMPROVE EMPLOYEE PRODUCTIVITY & REDUCE SKU DAMAGE

For improved pallet deposit in a tall rack storage position, paint stripes on your VNA forklift storage rack bay front load beam 2 pallet positions. Paint stripes for each storage rack bay pallet position improves forklift truck driver put-away/deposit productivity & minimizes sku damage. During a VNA forklift truck deposit to a storage rack bay with 2 pallet positions, an operator uses the nearest or adjacent upright position as a guide for a pallet deposit to a storage position. With a pallet in the nearest or adjacent position, pallet deposit to a vacant or far pallet position is difficult transaction for a VNA forklift truck driver to assure proper pallet alignment in a storage rack position. If you look at a VNA forklift truck full rack bays, most pallets that are deposited to a storage positions that are adjacent to an upright post are very close to an upright post due to a VNA forklift driver used an upright post as a deposit transaction or pallet alignment guide. Two paint stripes sets (1 set for each pallet or outside to outside distance between two pallet exterior stringers or blocks) on a storage rack bay front load beam are in an operator's view and serve as a guide for a forklift driver to complete a pallet deposit transaction. Paint stripes on a load beam improve forklift driver deposit productivity & minimizes sku damage. An option to paint strips is two tape strands.

TURNING AISLES IN A STORAGE AREA
INCREASE STORAGE POSITION NUMBER & IMPROVE EMPLOYEE PRODUCTIVITY

Turning aisles in a storage area is a manual controlled forklift truck storage area design factor that increases employee productivity. Aisle number per storage area design options are (1) front turning aisle is common in a conventional storage operation with a WA, NA forklift truck & VNA forklift truck, (2) front & rear turning aisle storage concept is used with a WA or NA or VNA forklift truck concept. In a manual controlled forklift truck operation, front & rear turning aisles allow a forklift truck transfer from one aisle to another aisle. Features are reduces forklift truck travel time & distance that improves employee productivity & provides a lower pallet position number & (3) front, rear & middle aisle storage concept is common in a large pallet position storage concept with very long rack rows and aisle & has a WA or NA employee controlled forklift truck. Front, rear & middle aisle widths permit forklift trucks transfer from one aisle to another aisle & in-house transport vehicles to complete sku pick-up/delivery transactions that improves employee productivity & provide fewer pallet positions.

BUILDING COLUMN LOCATIONS
IMPROVE SPACE UTILIZATION & IMPROVE EMPLOYEE PRODUCTIVITY

Building columns locations are a warehouse storage area or rack row & aisle layout design factor that affects your sku storage position number, your space utilization and employee productivity. Your building column location options are (1) in a back to back rack row flue space is a common building column location. With a standard 8 in wide building column & an allowable 2 in open space on a column both sides, a back to back rack flue space is a 12 in space for an entire rack row. For a 150 ft long rack row with 40 ft building column spacing, a flue space occupies 150 sq. ft. (1 X 150) & provides 128 pallet positions (16 rack bays X 2 pallets wide X 4 pallets high = 128 pallet positions). If your facility is in a high seismic location, a building column increases to 3 ft. wide with 450 sq. ft of unused space, (2) building columns in a rack bay has a rack bay pallet position arranged to have a building occupy 1 pallet position. A typical pallet position is 4 ft X 4 ft. Based on a 150 ft. long rack row, your unused building column space is 36 sq. ft. (4 X 4 X 3 columns = 36) & provides 116 pallet positions (128 – 12 (3 columns X 4 pallets), (3) rack around a building has a rack row arranged in between 2 building columns. With a 32 ft building span, there are 4 rack bays with 2 pallets wide & 1 rack bay with 1 pallet wide. Based on a 150 ft. long rack row, your unused building column space is 64 sq. ft. (4 X 4 X 4 columns = 64) and provides 126 pallet positions (3.5 bays X 2 pallets wide X 4 pallets high X 4.5 sections = 126 pallet positions. With the concept there is some additional rack costs for additional posts & load beams & (4) building columns in a forklift truck aisle is a least preferred location. When a building column is in an aisle there is 148 sq. ft. of unused space (1 ft X 150 ft plus 33 sq. ft. blocked pallet positions that are blocked by building columns & provides 116 pallet position (128 - 12 blocked). With building columns in an aisle there is an increase for potential building damage & accidents. Space savings with a wide aisle forklift truck & 18 back to back rack rows storage area allows you to add 2 rack rows & 1 wide aisle forklift truck aisle. Space savings with a narrow aisle forklift truck & 16 back to back rack rows storage area allows you to add 2 rack rows & 1 narrow aisle forklift truck aisle.

HOW YOUR VNA FORKLIFT TRUCK OR HROS VEHICLE DRIVER ENTERS & TRAVELS IN AN AISLE
ENHANCE SAFETY, IMPROVE EMPLOYEE PRODUCTIVITY & MINIMIZE VEHICLE DAMAGE

How your VNA forklift truck or HROS vehicle driver enters and travels in an aisle enhances safety, improves employee productivity and minimizes vehicle damage. A VNA or HROS storage/pick concept has an aisle between two tall shelf/rack rows and a vehicle travel is guided by a rail or electric concept. Per your company policy, no other vehicle or employee has access to an aisle. As your driver enters a VNA or HROS, a driver is facing your main aisle that assures complete main aisle vision and as entering a main aisle minimizes vehicle accidents. With your driver in this position, your shelf/rack number pattern directs an employee to assigned position.

MAN-DOWN, MAN-UP OR NO-MAN VEHICLE
MATCH YOUR NEEDS

Man-down, man-up or no-man are your storage vehicle concepts that are used in a warehouse. A man-down vehicle has an operator sit or stand, mobile between aisles and has complete vehicle control for a pallet storage transaction completion in a large sq. ft building. When compared to the other vehicle groups, a man-down vehicle is able to perform other warehouse activities such as unload and in-house transport, less cost, all required electric battery (s) and WA is available with an internal combustion engine and is available as WA, NA or VNA vehicle type. When a man-down VNA vehicle is compared to a man-up VNA vehicle, a man-up is preferred due to same cost and higher employee productivity with less damage. A man-up VNA or HROS vehicle has an operator stand or sit and have complete vehicle control to complete a pallet or master carton storage/pick transaction in a very narrow aisle between two tall racks or shelves. For best performance, man-up vehicles have aisle end P/D stations, guided aisle travel with UPS, off-line stop feature and on-board lighting. Features are mobile between aisles, restricted travel to your storage area, higher cost than standard man-down vehicle, provides good space utilization in a medium sq ft building. A no-man vehicle is a computer controlled crane that travels in a captive aisle between two tall racks/shelves to complete a pallet or master carton/tote/tray storage transaction. Aisle end P/D assure sku queue. Features are high cost, 24 X 7 operation with minimal environmental cost such as aisle lighting and temperature, no labor, usually captive aisle but mobile with a transfer (T-car) car and provides best space utilization in a small sq. ft building that has a conventional or rack support design.

WIDE AISLE, NARROW AISLE & VERY NARROW AISLE FORKLIFT TRUCKS
AISLE SPACE, AIR SPACE UTILIZATION AND DENSE STORAGE

WA, NA or VNA forklift trucks are a warehouse employee controlled forklift truck options. A WA forklift truck features are (1) 3 or 4 wheel, (2) employee seats, (3) lift to a 20 ft height in a 10 to 13 ft wide aisle, (4) electric battery powered or internal combustion engine, (5) notched mast or level finder assist to complete an elevated storage transaction and (6) complete transport activities and handles most accessories. A NA forklift truck features are (1) employee stands, (2) lift to 25 ft in a 7 to 8 ft wide aisle with a bottom storage on floor level or load beams, (3) electric battery powered, (4) notched mast/level finder assists to complete an elevated storage transaction and (5) engulfs a pallet between two out-riggers. A VNA forklift truck features are (1) employee seats, (2) lift to 35 ft in a 6 to 6 ft 6 in guided wide aisle with a bottom storage on floor level or load beams, (3) electric battery powered, (4) man-up minimizes transaction problems, (5) best performance with a P/D station and (6) used as a pick vehicle.

HROS/VNA TRAVEL IN A TUNNEL WITH UPS, LINE DRIVER, OFF-GUIDANCE STOP & ON-BOARD LIGHTING
EMPLOYEE PRODUCTIVITY & REDUCE DAMAGE

HROS or VNA forklift truck aisle or a tunnel is a concept that has a vehicle driver travel horizontal and vertical in a very narrow aisle between two tall shelf or rack rows. When a HROS or VNA vehicle travels in an aisle it resembles travel in a tunnel. To maintain your employee productivity and reduce damage, if your VNA or HROS vehicle is wire guided you have a (1) UPS or battery back-up that provides sufficient electric power for a vehicle to exit and aisle, (2) line driver that sends an electric impulse through a guide wire to guide a vehicle, (3) off-guidance stop that if a vehicles goes off-line in an aisle, it stops vehicle travel and (4) on-board lighting has spot lights added to your vehicle that provides additional in aisle light.

WHERE ARE YOUR AISLE LIGHT FIXTURES
IMPROVE SAFETY, REDUCE SKU DAMAGE & IMPROVE EMPLOYEE PRODUCTIVITY

Your lights or light fixtures in your storage area improve safety, reduce sku damage and improve employee productivity. A storage area has aisles between two pallets, rails, shelves or rack rows. Rails, shelves, pallets and rack rows are sku storage positions & aisles allow employees, employee controlled forklift trucks or AS/RS cranes travel to a sku storage position & complete a storage transaction. When your light fixtures hang above your rails, shelves, pallets or rack rows, your top sku & light beam angle minimizes light in a storage aisle and minimizes an employee vision to a sku ID or storage position ID. Feature lowers your employee productivity, increases potential for sku & rack damage & creates safety concerns. When your light fixtures hang above your aisle middle, a light beam is proper & provides light to easily see a sku or storage position ID. Feature enhances your employee productivity, decreases potential for sku & rack damage & minimizes safety concerns.

WHEN TO TURN YOUR STORAGE AISLE LIGHTS ON AND OFF
LOWER ENERGY OR ELECTRICAL COST

When to turn your aisle lights on/off is a storage concept that is used with fluorescent light fixtures or fast illumination light fixtures that reduces your energy or electrical cost. Your aisle light turn on/off options are (1) all aisle lights remain turned whether an employee or forklift truck is traveling in an aisle or not traveling in an aisle. Feature is that your warehouse incurs an expense with no employee productivity to off-set the expense & (2) all aisle lights remain off except for a main aisle lights and as an employee or employee controlled forklift enters an aisle, an aisle motion detector senses or a light beam is broken by an employee or forklift truck aisle travel & activates an aisle lights. For a pre-determined time or as long as employee or forklift truck moves in an aisle, lights remain on. Most AS/RS crane concepts have an aisle's first & last light fixtures remain on. For safety purposes, your local code or insurance company underwriter requires at least an aisle first & last light fixture remain on.

SPRINKLERS ARE IN THE CEILING AND/OR RACKS
REDUCE RISK

Sprinklers are in a ceiling and/or racks and the final determination is per local code or insurance underwriter requirement for fire sprinklers in your new or existing storage facility. In most storage concepts above 20 ft, fire sprinkler systems require a water holding tank that is above ground or buried in the ground or pond, pump to assure per-determined cubic ft of water per minute or water pressure, sprinkler heads, piping & alarm system. A storage concept fire sprinkler locations are (1) in a rack bay opening top under a rack bay fire barrier, (2) in a flue space between back to back rack rows or rack row & wall, (3) extending downward from a ceiling at a pre-determined height above your highest sku & (4) under solid walkways.

CONTROL YOUR LIQUID RUN-OFF
RISK MANAGEMENT

Control your liquid run-off is a warehouse storage concept with a storage area that during a fire is designed to restrict liquid run-off from burning sku containers in your facility or onto local grounds. Your local government or insurance company ID skus that are assigned to a restricted liquid run-off storage area. A containment chamber & building wall siding has cubic capacity to contain your liquid sku run-off and sprinkler water amount. Restrict run-off concepts are (1) storage area perimeter that is at an approved height with a drain that directs liquid flow to a containment chamber or (2) along a storage area wall, there is leak proof siding, but the siding is design to allow forklift truck entry & exist.

STOP THE MISSILES
RISK MANAGEMENT

Stop the missiles is a warehouse storage concept with storage positions that during a fire are designed to restrict air pressured cans with flames from being propelled from one storage location to another storage location & spread a fire to a new location. Restriction concepts are (1) with a very large inventory quantity, enclosed storage rack rows

& aisles, (2) for a medium inventory quantity, storage bay has solid wood, solid metal sheets, small wire mesh or planks that are securely attached to rack posts & load beams & (3) for a small inventory quantity, a solid sheet metal cabinet with doors. Stop the missiles concept lowers your insurance costs.

NETS
IMPROVE SAFETY & REDUCE SKU DAMAGE

Nets are plastic or fabric meshed is option to improve employee safety and reduce sku damage. After a net is attached to a single pallet rack row upright posts, the net covers pallet positions with exposure to an aisle (employee walk aisle). The net meshed opening size prevents a small sku falling from a pallet into an aisle.

HEADACHE BARS AND GUARDS
REDUCE BUILDING DAMAGE

Headache bars and guards are options that are placed along a passage-way or door frame. A headache bar is a ceiling hung bar with chains that extend downward slightly beyond a door frame top. When a forklift truck carries a pallet that is above a door frame top, a pallet strikes the chains that serves as an alarm to a forklift truck driver. Guards are cement filled and anchored posts that are placed in a door way frame to sides. When a forklift truck travels off-path and strikes a guard, a guard stops a forklift truck movement and prevents door frame damage.

RESTRICT EMPLOYEES FROM AN AISLE
EMPLOYEE PRODUCTIVITY & IMPROVE SAFETY

Restrict employees from an aisle is VNA or HROS safety procedure. After an employee (such as inventory clerk) enters a VNA aisle, at an aisle entrance an employee extends a yellow, orange or bright green chain across an aisle and hooks the chain onto a rack post. When a chain is across an aisle entrance, it is sign to a powered VNA or HROS vehicle driver that an aisle is occupied with an employee.

CHAPTER 4
SET-UP OR REPLENISHMENT ACTIVITY COST REDUCTION IDEAS

MANUFACTURER LOT NUMBER CONTROL (See Pack Activity)

KNOW YOUR CUBES
  IMPROVE EMPLOYEE PRODUCTIVITY & ENHANCE SPACE UTILIZATION
Know your cubes (master carton/tote & pick position) is a small item or master carton warehouse concept factor that impacts your pick position set-up/replenishment employee productivity and pick position utilization. Your cube information includes your master/tote exterior dimensions (length, width & height) & your pick position dimensions (length, width & height). When considering a pick position height you allow sufficient open space from a master carton/tote in a pick position to an above pick position structural member bottom. An open space permits a replenishment employee to easily transfer a master carton/tote to a pick position and a picker to easily remove a sku from a master carton/tote. Master carton/tote and pick position dimensions (length, width and height) determines a master carton/tote number per pick position. With accurate master carton/tote and pick position cube data in your WMS computer files and your customer order sku demand, your computer suggested replenishment transaction master carton/tote number matches your pick position capacity to assure 100% utilization and minimizes ready reserve positions in a pick area.

DO NOT LET YOUR VENDOR OVERSIZE A SKU MASTER CARTON
 IMPROVE REPLENISHMENT PRODUCTIVITY & ENHANCE INVENTORY CONTROL
Do not let your vendor oversize a sku master carton is a small item and master carton warehouse that assures a master carton size and sku quantity matches your pick position requirements to assure replenishment productivity and enhance inventory control. Do not oversize your master carton has your purchasing department request vendor to package skus into a master carton size that matches your pick concept design and are easily handled by an employee. With a small item pick concept, this means that your master carton size fits into your pick position that assures good replenishment productivity, master carton sku quantity permits accurate replenishment to an automatic pick machine lane/sleeve that assure good inventory control and a master carton is travels on a powered conveyor travel path that assures maximum picker productivity and is not picked as a manual picked master carton.

WHO DETERMINES YOUR CUSTOMER ORDER WAVE OR WORK DAY PIECES
   ASSURES REPLENISHMENT PRODUCTIVITY
Who determines your CO wave or work day piece quantity is an issue for a small item or GOH warehouse that determines your replenishment employee number and their productivity. A CO wave or work day piece quantity is determined by your warehouse staff and is based on your picker budgeted productivity rate that determines your picker employee number. From a CO wave, a WMS computer allocates sku quantity in inventory files and sends warehouse move messages for a sku quantity transfer (set-up/replenishment) from a storage area to a pick position. Each sku set-up/replenishment transaction assures sufficient sku quantity in a pick position to satisfy a CO wave (sku demand) & based on your replenishment productivity rates. it determines your replenishment employee number.

EMPLOYEE OR COMPUTER DIRECTED REPLENISHMENT
   IMPROVES REPLENISHMENT PRODUCTIVITY & INCREASES COMPLETED CUSTOMER ORDER NUMBER
Employee or computer directed replenishment transaction is a small item warehouse concept that has an employee complete a replenishment transaction to improve replenishment productivity and increase completed CO number. A dynamic catalog, direct mail, TV marketing or retail store pick concept with a very large sku number that requires numerous aisles and pick positions and covers a large area requires on time and accurate replenishment transactions. An employee directed replenishment activity has a replenishment or picker employee look at a sku quantity in a pick position, determine a sku replenishment quantity and transfer a sku quantity from a reserve position to a pick position. Features are (1) sku selected for replenishment has potential for no picks and if a picker completes a replenishment transaction means lower picker productivity and lower completed CO number. With a

computer suggested replenishment activity, for a CO wave your WMS computer identifies each sku with each sku quantity that requires a replenishment transaction. Features are (1) due to CO demand, only skus that require a replenishment are listed, (2) if a replenishment activity starts before the pick activity, improved picker productivity due to available skus in a pick position, (3) improved replenishment productivity due less aisle congestion and (4) with a replenishment activity sequenced by pick zones/aisles from highest to lowest sku number and time due to complete COs, increased completed CO number.

ONE OR DOUBLE SLOT SKUS TO PICK POSITIONS
   INCREASE COMPLETED CUSTOMER ORDER NUMBER & REDUCE READY RESERVE REQUIREMENT
One or double slot skus to pick positions is a small item warehouse pick line/aisle strategy that is used to increase your completed customer order number, reduce ready reserve requirement and replenishment transactions to 1 position. A double slot concept has a sku scanned and placed into 2 WMS ID pick positions. To control your pick activity, your pick instruction computer program directs a pick to a first scanned pick position. After a sku quantity is depleted, a WMS computer directs your next pick transaction to a second scanned pick position.

IN A PICK POSITION, NARROW CARTON WIDTH FACES A PICK AISLE
  IMPROVE PICKER PRODUCTIVITY, SPACE UTILIZATION & MINIMIZE SKU LOOSE/DAMAGE
In a pick position, your narrow carton width is a warehouse idea that has your master carton placed into your pick position with narrow carton width facing a picker to improve picker productivity, space utilization and reduce sku damage/lost. With a master carton dimension facing a picker aisle, it provides potential for the greatest sku number between two pick position posts that increases (1) hit concentration and density to improve picker productivity with a shortest walk distance between two picks, (2) enhances space utilization with the greatest sku number per inch ft and (3) in a carton flow rack lane, master carton bottom flaps run in a carton long dimension that assure smooth travel.

REDUCE SKU REPLENISHMENT ERRORS AND LOWER PROBLEM CUSTOMER ORDERS
  IMPROVE PICKER/PACKER PRODUCTIVITY & IMPROVES CUSTOMER SERVICE
Reduce sku replenishment errors and lower problem COs means that your CO package is sent to a customer with a damaged, wrong sku, short sku or extra sku quantity. The situation occurs in a small item warehouse and when a CO is received at a delivery address it creates a dissatisfied customer. To minimize problem COs, a replenishment objective is to have your replenishment employee place a correct sku into a pick position and to have pickers pick correct and quality skus in a correct quantity from a pick position into a CO container. In other words, for your warehouse to maintain your customer service standard, it starts at your replenishment position or activity.

CONSIGNMENT SKUS
   ASSURE CONSIGNMENT POLICY, PICKER PRODUCTIVITY & ENHANCE INVENTORY CONTROL
Consignment skus is a unique vendor arrangement that requires your replenishment employees or pickers to only open one sku master carton. With standard WMS replenishment program that does not suggest a master carton quantity, your replenishment employee and pickers only open one master carton. With a CO wave WMS computer program that suggests a master carton replenishment quantity to match your CO skus, your replenishment employee opens your WMS computer program suggested master carton quantity.

DEFAULT YOUR HAND HELD SCANNER TO ONE (See Customer Returns Chapter)

EACH PICK POSITION IS OCCUPIED
 IMPROVE PICKER PRODUCTIVITY & INCREASES COMPLETED CUSTOMER ORDER NUMBER
Each pick position is occupied is a small item or GOH operation replenishment that improves picker productivity and increases completed CO number. Your replenishment concept has a replenishment employee transfer and WMS scan a sku quantity to a WMS ID pick position and scan transactions are sent to a WMS computer program to update sku and pick position status. After a sku quantity and position update, a WMS computer program releases a customer order number that matches sku replenishment quantity. Features are (1) for 'A' fast moving skus in a pick

position increases hit concentration & density that improves picker productivity, (2) minimizes no stock or stock and (3) requires on-line replenishment transaction transfer to a WMS computer.

NO STOCK
IMPROVES PICKER PRODUCTIVITY & ENHANCES INVENTORY CONTROL

A "no stock" condition occurs in a warehouse when a sku physical inventory is physically in a pick position but a WMS computer inventory file does not reflect sku inventory in a pick position. When the situation occurs with a customer order, a WMS computer does not release COs to print a CO pick transaction instruction for a picker or pick machine. In a warehouse, the situation is falls below a company standard for customer service and it creates an inventory control problem that requires a sku count and allocation to another pick position.

STOCK OUT
IMPROVES PICKER PRODUCTIVITY & ENHANCES INVENTORY CONTROL

A "stock out" or "out of stock" condition occurs in a warehouse when a sku inventory file shows inventory in a pick position when there is no sku quantity. A "stock out" or "out of stock" condition creates nonproductive picker/pick machine activity because a picker/pick device traveled to a pick position but could not complete a pick transaction.

RE-ORGANIZE OR RE-PROFILE YOUR 'A' FAST MOVING SKUS
IMPROVE PICKER PRODUCTIVITY & INCREASE COMPLETED CUSTOMER ORDER NUMBER

Re-organize or re-profile your 'A'/fast moving skus is small item or master carton warehouse strategy that improves your picker productivity and increases your completed CO number. A re-organize or re-profile strategy requires your set-up or replenishment employee to allocate 'A'/fast moving skus to one pick zone or aisle and as required to relocate 'B' or medium moving skus to another pick zone or aisle. With your 'A'/fast moving skus in one pick zone or aisle that matches your budgeted picker productivity, it increases your sku hit concentration and density that improves your picker and replenishment employee productivity due to short travel distances between two positions.

YOUR 'A'/FAST MOVING SKUS ARE FIXED OR REMAIN
LOWERS PICKER PRODUCTIVITY & ENHANCES SKU INVENTORY CONTROL

If your 'A'/fast moving skus are fixed or remain in one position, it is a small item or master carton warehouse strategy for all your CO waves that has your 'A'/fast moving skus assigned to one pick zone or pick aisle pick positions. With all your 'A' fast moving skus in one pick zone or aisle (matches your budgeted picker productivity rate), a sku set-up or replenishment strategy that increases picker productivity and enhances sku inventory control. With a fixed or remain sku allocation to pick zone or pick aisle concept, after sku quantity becomes depleted in a pick position, a WMS/inventory control program directs a sku quantity replenishment transaction to move a sku from a storage area to the same pick position. If new 'A'/fast moving sku is allocated to a pick position that is adjacent to a slower moving sku, your pick productivity is lower due to additional travel distance between two picks. A fixed or remain sku pick position strategy is preferred for your B, C & D moving skus.

ROTATE YOUR 'A'/FAST MOVING SKUS
IMPROVES REPLENISHMENT & PICKER PRODUCTIVITY & ENHANCES SKU INVENTORY CONTROL

Rotate your 'A'/ fast moving skus is used in a small item or GOH warehouse and has your 'A'/fast moving skus that are assigned to 1 pick zone or pick aisle strategy (matches your budgeted picker productivity rate) that improves your replenishment and picker productivity and enhances sku inventory control. The concept has for DAY 1 CO wave all your 'A'/fast moving skus assigned to 1 pick zone or pick aisle that minimizes a picker walk distance between two picks. At DAY 1 CO wave end from all your 'A' pick positions any residual sku quantity is transferred from your pick zone pick positions to another pick zone or pick aisle. After a pick position zero scan transaction completion, DAY 1 'A'/fast moving sku rotation creates vacate pick positions in your pick zone for DAY 2 CO wave 'A'/fast moving skus. Features are (1) additional employee activity to relocate skus that is minimized with rounded down master carton concept and for DAY 1 'A' fast moving sku presence in another pick section pick position (1 master carton), (2) requires a zero scan transaction to assure sku inventory control, (3) requires pick position profile and set-up for hit concentration and density & high picker productivity & (4) is preferred for your 'A'/fast moving skus.

WHAT IS YOUR PICK POSITION CAPACITY
SPACE UTILIZATION & ENHANCES INVENTORY CONTROL

What is your pick position capacity is a small item or GOH warehouse concept that determines your pick position small item, GOH, master carton or pallet capacity or sku number that fits in each pick position and assures maximum space utilization and enhances inventory control. Your pick position capacity is determined by (1) cube space or sku number that fits into each pick position, (2) residual sku quantity or cube in each pick position and (3) your computer program calculates a sku replenishment quantity that is a master carton/pallet rounded-up, rounded-down or exact piece number. To have an efficient and cost effective replenishment activity, your computer replenishment program calculates your sku replenishment quantity on full master cartons and full pallets that satisfies your CO wave sku demand and minimizes sku handlings/scan transactions.

SOME 'A' FAST MOVING SKUS REQUIRE MULTIPLE FRONTS/ZONES
IMPROVES PICKER PRODUCTIVITY & INCREASE COMPLETED CUSTOMER ORDER NUMBER

Some 'A'/fast moving sku require multiple fronts/zones is a small item or GOH warehouse pick area design that separates a 'A'/fast moving sku into multiple pick front/zones in separate pick sections to improve picker productivity and increase your completed CO number. When your CO wave sku quantity exceeds your budgeted picker productivity, a sku in 1 pick position creates good picker productivity but your picker completes a CO wave sku pick requirements. Multiple pick fronts/zones for your 'A'/fast moving skus (sku demand exceeds picker productivity) has you creates two 'A'/fast moving pick fronts/zones/sections that are entered into your WMS computer program as separate WMS identified pick activity sections. With two separate WMS identified pick activity sections and with the same 'A'/fast moving skus, it allows your WMS computer program to direct COs to two pick areas that from both pick areas assures good picker productivity and higher completed CO number.

DELAYED OR ON-LINE REPLENISHMENT TRANSACTION COMMUNICATION
ENHANCES INVENTORY CONTROL

Delayed or on-line replenishment transaction communication is a warehouse option has a sku replenishment transaction sent to a WMS computer program that updates a sku position and quantity status. A delayed communication concept has a sku replenishment transaction sent to a warehouse computer that groups/batches transaction messages and at a pre-determined time are transferred from a warehouse computer to a WMS computer program. If a warehouse requires a WMS ID sku quantity in a WMS ID pick position are updated in a WMS computer program before release of a wave COs, the concept has a potential of adding time to CO delivery cycle time but a WMS computer with a lower capacity/cost due to when a computer has free time it handles the batched sku replenishment transactions. When a warehouse rotates 'A'/fast moving skus in pick zones and to maintain a customer service standard or CO delivery cycle time an on-line transfer from a pick position to a WMS computer program allows minimal time for a wave CO release to a pick concept but requires a WMS computer to have a larger capacity/cost to handle multiple transactions.

PICK CLEAN
IMPROVES REPLENISHMENT & PICKER PRODUCTIVITY & ENHANCES SKU INVENTORY CONTROL

Pick clean is a small item or GOH pick activity that improves your picker and replenishment employee productivity and enhances your 'A'/fast moving sku inventory control. Pick clean is used when you group your 'A'/fast moving skus in one pick zone or aisle (matches your budgeted pick productivity) and occurs when your pick activity depletes a sku quantity in a pick position to zero. After a pick position sku quantity has been depleted to zero, prior to a sku replenishment to a pick position a zero WMS scan transaction is completed and sent to a WMS computer to assure that an old sku is depleted from a pick position. With a completed zero scan transaction, a new sku is WMS scanned and physically set-up/replenished to a pick position.

ZERO SCAN
ENHANCES INVENTORY CONTROL

Zero scan is a WMS identified pick position scan transaction that enhances inventory control and assures good pick position management. After a pick position is picked clean (skus are depleted to a zero quantity) and prior to a new

WMS identified sku transfer and WMS scan to a pick position, your set-up employee completes a zero scan transaction. A zero scan transaction is sent to your WMS computer that updates a WMS ID sku quantity in a pick position as zero. Per your pick area design, a zero scan transaction assures that in a WMS computer that there are not 2 WMS ID skus in 1 pick position. With no zero scan of a pick position, there is potential for pick errors due to a customer order pick was directed and completed for a sku (old sku) but was another sku (new sku) in the pick position. If you have your pickers read each pick instruction sku description/inventory number and compare it to an actual sku description/inventory number, you have low picker productivity.

SMALL INVENTORY QUANTITY SKU & OLD SKU CONSOLIDATION
IMPROVES PICKER PRODUCTIVITY & SPACE UTILIZATION & ENHANCES INVENTORY CONTROL

Small inventory quantity sku & old sku consolidation is a sku profile strategy that consolidates your small sku quantity and old skus into 1 pick zone or pick aisle that improves your picker productivity, space utilization and enhances inventory control. A small inventory quantity sku and old sku situation occurs in a catalog, direct marketing or TV marketing warehouse that has a requirement for a minimum on-hand sku quantity to be advertised and old/out of season skus that have COs. When skus with a small inventory quantity (less than allowed to appear in a catalog or TV program) or an old skus are located in prime pick positions that are adjacent to pick positions with 'A' & 'B' moving skus, it creates low sku set-up/replenishment and pick productivity due to additional travel distance between two transactions and low pick position/space utilization. To improve your picker productivity and space utilization, you relocate your small inventory quantity sku and old skus from prime pick positions to a pick zone or pick aisle pick positions in a non-prime area.

LOOSE, BAGGED/BOXED/BINNED OR MASTER CARTON SKUS
IMPROVES REPLENISHMENT PRODUCTIVITY & ENHANCES INVENTORY CONTROL

Loose, bagged, boxed/bin or master carton skus are a small item warehouse sku characteristics and replenishment options that improve replenishment productivity and enhance inventory control. A sku's replenishment characteristics are determined by your (1) CO wave sku quantity, (2) pick position capacity and type, (3) WMS ID sku quantity (pack key) per bag, box/bin or master carton and (4) sku handling concept. A loose sku replenishment features are (1) an employee physically count a sku quantity, (2) sku is placed into a captive pick position bin or is stackable in a shelf or decked rack, (3) potential for sku damage or lose and (4) low replenishment employee productivity. Bagged, boxed or binned small sku replenishment quantity uses repacked skus that have a WMS ID in your computer program. When required to complete a replenishment transaction, a bagged/boxed/binned is transferred from a storage position to a pick position. Features are (1) requires a repack activity and labor, (2) bag/box/bin is placed into a pick position, (3) minimal replenishment employee count activity, (4) minimal sku damage and lose & (5) good employee productivity. Master carton replenishment quantity uses a vendor carton that has a WMS sku ID in your computer program. Features are the same as bag/box/bin replenishment sku concept except no re-pack activity and labor.

KNOW YOUR SKU PAIRS OR FAMILY GROUP
IMPROVES PRODUCTIVITY & INCREASES COMPLETED CUSTOMER ORDER NUMBER

Know your skus pairs or family group is a small item or GOH warehouse replenishment concept that improves pick and replenishment productivity and increases completed CO number. Skus pairs or family group replenishment means that one sku creates sales for another sku (salt and pepper items), common components for an end product or several skus with a common language. When skus pairs or family group are profiled or assigned to pick positions in one aisle, pick zone or pick cell, it creates (1) multiple sku replenishment transactions to one pick aisle, zone or cell that means less time to set-up a pick line and faster CO release, (2) hit sku hit concentration & density to improve picker productivity and (3) less picker travel distance and time that increases your completed CO number.

FIFO SKU
ENHANCES INVENTORY CONTROL

FIFO sku is a small item, master carton or pallet inventory flow that enhances inventory control with the oldest sku in a pick position as first picked sku for a CO. When a FIFO sku replenishment is made to a pick position with some residual sku quantity, it means that any residual sku quantity is the oldest inventory. To have a FIFO rotation with a fixed pick position concept, a residual sku quantity in a shelf, decked, basket, slide, pegboard, drive-in or standard pallet rack pick position is removed from a pick position, replenishment sku quantity placed into a pick position and old/residual quantity returned to a pick position. Features are additional labor activity and potential sku damage or lose. With a carton or pallet or drive-thru flow rack, a residual sku quantity is at a pick position front and replenishment sku quantity is placed into a flow lane or drive-thru rack charge end. Features are no additional labor activity or minimal potential sku damage. With a floating pick position & FIFO sku rotation, you place 1 sku quantity as the oldest sku quantity in 1 pick position (A100) and a second sku quantity as the newest sku quantity in pick position (C230) and updates are made to your WMS computer program. To complete COs, your computer program directs pick transactions from position A100. When position A100 sku quantity is depleted, your WMS computer directs CO pick transactions to position C230. Features assures FIFO rotation, no additional labor or sku handling but additional pick positions with some potential for low pick productivity due to low hit concentration or density.

YOUR REPLENISHMENT TOOLS
  IMPROVE EMPLOYEE PRODUCTIVITY & SAFETY
Your replenishment tools asks the question what are your replenishment tools that are required for proper master carton presentation and transfer to a pick position. In a small item warehouse, replenishment tools are (1) for employee safety, safety rubber tip gloves and safety shoes, (2) for productivity, a knife with a replaceable/retractable blade and a blade is rigid, (3) tool holder on a cart or employee belt that has a knife, pencil, scanner and other items sleeves/holsters, (4) sku symbology faces a replenishment position, (5) use a cart or pallet as a work surface and (6) access to trash removal device.

WHAT IS YOUR REPLENISHMENT SIGNAL
  IMPROVE EMPLOYEE PRODUCTIVITY & ENHANCE SPACE UTILIZATION
What is your replenishment signal is a warehouse idea that is used to improve replenishment employee productivity and enhance pick position utilization. After a pick position has a sku quantity set-up or WMS scanned and physically transferred to a pick position, sku quantity and pick position and sku WMS IDs are sent to a WMS computer update and for CO release. Completed COs deplete skus from a pick position and a depleted sku quantity is sent to your WMS computer. If a sku set-up quantity is less than a customer order sku quantity, a sku replenishment is required at a pick position. With a WMS program (computer suggested), as a pick position requires a replenishment a WMS program sends a message as a paper document or paper less message on a RF device or scoreboard. With a manual operation (employee suggested), as a pick position requires a replenishment, an employee recognizes that a pick position has capacity for a master carton or a colored mark appears on a pick position sleeve/lane. A mark indicates that an average master carton quantity fits into a pick position.

WHAT ARE YOUR PROFILE STRATEGIES (See Pick Chapter)

PROFILE OR PICK LINE/AISLE SET-UP
  IMPROVES PICKER PRODUCTIVITY & INCREASE COMPLETED CUSTOMER ORDER NUMBER
Profile or pick line/aisle set-up is used in any warehouse and is plan that has your skus assigned to specific pick positions. You complete a pick line/aisle pick position profile to obtain your budgeted picker productivity, increase completed CO number and serves as a road map for your set-up/replenishment employee to transfer and WMS scan skus to pick positions. A pick line/aisle profile is most frequently used for you 'A'/fast moving skus that account for 80% of your picks and for a pick activity that has two pick sections. For additional profile information, we refer the reader to the pick section.

HUMAN OR COMPUTER SUGGESTED REPLENISHMENT QUANTITY
  IMPROVE EMPLOYEE PRODUCTIVITY & ENHANCE SPACE UTILIZATION
Human or computer suggested replenishment quantity is a basic question in a small item warehouse for a sku quantity for set-up or replenishment to a pick position. When a human determines a sku replenishment quantity, there is potential for a sku replenishment quantity not to match a pick position capacity. If a human replenishment sku quantity is less than a pick position capacity or CO requirement and to satisfy a CO wave it requires another

sku replenishment transaction. An additional transaction lowers your employee productivity. If a human replenishment sku quantity exceeds a pick position capacity or CO wave requirement, it requires extra sku quantity WMS scanned and transferred to a ready reserve position. Features are additional employee activity that lowers productivity and additional reserve position has low space utilization. A computer suggested sku replenishment quantity matches a sku pick position capacity. With 1 replenishment transaction, it means good employee productivity and enhanced pick position space utilization and minimal ready reserve position for enhanced space utilization.

SKU REPLENISHMENT QUANTITY MASTER CARTON ROUND-UP, ROUND-DOWN OR EXACT
IMPROVES REPLENISHMENT PRODUCTIVITY & ENHANCES INVENTORY CONTROL

Sku replenishment quantity master carton round-up, round-down or exact are a warehouse master carton replenishment quantity options that are calculated by your WMS computer program to improve replenishment productivity and enhance inventory control. Per your CO wave, a WMS computer program determines each WMS identified sku quantity and from each sku quantity a WMS program calculates each sku rounded-up, rounded-down or exact sku (full and partial full cartons) master carton quantity. With a rounded-up master carton sku quantity, if a WMS identified sku quantity exceeds a CO wave sku demand, full master cartons are transferred from your storage area to your pick position. It is anticipated that your CO wave end that a sku pick position has a residual sku quantity. For your next CO wave a residual sku quantity in a prime pick position options are (1) to relocate a residual sku quantity from one pick position to another pick section pick position that creates a vacate pick position in your prime pick zone. For your next CO wave, the approach assures good sku hit concentration and density for good picker productivity but requires additional replenishment labor and a second pick zone (2) to have a sku remain in a prime zone pick position and profile your new skus around existing skus. For your next CO wave, the approach creates additional walk distance and time between 2 picks that creates low picker productivity but does not require additional replenishment labor. With a rounded-down master carton concept, for a CO wave skus your WMS computer program calculates only full master cartons are sent to your prime pick zone and one full master carton sent to a second pick zone that at a CO wave end would contain your residual sku quantity. With rounded-down approach, your prime pick zone pick positions are picked clean and with zero scan transactions are ready to receive your next CO wave skus, assures good prime zone pick line profile for good picker productivity, no relocate/replenishment labor, with skus in a second pick zone completion of all COs. An exact sku quantity is a master carton replenishment concept that has your storage area employee in transfer full master cartons and in a storage position to open, count and transfer a required skus from a master carton into a carton for replenishment to a pick position. With exact sku approach, each prime pick zone pick position is picked clean & with a zero scan transaction is ready to receive your next CO wave skus, assures good prime zone pick line profile for good picker productivity, no relocate/replenishment labor, but low replenishment labor due to open and count activity, trash (empty master carton) in a storage area and open master carton in a storage position that means potential sku damage or lose.

HUMAN OR BAR CODE SCAN/RF TAG READ TO VERIFY REPLENISHMENT TRANSACTION COMPLETION
IMPROVES REPLENISHMENT PRODUCTIVITY & ENHANCES INVENTORY CONTROL

Human or bar code scan/RF tag read to verify set-up or replenishment transaction completion has an impact on your replenishment employee productivity, accuracy, on-time and enhances inventory control. To minimize 'no stock' pick position condition, a WMS computer program does not release CO until a sku quantity is physically and WMS scanned to a pick position and sku WMS ID, pick position ID and sku quantity are send to and update in a WMS computer program. With a human verification concept, each sku set-up/replenishment employee writes onto a document each sku ID, quantity and pick position ID. Later in a work day, an employee enters a document data into a computer program for sku and position update. Features are (1) potential transposition errors and entries, (2) delayed data transfer activity, (3) paper document expense, (4) potential document damage or loss and (5) delayed CO release. With a bar code scan/RF tag read concept, each sku set-up/replenishment activity has an employee scan/read a sku symbology, pick position symbology and enter a sku quantity in a RF wave device. After a completed replenishment transaction, replenishment data is sent via wire or wireless from a replenishment location to a WMS computer program for sku and position update. Features are (1) accurate entry, (2) on-line or delayed data transfer activity, (3) wireless installation expense and (4) on-time CO release.

REPLENISHMENT POSITION ROUTING
  IMPROVES REPLENISHMENT PRODUCTIVITY
Replenishment position routing is a small item or GOH pick area concept that is used to sequentially direct a replenishment employee or AS/RS crane through a pick aisle/zone, arrive at a pick position and complete a replenishment to a correct pick position. A routing concept improves replenishment productivity due to minimal double travel past positions & is easy to understand. For routing concepts, we refer a reader to the pick section.

WHEN & HOW TO SCAN YOUR REPLENISHMENT SKU
  IMPROVES PICKER PRODUCTIVITY & ENHANCES INVENTORY CONTROL
When and how to scan your replenishment sku is small item or GOH employee activity that completes a sku set-up or replenishment transaction to a pick position by sending a sku quantity and pick position to a WMS computer. A WMS computer updates a sku quantity and position in a WMS computer program and is ready for CO pick activity. After a sku quantity is in a pick position, a WMS computer program releases COs to a pick area means higher picker productivity and enhances inventory control. In all pick position concepts a sku physical placement into a pick position have similar activities that have an employee scan a sku symbology, transfer a sku to a pick position, scan a pick position symbology and send a scan transactions to a WMS computer program. As a sku is transferred into a pick position, a sku symbology faces a pick aisle. With AS/RS crane sku replenishment to a pick position has an AS/RS crane computer send a sku quantity and pick position ID to a WMS computer that updates a sku quantity and pick position status.

REPLENISHMENT SKU QUANTITY IS SENT ALL AT ONCE OR IN SECTIONS
  IMPROVES REPLENISHMENT PRODUCTIVITY & ENHANCES INVENTORY CONTROL
Replenishment sku quantity is sent all at once or in sections is a small item, master or pallet CO wave WMS identified sku replenishment strategy that improves replenishment productivity and enhances inventory control. When a high volume or high cube sku is a replenishment sku, there is potential for a CO wave sku replenishment quantity to exceed a pick position capacity. If you send all or entire sku replenishment quantity to a pick area, features are (1) extra sku quantity require a ready reserve position and physical transfer and scan transaction and (2) additional sku quantity and potential queue on an in-house transport concept that delays an entire pick line set-up and in an early pick time fewer WMS computer released and completed CO number. If you send a sku replenishment quantity in sections or quantity that fits into a pick position, features are (1) minimal ready reserve position and transfer/scan transactions, (2) your replenishment labor focuses on a pick line set-up, (3) minimal queues on an in-house transport concept, (4) greater sku set-up number on a pick line means a greater WMS computer release and completed CO number in a short time.

REPLENISH FIRST WITH A PARTIAL OR FULL PALLET FIRST
    IMPROVES REPLENISHMENT/ PICKER PRODUCTIVITY & INCREASES COMPLETED CUSTOMER ORDERS
Replenish first with a partial or full pallet first is related to an 'A'/fast moving small item carton or pallet flow rack warehouse with a WMS computer program that suggests sku pallet quantity for replenishment to a pick position. To complete a CO wave, an 'A'/fast moving sku requires multiple pallets and in a storage area. In a most storage operations, there are at least 1 partial full pallet and full pallets. Your pallet replenishment options are to have your (1) first pallet replenishment as a partial pallet. To complete a sku move transaction, a conventional or VNA forklift or AS/RS crane withdraws both a partial pallet and full pallets from a storage position. In a standard WMS program, a sku allocation sequence is based on a pallet received date (oldest sku is allocate first) that is regardless whether a pallet is partial or full. In most warehouses, partial pallet is the most frequent first pallet transfer occurrence. When a partial pallet arrives at a transfer station, an employee completes a sku move transaction that transfers master cartons to another pallet and places a label on each master carton for transfer to warehouse transport concept or transfers a partial pallet to a temporary hold position. When a full pallet arrives at a transfer station, an employee either completes a sku moves and transfers master cartons from a full pallet to a temporary hold position or onto a partial pallet or transfers each master carton to an in-house transport concept. Features are (a) standard WMS program, with minimal computer calculations, (b) FIFO sku rotation, (c) at an early time, picker handles an empty

pallet, (d) at an early time, another replenishment activity is required at a pick position & (e) at a CO wave completion, partial pallet is returned to a storage area and (2) withdrawing a full pallet and withdrawing a partial pallet as required. In the option, a WMS program determines skus that require a full pallet quantity and matches a needed full pallet quantity to sku pallet. In response to a CO wave need, a full pallet is allocated and is withdrawn from a storage area. If a CO wave requires a partial pallet quantity, a WMS program allocates an existing partial pallet. A partial pallet is a last pallet withdrawn from a storage area and sent to a transfer station. At a transfer station or replenishment position, a full pallet is handled as described above. Features are (a) dynamic WMS program with some additional WMS computer processing time, (b) accurate pallet master-carton quantity, (c) at an early start, picker handles a minimal empty pallet number, (d) at an early start, other pick positions are set-up due to one less replenishment at the pallet position, (e) at an early start, an in-house transport concept handles full pallets & (f) CO wave end, a partial pallet has minimal master cartons.

MARK YOUR LANE/SLEEVE/BASKET
IMPROVE EMPLOYEE PRODUCTIVITY

Mark your sku lane/sleeve or basket is used in a small item warehouse with automatic pick machines or horizontal carousel pick concept to improve a replenishment employee productivity. After you determine a master carton sky quantity that fits into an automatic pick machine sleeve/lane or horizontal basket, from a pick machine sleeve/lane or carousel basket top you place a mark. The space between a pick machine sleeve/lane to carousel basket top and mark represents one master carton sku quantity. During a CO pick activity, as a mark appears in a pick position, it is a signal for a replenishment employee to complete a master carton transfer.

SKU SET-UP OR REPLENISHMENT BEFORE OR DURING YOUR PICK ACTIVITY
IMPROVE EMPLOYEE PRODUCTIVITY

The **Sku pick position set-up or replenishment before or during your pick activity** is a small item warehouse issue that focuses on when your set-up or replenishment employee transfers a master carton to a pick position. If your warehouse with a WMS program requires a sku quantity in a pick position to match a CO wave sku quantity for a WMS computer program to release COs for your pick activity, you require an entire CO demand for a sku quantity that is WMS scanned and transferred to a pick position and sent to a WMS computer program. Features are (1) creates good pick productivity, (2) minimizes stock outs & (3) with 1 aisle for both replenishment and pick activities, reduces aisle congestion and assures good productivity. If your warehouse has a sku replenishment activity occur during a pick activity, it means that your replenishment activity is human controlled and potential for your CO wave requirement quantity to exceed a pick position capacity. To assure on-time CO completion and as a sku quantity becomes depleted, a WMS program suggests a replenishment activity prior to additional CO release to a pick concept or prior to a zero quantity in a pick position. Features are (1) slow completed COs, (2) potential stock outs, and (3) with 1 aisle for both replenishment and pick activities, increase potential aisle congestion & low productivity.

HOW MUCH TO REPLENISH
IMPROVE EMPLOYEE PRODUCTIVITY & ENHANCE SKU INVENTORY CONTROL

How much to replenish is small item or master carton warehouse pick position set-up or replenishment sku transfer quantity that improves employee productivity and enhances sku inventory control. Sku quantity options are (1) CO wave requirement. When a total CO wave sku requirement is transferred and fits into a pick position, with 1 replenishment activity it assures good replenishment employee productivity, inventory control and high completed CO number. If a total CO wave sku requirement exceeds a pick position capacity, it requires your replenishment employee to locate and transfer a sku quantity to a ready reserve location that lowers your productivity due to double handling and requires additional space and (2) pick position capacity that has a sku replenishment quantity match available space in a pick position. Features are minimizes your ready reserve position requirement, improves space utilization, maintains your employee productivity.

WHEN YOUR SKU REPLENISHMENT QUANTITY EXCEEDS A PICK POSITION CAPACITY
IMPROVES SPACE UTILIZATION & ENHANCES INVENTORY CONTROL

When your sku replenishment quantity exceeds a pick position capacity describes a computer suggested sku replenishment quantity that is based on a CO withdrawal and exceeds a WMS ID pick position capacity. In a pick area, a sku replenishment overflow quantity requires a ready reserve position and sku physical deposit and scan transaction to a ready reserve position that are sent to a WMS computer for sku update. To assure accurate sku inventory control & CO completion, a pick position sku quantity is scanned & sent to a WMS computer for sku update.

WHERE TO PUT THE EXTRA
IMPROVE EMPLOYEE PRODUCTIVITY & ENHANCE SKU INVENTORY CONTROL

Where to put the extra is a small item or master carton warehouse set-up or replenishment employee idea to handle extra sku replenishment quantity that exceeds a pick position capacity. If a sku replenishment quantity exceeds a pick position capacity, extra sku quantity is placed into a ready reserve position. With a shelf or decked rack pick concept, ready reserve positions are above a top (highest) or bottom (pigeon hole) pick position or at another shelf/decked rack position location. With flow rack pick concept, reserve positions are decked positions on a flow rack top structural members, below the bottom flow rack lane on decked positions or in ready reserve racks behind a replenishment aisle. With an automatic pick machine or carousel pick concept, ready reserve positions are shelves or flow racks along a replenishment aisle.

MASTER CARTON REPLENISHMENT FROM A PALLET
IMPROVE EMPLOYEE PRODUCTIVITY, SKU REDUCE DAMAGE & IMPROVE SAFETY

For high volume master carton replenishment from a pallet to a flow rack position improves employee productivity, reduces damage and improves safety. Master cartons on a pallet provides a smooth flat surface for a replenishment employee to open a master carton and allows easy/quick open master carton transfer to a pick position.

INDIVIDUAL MASTER CARTON REPLENISHMENT FROM A CONVEYOR OR PALLET USE A CART
IMPROVE EMPLOYEE PRODUCTIVITY, REDUCE SKU/CART DAMAGE & IMRPOVE SAFETY

Individual master carton replenishment from a conveyor or pallet use a cart is a warehouse small item replenishment idea that improves replenishment employee productivity. In a shelf, decked rack or flow rack pick concept and after a master carton conveyor or pallet with mixed skus (master cartons) arrives in a replenishment aisle, a replenishment cart is used to transfer a master carton from a conveyor or pallet to a pick position. Cart features are (1) top shelf is a solid and structural deck/surface to open a master carton top, (2) cart deck/surface with no lips allows easy and quick open master carton transfer to a pick position, (3) lower shelf holds trash container for a removed master carton top, (4) for easy steering/turning front swivel casters/wheels & (5) push handle & tool (knife & scanner) holder. For maximum replenishment employee efficiency and easy master carton transfer to pick position, a cart shelf is set at an elevation above the floor surface to match a Golden Zone shelf, decked rack or flow rack position. With a flow rack pick concept for easy and quick aisle travel, cart travel in a replenishment aisle guided by a cart with a double wheel/'C' channel that interfaces with an angle iron guide that is attached full length to a flow rack upright posts.

MASTER CARTON IN A PICK POSITION HAS SMILE OR NO SMILE
IMPROVES PICKER PRODUCTIVITY & INCREASE COMPLETED CUSTOMER ORDER NUMBER

Master carton in a pick position has a smile or no smile are a small item warehouse master carton replenishment to a pick position concept that improves picker productivity and increase your completed CO number. A no smile face master carton in a pick position means that a master carton has a solid front/top and requires a picker to cut/rip open a master carton front/top. A master carton open activity is a non-productive activity that lowers your completed CO number and on a pick/pass line creates potential congestion. When compared to a replenishment employee opening a master carton, a picker master carton open activity requires additional time due a more difficult time to access a master carton front/top in a shelf or carton flow rack pick position. When a replenishment employee creates a smile face master carton or removes a master carton top, it adds time to a replenishment activity that is not a critical activity. Additional time is offset by increased picker productivity, replenishment employee has a solid work surface, safety gloves & quality knife, easier to handle carton trash and remove filler material and with multiple cartons per position is consider a repetitive activity. A smile face on a master carton has top flaps removed and a front has a 'V' or half circle cut front. To minimize potential of skus falling from an open master carton, a removed front section is inserted into a carton front and serve a sku retainer & top flaps placed on a top to retain skus.

WHEN TO CUT YOUR MASTER CARTON OR WHO OPENS
IMPROVE EMPLOYEE PRODUCTIVITY

When to cut your master carton or who opens a master carton in a pick position is a small item warehouse question to assure good replenishment and picker productivity. As a sku flows through your warehouse, pre-pick activities are less time critical and pick activities are time critical. Your master carton cut open options are (1) by your picker employee. Your picker focuses attention on a pick instruction that is a sku pick position, pick quantity, CO container and to transfer a sku into a CO container that is in a cart, on a conveyor or in a basket. A non-open master carton in a pick position has minimal clearances that requires additional time to handle a carton and dispose of a carton top into the trash or to leave a master carton open with flaps has potential to obstruct sku removal from a master carton. For a picker to open a master carton, it is considered a non-repetitive activity for 1 master carton that requires additional non-productive picker time to locate a knife and open a carton or tear open a carton or (2) by your replenishment employee. In a replenishment activity in most situations a master carton is on a conveyor travel path, pallet or cart deck that has solid, flat and smooth surface with sufficient clear space to handle a master carton and to remove a master carton's top flaps. A replenishment employee open master carton activity is a repetitive activity that most frequently involves several master cartons that assures good productivity and is considered simply activity with protective gloves.

If you complete a master carton open time study, a master carton open activity requires from a picker to notice an empty carton in a pick position, obtain a knife from a holster and cut open master carton in a pick position. The total non-productive time requires 1 to 1 ½ minutes. With a pick/pass concept, one to 1 ½ minutes of picker non-productive time can congest a pick line and lower your completed CO number. A replenishment employee open master carton activity involves 30 to 40 seconds per master carton with no pick line down time.

If we accept that customer on-time service and high completed CO number is an operation objective, your replenishment employee cuts a master carton as part of a replenishment activity.

SAVE & REUSE A MASTER CARTON TOP/FRONT
IMPROVE EMPLOYEE PRODUCTIVITY & REDUCE SKU DAMAGE

Save & reuse a master carton top/front is a small item warehouse idea that has a replenishment employee cut a master carton top or front (smiley face). After a master carton has a cut top or front and is transferred to a pick position, there is potential for skus to fall from a master carton to the floor. To reduce falling sku potential, your replenishment employee transfers as master carton cut top/front that serves as a sku barrier to retain skus in a master carton. After a master carton is in a pick position and skus become partial depleted, as required a picker removes a cut top/front.

NO MASTER CARTON FLAPS
IMPROVE EMPLOYEE PRODUCTIVITY & REDUCE SKU DAMAGE

No master carton flaps is a small item warehouse idea that improves replenishment and picker productivity and reduces sku damage. A master carton with no top flaps transferred means that your replenishment employee has removed a master carton's top flaps. Features are (1) improved picker productivity due clear and unobstructed access to a master carton, (2) minimal potential for master carton hang-up in a flow lane, (3) standard width clearance in a pick position, (4) during a replenishment activity, minimizes potential carton flap hang-up on a pick position structural member and (5) on a trash conveyor or in a trash wagon lower trash master carton cube that increases master carton quantity per inch ft or per wagon.

REMOVE THE FILLER MATERIAL
IMPROVES PICKER PRODUCTIVITY

Remove the filler material from a master carton is replenishment activity in a small item warehouse to improve order picker productivity that results from a picker's easy and unobstructed access to master carton skus. Remove a master carton filler material occurs as replenishment employee opens a master carton. After a master carton top is removed a replenishment employee removes any filler material such as padding, sheets, cardboard, chipboard or other items from a master carton. In a replenishment aisle, removed filler material is transferred to a trash container. If filler material remains in a master carton, it becomes difficult (obstruction) to pick skus and with a depleted carton becomes trash in a pick aisle that lower picker productivity and decreases your completed CO number.

MASTER CARTON FLOW LANE JAMS OR HANG-UPS
IMPROVES PICKER PRODUCTIVITY & ENHANCES INVENTORY CONTROL

Master carton flow lane jams or hang-ups is a small item or master carton flow rack situation that occurs as a tote/master carton does not travel/move over a flow lane. When a master carton/tote does not travel over a gravity flow travel path it is considered a jam or hang-up that is resolved by a picker or replenishment employee. The resolution time is non-productive picker time and lowers your completed CO number due to a sku was not available in a pick position. To minimize future hang-ups or jams in a carton flow rack, you quantify reasons & take corrective action to un-clog master carton jams/hang-ups with a long pole that has a curved end. Some reasons are (1) poor quality carton bottom surface or bowed carton, (2) carton length was too narrow for flow lane number, (3) flap hang-up, (4) carton edge in one flow lane hangs-up/jams on an adjacent carton or flow rack member, (5) carton weight was too low, (6) carton weight was too heavy and cause sku damage & (7) skus fall from a carton.

SHELF OR DECKED RACK PICK POSITION DIVIDERS
IMPROVES PICKER PRODUCTIVITY & SPACE UTILIZATION & ENHANCES INVENTORY CONTROL

Shelf or decked rack pick position dividers or separators are used in a small item order fulfillment operation to separate skus in a pick position bay that improves picker productivity, space utilization and enhances inventory control. A pick position divider is used in a shelf, decked rack or carton pick position. When your skus are difficult to stack or are loose, full depth dividers are used to restrict sku mix in a wide pick position. To create very small size sku multiple pick positions in a bin/tote, dividers are placed into a bin/tote interior. To assure master cartons in a flow rack lane remain in a lane, a lane divider is placed full length between 2 carton flow rack pick positions.

CARTON FLOW LANE CARTON UN-JAM DEVICE
IMPROVES PICKER & REPLENISHMENT PRODUCTIVITY & MINIMIZES SKU DAMAGE

Carton flow lane carton un-jam device (a.k.a. a shepherd's hook) is a small item warehouse idea that improves picker/replenishment employee productivity and minimizes sku damage. As master cartons are transferred onto a carton flow lane, gravity force and replenishment employee forward pressure on a last master carton moves all cartons through a flow lane. On some occasions, a master carton is hung-up in a flow lane and does not arrive at a pick position front. To move a hung-up master carton in a flow lane, a replenishment employee or picker uses a Sheppard hook or pole with curved end to push or pull a carton forward in a flow lane to a pick position front. When not in use to un-jam a flow lane, a hook shaped pole is hung on a flow rack member.

LOOK FOR CARTON JAMS IN A LANE
IMPROVES PICKER PRODUCTIVITY & SPACE UTILIZATION & ENHANCES INVENTORY CONTROL

Look for carton jams in a lane is a term that refers to a small item warehouse that uses a carton flow rack pick concept. If a carton jam occurs in a flow rack lane, a picker cannot complete a pick transaction that lowers your picker productivity and completed CO number, lowers pick position utilization and has potential sku damage or loose. When a carton jam occurs, a picker has non-productive time to unclog a jam. To minimize future carton jams, you have your replenishment employee or picker identify a carton jam reason such as a (1) carton flaps hung-up on another carton or structural support member that requires a (a) replenishment employee removes master carton flaps or (b) lane guides in your flow rack bays or (2) carton side falls between two wheel lanes that requires

(a) additional wheel lane in your flow rack bay, (b) sku is transferred to standard carton/tote or (c) sku is profiled to another pick position.

CARTON FLOW RACK WITH GUIDES
IMPROVES PICKER PRODUCTIVITY & SPACE UTILIZATION & ENHANCES INVENTORY CONTROL

Carton flow rack guides are an option that is used in a small item warehouse with carton flow rack pick positions to improve picker productivity, space utilization and enhances sku inventory control. Carton flow rack guides are used full length in a flow rack bay and inverted 'U' shaped member extends an estimate 1/8 in above the flow lane wheels to create a lane guide between two pick positions or a pick position side structural member. When compared to no-guides in a flow lane bay, two flow lane guides your add 1 in to your widest master carton width that sets your flow lane width characteristics. As gravity moves a carton over a flow lane wheels, flow lane guides direct carton travel from a flow rack charge end to a pick position front. If a master carton width exceeds the open space between two guides, it is extremely difficult to move a master carton through a flow lane. It is noted that flow lane guides are not easily removed from a flow lane bay. To resolve an oversized master carton situation, wide master carton options are (1) assigned to another pick position type or (2) skus transferred into standard flow rack carton/tote. Another feature is that the space between two flow lane guides serves as a replenishment ID location on a flow rack impact bar or structural support member.

CARTON FLOW RACK BAY WITH NO LANE GUIDES
PICK POSITION FLEXIBILITY & SPACE UTILIZATION

Carton flow rack bay with no lane guides is a carton flow option that has each carton flow rack level with no lane dividers or guides. No lane guides permits your carton flow rack to handle a wider carton size mix. To assure accurate replenishment employee activity, you add tape or paint lines on each carton flow rack flow rack impact bar/conveyor end member that serves as a guide. Features are low cost, pick position flexibility and improve pick position utilization.

CARTON FLOW RACK IMPACT BAR
IMPROVES REPLENISHMENT PRODUCTIVITY & REDUCES DAMAGE

A carton flow rack impact bar is a small item warehouse with a carton flow rack pick position idea that improves your replenishment employee productivity and reduces replenishment flow lane wheel damage. Carton flow rack impact bar options are (1) horizontal structural member that is a flow rack bay full width, 4 to 8 inch depth and installed on a flow rack change end or (2) solid metal member that is structural attached to a flow rack end and extends 12 ins into a flow rack bay. When a replenishment employee transfers a master carton to a flow rack lane, it provides a solid surface for a master carton & allows a master carton push gently onto a flow rack wheels. Features are protects flow lane wheels from damage as a replenishment employee transfers a carton into a carton flow lane, serves as a location for replenishment (pick position) ID & location for you to apply tape that indicates a flow lane width.

MARK YOUR REPLENISHMENT SIDE CARTON FLOW LANE WIDTH
IMPROVES PICKER PRODUCTIVITY & SPACE UTILIZATION & ENHANCES INVENTORY CONTROL

Mark your replenishment side carton flow lane width is an idea that is used in a warehouse to separate skus in a carton flow rack pick position to improve picker productivity, space utilization and enhance inventory control. Mark your carton flow rack lane has an employee place colored tape onto a flow rack impact bar or structural support member. Distance between 2 marks is width for a pick position and is set for your widest master carton width. If your flow rack lane has guides or no guides, a replenishment employee marks each flow lane to identify a pick position width. With narrow master cartons on required flow lane number, it allows 2 cartons wide in a pick position.

IN A CARTON FLOW LANE THREE SKATE-WHEELS OR ROLLERS UNDER YOUR SHORTEST CARTON
MINIMIZE SKU DAMAGE/LOST & IMPROVE PICKER PRODUCTIVITY

Three skate-wheels or rollers under your shortest carton is a small item warehouse idea for master carton flow lane that minimizes sku damage/lost and improves picker productivity. To assure master carton travel over your flow lane travel, flow lane wheels/rollers requires at least 3 wheels under your shortest carton.

PALLET FLOW LANE ENTRY GUIDES & FORKLIFT TRUCK STOP
IMPROVES REPLENISHMENT PRODUCTIVITY & REDUCES DAMAGE

Pallet flow lane entry guides & forklift truck stop is used on a pallet flow lane entrance to improve your forklift truck pallet transfer productivity and to minimize flow lane damage. Pallet flow lane entry guides are hardened metal angled shaped members on both flow lane sides. Each angle is pitched toward a flow lane and serves as a guide to assure a pallet is easily and properly placed onto a flow lane wheels. A forklift truck stop is an inverted 'V' shaped metal member that is anchored to the floor with an inverted 'V' shaped member crown extending upward. In the position as a counterbalanced forklift truck is completing a pallet transfer to a pallet flow lane, an inverted 'V' shaped serves as a stop for a counterbalanced forklift's front wheels. Features are assure proper pallet placement onto a flow lane & minimizes flow lane damage.

CAN YOUR REPLENISHMENT EMPLOYEE REACH A TOP REPLENISHMENT POSITION
IMPROVES REPLENISHMENT PRODUCTIVITY & ENHANCE SPACE UTILIZATION

Can your replenishment employee reach a top replenishment position is a concern for a warehouse to assure that your replenishment employee can complete a replenishment transaction to a top position above a floor surface that improves employee productivity & enhances space utilization. To complete a master carton or GOH replenishment transaction, an employee is required to lift a full master carton or GOH to an elevation above a floor surface and push a master carton onto a shelf, conveyor or basket or GOH onto rail. In most applications, a top shelf, conveyor, basket or GOH rail is above an employee's head, a master carton has a smiley face and a replenishment transaction is completed with no skus falling to a floor. When you design a shelf, decked rack, horizontal carousel basket or static GOH rail your pick position height has same replenishment height above a floor surface. If you have a 5'-6" employee and your top position is 6'-0" to 6'-1" above a floor surface, a mobile cart with a safety step ladder, safety stool, safety step ladder permits your employee to complete a top position replenishment transaction. If a work assist or HROS vehicle is used, your pick area has restricted aisle travel or replenishments are made from a separate aisle. With carton gravity flow rack or sloped conveyor pick concepts, replenishment top position elevation is a nominal 8 ins higher that the top pick position elevation. The situation requires a concept to increase a replenishment elevation above the floor. With an AS/RS crane your highest replenishment elevation above a floor surface is determined by your maximum crane elevation.

HOW TO INCREASE YOUR EMPLOYEE REACH FOR ACCESS TO YOUR TOP REPLENISHMENT POSITIONS
IMPROVES REPLENISHMENT PRODUCTIVITY & ENHANCE SPACE UTILIZATION & MINIMIZE DAMAGE

How to increase your employee reach for access to your top replenishment positions is a question that a warehouse manage answers that allows your shelf, decked rack or horizontal replenishment positions to improve employee productivity, enhance space utilization and minimize equipment damage and employee injury. When we consider positions for your 'C' & 'D' skus, we assure that a replenishment employee quickly, easily and safely completes a sku set-up or replenishment transaction. Various concepts to increase a replenishment employee ability to complete a transaction above an employee normal reach are (1) mobile stool with safety pads that is a low cost item but an elevation change is 8 ins, it requires additional employee time to locate and transfer to required location, (2) cart with safety step ladder that has 24 in elevation change additional cart counterweight cost and reduces an employee time to use, (3) mobile safety step with permanent or collapsible top or that is attached to a position top structural member have an added cost, requires time to relocate and has an elevation change to a top position, (4) work assist or HROS vehicle that has a high cost and separate aisle or when being used in a pick aisle for maximum safety pickers are restricted from an aisle, (5) shelf or deck rack pick positions with a step along a front that has a higher cost, wider aisle, 12 in elevation change but no relocation time, (6) re-enforced lower shelf position that has a higher shelf cost, 12 in elevation change but no relocation time, (7) with GOH static rail concepts to have an elevated walkway or GOH hangs into a cavity that has structural capacity to hold an employee. Both have safety rails, kick-plates and increase an employee ability to reach top rails & (8) with an automatic pick machine a platform in a replenishment aisle allows an employee to easily reach a sleeve or lane top.

REPLENISHMENT CONVEYOR TRAVEL TO CARTON FLOW RACK REPLENISHMENT LOCATIONS
IMPROVES PICKER & REPLENISHMENT PRODUCTIVITY

Replenishment conveyor travel path and divert master cartons/totes to carton flow rack replenishment locations that has an impact on your master carton replenishment to pick positions, queue area and replenishment employee productivity and reduces an operation 'A' & 'B' sku pick line set-up. A replenishment conveyor travel path divert locations to a carton flow rack pick concept are (1) at your pick zone start and a diverted carton travel on a pick zone replenishment conveyor has forward travel on a conveyor travel. The option with an ABC profile has diverted master cartons travel on a replenishment conveyor from highest volume sku pick positions to lower volume sku pick positions. With the option, if a replenishment employee does not complete a replenishment transaction, high volume master cartons travel to a replenishment conveyor travel path end that means additional employee walk time and distance to complete a master carton replenishment transaction and in a pick zone minimal master carton queue for high volume cartons on a replenishment conveyor and (2) at your pick zone end with an ABC profile and a diverted carton travel on a pick zone replenishment conveyor is from a low volume sku section to a high volume section. With the concept master cartons are diverted at a pick zone low volume sku end and master cartons move to a pick zone high volume end. Features are provides maximum fast moving master carton queue and less employee walk time and distance to complete replenishment transactions. With both concepts, your master carton divert from a main conveyor travel path assures each master carton faces a replenishment aisle and a main travel path has master carton re-circulation.

HUMAN OR CARTON AS/RS CRANE PICK POSITION SET-UP/REPLENISHMENT
IMPROVES PRODUCTIVITY & SPACE UTILIZATION & ENHANCES INVENTORY CONTROL

Human or carton AS/RS crane pick position set-up or replenishment is a master carton/tote warehouse replenishment options to carton flow rack or horizontal carousel that improves productivity, enhances space utilization and enhances inventory control. A human set-up/replenishment concept has an employee complete a sku transfers to a flow rack or carousel pick position and with a paper document or RF device for replenishment transaction transfer to a WMS computer program. With an 'A'/fast moving sku rotation to a pick concept allows an employee to determine a sku pick position, employee activity and handles all sku container types. A machine replenishment concept has a carton AS/RS crane complete a replenishment from a storage position/conveyor to a flow rack pick position. With an AS/RS crane carrier your opened master carton sku is handled by itself or in a tray or tote. With a horizontal carousel pick concept, a robotic and elevating sku carrier receives a sku opened master carton/tray/tote from a conveyor travel path. Per a computer suggested pick position elevates the sku to a pick position elevation for transfer into carousel pick position. A pallet AS/RS crane has ability to complete a sku replenishment transaction direct to a pick position or onto a carrier for transfer to a pallet pick position. AS/RS crane replenishment concept features are (1) crane communicates replenishment transaction (sku and sku pick position) direct to a WMS computer program, (2) accurate and on-time replenishment transaction communication, (3) sku set-up/replenishment occurs 24 X 7 that allows a pick activity warm start, (4) higher capital cost, (5) high employee productivity & (6) additional employee safety features such as meshed fence area.

WHERE DO YOU TRANSFER YOUR MASTER CARTONS FROM A PALLET TO A PICK POSITION
IMPROVES REPLENISHMENT PRODUCTIVITY & ENHANCES INVENTORY CONTROL

Where do you transfer your master cartons from a pallet to a pick position in a master carton or small item warehouse assures that a sku is replenished to a pick position to improve replenisher productivity and enhance inventory control. First option is at a storage position to transfer a master carton quantity from a storage pallet onto a cart or pallet that has an employee incur some master carton double handling to unitize onto a transport cart or pallet. Features are increases transfer quantity, requires fewer replenishment trips, cart or pallet cartons serve as a master carton open surface and less replenishment aisle congestion. The concept is preferred for B, C & D moving skus with 1 or 2 master carton quantities that are replenished to shelf or decked rack positions. Second option is to transfer master carton quantity from a pallet that is deposited in a replenish aisle and at this location an employee transfers master cartons to a pick position. After a replenishment activity, a partial pallet is returned from a replenishment aisle to a storage position. The concept is preferred for 'A'/fast moving skus with multiple master cartons that are replenished to carton flow rack positions. Features are requires a pallet moving vehicle, minimal double handling, pallet cartons serve as a master carton open surface & moves a large master carton quantity.

REPLENISHMENT POSITION IDENTIFICATION
IMPROVES REPLENISHMENT PRODUCTIVITY & ENHANCES INVENTORY CONTROL

Replenishment position identification is a small item or GOH warehouse ID on a pick position structural member that IDs a pick position replenishment location to improve replenishment productivity and enhance inventory control. Each replenishment position ID is a human or human/machine readable symbology that allows an employee or RF device to match an employee or computer directed replenishment activity to an appropriate pick position. With a shelf, decked rack, standard rack, carousel basket, GOH rail, drive-in rack, slide, peg board, stacking frame and floor stack rack a pick position ID is a replenishment position ID that is placed onto a shelf, load beam, rail or post that is above, below or adjacent to a pick position. Whenever possible, an ID is placed in a pick position middle to keep all pick positions in a consistent location. With some ID locations, directional arrows or colored labels assure proper pick/replenishment position ID. With some small item automatic pick machines, replenishment ID is attached to a sleeve or lane structural member and a shelf or flow rack ready reserve position is related to each sleeve or lane ID. In a carton or pallet AS/RS crane concept, all replenishment transactions are completed by a computer controlled crane that requires all replenishment/pick position IDs entered in a computer program. With a carton or pallet flow rack and drive thru concept, there is a pick aisle with pick position IDs that a progression along a pick zone front and a replenishment aisle with replenishment IDs along a same front. With the concept, during replenishment position ID attachment you make sure that each pick position ID and replenishment position ID match.

REPLENISHMENT TO AN AUTOMATIC PICK MACHINE
IMPROVES REPLENISHMENT PRODUCTIVITY & ENHANCES INVENTORY CONTROL

Replenishment to an automatic pick machine is a small item or master carton warehouse activity that assures good productivity and enhances inventory control but requires on-time replenishment transactions to assure maximum completed CO number. A small item automatic pick machine requires an employee from a replenishment aisle to transfer an individual sku quantity from a master carton into an automatic pick machine pick sleeve or lane. To have an effective, cost efficient and on-time replenishment to a pick position your replenishment activity is computer program suggested, for some 'A'/fast moving skus you use a floating slot concept and a non-powered conveyor is along a pick machine replenishment side to serve a work surface and back-up pick lane. With some pick machines that have an elevated base, a replenishment aisle is an elevated platform that increases an employee ability to reach a sleeve or lane top. For easy and quick empty master carton & filler material removal, a replenishment aisle has an elevated powered trash conveyor concept. Small item automatic pick machine replenishments are made from an aisle that is between a pick machine and carton flow rack and shelf ready reserve positions. Reserve position front configurations are (1) parallel to a replenishment aisle that provides fewest fronts per aisle but less employee walk distance and time to complete a replenishment transaction & (2) perpendicular flow rack and shelf bays to a replenishment aisle that provides greatest front number per replenishment aisle but additional employee walk distance and time to complete a replenishment transaction.

REPLENISHMENT TO CARTON FLOW RACK LOCATION
IMPROVES REPLENISHMENT PRODUCTIVITY & ENHANCES INVENTORY CONTROL

Replenishment to carton flow rack location is a small item warehouse activity that assures sufficient sku quantity in a pick position to improve replenishment productivity and enhances inventory control. For high picker productivity with minimal travel problems over a flow lane, master cartons have open tops & cut fronts. Your carton replenishment options are (1) replenishment from floor position pallet is made from an aisle between a flow rack and pallet and has all master cartons transferred from a pallet to a flow rack. Features are few pallet positions behind a flow rack bay, used for fast moving or high cube skus, requires on-time powered vehicle pallet transfer and for a pallet set-down spot painted lines improve safety and replenishment productivity, (2) for 'A'/fast moving skus replenishment from pallet flow lane is made by an employee who assures that each master carton is open and transfer a master carton from a flow lane pallet to a carton flow lane pick positions. Features are a pallet flow lane services one carton pick position and you require an empty pallet flow lane, (3) for 'B' & 'C' medium moving skus a conveyor transports master carton to a replenishment conveyor that is directly behind a flow rack replenishment aisle. As a carton arrives at a replenishment position, an employee assures that the sku is assigned to a pick position and transfers an open carton into a pick position. A conveyor travel path serves as a work surface and (4) for slow moving skus or few skus/master cartons, replenishment master cartons are picked mixed onto a cart or pallet. A cart or pallet is moved a floor position that is directly behind a flow rack. From a replenishment aisle an employee opens and transfers a master carton from a cart or pallet into a flow lane. Features are requires on-time replenishment carton pick transactions, a small carrying surface requires several trips and for a pallet or cart set-down spot painted lines improve safety and replenishment productivity,.

REPLENISHMENT TO STANDARD PALLET RACK POSITION
IMPROVES REPLENISHMENT PRODUCTIVITY & ENHANCES INVENTORY CONTROL

Replenishment to a standard pallet rack position is used in a small item or master carton warehouse that improves replenishment productivity and enhances inventory control. In a small item or master carton pick concept from standard pallet rack, nominal pick positions are 1 and 2 pick position levels and 3 and 4 pallet rack positions are used for reserve pallets. If a replenishment is made to 1 or 2 pick position levels, any residual master cartons are placed into a rack bay between two pallets or onto a pallet. With a manual forklift truck replenishment activity to a standard pallet rack position with only one pick level that has extra top open space, any residual master cartons in a pick position from a previous pallet are placed onto a new pallet. Features are extra high pick position opening reduces employee injury and minimizes potential sku damage.

REPLENISHMENT TO A HORIZONTAL CAROUSEL BASKET
IMPROVES REPLENISHMENT PRODUCTIVITY & ENHANCES INVENTORY CONTROL

Replenishment to a horizontal carousel basket small item pick position (horizontal carousel basket) is a disciplined activity to assure good employee productivity and enhances inventory control. An employee or computer commands a horizontal carousel to revolve a basket to a replenishment station. Replenishment to a horizontal carousel has an ecliptic layout with two ends as possible replenishment locations. A replenishment transaction assures that a sku is secured in a basket position, to access higher pick positions requires a picker elevating device and 'A'/fast moving skus that require a floating slot concept. Replenishment transactions at a pick station occurs on a separate shift, there is potential for lower picker productivity, inbound sku and outbound sku travel paths, separate trash handling concepts and minimal requirement for interlock controls. Replenishment transactions at the other end and occurs on same shift or separate shift. Interlock controls assure that a carousel basket movement minimizes potential employee injury by allowing one station to access a carousel basket. Replenishment on same shift concept features are lowers replenishment and picker productivity due to limited access to a carousel and lower completed CO number. Replenishment on a separate shift improves both picker and replenishment productivity due unlimited carousel access, higher completed CO number and lower cost with one trash handling concept.

HORIZONTAL CAROUSEL POSITION SLOPE & BARRIER
REDUCE SKU DAMAGE & IMPROVE SAFETY

Horizontal carousel position slope & barrier are a horizontal carousel pick concept ideas to reduce sku damage & improve safety. As a horizontal carousel rotates with flat bottom pick positions, there is potential for skus to slip from a pick position & fall to the floor or onto an employee. A 5% sloped pick position bottom to the rear is an option to retain skus in a pick position. A second option is to use a pick position front barrier of Velcro stripes that span a pick position front. As a pick position becomes depleted, a Velcro stripe is secured to a pick position side.

REPLENISHMENT TO SHELF, DECKED RACK, PEGBOARD, DRAWER OR SLIDE POSITIONS
IMPROVES REPLENISHMENT PRODUCTIVITY & ENHANCES INVENTORY ACCURACY/CONTROL

Replenishment to shelf, decked rack, pegboard, drawer or slide pick positions is used in a small item warehouse assures replenishment productivity and enhances inventory accuracy/control. With the pick concepts, a replenishment activity occurs in the same aisle as your pick activity. In most operations, a picker has depleted a pick position quantity. With a zero sku quantity in a pick position, to assure accurate inventory control a replenishment employee completes a zero scan transaction that is sent to a WMS computer program for sku and pick position update. To assure budgeted picker productivity, prior to master carton transfer a replenishment employee opens each master carton. For maximum replenishment productivity, a 4-wheel cart with a solid surface permits carton opening activity and on a bottom shelf has a trash container.

PALLET AS/RS CRANE OR VNA FORKLIFT TRUCK DIRECT REPLENISHMENT TO A PICK POSITION
  IMPROVES PICKER PRODUCTIVITY & ACCURATE TRANSACTIONS

Pallet AS/RS crane or VNA forklift truck replenishment to a pick position is warehouse idea to improve employee productivity and assure accurate transactions. With a computer controlled AS/RS concept, an AS/RS crane withdraws a computer suggested 'A'/fast moving sku pallet from a storage position and transfers a pallet to a computer suggested pick position. After each pallet transfer transaction, an AS/RS crane computer sends an update message to a WMS computer. With a VNA forklift truck concept, a VNA forklift truck completes a computer suggested withdrawal transaction and completes a deposit transaction to a pick position. WMS scan transactions are sent to a WMS computer. With an AS/RS crane that operates on 24 X 7 schedule, flow lane or standard rack pick positions with pick position capacity know in a WMS computer, employee safety with devices that restricts access to an AS/RS crane area such as a pallet pass through a pick position charge end bi-parting gate, an AS/RS crane and early start to a VNA forklift truck concept completes a 'A'/fast moving sku pick position set-up that means a warm start to pick activity with pallet queue in a flow lane or adjacent storage positions.

CARTON AS/RS CRANE REPLENISHMENT
   IMPROVES REPLENISHMENT PRODUCTIVITY & ENHANCES INVENTORY CONTROL

Carton AS/RS crane replenishment is a small item warehouse concept with an AS/RS crane complete master carton or tote replenishments to a gravity flow rack pick concept that improves replenishment productivity and enhances inventory control. From a storage position or from a P/D station, an AS/RS crane picks-up an open master carton or tote, travels in aisle to a pick position, transfer a master carton/tote to a pick position and an AS/RS crane computer communicates a completed replenishment transaction to your WMS computer. To assure a completed master carton/tote replenishment transaction and flow through a gravity flow lane, your master carton/tote has quality bottom surface that matches your flow lane requirements and no-flaps to create hang-ups. Your AS/RS crane carrier handler determines whether your master carton is open or closed and whether your AS/RS crane carries one or two master cartons/totes. If you use totes, your pick concept has a means for empty tote transport from a pick aisle. An AS/RS crane replenishment features are operates 24 X 7, requires minimal labor and assures accurate and on-time replenishments.

TRASH CONTAINER OR TRASH CONVEYOR LOCATION
   IMPROVES REPLENISHMENT/PICKER PRODUCTIVITY & INCREASED COMPLETED CUSTOMER ORDERS

Trash container or conveyor location is a small item warehouse layout idea that improves replenishment or pick productivity and increases completed CO number. A trash container or conveyor assures a constant trash flow from a pick or replenishment area, employee access and low cost. A replenishment or pick activity creates trash that is master carton tops or front sections and filler material. With a shelf and decked rack pick concept, replenishment container locations are on a cart bottom shelf or along a pick aisle. Features are requires an employee to replace full container with empty container, potential to mix cardboard and plastic trash, low capacity and handles a low volume. With a carton flow rack or automatic pick machine concept for 'A'/fast moving skus creates a high trash volume. If your flow rack replenishment employee removes a master carton top/front and filler material, the replenishment aisle has a separate container for plastic trash and a replenishment employee accumulates cardboard master carton tops/fronts in a large box/tote and transfers the cardboard trash onto an elevated trash conveyor. With an automatic pick machine or horizontal carousel concept, a replenishment employee has direct access to a trash conveyor for cardboard trash and a separate container for plastic trash. With a master carton warehouse, a pick aisle has trash container in a pick position for pallet plastic wrap trash.

CHAPTER 5
PICK ACTIVITY COST REDUCTION IDEAS

YOUR CUSTOMER ORDER SERVICE STANDARD
   IMPROVE PICKER PRODUCTIVITY & CUSTOMER SERVICE
Your customer order service standard is a company warehouse policy that a work day COs/CO wave are completed and CO packages on a freight delivery truck to assures customer service. To assure good customer service and on-time delivery, a catalog, direct mail or TV marketing warehouse determines a CO wave/work day COs based on several factors. The factors are (1) time require to complete all I T computer CO processing or time that COs as pick instructions are on your pick floor or available for your pick and pack activity, (2) your pick and pack employee budgeted productivity and actual employee number and (3) time for a delivery truck to travel from your operation to a freight terminal and arrive for freight company sort time.

ACCURATE PICKS REDUCES PROBLEM CUSTOMER ORDERS
   IMPROVE PICKER/PACKER PRODUCTIVITY & IMPROVES CUSTOMER SERVICE
Accurate picks reduces problem COs. A problems CO package is sent to a customer with a damaged, wrong sku, short sku or extra sku quantity. The situation occurs in a small item or GOH warehouse and when a CO is received at a delivery address it creates a dissatisfied customer. To minimize problem COs, a pick activity objective has your pickers pick correct and quality skus in the correct quantity from a pick position into a CO container. In other words, for your warehouse to maintain your customer service standard, it starts at your pick position or pick activity.

YOUR PICK OR PACK ACTIVITY WARM OR COLD START
   IMPROVE PICKER PRODUCTIVITY & ASSURE A CONSTANT CUSTOMER ORDER FLOW
Warm or cold start is a small item or GOH warehouse strategy to have sku quantity for a CO wave in pick positions that assures good picker/packer productivity and constant CO flow. A cold start has your replenishment, pick and pack activities start at the same time. Features are delayed pick activity start due to skus are replenished and scanned to a pick position that is updated in your WMS computer program. Time that is required to complete these activities, delays CO release to a pick area and low employee productivity due to non-productive waiting time or time to change an employee activity from replenishment to picker. A warehouse with a warm start has your set-up employee start at an early time to assure that skus are physically transferred and scanned to pick positions that allows a WMS computer program to on-time release COs to a pick concept. Feature is your 'A' moving skus are in pick positions that allows a pick activity warm start-up with a high completed CO number. After your pick activity has completed COs and they are queued on your pack area transport concept, your packers start at a later time to assure a warm start-up with COs ready for your pack activity.

CUSTOMER ORDER CARRY-OVER
   IMPROVE PICKER PRODUCTIVITY & ASSURE A CONSTANT CUSTOMER ORDER FLOW
CO carry-over is Day 1 CO wave COs that are not completed in Day 1 due to low productivity from unexpected volume increase with no additional employees, employee sickness, pick electrical/mechanical or I T computer process problems. If you rotate skus in pick positions, Day 1 CO carry-over is picked before Day 2 CO wave sku set-up in pick positions & Day 2 CO release to pick concept. This is due to Day 1 sku residual is in a pick position, Day 2 sku pick position set-up to same pick position that is scanned/sent to a WMS computer that have potential mis-picks. If skus remain in pick positions, Day 2 CO wave sku set-up is in same pick position with same sku & Day 2 CO release to pick concept with potential pick & replenishment activity occurring together.

CUSTOMER ORDER POOL
   IMPROVE PICKER PRODUCTIVITY & ASSURE A CONSTANT CUSTOMER ORDER FLOW
CO pool equals existing COs in a WMS computer that are not released to a previous work day/CO wave & new COs that are sent from a Host computer to a WMS computer and are not included a previous CO wave. CO pool are COs available to a warehouse staff for creation of a CO wave.

WHAT CUSTOMER ORDERS ARE FIRST IN YOUR CUSTOMER ORDER POOL
  IMPROVE CUSTOMER SERVICE & INCREASE COMPLETED CUSTOMER ORDER NUMBER
What COs are first in your order pool is a warehouse with an existing CO pool (COs not been released to your pick activity) and can have an impact on your customer service standard. As new COs are received by your warehouse, after CO processing and approval new COs are added to your CO pool. To achieve your company customer service objectives from your CO pool & per your company criteria your warehouse staff creates a CO wave/work day CO number. Per your employee number, productivity rates & CO pool order type, your CO wave selection factors are (1) single line/single sku that includes pre-packed & if you use a slapper label, vendor ready to ship cartons & single line/multiple pieces that assures your highest completed CO number, (2) age/oldest CO to assure customer service, (3) new customers to retain customers, (4) promotional/special value for high volume, (5) carton size, (6) delivery company or CO delivery address, (7) multiple lines/single or multiple skus, (8) combination & (9) foreign country.

YOUR CUSTOMER ORDER WAVE
   IMPROVE PICKER PRODUCTIVITY & CONTROL CUSTOMER ORDERS
A customer order wave is a small item or GOH warehouse staff activity that has your staff selects COs from an existing CO pool in your WMS program computer for an operation work day COs. Based on your company CO priority and your budgeted picker/sorter/packer productivity, your warehouse staff selects COs for a work day/wave and sends it your WMS computer. Your WMS computer allocates skus and suggests WMS ID sku moves to satisfy your CO wave. After skus are physically placed and scanned in pick positions, scan messages are sent to a WMS computer that releases COs to your pick concept. The arrangement assures CO control, due to only a wave's COs that can be completed are issued to a warehouse.

YOUR CUSTOMER ORDER PACK SLIPS/INVOICES GO ONTO YOUR PICK FLOOR
   IMPROVE CUSTOMER OREER PACK SLIPS/INVOICES ACCOUNTABILITY & REDUCE PRINT EXPENSES
Your CO pack slips/invoices go onto your pick floor means that your WMS computer program printed CO pack slips/invoices are used by your picker/sorter or final picker. With a bulk pick/sort to a CO carton/tote, a CO pack slip/invoice is placed into a CO carton/tote that is in a cart sort position. After your picker pick/sort activity completion, a completed pick/sort cart with picked skus and CO pack slips/invoices are delivered to a pack station. With a bulk pick, sort and final pick concept, a CO pack slips/invoices are printed and sorted by sort position sequence (first digit, last digit) and each CO pack slip/invoice group is distributed to each sort position number. From each sort position, a final picker with a CO pack slip/invoice a customer order completes final pick. A completed CO in a carton/tote with picked skus and CO pack slip/invoice are sent to a check/pack station. To assure all CO pack slips/invoices are accounted, your WMS computer program has your CO pack slip/invoice total that is compared to a manifested CO pack slip/invoice. If there is a variance, your pick and pack activities search for a missing CO pack slip/invoice. Features are (1) improves packer productivity, (2) with pick, sort and final pick lowers pick instruction cost, (3) with pick, sort and final pick concept that has CO pack slips/invoices separated by sort location improves picker productivity and (4) computer compares printed total to manifested total improves control and accountability.

HOW TO COMMUNICATE A PICK TRANSACTION TO YOUR WMS COMPUTER
   IMPROVE PICKER PRODUCTIVITY & ENHANCE INVENTORY CONTROL
How to communicate a pick transaction to your WMS computer is a warehouse activity that has a picker send a sku pick transaction completion message to your WMS computer program that assures good picker productivity, enhances sku inventory control and depletes a sku quantity from a pick position. Picked sku depletion from a pick position assures accurate inventory count in a pick position and WMS computer program on-time replenishment transaction. Picked sku communication options are (1) with a paper pick instruction that is printed by your warehouse computer and occurs after pick instruction preparation but does not assure on-time sku replenishment and accurate pick transaction, (2) with a pick to light pick instruction, after your sku pick light pick button is pressed or laser beam is broken, your warehouse computer sends a pick completion message to your WMS computer program, (3) an automatic pick machine sku release, your warehouse computer sends a pick completion message

to your WMS computer program. Features are (1) on-line communication, (2) requires a communication network and (3) with any pick concept between your pick and pack areas, on a travel path or at a pack station you have an employee or machine complete a picked sku check scan transaction for each CO picked sku that is sent on-line to your WMS computer program.

AT A PICK ACTIVITY START HAVE EMPTY CART, TROLLEY & CARTON/TOTE QUEUE
IMPROVE PICKER PRODUCTIVITY & MINIMIZE BUILDING/EQUIPMENT DAMAGE

At a pick activity start have empty cart, trolley & empty carton/tote queue lanes are used in a small item or GOH pick concept to assure a picker with a new CO has an empty CO container to improve picker productivity. A small item and GOH pick concept designs are (1) at a pick/pass line or automatic pick machine entry have an empty carton or tote queue conveyor prior to a pick line start station or automatic pick machine first pick position and (2) with a small item or GOH pick into/onto a cart/trolley, at a control/dispatch desk has an empty cart/trolley queue. If a cart uses cartons/totes in pick/sort position, there are empty carton/tote stacks.

PICK AREA/LINE SKU PROFILE
IMPROVE PICKER PRODUCTIVITY & INCREASE COMPLETED CUSTOMER ORDER NUMBER

Profile is a small item or GOH sku allocation to a pick position strategy that assures your skus are in pick positions for your employee, mechanized or automatic pick machine actual pick productivity to match your budgeted productivity. To complete a pick aisle/line/zone, carousel or automatic pick machine profile you require your sku historical sales, estimated sales, sku weight/physical characteristics, your budgeted picker productivity, your selected profile strategy and a spread sheet that shows your pick positions. Various profile strategies are by budgeted picker productivity, 'A' skus to your Golden Zone or Golden Highway, prime real estate, family group and random. With a PC or paper spread sheet that mirrors your pick concept, you allocate your skus to pick positions. After PC or spread sheet completion, you enter your selected profile strategy into your WMS computer program that directs your sku set-up or replenishment transactions for your pick activity.

WHAT ARE YOUR CUSTOMER ORDER TYPES
IMPROVE PICKER PRODUCTIVITY

What are your customer order types are important to a small item or GOH warehouse and has an impact on your picker productivity. In a warehouse your CO types are single line/single piece, single line/multiple pieces, multiple lines/single or multiple pieces or combination. If your CO computer program has the ability to separate your COs into CO waves for each group, you have potential to improve your picker/packer productivity, reduce sku damage and increase completed CO number. With single line/single sku COs, you have an opportunity to set-up fast pack lines with a sku bulk pick activity. With multiple line/multiple sku COs, you have an opportunity to bulk pick sku for sort to a temporary hold position and final CO assembly.

PICK SINGLE CUSTOMER ORDERS
PICKER ACCOUNTABILITY

Pick singles is a warehouse that has one picker or pick machine pick one CO's total sku number. A single CO pick approach has good picker accountability, easy to identify problem pickers, handles a small CO number, minimal computer program requirement and low picker productivity.

BULK OR BATCH PICK CUSTOMER ORDERS
IMPROVE PICKER PRODUCTIVITY & INCREASES COMPLETED CUSTOMER ORDER NUMBER

Batch pick is a small item or GOH pick concept that has your CO computer program separate COs into pre-determined groups. After your CO skus are picked as a group, later your CO picked skus are sorted to a CO holding position that increases picker productivity and your CO number. Picker productivity increase is due to at one pick position a picker has potential to pick multiple skus and off-sets your sort activity. Each sku has a sku or CO ID that is used in a sort area to separate skus to CO collection/hold positions. Batch pick concepts are (1) small item or GOH pick/sort activity completed at the pick position that has a picked sku sorted to a CO hold position on a cart/trolley/tote. Each cart/trolley/tote capacity determines your batch size, (2) small item or GOH bulk pick, transport, sort and final pick activity that has in a separate area, skus sorted to temporary sort/hold position. From skus temporary hold positions, a final CO picker with a CO pack slip/invoice completes a final CO pick transaction. A separate sku bulk pick document and CO pack slip/invoice minimizes a computer program cost, (3) small item or GOH bulk pick, transport, sort and final sort activity that has in a separate area, picked skus sorted to CO temporary hold positions. Each batch has a separate sort area/lane and picked skus are transported on a belt conveyor or in totes. After sort, a packer with a CO pack slip/invoice verifies a CO accurate completion and (4) small item or master carton bulk pick, transport, sort and final sort activity that has a pre-determined CO group small item skus sorted to a CO temporary hold position. Per position has a nominal 50 piece quantity. A packer with a CO pack slip/invoice complete a final CO sort. To handle a high pick volume, a powered conveyor moves skus loose or in totes to an induction location for sku transfer onto a powered/mechanized scan and sort concept. To assure maximum completed CO number, you assure a constant sku flow that is based on your picker/packer budgeted productivity rates and available employee number at each work station.

SINGLE CUSTOMER ORDER PICK ACTIVITY
PICKER ACCOUNTABILITY
Single CO pick activity has one picker complete all picks for a CO. A manual single CO pick concept has good picker accountability but low picker productivity due to greatest travel distances and is not preferred in a warehouse.

MANUAL PICK & SORT IN A PICK AREA
IMPROVE PICKER PRODUCTIVITY & MINIMIZE ERRORS
Manual pick and sort in a pick area is a grouped CO pick and sort concept that is used in a small item warehouse to increase picker productivity and your completed CO number. When compared to a single order pick concept, your picker productivity increase off-sets your picker's sort expense. After your computer program batches your COs into a pre-determined CO number per group (match your 4-wheel cart sort positions), for each pick/sort cart, it prints one pick & sort instruction/document and a batch CO pack slips/invoices. Each pick/sort cart is ID with your computer batch pick number. On a pick/sort document, for each batch each sku's pick position is printed down a page, across a page top is there are several columns. Each column starts with a sort location number, under a sort location number is a CO number and under each CO number is listed a CO sku quantity. Your sort location number are arithmetic from to required number (typically from 1 to 9 or 12). Your pick & sort cart positions are pre-numbered and your places a CO ID carton/tote into each position. Next, your picker places a CO pack slip/invoice into a corresponding CO sort position/cart/tote. At each pick position with a pick/sort cart and pick/sort instruction, a picker completes a bulk sku pick activity. Per your batch pick/sort instruction and from a sku bulk picked quantity a picker sorts a CO sku quantity to each CO location. Per your pick concept, for one batch cart one picker completes all pick transactions or one batch cart/tote is pushed from one assigned pick zone to another picker's assigned pick zone. After completion of all picks, a picker pushes a cart/tote to a pack area.

TRAVEL EMPTY TO YOUR FIRST PICK POSITION
IMPROVE PICKER PRODUCTIVITY
Travel empty to your first pick position is a manual small item or GOH warehouse that has a picker travel with an empty pick tote/carton/cart/trolley from a dispatch desk to a first pick position for improved picker productivity and minimal sku damage. Picker travel with an empty pick tote/carton/cart/trolley to the furthest position concept has a picker with an empty tote/carton/cart/trolley/vehicle to travel from a dispatch desk with a CO pick instructions to the furthest pick position. Feature allows a picker to travel at the fast travel speed with no sku on a tote/carton/cart/trolley. From a furthest pick aisle, each aisle and position routing pattern has an arithmetic progression that leads a picker to a discharge/dispatch desk. During pick activity, as picked skus accumulate in tote/carton/cart/trolley, it minimizes a picker physical effort and minimizes potential sku damage.

SMALL ITEM APRON OR SMALL CARTON/TOTE WITH HANDLES/HOLES
IMPROVE PICKER PRODUCTIVITY & MINIMZE DAMAGED SKUS
Small item apron or small carton/tote with handles/holes is used in a small item warehouse that improves picker productivity and minimize sku damage. Using an apron or small carton/tote increases a picker's ability to transfer a multiple picked sku quantity between a pick position and CO container that decreases the walk distance and permits handling a larger sku quantity.

PICKER CLIPBOARD
IMPROVE PICKER PRODUCTIVITY & REDUCE POSSIBLE PAPER DAMAGE/LOST

A picker clipboard is used in a small item warehouse with a paper pick document that improves picker productivity, reduce possible paper pick document damage/lost and reduce sku damage. When picking with a paper document, a clipboard provides a picker with a device to maintain a paper pick document in one location and to have a solid surface for easy and quick picker marking on a document that assures a pick transaction completion. Also, a clipboard is solid surface that is used to transfer multiple skus from a pick position to a CO container.

SKUS ARE SET-UP IN PICK POSITIONS
IMPROVE PICKER PRODUCTIVITY & INCREASE COMPLETED CUSTOMER ORDER NUMBER

Skus are set-up in pick positions with sufficient sku quantity for your CO wave number. With a proper sku quantity in all pick positions, it assures high picker productivity and high completed CO number. After your CO wave creation, your WMS computer program directs your storage activity to transfer skus from your storage area to pick positions or ready reserve positions. In some operations, after a WMS computer program has received a sku transfer to a pick position message, it releases COs to a pick concept. As COs deplete a sku quantity from a pick position, a WMS computer program suggests a sku replenishment transaction from a storage or ready reserve position.

PICK SKUS FROM MIXED SKUS IN TOTES/TRAYS/RAILS
IMPROVE PICKER PRODUCTIVITY

Pick skus from mixed skus in totes/trays/rail is a small item or GOH pick concept that has different skus mixed with no separation in one container or on one GOH rail. When a picker completes a pick transaction from a mixed skus tote/tray/rail, a picker has non-productive time searching and locating a sku for a pick transaction completion. This lowers picker productivity and the completed CO number. Since your pick activity is a time critical activity and for good customer service, it is more productive for your replenishment employee to physically separate skus in a mixed tote/tray/rail. Mixed skus in a container concept is used to improved space utilization for 'C' and 'D' moving skus, consider one sku per pick position with a narrower or shorter tote/tray.

WHAT IS YOUR PICK AREA LAYOUT PHILOSOHPY
IMPROVE PICKER PRODUCTIVITY & INCREASE COMPLETED CUSTOMER ORDER NUMBER

What is your pick area layout philosophy has a major impact on your picker productivity, assures proper sku rotation and increases your completed CO number. Your pick area layout philosophy is how you profiled your skus to pick positions in your pick concept. Whether you have a small item or GOH manual, mechanized or automatic pick machine pick activity, your pick area has a layout philosophy. Pick area philosophies are (1) ABCD or Pareto's Law that groups your 'A'/fast moving skus in one pick aisle/zone to improve hit concentration & density, (2) Pairs, Cell, Kit or Family Group that groups sku with specific characteristics in adjacent pick positions, (3) FIFO Rotation that has your oldest skus picked first & (4) Random that has your skus assigned to pick positions with no discipline.

SKU HIT CONCENTRATION & DENSITY
IMPROVE PICKER PRODUCTIVITY & INCREASE COMPLETED CUSTOMER ORDER NUMBER

Hit concentration and density is a small item or GOH warehouse factor that groups your 'A' fast moving skus in one pick aisle/zone to improve your picker productivity sku and increase completed CO number. Good hit concentration is a high sku pick number per aisle/zone/pick machine and good hit density is a high sku pieces picked per pick position. With good hit concentration and density, you minimize a picker non-productive travel distance between two picks and within one pick aisle/zone/pick machine, you increase the potential for completed COs.

VALUE SKU PROFILE STRATEGY
IMPROVE SECURITY

Value sku profile strategy assignment to pick position within a specific area/cell by a sku value improves security. With your high value skus in one solid or meshed enclosure and secured area or solid shelves with lockable doors, you have controlled and restricted access to your value sku pick area. To increase security, you have cameras and entrance locks with issued keys/pass cards to listed employees.

HOW TO HANDLE SPECIAL GIFTS & SALES LITERATURE INSERT INTO A CUSTOMER ORDER PACKAGE
 (See Pack Chapter)

SPECIAL, PROMOTIONAL, SEASONAL, CATALOG OR TV SOLD SKU LOCATION ON A PICK LINE
   IMPROVE PICKER PRODUCTIVITY & INCREASE COMPLETED CUSTOMER ORDER NUMBER
Special, promotional, seasonal, catalog or TV sold sku location on a pick is a sku layout strategy with your small item, GOH, or master carton skus that are historical or estimated (based on sale promotion) 'A'/fast moving skus in one pick aisle/zone. When you consolidated 'A'/fast moving skus in one pick aisle/zone, you increase your hit concentration and density to improve your picker productivity and density. If your sku profile/assignment to a pick aisle/zone exceeds your picker productivity, you add a second unique ID WMS computer program pick aisle/line that allows you to profile 'A' fasting moving over two pick lines and your computer program to direct your pickers to pick CO skus from two pick line pick positions.

ABCD OR PARETO'S LAW PROFILE STRATEGY
   IMPROVE PICKER PRODUCTIVITY
ABCD or Pareto's Law profile strategy is a small item or GOH sku profile strategy that has your skus separated into 4 major groups to improve your picker productivity. Your sku classification groups are established by each sku's historical sales or CO wave/work day sales. When sku is profiled or allocated by sales volume classification to 'A' fast moving pick aisle or pick zone within an aisle (group or adjacent pick positions) it creates high hit concentration and density and reduces travel distance and time between 2 picks that improves picker and replenishment employee productivity. When Pareto's law is applied to sku movement, it means that 85% of your sales are generated from 15% of your skus. In recent study results show that 95% of your sales are generated from 5% of your sales. With the sku movement analysis, your skus are separated into 4 groups. Groups are (1) 'A' fast moving skus (special value or promotional) that have high pick number and few sku number with a high inventory. When consolidated into one pick aisle or required pick zones at a pick aisle/line front that do not exceed your budgeted picker productivity, it creates higher picker productivity and increases completed CO number, (2) 'B' medium moving skus that were last week special or promotional skus or frequently purchased skus. Skus are allocated to a pick aisle middle or required pick zones, (3) 'C' slow moving skus that appear on few CO and skus are allocated to a pick aisle rear and (4) 'D' very slow moving or obsolete skus that appear on fewest Cos and skus are allocated to an aisle rear most positions. With your 'B', 'C' & 'D' moving sku consolidation in groups does minimize a picker walk distance & time between 2 picks that improves picker productivity & increases completed CO number.

'D' MOVING SKU HAVE FEW PICKS
    IMPROVE PICKER PRODUCTIVITY & ENHANCE SPACE UTILIZATION
'D' moving or old sku means in any warehouse that there is low CO demand for a sku. When COs have a 'D' moving skus, due to low pick frequency, it lowers your picker productivity and space utilization. A 'D' moving sku is classified as a seasonal sku, a sku that does not appear in a catalog & TV promotion or a sku inventory level does not satisfy your TV sales sku inventory quantity guide. To identify 'D' moving skus, you have your computer program print a sku historical movement report from high volume to low volume that shows each sku inventory level. If a warehouse has in one pick aisle/zone your 'D' moving skus in pick positions mixed with 'A'/fast moving skus in adjacent pick positions, features are (1) low hit concentration and density that means low picker productivity and (2) with a large inventory in a prime pick area means poor space utilization. 'D' moving sku consolidation into one pick aisle with 'D' moving skus in adjacent skus. Features are (1) frees-up prime pick positions for your 'A' moving skus that improves picker productivity, (2) with a few pieces in a short depth & narrow width pick position enhances space utilization or increases pick fronts per bay & (3) with a batch or bulk pick concept, increases 'D' moving sku pick concentration & density.

SET-UP YOUR PICK EQUIPMENT & PICK LINE SKUS FOR YOUR NEXT CUSTOMER ORDER WAVE
IMPROVE PICKER PRODUCTIVITY & INCREASE COMPLETED CUSTOMER ORDER NUMBER

Set-up your pick equipment & pick line skus for your next CO wave is designed to improve your picker productivity and increase your completed CO number. Set-up your pick equipment means that you match your pick position type to your pick volume. If your CO wave has high volume skus, you use pallet flow rack or carton flow rack pick positions with 1 sku per level or 2 skus per level. If your CO wave has medium volume skus, you use carton flow rack position with standard skus per level. If your CO wave has slow moving skus, you use shelf pick positions with 3 skus per level.

PAIRS, CELL, KIT OR FAMILY GROUP PROFILE STRATEGY
IMPROVE PICKER PRODUCTIVITY

Pairs, cell, kit or family group profile strategy is a small item or GOH sku profile strategy that places skus with similar features to one aisle or pick zone adjacent pick positions and is designed to improve picker productivity and completed CO number. From your sales program you identify pairs, cells, kit or family group skus. With the sku information, your sku pick aisle/line profile assigns skus to adjacent pick positions. Good picker productivity and increased completed CO number results from minimal walk distance and time between two picks. Pairs are skus that complement each other such as salt and pepper shakers or battery powered toy and battery. Cell skus are unique skus that are intended for a specific customer group such as a specific language or ethic group. Kit skus are components for one sku that is being manufactured on a production line. Family group skus are sku for one retail store aisle that also minimizes your retail store labor to get a sku onto a retail shelf.

SKU FIFO ROTATION
MINIMIZE SKU DAMAGE

Sku FIFO or first-in first-out sku rotation is used in a small item warehouse that handles a sku with a saleable date on each sku or oldest sku inventory is sold first. If a company has a criteria for good picker productivity and FIFO sku rotation, your options are (1) with a single deep shelf, decked rack or standard rack pick position use a floating pick position concept that has your computer deplete inventory in one pick position (A100) before have pick transactions occur from pick position (B200). Features are less replenishment activities, lower picker productivity due to increased walk distance between two picks, difficult to profile for high pick concentration and density and additional computer program or (2) with a dense/gravity flow pick position concept that has a replenishment employee transfer the oldest sku first into a flow lane and next transfer another sku. At a pick position, the oldest sku is the first available sku at a pick position. Features are additional replenishment activities, higher picker productivity due to minimal walk distance between two picks, easy to profile for high pick concentration and density and standard computer program and cost.

MANUFACTURER LOT NUMBER REGISTRATION
IMPROVE CUSTOMER SATISFICATION

Manufacturer lot number registration is very important in some industries (drugs, appliance & medical) that requires a CO picked sku ID (manufacturer lot number) recorded in your files. If you rely on your picker to register a sku manufacturer lot number and WMS CO ID onto a separate document, you have decrease your picker productivity due to additional time for a picker to locate and write a sku lot number and WMS CO ID number onto a separate document. With a pick into a warehouse ID tote, bulk pick or batched pick & sort concept, it is more efficient and cost effective for a packer to register a sku manufacturer lot number onto a separate document with a CO pack slip/invoice number and a packer has table work surface.

RANDOM SKU ASSIGNMENT OR NO PROFILE STRATEGY
LOW PICKER PRODUCTIVITY

Random sku assignment or no profile strategy to a pick position means that your sku is placed in any pick position. With seasonal, catalog, TV marketing or special promotion skus, the approach has potential to mix 'A'/fast moving skus with 'B' or 'C' medium moving skus. Features are low picker productivity due to low hit concentration and density, increased non-productive walk distances and low completed CO number.

EDIBLE SKU ALLOCATION TO PICK POSITIONS
MINIMIZE SKU DAMAGE
Edible skus allocation to pick positions by some local codes or company policy that require edible skus allocated to separate pick positions from non-edible sku pick positions. With the procedure, you basically assign non-edible skus to separate pick positions.

FLAMMABLE SKU ALLOCATION TO PICK POSITIONS
MINIMIZE SKU DAMAGE
Flammable skus allocation to pick positions by some local codes or company policy that require flammable skus allocated to separate pick positions that are in a solid enclosed area with a drain and any liquid run-off flows to a containment chamber. During a fire, a solid wall minimizes potential sku flow and a drain directs sku flow to a containment chamber. For your pick activity skus are assigned to specific pick zones or a cell pick concept that is designed for flammable skus. With the approach a picker or CO carton/tote sent to the specific pick positions or cell.

85/15 15/85 PICK AREA/LINE PROFILE STRATEGY
IMPROVE PICKER PRODUCTIVITY & INCREASE COMPLETED CUSTOMER ORDER NUMBER
85/15 15/85 refers to Pareto's Law that states 15% of the population has 85% of the wealth. In the warehouse industry, Pareto's Law means that 15% of your skus account for 85% of your COs. When you profile you 15% of skus ('A' fast moving skus) to a Golden Highway, Golden Zone or prime real estate/front pick positions, you have increase your hit concentration and density that improves your pick productivity and increases your completed CO number. When you profile your skus to one pick zone, your picks must equal your pickers budgeted productivity. If your CO picks exceed your picker budgeted productivity, there is potential congestion and pick line down time. To assure picker budgeted productivity, you design two pick section and your WMS computer spreads your pick volume to each pick section and matches your picker budgeted productivity.

SKU PAIRS STRATEGY
IMPROVE PICKER PRODUCTIVITY & INCREASE COMPLETED CUSTOMER ORDER NUMBER
Pairs or two by two is a small item or GOH sku allocation to your pick positions for good sku hit concentration and density that improves your picker productivity and increases your completed CO number. A pair or two by two sku concept has one sku create a sale for another sku. If you profile air skus adjacent to each other, a picker has an increase potential for multiple picks with minimal walk distance that increases picker productivity. Examples are battery powered toy with batteries, slacks with the top and peanut butter and jelly.

GOLDEN HIGHWAY SKU PROFILE STRATEGY
IMPROVE PICKER PRODUCTIVITY & INCREASE COMPLETED CUSTOMER ORDER NUMBER
A Golden Highway is a small item or GOH warehouse profile strategy to assign your 'A'/fast moving skus into one pick aisle/zone to increase your hit concentration and density that improves your picker productivity and increases completed CO number. In a manual, pick/pass, horizontal or automatic pick machine concept you use your historical sales or estimated sales to identify your candidate skus. With your sku movement data, you separate skus into A,B,C & D groups. In most companies, an 'A' moving sku is a promotional sku and 'B' moving sku is a sku with repeat COs. Your Golden Highway options are to allocate (1) all 'A' moving skus to one pick aisle, pick zone, horizontal carousel or automatic pick machine and (2) if your 'A' moving skus do not fill your pick position, you allocate your top moving 'B' moving skus to vacate pick positions. If your profiled Golden Highway sku picks exceed your budgeted picker productivity, in your warehouse and in your WMS computer you create a second Golden Highway pick section that spreads your sku picks to match your budgeted picker productivity.

GOLDEN ZONE SKU PROFILE STRATEGY
IMPROVE PICKER PRODUCTIVITY & INCREASE COMPLETED CUSTOMER ORDER NUMBER
A Golden Zone is a small item or GOH pick position strategy for sku profile to pick positions above a floor that improves picker productivity and increases completed CO number. For most manual pickers, a Golden Zone is between a picker's knees and shoulders. With pick position elevations above a floor surface, a picker physical

requirement (effort & time) to complete a pick transaction is minimal. With a standard high pick position shelf, 4 pick position carton flow rack or 5 basket level high horizontal carousel pick concept, your Golden Zone pick positions are levels 2, 3 & 4. With a 5 level shelf or horizontal carousel pick concept, your Golden Zone pick positions are levels 2, 3 & 4. With a 4 level carton flow rack, your Golden Zone pick positions levels are 2 & 3. With a 3 level decked standard pallet rack with access to both sides pick concept, your Golden Zone pick positions are levels 2 & 3. With a 2 level standard pallet rack pick concept, after partial pallet depletion both levels are not considered a Golden Zone. With a 1 level standard pallet rack pick concept, it is considered a Golden Zone. With a standard 1 long GOH rail and 1 short GOH rail, a long GOH is nearest to the floor and is the Golden Zone. With a standard 3 level short GOH rails, a levels 1 & 2 & are the Golden Zone.

PRIME REAL ESTATE OR PICK POSITIONS
IMPROVE PICKER PRODUCTIVITY & INCREASE COMPLETED CUSTOMER ORDER NUMBER
Prime real estate is a warehouse pick position strategy that focuses on your pick positions that are nearest your pack or sort area that are considered prime real estate & the most distance pick positions are low real estate. When you allocate your 'A'/fast moving skus to prime real estate positions and you consider that 85% of your COs are completed from 15% of your skus, it improves your picker productivity & increases your completed CO number due to a short non-productive distance between 2 pick positions & short travel distance from pick area to pack/sort area.

PICK AREA PICK POSITION ROWS AND AISLES HAVE A PARALLEL OR PERPENDICULAR LAYOUT
IMPROVE PICKER PRODUCTIVITY & REDUCE DAMAGE
Pick area pick position rows and aisles with a parallel or perpendicular layout are small item or GOH pick area layout options that have completed COs flow from a pick area to a pack area to improve picker productivity. Your selected pick position row and aisle layout is determined by your facility shape/sq. ft. area, sku pick position number and pick concept. A parallel pick position row and aisle layout has turning aisles at both row and aisle ends that face a wall. With a parallel pick position row and aisle layout, a picker with a full pick cart/trolley has additional travel time and walk distance to move from a pick aisle to a pack area. Feature is lower picker productivity due to increased walk distance and time. A perpendicular pick position row and aisles layout has turning aisles at both row and aisle ends. One turning aisle is adjacent to your pack station area. A picker with a full pick cart/trolley has minimal travel time and walk distance to move from a pick aisle to your pack station area. Feature is higher picker productivity due to decreased walk distance and time.

IN A PICK AREA HAVE A CROSS AISLE
IMPROVE PICKER PRODUCTIVITY
In a pick area a cross aisle is a manual small item or GOH pick area design to improve your picker productivity and increase your completed CO number. If we consider Pareto's law applies to most warehouses that has 80% of your picks are from 20% of your skus/'A' moving skus, after an 'A' fast moving sku pick section, you have few picks and there is a great walk distance between picks. With a long pick aisle that has your 'A' fast moving skus in a front pick section and 'B', 'C' & 'D' medium to slow moving skus in your rear pick section and for your pick aisle a progressive/arithmetic picker routing pattern, there is a need for a cross aisle that permits an employee with no picks in the present or adjacent aisles' 'B', 'C' & 'D' section to transfer from one pick aisle to another pick aisle without walking/traveling to an aisle end. The arrangement allows a picker to complete all picks from both aisles' 'A' fast moving section with the shortest travel distance. For maximum picker travel efficiency and minimal aisle congestion, your pick and cross aisle widths allows two vehicles per aisle.

DECK YOUR BOTTOM HAND STACKED/DECKED STANDARD PALLET RACK LEVEL
IMPROVE PICKER PRODUCTIVITY & ENHANCE SPACE UTILIZATION
Deck your bottom hand stacked/decked standard pallet rack level has your bottom (floor) level skus hand stacked onto a deck instead of 2 pallets. A deck is a solid wood, harden plastic or metal member with 1 or 2 in high bottom full depth runners evenly spaced to assure minimal deck bow. When compared to hand stack on 2 pallets, a deck concept increases vertical open space by a nominal 4 ins and allows a rack bay entire area used for skus that

increases usable space by 8 to 12 ins or 1 standard master carton width. Deck & runner cost is equal to 2 pallets cost.

PICK POSITION CELL
IMPROVE PICKER PRODUCTIVITY & INCREASES COMPLETED CUSTOMER ORDER NUMBER

Pick cell is a small item warehouse pick area configuration with pre-determined sku (language, preferred customer gift, nationality) that increases sku hit concentration and density to improve picker productivity and increase completed CO number. A pick cell is a pick positions that are adjacent to each other and have skus WMS scanned in pick positions for specific CO characteristics such as language, retail store aisle. special catalog or special customers. When a CO has a pick for one sku in a pick cell and with a family sku group in a pick cell a CO has a high potential for other skus to appear on a CO in a pick cell pick position that reduces a picker walk distance and time between 2 picks. Pick cells designs are (1) selected pick aisle or zone, (2) selected carousel, (3) selected automatic pick machine and (4) with a pick/pass concept, options are specific (a) shelves parallel to a pick conveyor, (b) shelves perpendicular to a pick conveyor with open aisle end and (c) shelves perpendicular to pick conveyor with mobile shelf at aisle end.

STOP THE PRESSURIZED SKU TRAVEL (MISSILES)
MINIMIZE SKU DAMAGE

Stop the pressurized sku travel (missiles) is a term that has your skus in pressurized cans stored in special pick position. Local codes or company policy require pressurized skus allocated to separate pick positions that are enclosed in meshed or solid enclosed pick positions. If a pressurized vessel or can 'fails" or during a fire, a solid or meshed enclosure minimizes potential sku (propelled or air borne) movement. For your pick activity skus are assigned to specific pick zones or a cell pick concept. With this approach a picker or CO carton/tote sent to the specific pick positions or cell.

YOUR PICKER OR REPLENISHMENT HEAD HEIGHT IS YOUR PICK POSITION MAXIMUM HEIGHT
IMPROVE PICKER PRODUCTIVITY

Head high is a manual or mechanized small item or GOH pick position maximum elevation above your floor to assure good picker productivity. Head high is an elevation with no employee restriction or difficulty to transfer a sku from a shelf, decked rack, standard pallet rack, GOH rail or horizontal carousel basket pick position into a CO container/cart rail/vehicle carrying surface. Above a head high, a picker productivity is lower due to increased picker physical effort to reach a sku pick position or obtain a device to elevate a picker. If 'C' or 'D' moving skus are allocate to above head high pick positions, means less potential for lower picker productivity due to few picks.

YOUR LOWEST OR PIGEON HOLE LOWER PICKER PRODUCTIVITY
IMPROVE PICKER PRODUCTIVITY

No squats or pigeon hole pick positions is not good in a manual small item pick position location. A pigeon hole is lowest pick level (3 in) above the floor that lowers picker productivity. To access a sku from a pigeon hole pick position, a picker squats or bends that is difficult to transfer a sku from a pick position into a CO container or vehicle carrying surface. A picker time and physical effort to complete a pick transaction creates lower picker productivity. If 'C' or 'D' moving skus are allocate to above head high pick positions, there is less potential to lower picker productivity due to few picks.

INCREASE TRAVEL DISTANCE DECREASES YOUR PICKER PRODUCTIVITY
IMPROVE PICKER PRODUCTIVITY & INCREASE COMPLETED CUSTOMER ORDER NUMBER

Travel distance is an important pick concept factor that impacts your picker productivity. With a manual push cart pick concept, your travel distance factors are walk distance and time (1) between two pick positions and (2) between your pick area and pack/sort area. With a multiple horizontal carousel pick concept your travel distance/time is the time that is required to rotate a basket to your pick station. To improve your manual picker, you minimize a manual picker non-productivity walk distance and time or horizontal basket rotation time. To minimize the distance between two pick positions or horizontal basket rotation time, you consider an 'ABCD' sku moving profile strategy that consolidates 'A'/fast moving skus with 'B'/medium moving skus in few pick aisles/zones, one horizontal carousel or prime real estate that completes 85% of your COs and 'C' & 'D' moving skus in your other pick aisles/zone, a second horizontal carousel or low value real estate that completes 15% of your COs. Features are to increase hit concentration & density that improves your picker productivity. With a manual pick concept to minimize your picker travel distance/time & physical effort, after a picker receives pick instructions you start your picker first pick position most distant from your pack/sort area. Features are (1) to start a picker pushes an empty pick vehicle to the first pick position that requires minimal employee physical effort, (2) picker routing pattern directs a picker toward your pack/sort area that reduces complete CO or full cart travel distance from a pick area to a pack/sort area & (3) with a completed CO or full cart travel distance to pack/sort area is short but requires a picker physical effort to push a cart.

MANUAL PICK SMALL ITEMS
  IMPROVE PICKER PRODUCTIVITY & INCREASE COMPLETED CUSTOMER ORDER NUMBER
Manual pick small items has your picker push a 4-wheel cart through storage/pick aisles. Manual pick small items requires an employee to have a printed document or RF device that shows a picker each CO sku. Each pick document shows pick position, pick quantity and sku description. A manual pick concept is used to pick single COs, bulk or 'en masse' picked skus for later sort and bulk pick and sort skus. Features are (1) easy to implement, (2) used with various pick concepts and (3) low equipment cost.

WHAT ARE YOUR PICK INSTRUCTION COMPONENTS
  IMPROVE PICKER PRODUCTIVITY
What are your pick instruction components is your pick instruction format that is used to direct an employee or pick machine for sku transfer from a pick position into a picker hands, container or onto a conveyor belt. A clear and understandable pick instruction assures good picker productivity and accurate picks. Your pick instruction components identifies your pick aisle, in an aisle a shelf/rack bay, in a shelf/rack bay a level and on a shelf/bay level a pick position. With an employee picker concept your options are (1) alpha characters, (2) digits or (3) combination of both. Alpha characters and digits combination option features are unlimited pick position identifications, easy to print, easy to read due to an employee deals with numbers in their everyday life, easy to have an arithmetic progression and matches most picker routing patterns. Most computer controlled/automatic pick machines use a numeric pick instruction.

PAPER OR PAPERLESS PICK INSTRUCTION
  IMPROVE PICKER PRODUCTIVITY & MINIMIZE ERRORS
Paper or paperless pick instruction are a warehouse options to direct a picker to a pick position and complete a pick transaction to assure your picker productivity and minimize errors. A paper pick instruction options are (1) paper document that requires your computer program to print a document and your picker to read. A paper document preferred print sequence has pick position first, pick quantity second, sku description and other company information. Features are a picker carries a pick document, print has clear and large as possible printed digits & characters, associated print paper/ink expenses and requires a printer and (2) paper labels that are used in a pick, transport and sort CO concept with one label equals one pick transaction. On each label is printed a sku pick position, human/machine readable CO ID, sku description and other company information. When compared to a paper document, labels are printed in pick position sequence as a roll or paper sheets that are difficult to handle, minimal reading requirement and for sort activity requires human/machine readable CO ID. A paper-less pick instruction options are (1) a display screen (pick to light) above or below a pick position or finger, wrist or hand held RF device with a display that has an employee read a CO sku pick quantity. With a paper-less instruction and pick concepts an employee walks to a pick position, transfers a sku from a pick position to a CO container and presses a pick to light button, breaks a laser beam or presses a RF device button to register a pick transaction completion. Features are increase picker productivity and accuracy and high cost or (2) computer controlled message to activate a mechanical device to release a small item or GOH for a CO pick transaction. After a pick transaction completion, a small item or GOH pick machine release device computer sends a message to WMS computer that register a completed pick transaction. A picked sku is transferred into a carton/tote or loose onto a conveyor for travel to a pack station. Features are increased picker productivity, with outbound queue works on a 24 X 7 schedule, requires a conveyor in-feed and out-feed concept and highest cost.

PAPER PICK (See Pick Instruction Paper or Paperless)

PICK TO LIGHT OR SORT TO LIGHT (See Pick Instruction Paper or Paperless & Pick By Light)

PICK BY LIGHT OPTIONS
IMPROVE PICKER PRODUCTIVITY & LOWER COST

Pick by light options are standard shelf and carton flow rack pick to light placed onto pick position to improve picker productivity and lower cost. A pick by light concept has (1) horizontal pick pattern in a shelf or carton flow rack bay that starts at each bay upper right pick position, across a horizontal level and to a next lower level right most position and (2) computer activated pick position display screen that shows a sku customer order quantity. With a standard shelf design, your design options are (1) shelf rows are perpendicular to pick conveyor. Your options are (1) a bay lamp at each shelf row end to indicate a pick transaction in a shelf row & a second bay light indicator on a shelf post for each level to show a pick transaction on a shelf level, (b) a bay lamp at each shelf row end to indicate a pick transaction each shelf bay has a light indicator and each shelf level pick position has a light to show a pick transaction and (c) a bay lamp at each shelf row end to indicate a pick transaction in a shelf row each shelf level pick position has a human readable pick position identification and after a picker removes a pick document from a customer order container, a sku pick position is matched to a paper pick document. After a pick transaction, a paper pick document is returned to a customer order carton/tote and (2) shelf row is parallel to pick conveyor that has a bay lamp and each pick position with a pick light. Carton flow rack pick to light options are for (1) high volume & large size sku has 1 sku per carton flow rack level. Your options are to have one pick position with one pick light or to have 4 pick positions with 4 pick lights and your cover three pick lights and three associated replenishment IDs, (2) high volume & medium size sku has 1 or 2 skus per carton flow rack level. Your options are to have 2 pick positions with 2 pick lights or to have 4 pick positions with 4 pick lights and your cover two pick lights and two associated replenishment IDs, & (3) medium & small size sku has 3 to 7 skus per carton flow rack level and each pick position has a pick light and associated replenishment IDs.

CARTON FLOW RACK BAY PICK TO LIGHT DISPLAYS
IMPROVE PICKER PRODUCTIVITY & MINIMIZE DAMAGE

Carton flow rack bay pick to light displays are attached to each carton flow rack level and improve picker productivity due to a picker quickly and easily reads a pick position display and minimize damage. Each carton flow rack level has a 'C' Channel on each pick level that holds & protects pick to light display from damage & shows pick position   number & sku quantity & permits display directed to a picker with (1) top pick level angled downward, (2) middle levels face outward & (3) lower level directed upward.

CARTON FLOW RACK BAY
IMPROVE PICKER PRODUCTIVITY & MINIMIZE SKU DAMAGE

Carton flow rack bay has an impacts on your picker productivity and minimizes sku damage. Your carton flow rack bay options are (1) titled front end is excellent for pick loose skus from opened master cartons/totes and for good picker productivity slant & tilt back front flow racks are preferred, (2) slanted front is excellent for pick loose skus from master cartons/totes & (3) straight preferred for full master carton picking.

CARTON FLOW RACK FRONT END
IMPROVE PICKER PRODUCTIVITY & MINIMIZE SKU DAMAGE

Carton flow rack front end assures that a carton is properly presented to a picker that improves picker productivity and minimizes sku damage. Your carton flow rack end options are (1) solid sheet metal that minimize sku damage or (2) short strand conveyors with open space between conveyor lanes that increase potential for sku damage.

YOUR PRINTER CAPACITY
IMPROVE PICKER PRODUCTIVITY & CUSTOMER ORDER CONTROL

Printer capacity is a warehouse computer controlled printer ability to print a CO wave/work day pick/pack/ship documents. A computer controlled printer ability (memory and capacity) to print your CO wave line numbers assures on-time CO pick instructions on your pick floor and pack slips/invoices with delivery labels at your pack stations. If a printer capacity cannot handle a memory or print requirement, there is potential for printer problem, late start-up, low employee productivity and poor customer service. Possible solutions are additional printers, new printer or earlier print time that could be difficult due to a time critical factor between a host computer final process time and COs available for print and your operation required start-up time.

PICK LABELS AS A ROLL OR SHEETS IN A DISPENSER
IMPROVE PICKER PRODUCTIVITY & MINIMIZE DAMAGE LABELS & LOST LABELS

Pick labels as a roll or sheets in a dispenser are used in a batched pick concept that is designed to increase picker productivity to off-set your sort labor expense and increase your completed CO number. All pick labels are printed in pick position sequence to assure minimal picker walk distance. A label fits onto a sku and a label adhesive secures a label onto a sku. During a batch pick activity that uses a CO ID as a sort instruction, each sku receives a label. With labels as a roll or sheets, during a pick activity there is potential for labels to become lost, misplaced, damaged or out-of-sequence and to re-group creates picker non-productive time. To assure good picker productivity and minimize potential label problems, a label roll is placed into a dispenser or label sheets are placed into pouch. The devices are attached to a picker belt and assure that labels are readily available to a picker. To assure a clean pick area, a picker has a trash pouch for a label self- adhesive back.

PAPER PICK DOCUMENT HAVE FAST SKUS AT A PAGE TOP
IMPROVE PICKER PRODUCTIVITY & INCREASE COMPLETED CUSTOMER ORDER NUMBER

Paper pick document fast skus at a page top has your 'A' moving sku assignment to pick positions that are first in your pick area/routing pattern. The arrangement has your printer print your CO 'A' moving skus as first picks on a paper document. Features are improves your picker productivity and accuracy due to minimal reading requirement, easy reading at a page top and increases your completed CO number.

PAPER PICK DOCUMENT SKU NUMBER
IMPROVE PICKER PRODUCTIVITY & INCREASE COMPLETED CUSTOMER ORDER NUMBER

Paper pick document sku number is the sku number that is printed each picker page. The sku number determination factors are (1) printer ability, (2) page length, (3) skus required to cube a ship carton and (4) print size. To assure picker productivity, your print lines per page are usually 15 to 20 and most catalog COs have 1 to 5 skus/lines. Features are easily read and handled by an employee

PICK LABEL HOLDER
IMPROVE PICKER PRODUCTIVITY & MINIMZE DAMAGED/LOST LABELS

Pick label holder is used in any warehouse that applies a label to a picked sku that improves picker productivity and minimizes damaged/lost labels. In any pick concept, a label stack or label sheets are difficult to handle as a picker or a pick line start employee. To complete a label pick activity, a picker arrives at a pick position, sets a label stack in one hand, removes a label, removes a self-adhesive back and places a label onto a sku, transfers a labeled sku into a tote or onto a conveyor and a backing that is placed into a trash holder. Most situations, a picker sets a label stack in a pick position that provides two hands to complete a pick activity. Features are potential for labels to fall and become out-of-pick sequence or become damaged/lost that creates non-productive picker time. For a label roll, a label holder is attached to a picker belt and as a picker removes a label from a holder a label self adhesive back is removed and a picker has two hands to complete a pick transaction. If you have a pick/pass concept with a disposal CO label on a CO carton, at your pick line start station an employee adds a CO ID label to a pick/ship carton. If your pick/pass computer CO sequence is the same as your printed label sequence, at your pick line start station you assure that your CO labels maintain the same sequence. With a high volume pick line and labels in a stack, there is potential for a label stack to fall that creates pick line down time. With a label holder, labels out-of-sequence problem is minimized.

PRE-LABEL SKUS
IMPROVE PICKER PRODUCTIVITY & ENHANCE INVENTORY CONTROL

Pre-labeled or non-labeled sku are a small item or GOH (vendor ready to ship) warehouse sku ID that increases your picker/sorter/customer returns process employee productivity & enhances inventory control. It is clearly understood for good sku inventory control that each sku requires a discreet WMS ID that is attached to a sku by your vendor, your receiving department or picker. With a pick & sort concept, a pre-labeled sku inventory ID serves as part of your sort instruction. In a small item or GOH batched pick, transport, sort & final sort concept, each sku requires a CO ID that is applied by a picker. Feature is additional print time and label/ink expense but handles a large volume.

KISS IT PICK INSTRUCTION
IMPROVE PICKER PRODUCTIVITY

Kiss it pick instruction is a term to describe a picker transaction instruction. To assure good picker productivity, your pick transaction instruction approach is to keep it simple that decreases your picker non-productive time.

LARGE OR SMALL PICK POSITION IDENTIFICATION HUMAN & MACHINE READABLE SYMBOLOGIES
IMPROVE PICKER PRODUCTIVITY

Large or small pick position ID human readable symbology or machine readable symbology are a small item, GOH manual, mechanized or automatic pick machine replenishment pick concept pick position ID options. To complete a pick transaction, a pick position ID allows a picker to read and identify a pick position. A pick position ID has human (alpha characters and digits) or human/machine readable (bar code) symbologies that are considered part of a picker CO pick instruction. To complete a human pick transaction, from an aisle or pick station an employee reads pick position ID that is attached to a shelf, decked rack, standard pallet rack, carousel basket or carton flow rack member. To read or scan a small human/machine readable pick position ID, a picker walks from an aisle middle next to a pick position that creates non-productive time. To read or scan a large human/machine readable pick position ID, a picker remains in an aisle middle that minimizes non-productive time. Your pick position ID size is determined by your pick position member dimension and your pick position ID label/light.

ON A PICK BAY WHERE IS EACH PICK POSITION IDENTIFICATION LOCATION
IMPROVE PICKER PRODUCTIVITY

On a pick bay where is each pick position ID is used to identify a pick position and is a factor that affects your picker productivity by reducing a picker non-productive time to have line of sight and read a pick position ID. In a decked standard pallet rack concept, as you face a decked pallet rack bay a pick position ID is located for each pick position in a decked rack bay and is under each pick position. If there are two pick position IDs on one load beam, a top ID refers to the above pick position and lower ID refers to the below pick position. In a GOH static rail concept, as you walk in an aisle and face a GOH rail, a moveable (slides or employee moved clip) pick position ID is on a rail in front of a GOH. In a small item shelf pick concept with 3 to 10 shelves. Carton flow racks with 4 to 5 levels high or a horizontal carousel basket, as you face a pick bay, pick position IDs are attached to a shelf/flow lane end member/basket and are located directly below a pick position. With shelf. flow rack and carousel basket concepts to improve line of sight your options are (1) bottom shelf, flow rack lane or basket ID upward and for protection is enclosed in a harden plastic/metal low profile 'C' member and (2) top two flow rack levels are angled downward. With a pegboard or drawer pick concept, pick position ID locations are same as a shelf pick position ID features.

YOUR PICK/SHIP CARTON WMS CUSTOMER ORDER IDENTIFICATION LOCATION
IMPROVE PICKER PRODUCTIVITY, NO TOTE COST & MINIMIZE ERRORS

Your pick/ship carton WMS CO ID location is used in a small item pick/pass, pick/sort or automatic pick machine warehouse to assure a picker or automatic pick machine bar code scanner has CO ID line of sight. Feature is to improve picker productivity, no tote cost and minimize errors. After an employee or machine applies a WMS CO ID to pick/ship carton/tote, it enters your pick area and travels through your pick/sort area. On a pick/pass line or on your automatic pick machine conveyor travel path it is considered a CO container. A pick/ship carton/tote WMS CO ID and location is consider part of your picker or automatic pick machine instruction component that allows a picker to match a pick/ship CO ID with a paper document printed CO ID, CO ID on a zone display light or causes a message sent to your automatic pick machine computer to have a sku released for a CO. A basic pick/ship WMS CO ID rule is in a pick area that a pick/ship CO ID faces a picker or automatic pick machine bar code scanner. Each pick/ship has one CO ID location. A WMS CO ID objectives are (1) in your pick activity to have clear employee and bar code scanner line of sight, (2) in your CO seal activity, have tape strands applied to a carton top that do not reduce a CO ID readability and (3) by your freight delivery company as your CO package delivery label. With a pick/sort concept, in a pick/sort position a pick/ship carton CO ID is on a carton side or flap that faces a picker. With an automatic pick machine concept, on an automatic pick machine conveyor travel path a CO ID is on a carton side that faces a bar code scanner. In a pick/pass concept, on a pick conveyor travel path a pick/ship carton a CO ID is on a carton side or flap that faces a picker. It is noted a pick/ship carton WMS CO ID is a disposal ID that is used by your freight company for CO package address. At a CO picked sku pack station or machine tape station, your employee or machine applies tape to secure a carton top flaps and tape strands do not reduce a CO ID readability. After a complete CO package, a pick/ship carton WMS CO ID is manifest scanned (scan message sent to your WMS computer) and is sent from your warehouse to a CO package delivery address. This means that a pick/ship carton WMS CO ID is not reused in your warehouse and does not require a zero scan transaction.

YOUR CUSTOMER ORDER CAPTIVE TOTE WAREHOUSE IDENTIFICATION LOCATIONS
    IMPROVE PICKER PRODUCTIVITY & MINIMIZE ERRORS
Your captive tote warehouse IDs is a small item pick/pass warehouse with a pick to light or automatic pick machine to have a captive pick tote warehouse ID in multiple locations that are quickly and easily reader by your pickers or bar code scanners. Feature improves picker productivity and minimizes errors. At your pick line or automatic pick machine entry, an employee or mechanical scanner attaches a WMS CO ID to your captive (warehouse) ID. After your pick computer relates a captive tote warehouse ID to a WMS CO ID, a warehouse ID tote travels through your pick/pass line or on your automatic pick machine conveyor travel path it is considered a CO container. A captive pick tote warehouse ID and location is consider part of your picker or automatic pick machine instruction component that allows a picker to match a captive tote warehouse ID to a CO ID on a zone light or causes a message sent to your automatic pick machine computer to have a sku released for a CO. A basic captive tote warehouse ID rule is in a pick area that a captive tote warehouse ID faces a picker or automatic pick machine bar code scanner. To have maximum tote flexibility and readability, a tote warehouse ID is preferred on all 4 tote exterior and 2 interior sides. Each tote warehouse ID location has clear employee and bar code scanner line of sight. With a pick/pass concept, a captive tote warehouse IDs are located at the highest possible location on a tote 4 exterior sides and on a rectangle shaped tote long 2 interior sides. On a pick/pass conveyor, warehouse ID locations assure picker line of sight as a tote moves on a conveyor travel path and when a picker is directly in front of a tote, an interior warehouse ID is easily read. It is noted a captive tote warehouse ID is a permanent ID that is related to a WMS CO ID. At a CO pack station or transfer station, your employee or bar code scanner zero scans a captive tote warehouse ID. A zero scan transaction is sent to your WMS computer that breaks the relationship between a captive tote warehouse (permanent) ID and WMS CO ID and allows a captive tote warehouse (permanent) ID used for another WMS CO ID.

ONE CUSTOMER ORDER OR MULTIPLE CUSTOMER ORDERS PER PICK TOTE (See Pack Chapter)

YOUR PICK VEHICLE MATCHES YOUR PICK CONCEPT
    IMPROVE PICKER PRODUCTIVITY & INCREASE COMPLETED CUSTOMER ORDER NUMBER
Your pick vehicle matches your pick concept assures good picker productivity. A good pick vehicle characteristics are (1) load carrying surface permits picked sku transfer, (2) carries maximum picked sku and CO number, (3) assures skus are retained on the carrying surface, (4) wheel/caster and vehicle permits unobstructed one or two-way vehicle travel in an aisle and accurate steering and (5) allows picked sku transfer onto a pack table.

PICK CART SIDE & REAR NETS
IMPROVE PICKER PRODUCTIVITY & REDUCE SKU DAMAGE
Cart side and rear nets are used in a manual small item bulk or pick/sort pick concept that improves picker productivity, reduces sku damage and increases a cart carrying capacity. With an open shelf cart and a loose sku pick concept, as a cart is pushed through pick aisle with loose skus on a shelf, there is potential for skus to fall from a cart shelf onto the floor. Feature has a picker to have a tendency not transfer a large sku quantity onto a cart. After a plastic or fabric netting is secured to a cart sides and rear, it creates a sku barrier and allows a picker to see and utilize an entire cart shelf.

CART CASTERS/WHEELS TYPES
IMPROVE PICKER PRODUCTIVITY & REDUCE EQUIPMENT DAMAGE
Cart casters/wheels are an important cart design factor for a small item or GOH manual push cart pick concept that improves picker productivity and reduces equipment damage. The preferred casters/wheels arrangement is swivel in the front and fixed in the rear that improves picker guiding a cart in a straight line and is easy to push a cart through a turn. Other caster/wheel options are difficult to guide and steer and include (1) all swivel casters/wheels with an exception of a 'Z' bottom frame GOH cart that is used to couple two carts together, (2) swivel casters/wheels in rear and fixed casters/wheels in the front and (3) fixed casters/wheels on a cart one side and swivel casters/wheels on a cart other side.

PUSH CART SWIVEL CASTERS/WHEESL IN A CART FRONT & FIXED IN THE REAR
IMPROVE PICKER PRODUCTIVITY & MINIMAL DAMAGE
Push cart swivel casters/wheels in a cart front and fixed in the rear are a small item or GOH pick cart caster/wheel arrangement that improves picker productivity and assures minimal damage. A cart swivel caster/wheel arrangement with cart push handles make it easier for an employee to steer and turn a cart through pick aisles, travel straight sections and curves. When compared to other cart caster/wheel arrangements, swivel casters/wheels in a cart front and fixed in the rear requires less employee effort to turn a cart.

PUSH CART WITH ALL SWIVEL CASTERS/WHEELS
IMPROVE PICKER PRODUCTIVITY & REDUCE DAMAGE
Push cart with all swivel casters/wheels are a cart casters/wheels arrangement on a pick carton that creates a cart steering problems with lower picker productivity and potential damage. A cart with all swivel casters/wheels an employee easily parks a cart adjacent to a work station but it is difficult to steer cart a straight through an aisle or curve. An all swivel casters/wheels cart is not preferred for a small item pick cart.

SHOPPING CART AS AN EMPLOYEE PICK CART
IMPROVE PICKER PRODUCTIVITY & REDUCE DAMAGE
Shopping cart as an employee pick cart means that a shopping cart is used in your small item warehouse. A retail shopping cart with a deep cavity and meshed side walls and bottom lowers picker productivity and potential sku damage and is not preferred in a pick activity. Many operations use a shopping cart due to employees are familiar with a shopping cart, swivel casters/wheels in the front and it is easily pushed through a pick aisle straight sections and curves. Features are low cost, low picker productivity due to a deep cavity requires a picker to bend/reach to complete a sku transfer, potential for skus to become hung-up on mesh openings and low carrying capacity.

MULTI-SHELF PICK CART
IMPROVE PICKER PRODUCTIVITY, PERMITS PICK AND SORT ACTIVITY & MINIMAL DAMAGE
Multi-shelf pick cart is a small item warehouse cart that is used as a pick vehicle in a manual pick & sort or bulk pick concept. A multi-shelf cart improves picker productivity due to increased carrying capacity or sort locations and reduced pick trips. A multi-shelf cart has 4 to 5 shelf levels that permits sku transfer, each level retains skus on a shelf (shelf lip faces upward or meshed plastic barrier that is secured Velcro and push/steer handles) and allows 3 pick & sort locations per shelf level. Features are when not being used empty carts require a storage area. With one cart per aisle, an aisle width that is 6 ins wider than a cart width or two vehicles per aisle, an aisle width includes two carts and 18 ins for clearance.

CART PICK FRONT FACES A PICKER
IMPROVE PICKER PRODUCTIVITY

Cart pick front faces a picker is a small item pick cart design that increases a picker productivity and decreases aisle congestion. A pick cart front is a multi-level shelf cart with 4 wheels and 2 push handles/bar. As a cart with this design is pushed through a pick aisle, a picker is at a cart end. At a pick position, a picker remains at a cart end and is a simple activity for sku transfer from a pick position to a cart shelf. With limited cart width and multiple pickers per aisle, there is minimized aisle congestion. With a 36 in wide and 36 in long carrying surface, for a pick/sort activity there are few CO pick/sort locations but for a bulk pick, sort and final pick activity there is ample space for picked skus. With a pick/sort activity with multiple CO sort locations on a cart, a picker pushes a cart from the rear and from a cart side a picker completes a pick/sort activity.

PICK VEHICLE AISLE GUIDANCE
IMPROVE PICKER PRODUCTIVITY & MINIMIZE EQUIPMENT DAMAGE

Pick vehicle aisle guidance is used in a warehouse with a man-up powered vehicle that allows skus picked from very high pick positions and assures good employee productivity, space utilization and minimize damage. A man-up pick vehicle travels vertically and horizontally in an aisle between 2 shelf/rack rows. Aisle guidance matches your vehicle guidance concept and allows a picker/vehicle to travel at fast speeds with minimal employee effort. Aisle guidance starts at an aisle entrance and stops at an aisle end. Most aisle guidance concepts have entry guides that are harden metal members anchored to the floor and assist employee's vehicle aisle entrance and aisle end slow down/stop devices assure minimal accidents. Aisle guidance options are (1) rail guidance that are (a) single rail on the floor, (b) single rail on rack posts, (c) double rail on the floor, (d) double rail on an elevated floor and (e) double rail on rack posts & (2) electronic guidance that includes (a) wire, (b) magnetic tape, (c) magnetic paint and (d) laser.

PICK INTO YOUR MAN-UP HROS/VNA VEHICLE PICK CART OR CAGE
IMPROVE PICKER PRODUCTIVITY & MINIMIZE SKU DAMAGE

Pick into your man-up high rise order system (HROS picker)/very narrow aisle (VNA) truck pick cart and pack cage are small item or GOH warehouse device that improves employee productivity and minimize sku damage. With a HROS or VNA vehicle a picker and picked sku carrying device vertically and horizontally travels in an aisle to a pick position. At a pick position, a picker transfers a sku from a pick position on a cart shelf/tote or in a cage. A pick cage has a solid three wall pick device with fork openings and open side that faces a picker. After a shelf device is set onto a pallet and a pallet center stringer is secured by a vehicle claw and picked skus are placed onto a shelf level. During vehicle travel, a pick cage side walls restricts shelf and skus falling from a pallet. When picking GOH a hand bar is secured to a pick cage side walls. A pick cart has two long fork sleeves that permit a HROS or VNA vehicle forks to enter and secure a cart to a vehicle with a chain and lock that is used to hold a cart post to a vehicle. You pick skus into totes and mesh netting is placed on a cart two side walls and back side to retain totes on a cart surface that assures sku carrying capacity and minimize skus falling to the floor.

AT AN AISLE END SLOW DOWN YOUR HROS OR VNA TRAVEL
IMPROVE PICKER PRODUCTIVITY & MINIMIZE EQUIPMENT DAMAGE

At an aisle end slow down your HROS (high rise order system/truck) or VNA (very narrow aisle) vehicle travel is used for a man-up vertical and horizontal travel vehicle to improve employee productivity and minimize equipment damage. When a vehicle travels in a guided aisle between 2 tall shelf/rack pick position rows, your vehicle operator is facing an aisle entrance and not facing an aisle end. During travel to an aisle last pick position an operator has an order picker routing pattern help to determine an aisle location and to calculate the last pick position in a routing pattern. Slow down device is designed to have a vehicle leave a pick aisle and at a slow travel speed enter a main traffic aisle. Slow down devices are (1) manual that are (a) shelf/rack position posts/shelves/load beam painted a different color & (b) anchored barrier across an end aisle & (2) electric magnetic on a vehicle and in the floor.

LIGHT FIXTURE LOCATION IN A PICK AISLE
IMPROVE PICKER PRODUCTIVITY & PROPER ENERGY USAGE

Lights fixture location in your pick aisle is reference to where are your small item or GOH pick aisle light fixtures hung and to meet local code lighting. Most codes require X lumen number for 30 ins above the floor surface. Properly hung light fixtures in an aisle with proper lighting level improves picker productivity and accuracy. A paper document or label pick concept with a forklift truck activity, aisle light fixtures are chain hung from a ceiling in an aisle middle. With non-forklift truck activity or GOH aisle, light fixtures are chain hung from a ceiling or shelf/rack structural members to provide sufficient light to read a pick instruction. With a small item or GOH pick to light concept, light fixtures are hung from a chain or shelf/rack structural members and are at a minimum level due to your picker instruction is displayed on a lighted screen.

CLEAR PICK AISLES
IMPROVE PICKER PRODUCTIVITY & MINIMIZE EQUIPMENT/SKU DAMAGE

Clear pick aisles is a warehouse pick aisle situation that has no obstructions in a pick aisle between two pick rows and assures good picker productivity and minimizes equipment/sku damage. No obstructions in a pick aisle means there is no trash, empty carton/tote or debris that causes a picker or truck to stop travel or non-productive picker time to remove an obstruction from an aisle.

DO NOT LITER IN A PICK OR REPLENISHMENT AISLE
IMPROVE PICKER PRODUCTIVITY & IMPROVE SAFETY

Do not liter in a pick or replenishment aisle has a picker or replenishment employee transfer an empty master carton or filler material into a trash container or trash conveyor travel path to assure clear aisles that improves picker productivity and safety. To assure maximum picker productivity, a sku in a pick position has minimal residual liter. With a small item pick concept, a replenishment employee opens a master carton and removes filler material that is transferred to a trash container or trash conveyor. After master carton depletion, a picker transfers an empty master carton to trash container or conveyor. With an empty plastic tote in a pick position, a picker turns an empty plastic tote upside down that is a signal for replenishment employee to remove an empty tote. During a pallet replenishment activity to a pick position, a forklift truck driver or replenishment employee removes all plastic wrap that is transferred to a container and empty pallets are transferred onto an empty pallet return lane.

CUBE YOUR SKU EXTERIOR, SHIP CARTON INTERIOR AND PICK POSITION
IMPROVE PICKER PRODUCTIVITY & ENHANCE SPACE UTILIZATION

Cube your sku exterior, ship carton interior and pick position means that you have entered in your (1) CO processing program, each sku's exterior length, width and height dimensions, (2) CO processing program, each ship carton's interior dimensions, (3) in your replenishment program you have entered each vendor master carton's exterior length, width and height dimensions and (4) in your replenishment program each pick position's interior dimensions. When your CO computer program cubes a CO small item or GOH skus cube to a ship container cube, you have improved picker productivity due to each CO sku quantity fits into a computer suggested ship container. Cube your small item pick activity has your CO computer program that takes each CO sku quantity cube, ship carton utilization, filler material factor and matches it your pick vehicle capacity or one of your pick/ship containers. With a GOH pick activity, it determines GOH number per trolley hang bar that assures a full trolley per pick trip. With your master carton and pick position cube information, it determines a master carton number that fills your pick position to capacity with no overflow and assure maximum space utilization.

PICKER ROUTING OR NO ROUTING
IMPROVE PICKER PRODUCTIVITY

Picker routing or no routing are an employee picker or mechanized picker position sequence options that directs a picker through a pick aisle/line to a pick position or to have a carousel move a basket to a pick station. A pick concept that does not have a picker routing pattern or pick position ID sequence means that a pick position IDs are randomly location in an aisle. Features are low picker productivity due to potential double walking in an aisle, with two pickers in an aisle potential congestion or non-productive conversations and difficult to develop a pick aisle/line profile. A pick concept with a pick position ID routing pattern has an arithmetic progression from a pick aisle/line first pick position, through an aisle/line and to an aisle/line last pick position. Features are minimal potential for double walking, less potential for pick aisle/line congestion and easier to develop a pick aisle/line profile.

NON-SEQUENTIAL ROUTING
  LOWER PICKER PRODUCTIVITY
Non-sequential routing is a warehouse with pick position IDs that do not follow a pattern as a picker travels through a pick aisle. A non-sequential routing pattern creates low picker productivity due to poor instructions, double walking, walking past pick positions that have been picked and potential high aisle congestion.

SKU IDENTIFICATION NUMBER ROUTING PATTERN
  PICKER PRODUCTIVITY
Sku ID number as your picker routing pattern has each sku inventory ID number as your pick position number. With sku number routing pattern, your picker routing pattern is a random routing pattern. Features are (1) low picker productivity, (2) difficult to obtain a good pick line profile, (3) wide sku mix that are placed into a picker container and (4) difficult to expand.

SEQUENTIAL OR ARITHMETIC PROGRESSION THROUGH A PICK AISLE
  IMPROVE PICKER PRODUCTIVITY
Sequential or arithmetic progression through a pick aisle is used in a manual, mechanized or automated warehouse to identify pick positions that improves employee productivity & minimizes aisle congestion. Sequential or arithmetic pick position progression or pattern starts at an aisle entrance/first pick position & each additional pick position ID is increased by one. As an employee travels in an aisle with a pick instruction, it minimizes non-productive double travel (walking) time & with a manual concept reduces potential aisle congestion with other pickers.

PICK POSITIONS THAT END WITH EVEN NUMBERS & PICK POSITIONS THAT END WITH ODD NUMBERS
  IMPROVE PICKER PRODUCTIVITY
Pick positions that end with even numbers and pick positions that end with odd numbers is a manual storage or pick position numerical sequence that improves employee productivity and minimizes employee confusion. An even and odd position numerical sequence has all position identifications that end with odd digits on an aisle left side and all position identifications end with even digits on aisle right side. As an employee travels in an aisle, there is an arithmetic progression from an aisle first pick position identification to an aisle last pick position identification.

DRAWER PICK POSITION FRONT TO REAR PICKER ROUTING PATTERN
  IMPROVE PICKER PRODUCTIVITY & INCREASES COMPLETED CUSTOMER ORDER NUMBER
Front to rear routing pattern is a l item picker routing pattern that is used in a warehouse with drawer pick positions to improve picker productivity and increase completed CO number. A drawer pick concept is a solid wall container with 10 to 12 drawers per container. Each drawer is separated to make 20 to 30 pick positions. With a same size or different lengths/depths to pick positions, each position has capacity for a 'C' or 'D' moving sku with a very small inventory. With this feature and a front to rear picker pattern, your picker has increased potential for high hit concentration & density to improve picker productivity. A drawer is locked for improved security for high value skus.

HROS ROUTING PATTERN
  IMPROVE PICKER PRODUCTIVITY & INCREASES COMPLETED CUSTOMER ORDER NUMBER
HROS or high rise order picker vehicle/system routing pattern is employee controlled vehicle routing pattern that is a specialized picker pattern for picking 'C' or 'D' moving skus from shelf or rack pick positions. A routing pattern is used with a guided vehicle to travel vertical and horizontal in aisle between 2 pick position rows that improves picker productivity, increases completed CO number and minimizes sku/equipment damage. A HROS vehicle routing pattern is an arithmetic progression that starts at a high elevation to access highest pick positions and at the elevation, a pattern directs a vehicle through a pick aisle at an same elevation until all pick transactions completion or arrives at an aisle end. At an aisle end, a HROS vehicle lowers to a next pick level elevation and at the elevation directs a vehicle to an aisle entrance. During a HROS vehicle aisle stop to complete a pick transaction and without

vertical or horizontal moving a vehicle, routing pattern has potential to have CO picks from pick positions on an aisle both sides. A HROS pattern has positions that end with even numbers on a pick aisle right side and end with odd numbers on a pick aisle left side. Per your shelf or rack position vertical number, HROS picker patterns are 4, 8, 10 and 12 levels. Features are with good pick aisle profile, it increases picker productivity due to less vertical movement and at the pick activity beginning with a minimal picked sku number on a cart or in a pick cage, there is less potential for sku damage from falling from a cart or pick cage.

LOOP ROUTING PATTERN
   IMPROVE PICKER PRODUCTIVITY & INCREASES COMPLETED CUSTOMER ORDER NUMBER
Loop routing pattern is a small item, GOH or master carton picker pattern that is used for a pick to a powered tugger cart concept in a wide aisle forklift truck aisle from shelf or rack positions on an aisle both sides. With a loop pattern an arithmetic progression positions that end with even numbers on a pick aisle right side and end with odd numbers on a pick aisle left side. As a picker travels through an aisle, picks are made from aisle (A) pick positions on a pick aisle right side and at aisle (A) side completion, a picker enters aisle (B) to complete all picks from aisle (B) right side, returns to aisle (A) to complete all picks from aisle (A) left side, returns to aisle (B) to complete all picks from aisle (B) and enters aisle (C) to complete all pick from aisle (C) right side. With a powered tugger and cart train, in an aisle a picker is between a tugger and pick row. With a remote controlled tugger and cart train in an aisle a picker is between a cart and pick row. Features are with good pick aisle profile and minimal walk distance to complete a pick transaction that improves pick productivity, requires 2 aisle trips that can lower picker productivity and best for a cart customer delivery concept.

HORSESHOE OR 'U' ROUTING PATTERN
   IMPROVE PICKER PRODUCTIVITY & INCREASES COMPLETED CUSTOMER ORDER NUMBER
Horseshoe or 'U' routing pattern is a small item, GOH or master carton picker pattern that is used for a pick to a cart or pallet truck concept in a wide or narrow aisle forklift truck aisle. With a 'U' routing pattern has an arithmetic progression positions that end with even numbers on a pick aisle right side and end with odd numbers on a pick aisle left side. As a picker travels through an aisle, at each pre-determined aisle location, a picker stops and completes picks from an aisle right side positions to an aisle left side pick positions. The routing pattern is repeated for an entire aisle. Features are that with good pick aisle profile it requires one aisle trip but requires employee training and potential aisle congestion.

'Z' ROUTING PATTERN
   IMPROVE PICKER PRODUCTIVITY & INCREASES COMPLETED CUSTOMER ORDER NUMBER
'Z' routing pattern is a master carton picker pattern that is used for a pick to a cart or pallet truck concept in a wide or narrow aisle forklift truck aisle. With a 'Z' routing pattern has an arithmetic progression positions that end with even numbers on a pick aisle right side and end with odd numbers on a pick aisle left side. As a picker travels through an aisle, at each pre-determined aisle location, a picker stops and completes picks from an aisle 3 to 4 bays on right side and picks from an aisle 6 to 8 bays on the left side. The pattern is repeated for the entire aisle. Features are with good pick aisle profile it requires one aisle trip but requires employee training.

BLOCK ROUTING PATTERN
   IMPROVE PICKER PRODUCTIVITY & INCREASES COMPLETED CUSTOMER ORDER NUMBER
Block routing pattern is a small item, GOH master carton picker pattern that is used for a pick to a cart or pallet truck concept in a wide or narrow aisle forklift truck aisle. With a block pattern has an arithmetic progression positions that end with even numbers on a pick aisle right side and end with odd numbers on a pick aisle left side. As a picker travels through an aisle, at each pre-determined aisle location, a picker stops and completes from an aisle right side 2 bays and from an aisle left side 4 bays and the pattern is repeated for an entire aisle. Features are good pick aisle profile it requires one aisle trip with minimal walk distance between pick position and vehicle and requires some employee training.

STITCH ROUTING PATTERN
IMPROVE PICKER PRODUCTIVITY & INCREASES COMPLETED CUSTOMER ORDER NUMBER

Stitch routing pattern is a small item or GOH picker pattern that is used for a pick to a cart concept in aisle between two shelf or decked rack rows. An aisle width is for a short aisle a minimum width of a cart plus sufficient clearance on a cart both sides or for a long aisle a width for two carts plus sufficient clearance to assure no hang-ups. With an arithmetic progression positions that end with even numbers on a pick aisle right side and end with odd numbers on a pick aisle left side. As a picker travels through an aisle at each pick location there is a minimum distance to transfer a sku from a pick position to a cart. At each pick location, shelf or decked rack pick positions are on an aisle left and right sides with a minimum of 15 skus per side to a maximum of 120 skus per side. Features are with a good pick profile and high hit concentration and density improved picker productivity and one trip through an aisle increases completed custom order number.

SKUS AS SEPARATE OR MIXED SKUS IN PICK POSITIONS
IMPROVE PICKER PRODUCTIVITY & SPACE UTILIZATION

Skus as separate or mixed skus in pick positions is a small item/GOH pick position set-up or relocation strategy for your 'C', 'D' & obsolete/very slow moving skus to improve picker productivity and enhance space utilization. Skus in separate pick positions is based on a philosophy that your pick activity is time critical, most of your COs have multiple lines/multiple skus and your pick aisle/line profile minimizes a picker's walk distance between two picks. With 'C', 'D' & obsolete/very slow moving skus, to improve sku hit concentration and density, allocate the skus to one pick aisle in narrow pick positions. If your one pick aisle is considered in your WMS computer program as one pick section and where your multiple lines/multiple skus CO starts. your in-house transport concept moves a partial completed CO from your slowing sku section to your 'A' fasting moving section. Features are you maintain your budgeted 'A' fast moving picker productivity and assure good space utilization. When you mix 'C', 'D' & obsolete/very slow moving skus into a carton/tote or GOH on rail with no sku separation, you improve your sku re-location or set-up/replenishment employee productivity and space utilization but lowers your picker productivity due to non-productive time to search and locate a sku in a carton/tote on a rail. If you mix 'C', 'D' & obsolete/very slow moving skus into a carton/tote or GOH on rail with sku separation, you maintain your sku re-location or set-up/replenishment employee productivity and space utilization but slightly lower your picker productivity due to minimal time to search and located a sku in a carton/tote on a rail.

FLOATING OR FIXED SKU PICK POSITION LENGTH
IMPROVE PICKER PRODUCTIVITY

Floating or fixed sku pick position length is a term that is used in a manual small item or GOH manual , mechanized or automated warehouse for sku assignment to a pick position. A floating pick position concept has one sku allocated to two pick positions. Pick positions are adjacent to each other, separated by other skus or in different aisles. With a floating pick position concept, a sku quantity is placed into two pick positions that are A100 and B290. After CO picks deplete a sku quantity in one pick position (A100), your computer program has your next CO picked from pick position (B290). Features are requires additional pick positions, difficult to maintain a pick line/zone profile, requires a computer program, minimizes replenishment transactions and minimizes stock-outs. A fixed pick position concept has one sku allocated to one pick position (C250) with additional skus allocated to storage positions. After CO picks deplete a sku quantity in one pick position (C250), your computer program suggests a replenishment transaction from a storage position to a pick position (C250). Features are requires minimal pick positions but additional storage positions, easy to maintain a pick line/zone profile that improves picker productivity, minimizes computer program requirements and requires replenishment transactions.

ONE CUSTOMER ORDER OR MULTIPLE CUSTOMER ORDERS PER PICK TOTE (See Pack Chapter)

WHERE TO START CUSTOMER ORDERS WITH TWO WMS IDENTIFIED PICK SECTIONS
IMPROVE PICKER PRODUCTIVITY & MINIMIZE SKU DAMAGE

With two WMS computer program identified pick sections where to start COs with sku picks from both pick sections and how to assure good picker productivity with minimal sku damage is a question that is asked by small item or GOH warehouses. An operation with two WMS computer program identified pick section has one pick section that is profiled with 'A'/fast moving, high cube or heavy skus and account for 85% of your picks and a second pick section that is profiled with 'B' 'C' 'D' slow moving, small cube, light weight, fragile or crushable skus and account for 15% of your picks. When you start COs in a slow moving sku section, as a CO container arrives in your 'A' fast moving section, a picker is careful not to place heavy skus onto fragile skus, has potential to move skus (15% of your picks) inside a container for fast moving sku space that creates non-productive time and to assure smooth order flow you require in-house transport travel path queue and with some pick concept to scan CO container scan on prior to your second pick section. If you start COs in your 'A' fast moving section, your picker places skus (85% of your picks) into an empty container. Features are less CO congestion due to 15% of your picks/orders travel to your second pick section, with heavy/high cube skus in container bottom less fragile sku damage, higher completed CO number and all CO containers start in one section that means less congestion and lower in-house transport cost to move COs between two sections and less queue area and easier to scan CO IDs.

TOO MUCH OF ONE SKU IN ONE PICK ZONE CREATES PICK LINE CONGESTION OR SHUT-DOWN
IMPROVE PICKER PRODUCTIVITY & SPACE UTILIZATION

Too much of one sku (pick volume) in one pick zone/position creates pick line congestion or shut down is not good and lowers your picker productivity and space utilization. This statement refers to a pick concept that has for one sku with a very high pick volume that exceeds your standard pick position front or budgeted picker productivity. If you have one sku pick position with a high pick volume. it creates pick line or CO container congestion that has one picker achieve good productivity but lowers other pickers' productivity. To remedy a situation, in your WMS computer program and in your operation you have two separate pick sections or dual pick lines. Another too much situation occurs with your vendor master carton exceeds your standard shelf or decked rack pick position front and your over-sized master carton extends from one pick position into an adjacent pick position. The situation creates low picker productivity due to a vacate pick position (vendor carton extends into adjacent pick position) that increases a picker walk distance between two picks. To remedy the situation, you have skus transferred from a vendor oversize carton into a standard size carton for a pick position and sku quantity per new carton ID are updated in your WMS computer program and in the future your purchasing department advises your vendor to use a standard size carton.

IF YOU DAILY ROTATE YOUR 'A' SKUS WITH A SKEWED 2/4 DAY LIFE CYCLE CONSIDER TWO PICK SECTIONS
IMPROVE PICKER PRODUCTIVITY & SPACE UTILIZATION

If you daily rotate your 'A' skus with a skewed two/four day life cycle consider two pick sections improves your picker and replenishment productivity and space utilization. With two pick sections, for CO wave on Day 1 you have Day 1 skus in pick section A and pick Day 1 customer orders and on Day 2 you set-up pick section B with Day 2 skus. With Day 2 your CO wave, your picks are from both pick section A & B. After Day 2 CO wave completion, any residual sku quantity in pick section A is transferred to regular pick section and you set-up your Day 3 skus in pick section A.

HOW HIGH IS YOUR MAXIMUM SKU PICK POSITION HEIGHT
IMPROVE PICKER PRODUCTIVITY

How high is your maximum sku pick position height is a manual, mechanized or automatic warehouse consideration for a pick position height that impacts your picker reach height and assure good productivity. Your pick position height is a pick position with a sku master carton or GOH rail above the floor surface. A pick position height above the floor allows an employee picker or replenishment employee to complete a pick/replenishment transaction without stepping on a shelf or using an elevating device. A pick/replenishment transaction removes a sku from a master carton, picks a GOH from a rail or adds a sku to a pick lane. In most pick operations, your pick levels are shelf with 4 to 5 levels, decked rack with 3 levels, standard pallet rack with 2 levels, GOH with 2 to 3 levels and carton flow rack with 4 to 5 levels.

INCREASE YOUR PICKER REACH
IMPROVE PICKER PRODUCTIVITY & ENHANCE SPACE UTILIZATION

Reach higher is used in a small item or GOH warehouse for a picker ability to reach a pick position above the normal reach. Features are to improve picker productivity and enhance space utilization. Since most skus are classified as A,B,C or D moving skus, to have good picker productivity your 'D' moving skus are assigned to your highest pick positions or non-Golden Zone pick positions. Devices to increase a pickers reach height are (1) manual group that includes (a) mobile one step high stool with safety step, (b) mobile three or four safety step ladder that is attached to a pick cart with safety step, (c) fixed step that is attached to a pick position front, (d) mobile four wheel and six or seven step ladder with a safety step and (e) captive aisle two wheel and six or seven step that is attached on a rail to a pick position top and (2) mechanized group that includes (a) work assisted vehicle with limited carrying capacity, (b) high rise order pick vehicle with cart or pick cage with an attached GOH bar carry capacity, (c) man-up very narrow aisle vehicle with a pick cage or (d) decombe or pick car.

PICK BY SHIP CARTON SIZE
IMPROVE PICKER & PACKER PRODUCTIVITY & INCREASES COMPLETED CUSTOMER ORDER NUMBER

Pick by carton size is a small item warehouse option to release COs to a pick/sort and pick/pass pick train concept to improve picker/packer productivity, allows a picker to easily read a container CO ID, increase completed CO number and minimized conveyor travel path or cart pick position handling problems. A pick train pick/pass concept has a picker physically or powered queue conveyor travel path moves CO cartons over a pick zone and onto the next pick zone or onto a take-away conveyor. To have your COs arranged to enter a pick/pass pick conveyor by carton size you have your computer cube program determine each CO carton size and to release one carton size CO to your pick line (computer). At a pick line entry or a pick cart preparation station, you have your computer suggested carton size pre-made and available for pick concept entry. Features improves your employee or machine carton make-up activity and easier to control collapse carton in-feed to your carton make-up station. Your pick line computer assures that your COs are sequenced by carton size. Features are requires accurate sku and ship carton cube data and additional computer process time.

HOW TO PICK INTO A SMALL SIZE CUSTOMER ORDER SHIP CARTON
IMPROVE PICKER & PACKER PRODUCTIVITY & INCREASES COMPLETED CUSTOMER ORDER NUMBER

How to pick into a small size CO ship carton is a pick & sort, pick/pack or pick/pass concept that has your pickers transfer picked skus into a computer suggested CO small size carton. Picking into a CO ship carton improves your picker and packer productivity and increases your completed CO number. With a wide ship carton mixed in a pick/sort cart or on a powered conveyor or on a pick conveyor travel path, there are potential small size carton handling travel problems/jams or carton tipping that creates lost skus with non-productive employee to assure carton stays in a pick/sort position or travels on a conveyor and to correct a lost sku problem. Small size carton conveyor travel path options are (1) skew rollers that direct all carton travel onto one conveyor side for carton travel along a 'C' channel guard rail (s) and if possible have WMS computer program release customer orders as a group by carton size. Features are potential travel path problems that are minimized when pick by carton size, requires additional costs but each carton has CO ID and after all pick transactions completion, captive tote/large carton goes to your next activity station (check, pack or seal station), (2) place each small made-up carton onto a captive tray. Features are minimal travel path problems, requires additional employee time to handle/relocate empty trays and tray cost but each carton has CO ID and after all pick transactions completion, captive tote/large carton goes to your next activity station (check, pack or seal station), (3) pick into a captive tote/large carton with a peel-off label (WMS CO ID) and after all pick transactions completion, captive tote/large carton goes to your next activity station (check, pack or seal station). Features are minimal travel path problems, requires WMS CO ID relocated from captive tote/large carton onto a small size carton, additional tote/carton handling, pack station employee requires small cartons and carton make-up time or small size carton is picked into your captive tote/large carton & (4) pick into a captive tote/large carton with a warehouse ID that is associated to a WMS CO ID and (a) at a special carton/filler material pick station to have a collapsed or made-up small carton transferred into a captive tote/large carton or (b) pack station has small carton size & after all pick transactions completion, captive tote/large carton that goes to your next activity (check, pack or seal station). Features are requires WMS CO ID related to a warehouse ID, additional tote/carton handling, prior to captive tote/large carton reuse, zero scan a warehouse ID, high pack station employee productivity with minimal carton make-up time & less required space. Pick/sort cart position, a small size carton side wall handling options are (1) fold onto inside walls, (2) place with flaps-up and (3) fold to outside wall & secured with rubber band.

YOUR CUSTOMER ORDERS ARE SEPARATED BY SKUS
IMPROVE PICKER PRODUCTIVITY & INCREASE COMPLETED CUSTOMER ORDER NUMBER

Your COs are separated by skus is a small item final pick and CO pack slip/invoice preparation concept for a sku that is used in a bulk pick, transport, sort and final CO pick that improves picker productivity and increases completed CO number. To have a cost effective, efficient, accurate and good employee productivity for your final pick activity, you have (1) your WMS computer program arrange your CO wave CO pack slips/invoices for print by a first or last sku digit and (2) sort your bulk pick skus by WMS sku ID. Sku sort options are by (a) first and last digit and first digit that IDs a shelf or rack bay and last digit IDs a shelf level, (b) last and next to last digit and last digit that IDs a shelf or rack bay & next to last digit IDs a shelf level or to first & (c) first and second digit and first digit that IDs a shelf or rack bay & second digit IDs a shelf level. When your WMS computer program groups/prints your CO pack slips/invoices by your selected sku digit sequence and your printed CO pack slips/invoices as group are placed into a shelf /rack bay and shelf/rack level for the corresponding sku digit sequence, your final picker productivity is high due to a picker first CO pick transaction is at a shelf/rack bay position with no non-productive walk time.

YOUR REPLENISHMENT EMPLOYEE OR PICKER MAKES A MASTER CARTON SMILEY FACE
IMPROVE PICKER PRODUCTIVITY & IMPROVES TRASH HANDLING

Your replenishment employee or picker makes a master carton smiley face or cuts-off a master carton top/front end that is placed in a pick position to improve picker productivity and trash handling. A master carton properly opened or with a smiley face permits a manual picker to easily and quickly with minimal sku removal obstruction and complete a pick transaction or a replenishment transaction to fill an automatic pick machine pick lane/sleeve. An open master carton allows an employee to insert a hand into a master carton and remove a sku from a master carton without hanging-up on a carton top flaps. Your master carton open options are (1) picker that is time critical activity that focuses on completing a manual or mechanized pick transaction or sku transfer to an automatic pick machine or (b) replenishment person that is not as time critical. In most pick activities with a WMS computer program, after a sku is physically transferred and scanned to a pick position. After a WMS computer program updates a sku pick position status, it releases COs to a pick concept. In all pick concepts, a replenishment employee opens a master carton is the preferred activity. This is due to the fact (1) your replenishment activity is less time critical than a picker activity that is more time critical, (2) a replenishment employee is handling a master carton and in most replenishment activities a master carton is an employee has work station that is level and a solid surface and (3) with most standard WMS programs a master carton replenishment quantity is based on your CO wave and after a master carton is physically and WMS scanned to a pick position, a WMS computer program releases COs to your pick concept. Replenishment to an automatic pick machine sleeve/lane, a replenishment employee is not preferred to open master cartons but the storage employee who transfers a master carton to an automatic pick machine ready reserve position. We preferred that a picker or automatic pick machine pick position replenishment employee does not open cartons is due to the fact that (1) it requires a time critical employee (picker) to remove a carton from a pick or ready reserve position that is extra handling or with limited space leave a master carton in a pick position and open a carton, (2) it is a picker non-productive time that requires a 1 to 1 ½ minutes to open a master carton. This time includes aware that a master carton is empty, located open knife, remove a knife from a sleeve and open or rip master carton top, replace master carton to pick position and place trash in a container. Features are non-productive picker time lowers your picker or productivity, with an automatic pick machine slow CO release to a pick machine and in a pick/pass or pick cell concept potential to create CO container congestion on a pick conveyor or pick zone in-feed conveyor.

PICK/PASS SMALL ITEM PICK CONCEPT
IMPROVE PICKER PRODUCTIVITY & INCREASE COMPLETED CUSTOMER ORDER NUMBER

Pick/pass is a small item or GOH pick concept that improves picker productivity and increases completed CO. With a pick/pass concept, skus are picked from flow rack, shelf or rail pick positions that are adjacent to each other and on a pick aisle other side is a pick conveyor. From a 30 to 36 wide pick aisle between a pick/pass line (pick positions) and CO travel path, it minimizes a picker transfer distance for skus from pick positions into a CO carton/tote or onto a cart/trolley hang bar. For maximum productivity, your pick positions are profiled with 'A' moving skus and other skus are separated into pick zones by sku pick quantity that matches your budgeted picker productivity. Your pick/pass CO travel path is past each pick zone and assures a minimum distance to transfer a sku from a pick position to CO container.

PICK POSITION SEQUENCE HORIZONTAL OR VERTICAL ROUTING PATTERN
IMPROVE PICKER PRODUCTIVITY

Horizontal or vertical are a manual picker routing pattern for pick positions in a shelf bay, decked rack bay, standard pallet rack bat, carousel basket or carton flow rack bay. A picker routing pattern directs a picker to pick skus from pick positions that assures your picker productivity rate. A vertical picker routing pattern starts at a bay bottom level pick position and for each pick level progresses (arithmetically) upward. After a reaching the top level, a picker starts at the adjacent bottom pick position and repeats the upward progression. Features are (1) difficult to maintain a Golden Zone, (2) if a Golden Zone sku requires additional space, it is difficult to achieve a Golden Zone and (3) requires additional non-productive time for a picker to review a vertical path for additional picks. A horizontal picker routing pattern starts at a bay top level (or bottom level) and progresses horizontal across each pick level. At a pick level end, a picker moves to the next pick level start and repeats horizontal progression. Features are (1) easier to maintain a Golden Zone, (2) easier for a picker to review a level for additional picks and (3) if a fast moving sku requires additional space, a sku occupies additional lanes and remains in your Golden Zone.

PICK/PASS PICK TRAIN OR PICK CELL CONCEPT
IMPROVE PICKER PRODUCTIVITY

Pick/ass pick train or pick cell concept are alternative pick/pass CO carton/tote travel concepts for CO pick container travel past all CO pick positions to complete a CO and assure picker productivity. After CO container entry onto a pick conveyor, a pick train has several CO cartons/totes manual or powered conveyor moved over a pick conveyor past all pick positions to a pick line last pick position. Features are preferred for 'A'/fast moving skus, easy to develop a pick line profile to match your picker budgeted productivity, simple pick conveyor design, lower cost conveyor, manual pick conveyor requires a picker physical effort to move a pick train that is especially true with mixed carton sizes and with a powered pick conveyor pick zone end stops help control a pick train flow. If a pick/pass concept has a completed CO take-away conveyor, a completed CO is pushed from a pick train onto a CO take-away conveyor. Feature is that it reduces a pick train CO container number and minimizes picker physical effort to move a pick train. A pick cell concept has all CO cartons/totes travel on a main powered conveyor travel path. On a main conveyor travel path each pick cell has a scanner and divert device that diverts a CO container with a pick transaction from a main conveyor travel path to a pick cell. A pick cell is considered a picker zone with a pick conveyor, completed push-off access to main travel conveyor and pick positions. Within a pick cell a picker completes all picks and a completed CO is pushed forward from a pick conveyor onto a main conveyor travel path for travel on a main conveyor travel path to the next pick cell or pack station. If an 'A'/fast moving sku has a high pick requirement in 1 pick cell, there is potential for main conveyor travel path shut down or CO re-circulation on a main conveyor travel path that increases your CO container volume. Features are higher conveyor cost, difficult to profile a pick line for picker budgeted productivity, every pick cell has a picker and each pick cell has some a powered conveyor and queue pick line.

PICK POSITIONS OVER & UNDER A PICK/PASS PICK/TAKE-AWAY CONVEYOR
IMPROVE PICKER PRODUCTIVITY & INCREASE PICK FACES

Pick positions over and under a pick/pass pick/take-away conveyor has potential to increase your pick faces along a pick line. Pick positions over and under your pick/pass pick/take-away conveyor are carton flow rack positions that extend over and under your pick and take-away conveyors. The arrangement has one pick level below your pick conveyor frame and with one or two pick levels extend over your take-away conveyor and end above the take-away conveyor frame. In the pick positions, you profile light weight and small cube skus. If you have your 'A'/fast moving sku profile (budgeted picker productivity) to carton flow rack position on a pick aisle back, you have potential and additional pick positions over and under your pick conveyor line. Features are (1) lower your picker budgeted productivity due to an additional pick positions to review for 'A' fast moving skus, (2) lowest pick position is a pigeon hole reach and high pick position has a high reach that has potential to lower picker productivity, (3) additional pick position cost and (4) increases pick positions. If your pick/pass line has 'B' & 'C' moving skus that are difficult to profile for picker budgeted productivity, additional pick positions over and under your pick conveyor line are used for 'B' & 'C' skus. Features are (1) increases your pick zone hit concentration and density that improves picker productivity, (2) with fewer customer orders for 'B' & 'C' skus in a pick zone, minimal CO congestion and (3) increases your pick zone pick faces.

PICK/PASS CONCEPT PICK TRAIN
    IMPROVE PICKER PRODUCTIVITY
A pick train is a small item pick/pass concept with a pick positions on a pick line that has a CO containers continuously travel to your pick line entry location. As a customer order container enters pick line, each CO container ID is read by a scanner that assures CO sequence or an employee applies a customer CO ID label to a container. Your CO IDs are in your computer CO download sequence. A pick line is separated into multiple pick zones with a picker assigned to each pick zone. With a pick to light concept, for maximum pick zone flexibility, each flow rack bay, shelf or pallet pick position has a zone controller. To have your pick zone match your picker budgeted productivity your expand or reduce a pick zone length. To assist picker control, unique flags/banners identify each pick zone start and finish bay. With your pick/pass pick train on a pick conveyor only concept, your CO pick train is pushed by each picker from first pick zone to the next pick zone until a CO container train travels past the last pick position. This means that a CO container pick train is pushed past positions with no picks. If your pick/pass pick train on a pick conveyor and take-away conveyor concept, as a CO pick transactions are completed, a completed CO is pushed from a pick conveyor (pick train) onto a take-away conveyor that reduces your CO container number in a pick train. This means that CO containers that require picks are pushed to your last pick position. Pick train features are easier to profile for your budgeted picker productivity, increase employee physical push effort, mixed CO carton size has potential problems and potential for miss-picks or picked sku transfer to wrong CO container. When you use picker clips for a picker to attach a clip to an active CO container minimizes miss-picks or transfer to wrong CO container. If your pick/pass concept has a pick conveyor and completed CO take-away conveyor concept, after completion of a CO picks, a picker pushes a completed CO container from a pick train (conveyor) onto a take-away conveyor. Features are to reduce employee physical push effort, with fewer CO carton containers on a conveyor minimal potential problems and lower potential for miss-picks or picked sku transfer to wrong CO container.

PICK/PASS PICK CELL CONCEPT
    IMPROVE PICKER PRODUCTIVITY
A pick cell is a pick/pass concept with a unique CO ID on each container and has a main CO container conveyor with scanners and divert device and a series of pick cells with a pick conveyor adjacent to a main conveyor and pick position groups. After a CO container ID is scanned, a conveyor computer determines a CO container with required picks is diverted from a main conveyor onto a pick cell conveyor. Scanned CO ID sequence is transferred to your pick computer that assures CO sequence is in the appropriate pick cell. After completion of a CO picks, a cell picker pushes a completed CO container from a pick cell (conveyor) onto a main conveyor for travel to the next pick cell or work station. Features are less picker physical effort, difficult to profile to match your budgeted picker productivity, additional conveyor costs and short pick positions per picker.

PICK/PACK (See Pick/Pass)

MIRRORED PICK/PASS LINES
    IMPROVE PICKER PRODUCTIVITY & MAINTAIN CUSTOMER SERVICE
Mirrored pick/pass lines is a small item carton flow rack pick/pass layout with 2 WMS computer identified pick/pass lines that is used to handle a very high pick volume. If your 'A'/fast moving sku pick volume exceeds your one pick/pass line budgeted productivity, a mirrored pick/pass line concept has at least two pick/pass lines and each pick line has skus in the same pick positions. Two pick/pass lines/pick positions assures your picker productivity

matches your budgeted productivity, has a simple pick/pass line profile, assures constant CO flow and increases completed CO number. With a mirrored pick/pass line concept your computer program recognizes 2 pick/pass lines and your pick/pass line profile has each sku that is located in both pick lines same pick position. This means that sku 11102 is located in pick line 1 pick position A101 & in pick line 2 pick position A101.

WHAT IS A PICK CARTON/TOTE LICENSE PLATE
IMPROVE PICKER PRODUCTIVITY

What pick a carton/tote license plate (warehouse ID or WMS CO ID tote/carton to assure picker productivity and accurate pick transactions. In a pick to light or automatic pick machine pick concept, each pick tote/carton has a unique CO ID. During your pick activity, a pick tote/carton ID is considered a pick instruction component that is read by an employee or automatic pick machine scanner and directs a picker or automatic pick machine to transfer a sku from a pick position into a CO container. A warehouse ID on a CO tote is considered a permanent identification. To be effective, prior to your pick activity each tote warehouse ID is associated with a WMS CO ID that is sent to your WMS computer. As a warehouse ID tote travels through your pick area, a warehouse ID is a pick instruction component. At a pack station, a packer zero scans a tote warehouse ID that breaks a WMS CO ID association to a warehouse tote ID and allows a tote used for another WMS ID CO. Each completed/packed CO ship container receives a WMS CO ID and leaves your warehouse. With a WMS CO ID on a pick/ship carton, a WMS CO ID is a pick instruction component as a CO container travels through your pick area. At a pack station, your packer does not zero scan a WMS CO ID due to it is a disposal CO ID. After a packer completes a CO, a WMS COP ID remains on a CO ship container and leaves your warehouse.

YOUR PICK CONVEYOR SURFACE IS SET HIGH OR SET LOW
IMPROVE PICKER PRODUCTIVITY & ASSURE COMPLETED CUSTOMER ORDER FLOW

Your pick conveyor surface is set high or set low is a pick/pass line conveyor roller location on a conveyor frame that improves picker productivity and assure completed CO flow. Set high roller option has conveyor roller surfaces set at the same elevation as a conveyor frame top surface. Set low roller option has conveyor roller surfaces set below a conveyor frame top surface. A pick/pass pick train concept with only a pick conveyor, a set low roller concept has a pick conveyor frame serve as a guard rail. As a pick train is pushed over a pick conveyor, a conveyor frame retains a pick train cartons/totes on a conveyor. With a pick conveyor and completed CO take-away conveyor on a pick/pass pick train or cell concept, a pick conveyor roller surfaces are set high with a low profile near/picker side guard rail and take-away conveyor roller surfaces are set low with far side high guard rail. With both pick conveyor and take-away conveyor frames are set at the same elevation above a floor that allows a take-away conveyor frame serve as a guard rail to retain completed customer orders on a conveyor.

SKATE-WHEEL OR ROLLER PICK LINE
IMPROVE PICKER PRODUCTIVITY & MINIMZE JAMS

Skate-wheel or roller pick line are a pick/pass conveyor surface options that assure good pick productivity and minimize jams as CO containers are transferred from a pick conveyor onto a take-away conveyor. Both skate-wheel and roller conveyor surfaces assure CO container forward movement over a pick line. If your pick/pass concept does not have completed CO push-off concept, meshed skate-wheel conveyor serves as a pick line conveyor surface and is able to handle narrow cartons/wide carton size mix. If your pick/pass concept has a completed CO push-off concept, a roller conveyor surface with a solid, smooth and continuous surface spans an open distance between a pick conveyor two frames that minimizes a co-efficient of friction as a picker pushes a completed CO from a pick conveyor onto a take-away conveyor. A solid roller surface handles a wide carton size mix. Features improve picker productivity and minimize jams. If a skate-wheel conveyor surface is used on a completed CO push-off concept, skate wheels and open space between skate-wheels creates a co-efficient of friction as a picker pushes a completed CO container from a pick line onto a take-away conveyor. Open space between skate-wheels has potential for CO container hang-up on a skate-wheel or container tipping that means lower picker productivity and potential lost skus.

PICK/PASS PICK CONVEYOR FRAME EDGE & GUARDS
IMPROVE PICKER PRODUCTIVITY & INCREASED COMPLETED CUSTOMER ORDER NUMBER

Pick/pass pick conveyor frame edge or guards is an option that improves picker productivity and completed CO number. A pick/pass conveyor frame edge or guard serves to guide a pick carton/tote as it is moved over a pick conveyor and assures a pick carton/tote remains on a pick conveyor. A conveyor frame edge means that your pick conveyor roller conveyor surface is below your conveyor frame edge (roller set low). Features are (1) low cost and (2) guides cartons/totes. A pick conveyor guard is a conveyor accessory that is added to your pick conveyor near (picker) frame side and used with a conveyor roller or skate-wheel top surface is above a pick conveyor frame (rollers or skate-wheels set high). Features are (1) additional cost and (2) guides cartons/totes.

PICK/PASS PICK CONVEYOR PICK ZONE CONTROL
IMPROVE PICKER PRODUCTIVITY

Pick/pass pick conveyor pick zone control are options that assure a picker remains in an assigned picker zone (pre-determined shelf bay or carton flow rack bay number). Per your CO wave sku pick number, your pick zone profile (allocated picks) matches your budgeted picker productivity. Your pick zone control options are (1) variable zone has each pick zone start and end pick positions that vary. For each CO wave, a pick zone bay number is increased or decreased to assure each pick zone pick number matches you picker productivity rate. Features are (1) potential low picker productivity due to a pick zone is long and increases picker non-productive walk distance, (2) requires pick zone profile time, (3) difficult to control CO container travel on a pick conveyor and (4) potential for picked sku transfer errors and (2) fixed zone has each pick zone start and end pick position that are same pick position for each CO wave. For each CO wave, a pick zone bay number is the same number and does not fluctuate with a different pick volume. With a good pick line profile, you allocate sku picks to assure good picker productivity and some fixed pick zones with high volume picks have 1 or 2 bays and other pick zones with low volume picks have 3 to 4 bays. With a fixed pick zone concept, add banners/flags to identify a pick zone start & finish. Features are (1) potential high picker productivity due to a pick zone picks matches your budgeted productivity & decreases picker non-productive walk distance, (2) requires pick zone profile time, (3) improves CO container travel on a pick conveyor & (4) reduces picked sku transfer errors.

COMPLETED CUSTOMER ORDER IS PUSHED-AWAY OR CONTINUES AS PART OF A PICK TRAIN
IMPROVE PICKER PRODUCTIVITY & ACCURACY

Completed CO is pushed-away or continues as part of a pick train that describes your pick/pass concept completed CO travel path options that impact a picker productivity and accurate picked sku transfer into a CO carton/tote. Continues as part of a pick train option has a completed CO container remain on a pick/pass pick conveyor travel path and after a last pick position to exit. The situation means that each picker pushes a full pick train (CO cartons/totes) through each pick zone. With a great CO container number within a pick zone, it requires additional non-productive time to assure accurate picked sku transfer from a pick position to a proper CO container and potential for increased pick errors. Continues as part of a pick train board concept has minimal conveyor cost. Completed CO push-away concept has a completed CO take-away powered conveyor travel path that is adjacent and full length to a pick conveyor travel path. The design allows a picker to push a completed CO container from a pick conveyor onto a take-away conveyor travel path. With fewer CO containers on a pick conveyor, it minimizes a picker physical effort to move a pick train over a pick conveyor, lower potential to have a picked sku transfer from a pick position to an incorrect CO container and higher conveyor cost.

COMPLETED CUSTOMER ORDER PUSH-OFF CONCEPT, A GAP PLATE OR PICK & TAKE-AWAY CONVEYORS AT DIFFERENT ELEVATIONS
IMPROVE PICKER PRODUCTIVITY & MINIMZE JAMS

With a completed CO push-off concept to permit a picker to easily transfer a completed CO from a pick conveyor onto a completed CO take-away conveyor and on a completed CO travel path to guide completed CO container travel, your require a gap plate between your pick & take-away conveyors or pick conveyor and take-away conveyor travel paths have different elevations. A gap plate is basically a solid sheet metal member that has an inverted and flatten 'V' shape with a high middle section. When a gap plate low side is attached to a pick conveyor frame far side and high side attached to a take-away conveyor frame near side. A smooth gap plate side permits easy completed CO transfer and high middle serves as a completed CO carton travel guard rail. Features are minimal carton jams and additional cost. Different conveyor travel path elevation concept has a pick conveyor travel path set a ¼ in higher than a take-away conveyor travel path and your pick and take-away conveyor frames assure that there is no gap between two conveyor travel paths. After a CO completion, a picker pushes a completed CO from a high pick conveyor across both conveyor frames onto a low take-away conveyor. Conveyor frames serve as smooth transfer surface and elevated pick conveyor frame serves as a guide rail for CO container travel on a take-away conveyor. To have a pick conveyor and take-away conveyor set at different elevations above a floor has no additional cost and is stated in your conveyor specifications.

WITH PICK/PASS CONCEPT CYCLE PICKERS TO DIFFERENT PICK ZONES
IMPROVE PICKER PRODUCTIVITY & INCREASE COMPLETED CUSTOMER ORDER NUMBER

With a pick/pass concept cycle pickers is a manual small item, GOH pick cart or trolley concept that minimizes a picker's non-productive walk time and reduces picker fatigue to improve picker productivity, rotates pickers to short walk sections and increases completed CO number. Cycle your pickers from your pick/pass 'A' fast moving high volume section allows a picker to rotate to a slow moving/low volume section that is requires less physical effort to complete pick transactions. With a push cart or trolley concept and picking from a slow moving/low volume section requires a long walks distance with an empty pick cart/trolley from your dispatch station to your most distant pick position. From a picker's most distant pick position, your picker routing pattern progressively directs your pickers through the pick aisles toward your pack stations. After a picker starts with an empty cart, a picker travels through the pick area and as a picker approaches your pack station, there is greater potential for a picker to move a full pick cart from a pick area to a pack station. After dropping a full cart/trolley in your pack station area, from a control desk to cycle a picker, a picker is given an empty cart/trolley with a CO pick instructions for 'A' fast moving high volume section that has a shorter walk to the first pick position.

EMPLOYEE PICKER USE A GLOVE
IMPROVE PICKER PRODUCTIVITY & MINIMZE SKU DAMAGE

Employee picker use a glove is a manual small item pick concept to improve picker productivity and minimize sku damage. When a small item picker has to pick plastic bottles or plastic wrapped skus, there is potential damage from a sku to slip from a picker's hands. This is due to a sku exterior smooth and slick surface. With a pick/pass concept, to assure a CO ID on a container matches a pick zone CO ID a picker lifts a CO container. When lifting a plastic tote or new cardboard carton, there is potential for a picker to cut a hand but a glove minimizes injury possibility. In a small item pick concept and if your replenishment employee opens or cuts master cartons, safety gloves are used to minimize employee injury.

FLAG EACH PICK/PASS CONCEPT PICK ZONE START AND END PICK POSITION
IMPROVE PICKER PRODUCTIVITY

Flag each pick/pass concept pick zone start and end pick position is used in a small item pick/pass concept that improves your picker productivity. In most high volume pick/pass concepts a pick line is separated into picker zones that have sufficient sku picks for a picker to match budgeted picker productivity and each pick zone has a fixed start and end position. In a pick/pass aisle for each pick zone you use a different colored or numbered flag to identify a pick zone start and end position. Each flag extends down from a pick position top to the middle bottom and does not obstruct an picker walking in an aisle. Features are (1) allows a picker (especially new pickers) to easily identify a pick zone start and end pick position, (2) minimizes a picker non-productive walk and helps to determine no additional picks in a pick zone and (3) allows faster CO container transfer to the next pick zone.

FIXED OR VARIABLE PICK ZONE LENGTH
IMPROVE PICKER PRODUCTIVITY

Fixed or variable pick zone length are a small item pick/pass line length options that impact a picker productivity, pick line congestion and CO flow. On a pick line a pick zone is established by a picker start and end pick positions and determines a picker's pick position number and potential picks. Your pick line profile a pick number and sku volume influences a picker's ability to obtain budgeted pick rates. A fixed pick zone means for each CO wave that a pick zone has the same start pick and end pick positions. If you do not rotate and re-profile your skus, there is potential for low picker productivity due to mixing 'A'/fasting moving skus adjacent to 'B' medium & 'C' slow moving sku means low hit concentration and density and increases walk distance between 2 picks. If you rotate your skus with a good sku profile, there is potential for high picker productivity due to 'A'/fast moving skus are adjacent to each other that means high hit concentration and density and minimal walk distance between 2 picks. A variable pick zone has per each customer order wave different start and end pick positions. If a pick zone length increases and becomes too long, a picker has low productivity due to increase walk distance between 2 picks.

RUBBER MAT IN YOUR PICK/PASS AISLE
IMPROVE PICKER PRODUCTIVITY & REDUCE SKU DAMAGE

Rubber mat in your pick aisle is used in a small item pick/pass concept aisle that improves your pick productivity and reduces sku damage. In most pick/pass concepts, a pick aisle is 30 to 36 ins wide and is between your pick position row fronts and pick conveyor. In a pick aisle is a cement surface and within a pick zone a picker transfers a picked sku from a pick position into a CO container. Within a high volume pick zone, a picker has a 5 ft distance between a pick zone start and end pick positions that means a picker stands in one location for a work day majority. If a picker stands on a rubber mat, there is less fatigue from a cement floor and during winter, less cold feeling in a picker feet that means greater potential for good picker productivity. When humidity builds on a pick line cement floor, it becomes slippery. A rubber mat in a pick aisle minimizes potential for an employee to slip. During a picked sku transfer from a pick position to a CO container, there is potential for a sku to fall from a picker's hands onto a rubber mat. With a rubber mat surface, there is less potential sku damage.

YOUR STATIONARY PICKER ON A CEMENT PICK FLOOR LOWER PRODUCTIVITY USE A RUBBER MAT
IMPROVE PICKER PRODUCTIVITY & REDUCE SKU DAMAGE

To picker a cement is hard and rubber is soft/comforting. In a small item pick/pass aisle, horizontal carousel pick station or automatic pick machine replenishment aisle, a rubber mat on the floor surface improves employee productivity and reduces potential sku damage. If your pick/pass pick zone has a short walk distance (nominal 5 ft long by 30/36 in wide aisle) or if your fixed pick station in front of a horizontal carousel, your picker is standing on a cement floor. Many studies have indicated that a hard cement floor lowers a picker productivity by an estimated 5% due to employee fatigue from standing on a cement floor. Rubber mat features are (1) in cold winter months, a floor is cold that is fatigues an employee that is reduced by a rubber mat, (2) in hot humid months there is potential for a floor surface to become moist that has potential for employee injury and is minimized by a rubber mat and (3) during a picked sku transfer from a pick position to a CO container, a dropped sku onto a cement floor has high potential for damage that for most skus is reduced with a rubber mat. It is noted that a wood surface between the floor and rubber mat improves a cushion feature.

SECURE YOUR PICK CARTON FLAPS IN A PICK & SORT CART & PICK CONVEYOR
IMPROVE PICKER PRODUCTIVITY

Secure your pick carton flaps in a pick & sort cart and pick conveyor is an option to improve picker productivity. Secure your pick carton flaps means that your pick carton top flaps are folded down onto a carton interior side walls or against a carton exterior side walls. With a pick and sort concept, a pick carton flaps folded down creates a smaller pick/sort position and with a pick/pass concept creates a lower elevation to transfer picked skus. Your secure carton top flaps options are (1) fold flaps to a carton interior side walls. Features are (a) low cost and (b) requires packer double handling, (2) fold flaps on exterior side wall and secure with a rubber band. Features are (a) some additional cost and (b) requires packer to recycle, (3) fold picker side flap down onto exterior side and secure with a clip. Features are (a) some additional cost and (b) requires packer to recycle and (4) fold picker side flap down onto exterior side and secure with plastic rivet. Features are (a) additional equipment cost and activity and (b) additional packer activity.

IN A PICK ZONE USE A PICKER CLIP FOR YOUR PICKER'S ACTIVE CUSTOMER ORDER CARTON/TOTE
IMPROVE PICKER PRODUCTIVITY & MINIMIZE ERRORS

In a pick zone use a picker clip for your picker's active CO carton/tote is a small item pick/pass with a pick train or pick cell concept that helps to improve picker to identify a CO carton/tote, improves productivity and minimizes errors (transfer a picker sku to a correct CO container). In most pick/pack concepts, a CO container (carton/tote) is constantly moving into a pick zone and moved over a pick line to a next pick zone or take-away conveyor. As a CO container arrives at a pick zone start, a picker attaches a pick zone clip that becomes a picker's active CO container. During a pick zone pick activity with a pick train concept or queue on a pick line, a picker clip serves to identify an active CO container from other CO containers (cartons/totes) and helps to assure that CO picked skus are transferred to a correct CO container. After a CO completion, a picker transfers a pick zone clip from a completed CO container to the next CO container. With a pick train and different pick zones, different colored clips are useful for new pickers.

HOW A PICKER WALKS IN A PICK/PASS AISLE
IMPROVE PICKER PRODUCTIVITY

How a picker walks in a pick/pass line pick zone/cell is as your picker walks between pick positions and a pick conveyor your reads a pick positions IDs and CO ID on a pick conveyor. As a picker walks in a 30 to 36 wide aisle between pick positions and a pick conveyor, a picker transfers skus from pick positions into a CO container on a pick conveyor and maintains your budgeted picker productivity with accurate transactions. During your pick activity, your picker matches a pick position ID (paper label or pick to light) to a CO ID container (pack slip/invoice clipped to a container or label attached to a container). With a paper document pick concept, a picker reads a sku pick position and quantity and looks and reads a pick position paper ID. With a pick to light pick concept, a picker reviews a pick bay to locate a CO ID on a pick zone light and for each CO sku pick quantity on an activated pick position light. Your picker walk options are (1) parallel or picker faces a pick conveyor. When a picker faces a pick conveyor and to complete a pick transaction, a picker is required to twist or turn for a look at the pick positions and for sku transfer into a CO container. Features are increased picker physical effort, picker turns to review pick positions & CO container, potential difficulty to a track CO container and potential to drop picked skus & (2) perpendicular or picker faces a pick aisle. When a picker is perpendicular to a pick conveyor & pick positions, a picker simply turns their head to review required pick positions, easily to recognize a CO container & easy to transfer picked skus from a pick position into a CO container. Features are less picker physical effort, picker head turns to review pick positions & CO container, easier to a track CO container & less potential to drop picked skus.

PICKER WALKS PERPENDICULAR IN A PICK/PASS AISLE
IMPROVE PICKER PRODUCTIVITY

Picker walks perpendicular in a pick/pass aisle is used in a small item pick/pass pick to light zone that improves a picker productivity due to the fact that within a pick zone a picker has vision of each activated pick to light position and an active CO container. With 'A'/fast moving skus in a pick/pass pick zone, most frequent pick zone length is 1 bay (5 ft) or 2 carton flow rack bays (10 ft). In a pick zone, a picker walking perpendicular to a pick zone pick position and pick line conveyor allows a picker without turning/twisting to see each pick zone activated pick light and complete a pick transaction (pressing a pick button/breaking a laser beam) by transferring a picked sku from a pick position into a CO container.

HOW TO HANDLE A PICK POSITION EMPTY TOTE OR PALLET
IMPROVE PICKER PRODUCTIVITY & ENHANCE SAFETY

How to handle a pick position empty tote or pallet looks at your picker empty tote or wood/pallet handling options. To assure maximum picker productivity, after your WMS computer program receives a sku replenishment transaction completion to a pick position, your WMS computer program releases COs to your pick concept. In most pick concepts and with this approach a replenishment employee handles an empty tote. Tote handling options are (1) with a shelf/rack pick concept, a captive tote is transferred from a pick position to a temporary storage position that is at a shelf/rack top or bottom level position, (2) with a shelf/rack pick position, a tote remains in a pick position and is turned upside down or (3) with a flow rack pick position, a picker transfers an empty tote to non-powered conveyor, cart or holding position. A replenishment employee handles a full cart, removes totes from a conveyor or from a holding position. In most order warehouses, 'A' fast moving and medium/high sku has a pallet flow lane pick position and has a wood pallet as a sku bottom support device. In a pallet flow rack pick concept and after sku depletion, a picker physically tilts an empty pallet onto a narrow meshed skate-wheel or roller return flow lane with two high side guards and is floor level. A picker gently pushes a pallet into a two high sided guard rail travel path that maintains a pallet upright as it flows to a forklift truck location.

BULK OR 'EN MASSE' PICK 'A' MOVING SINGLE SKUS
IMPROVE PICKER PRODUCTIVITY & INCREASES COMPLETED CUSTOMER ORDER NUMBER

Bulk or 'en masse' pick 'A' moving single skus is a small item or GOH warehouse pick concept to improve picker and packer productivity and increase your completed CO number. To have a cost effective and efficient pick concept, your operation activities are (1) computer prints for a CO wave paper document single sku bulk or 'en masse' pick lists that are as a bulk pick instruction. Picked skus are delivered to an assigned pack station or fast pack line, (2) computer prints for each single sku quantity CO wave CO pack slips/invoices in the same sku sequence as on your paper bulk pick document sku print sequence, (3) at a CO and sku scan station, a picker delivers one sku piece for each bulk picked sku that appears on a picker's bulk pick list. This allows an employee to repetitively scan a sku to each CO and as required to insert each CO pack slip/invoice into a slapper envelop and (4) slapper envelopes are delivered to an assigned pack station or fast pack line.

MANUAL BULK PICK & SORT SMALL ITEMS
IMPROVE PICKER PRODUCTIVITY & INCREASE COMPLETED CUSTOMER ORDER NUMBER

Manual bulk pick, sort and final pick small items has your employee picker push a 4-wheel cart through storage/pick aisles. Manual bulk pick & sort small items requires an employee to have a printed document. Each pick document shows pick position, bulk pick quantity, each CO pick quantity and sku description. Prior to a pick activity, a picker identifies on a cart each CO sort position. At each sku pick position, a picker bulk picks a sku quantity and per your sort document sorts a sku to each CO holding position. A manual bulk pick & sort concept improves your total employee productivity but with your picker traveling the entire pick area potential to have lower CO completion number. Features are (1) requires a computer program to print bulk pick & sort documents, (2) easy to problem pickers and (3) easy to complete a pick check.

MANUAL BULK PICK, SORT & FINAL PICK SMALL ITEMS
IMPROVE PICKER PRODUCTIVITY & INCREASE COMPLETED CUSTOMER ORDER NUMBER

Manual bulk pick & sort small items has your employee picker push a 4-wheel cart through storage/pick aisles. Manual bulk pick & sort small items requires an employee to have a printed document. Each bulk pick document shows pick position, bulk pick quantity, and sku description. At each sku pick position, a picker bulk picks a sku quantity and transfers a sku onto a cart holding position. In a sku sort area, you identify each sort position by a position ID that corresponds to your sku inventory ID. Your sort locations are shelves and deck standard pallet rack positions. To have all possible sort locations, your sort area has 5 levels per shelf bay and two shelf bays per digit. Sort location sequences are (1) sku first digit is a shelf bay and last sku digit is a shelf level, (2) sku first digit is a bay and sku second digit is the shelf level & (3) sku last digit is a shelf digit and next to last digit is a shelf level. A manual bulk pick, sort and final pick concept with CO pack slip/invoice improves your total employee productivity & higher CO completion number. Features are (1) requires a computer program to print bulk pick documents, (2) CO pack slip/invoice documents are used in your final pick activity & (3) easy to complete a pick check.

MANUAL BULK PICK, SORT & FINAL PICK GOH SKUS
IMPROVE PICKER PRODUCTIVITY & INCREASE COMPLETED CUSTOMER ORDER NUMBER

Manual bulk pick & sort GOH skus has your employee picker push a 4-wheel cart with a load bar or trolley through storage/pick aisles. Manual bulk pick & sort GOH skus requires an employee to have a printed document. Each bulk pick document shows pick position, bulk pick quantity, and sku description. At each sku pick position, a picker bulk picks a sku quantity and transfers a sku onto a cart or trolley hold position. In a sku sort area, you identify each sort position by a position ID that corresponds to your sku inventory ID. Your sort locations are carts with a load bar and trolley rail lanes. To have all possible sort locations, your sort area has 10 to 20 carts or 10 to 20 trolley capacity that has 1 or 2 carts/trolley per digit. Possible sort location sequences are (1) sku first digit is a cart or trolley and on a load bar last sku digit is arranged in arithmetic sequence from 0 to 9, (2) sku first digit is a cart or trolley and on a load bar sku second digit is arranged in arithmetic sequence from 0 to 9 and (3) sku last digit is a cart or trolley and on a load bar next to last digit is arranged in arithmetic sequence from 0 to 9. A manual bulk pick, sort and final pick concept with CO pack slip/invoice improves your total employee productivity and higher CO completion number. Features are (1) requires a computer program to print bulk pick documents, (2) CO pack slip/invoice documents are used in your final pick activity and (3) easy to complete a pick check.

BULK PICK & MANUAL SORT & FINAL PICK BY SKU
 IMPROVE PICKER PRODUCTIVITY & INCREASE CUSTOMER ORDER NUMBER
Bulk pick, transport, manual sort & final pick by sku concept is used in a multi-line/multi-sku small item or GOH warehouse to improve picker productivity and increase your completed CO number. When compared to a single CO pick or pick & sort concept, a bulk pick, transport, manual sort & final pick by sku concept has fewer picker trips that increase a picker productivity and increases your CO number completed per day. Your picker productivity increase and completed CO number off-sets your sort expenses. To complete a bulk pick, transport, manual sort & final pick by sku activity, your computer program prints a bulk pick document that has each sku listed and in a pre-determined print sequence print your CO pack slips/invoices. Each CO pack slip/invoice indicates each sku WMS ID and quantity. In a sort section, shelves and decked pallet rack with position numbers are in a numerical sequence that allows your bulk sku pickers to sort skus to sort/pick positions and from the sort/pick positions permit your final CO pickers to complete CO picks. After a bulk picker with a sku, reads a sku WMS ID number, it serves as a sku sort instruction and sorts a sku to an appropriate position. From a sort/pick position & with CO pack slip/invoice as a CO final pick instruction that has a sku WMS ID number and sku quantity, a picker completes a CO final pick transaction.

MANUAL BULK PICK, TRANSPORT, MANUAL SORT & FINAL PICK BY CUSTOMER ORDER NUMBER
 IMPROVE PICKER PRODUCTIVITY & INCREASE COMPLETED CUSTOMER ORDER NUMBER
Manual bulk pick, transport, sort and final pick by CO number is a small item warehouse that is used to increase your picker productivity and your completed CO number. When compared to a single order pick concept, your picker productivity increase off-sets your sort expense. After your computer program batches your COs into a pre-determined CO number per group (match your sort positions), it prints one pick and sort instruction/label for each sku in a batch and print your batch CO pack slips/invoices. Your pick labels are printed in pick position sequence number and your CO pack slips/invoices are printed in an arithmetic sequence from a CO low number to a high number. With batch CO pack slips/invoices, a sorter employee writes each CO number on each cart/tote sort position that faces a sorter lane/aisle. Each sort aisle/lane is assigned to a batch and at each sort lane entrance is a batch color/digit ID. Per your pick, transport and sort concept, a CO carton/tote is placed into each position or a sort position is open (slide/chute) and places a CO pack slip/invoice into each CO sort position. On each batch pick label is printed a sku's pick position, CO number and other company required information. Each batch is assigned a color and batch digit ID, a batch colored tag and digit ID is placed onto each tote/carton/cart. As a picker travels with tote/carton/cart through all pick aisles, at each pick position a picker removes a sku, labels a sku and transfers a sku into a cart/tote/carton. After a cart/tote/carton is full or batch completion, a cart/tote/carton is transferred to a transport concept for travel to your sort area. In your sort area, each batch ID carton/tote/cart is pushed into an appropriate batch sort aisle/lane. As a batch cart/tote/carton moves through a sort aisle/lane, a sort employee removes a sku from a cart/tote/carton and matches a sku's CO number to a sort location CO number and a sku is transferred to an assigned CO sort location. Per your concept, sort location options are (1) one sort employee is assigned an entire sort aisle/lane or (2) sort aisle/lane is separated in sort zones with one employee is assigned to one sort zone. After all CO sku sorts, a pack employee removes a CO skus to a pack station and an empty tote is returned to your pick area.

BATCHED CUSTOMER ORDER PICK ACTIVITY
 IMPROVE PICKER PRODUCTIVITY & INCREASE COMPLETED CUSTOMER ORDER NUMBER
Batched CO pick activity is a small item or GOH warehouse paper pick concept that has your computer program group COs into pre-determined CO number per group. With a batched CO group, during one pick trip a picker picks for several COs that increases a sku hit concentration and density to increase your picker productivity and your completed CO number. It is your increased picker productivity that off-sets your additional batched picked sku sort labor and expenses. Your batched CO number is determined by your (1) manual pick & sort cart CO number and (2) mechanized sorter capacity that is based on (a) picker driven or your picker number and productivity rate or (b) active pack station number and productivity rate. After your computer program prints a (1) batched CO pick &

sort document that directs an employee to bulk pick a sku quantity. Per a pick & sort document CO sku, your picker sorts from a bulk picked sku quantity into a CO location on a cart, (2) pick labels that has a (a) picker place a label onto a sku. A labeled sku is placed onto a belt conveyor travel path or in a tote that is transported to a sort station where an employee reads a sku sort label and sorts a sku into a CO location (b) labeled sku is inducted onto a sort conveyor for travel under a scanner that sends a message to a sort computer for a sku sort onto a CO location and (3) with pre-labeled skus a paper pick document or RF device instructs a picker to transfer a pre-label sku quantity onto a belt conveyor travel path or in a tote that is transported to an induction station for sku transfer onto a sort conveyor for travel under a scanner that sends a message to a sort computer for a sku sorted onto a CO location.

LAST BATCHED PICKED TOTE/CART/TROLLEY SIGNAL
IMPROVE PICKER/SORTER PRODUCTIVITY & MINIMIZE ERRORS

Last batched picked tote/cart/trolley signal is a human readable code that is used on a batch pick tote/cart/trolley pick, transport, sort and final pick concept to signal a last picked sku in a batch. In your sort area, a last batch picked tote/cart/trolley signals to a sort employee/bar code scanner/RF tag reader that a batch is completed and your sort area supervisor signals that your next batch totes/carts/trolleys can flow to the sort area. Most last batch signals are colored tag with a human/machine readable symbology.

BATCH PICK & SORT IMBALANCED PLAN
IMPROVE PICKER/SORTER PRODUCTIVITY & MINIMIZE ERRORS

Batch pick & sort imbalance plan is your small item or GOH pick and sort/pack area plans to handle a batched pick/sort concept imbalance between your pick area and sort/pack area. An imbalance plan allow you to maintain your picker/sorter productivity and minimize errors. With a batched customer order pick imbalance occurs between a pick area and sort/pack area, it creates an uncontrolled sku accumulation at a sort/pack area or there is insufficient pieces delivered to your sort/pack area. Your measures to minimize an imbalance situation are (1) for each customer order wave, plan your picker and sorter/packer employee number. Your employee number is based on your picker productivity rate and your sorter/packer productivity rate that provides you with the proper employee number to assure a smooth customer order flow, (2) your pick operation tote, trolley, cart or conveyor travel path concept design number has a safety factor (extra quantity) to compensate for an imbalance and allows pickers to pick the next batch and maintain their productivity and your pick area design your have sufficient picked sku set-down area or queue conveyor lanes. If pickers pick a batch in advance, each next batch tote/cart/trolley/master carton has a proper batch identification with a human/machine readable symbology and is placed in the set-down area. Some potential pick area set-down areas are (a) under or over a conveyor travel path and (b) wider aisle along a conveyor travel path, (3) in your sort/pack area (a) each mechanical sort location design has three windows (one window for present batch/second window for next batch/third window for next batch), (b) with manual sorted small items, have an additional sort lane with sort/pack locations, (c) additional tote/cart/trolley carton queue lanes or conveyor travel paths and (c) manual sort concept or a mechanical sorter is designed with sku re-circulation.

1, 2 OR 3 PICK/PASS PICK LINES OR SECTIONS
IMPROVE PICKER PRODUCTIVITY & INCREASE COMPLETED CUSTOMER ORDER NUMBER

1, 2 or 3 pick lines or sections is a small item warehouse pick/pass line layout option that has your 'A'/fast moving skus profiled to multiple pick lines or sections. When your 'A'/fast moving skus pick volume exceeds your budgeted picker productivity rate, you have potential for pick line congestion or CO flow problems. To resolve your pick line situation, spread your 'A' fast moving sku pick volume over multiple pick lines or sections. Each pick line has a unique WMS ID that allows your set-up/replenishment employees to transfer skus to pick positions and for your WMS computer program to release CO to specific pick lines. Features are per shift high picker productivity, continuous CO flow, high completed CO number, sku set-up replenishment to multiple pick lines and easily handles high volume multiple line/multiple skus COs.

BULK PICK & BULK PICK, SORT & FINAL PICK CUSTOMER ORDER PACK SLIPS/INVOICES PREPARATION
IMPROVE PICKER/SORTER PRODUCTIVITY & MINIMIZE ERRORS

How do you prepare your bulk pick & sort and bulk, sort and final pick CO pack slips/invoices is designed to improve your picker/pack productivity and minimize errors. With a bulk pick/sort to a CO carton/tote, a CO pack slip/invoice is placed into a CO carton/tote that is in a cart sort position. Most bulk pick & sort carts have 9 to 12 CO sort positions that requires your WMS computer program to batch COs into groups that have a CO number that matches your cart sort position number. To assure accurate CO pack slip/invoice handling, for each batch/group each batch number is included on each CO pack slip/invoice of a batch/group. With a bulk pick/sort to a CO carton/tote, a CO pack slip/invoice is placed into a CO carton/tote that is in a cart sort position. Features are (1) improves picker productivity, (2) matches your pick/sort activity to your cart sort positions and (3) improves CO pack slip/invoice control and accountability. With a bulk pick, sort and final pick concept, per your CO wave/group your WMS computer prints a bulk pick document in pick position sequence. Your CO wave/group CO pack slips/invoices are printed and sorted by sort position sequence (first digit, last digit) and each CO pack slip/invoice group is distributed to each sort position number. From each sort position, a final picker with a CO pack slip/invoice a CO completes final pick. If CO pack slips/invoices are randomly printed and distributed to sort positions, your picker productivity is low due to additional walk distance and time to the first pick position. Features are (1) improves packer productivity, (2) with pick, sort and final pick lowers pick instruction cost, (3) with pick, sort and final pick concept that has CO pack slips/invoices separated by sort location improves picker productivity and (4) improves CO pack slip/invoice control and accountability.

YOUR BATCHED PICK SORT CUSTOMER IDENTIFICATION ON A LABEL
 IMPROVE PICKER/SORTER PRODUCTIVITY & MINIMIZE ERRORS
Your batched pick sort CO ID on a label is used in a manual small item or GOH batched CO pick concept to improve picker/sorter productivity and minimize sort errors. After a picker applies a pick/sort label to sku, a labeled sku is placed into a tote, onto a belt conveyor or trolley for transport from a pick area to a sort area. In a sort area, an employee or mechanical scanner requires a sku label with a CO sort ID line of sight to complete a sort transaction. To assure maximum sorter productivity, your CO sort ID is printed as large as possible and is on a label front right and top section. CO sort ID location features are (1) easy to read and (2) first alpha character or digit on a label.

BATCH PICK ONTO A BELT OR INTO A CARTON/TOTE FOR MANUAL SORT OR MECHANIZED INDUCTION
   IMPROVE PICKER PRODUCTIVITY & MINIMIZE SKU DAMAGE
Batch pick onto a belt conveyor or into a carton/tote for manual sort or mechanized induction sort activity are a small item warehouse pick and transport options to assure good employee productivity and minimize sku damage. When your pick, transport and sort warehouse handles skus that are fragile, crushable, have sharp edges, heavy weight, cannot have damaged edges or liquid skus, your picked skus are placed into a tote/carton. Totes/cartons are transported from a pick area to your sort/induction area. To assure empty totes/cartons are in a pick area, totes/cartons are transported to a pick area and strategically stacked in a pick area. Features are additional conveyor costs, tote/carton cost, queue areas, increased potential for a pick/sort label to remain on sku and protects skus. If your operation handles durable skus, your pickers places skus directly or transfers from a self-dumping cart onto a belt conveyor. A belt conveyor transports loose skus to your sort/induction area. Features are lower conveyor cost, no tote/carton cost, potential sku damage or lost pick/sort label and minimal queue capacity.

HOW TO CONTROL YOUR BATCHED PICK ACTIVITY
  IMPROVE PICKER/SORTER PRODUCTIVITY & MINIMIZE ERRORS
How to control your batch CO pick activity is a small item or master carton warehouse method to assure that a batched and picker CO skus are released on-time from a pick area for transport to your sort/induction area. Features are to improve picker/sorter productivity, minimize errors and assure maximum completed CO number. In your pick area on scheduled batched CO picked sku release/control options are to have a (1) clock and batch release time that is printed on each pick label. Feature is relies on picker, (2) score board that shows an active batch for pick/release batch number and each batch number is printed each label. Feature is relies on picker and (3) clerk to issue batch labels to pickers. Feature is relies on a clerk that is additional control and cost. If you desire to maintain your picker activity with an imbalance between a pick and sort/induction area, in your pick area you design advance picked sku set-down area.

HOW TO IDENTIFY YOUR BATCHED PICK ACTIVITY LAST PICK
IMPROVE PICKER/SORTER PRODUCTIVITY & MINIMIZE ERRORS

How to identify your batched pick activity last pick is a consideration for a small item batch pick warehouse to assure picker/sorter productivity, a smooth CO flow and minimize pick/sort errors. Your completed batch CO pick options are (1) if you use a tote/carton transport concept, a colored tote with a human/machine readable pick zone identification tag that is used to identify a last pick from a pick zone. In a sort/induction area, your sort/induction area collects tags until all pick zone tags are received that means a completed batch and (2) with a pick to conveyor concept, your last pick zone has a colored marked and human/machine readable ID on your last pick label. As each pick zone colored label arrives in a sort/induction area, each completed pick zone is listed until a sort/induction area collects all pick zone tags.

HORIZONTAL CAROUSEL CONSIDERATIONS
IMPROVE PICKER PRODUCTIVITY & INCREASE COMPLETED CUSTOMER ORDER NUMBER

Horizontal carousel considerations are ideas to improve your picker productivity and increase your completed CO number. The ideas are (1) forward & reverse or 2-way travel that has a carousel carriers/baskets move in a forward & reverse direction past a pick/sort station. Features are increase computer program cost, minimizes potential picker non-productive time due to minimal waiting time for next sku or CO carrier/basket rotate & arrive at a pick/sort station, (2) carousel controls command a carousel to move an assigned carrier/basket to a pick station that is computer controlled that per your customer order down load has your carousel rotate carriers/baskets with skus or COs to arrive at your pick/sort station. Features are maximum productive sku or customer order basket/carrier rotation due to rotation that is based on sku or CO basket/carrier numerical sequence, maintains good picker/sorter productivity with no carousel move command activity, minimal non-productive employee waiting time & capable to command multiple carousels for maximum picker/sorter productivity, (3) 3 or multiple horizontal carousels service 1 pick/sort station. 3 carousel pick/sort station concept is designed with 3 horizontal carousel in a horse shaped pattern to service 1 pick/sort station that permits 1 picker/sorter employee access to 3 carousels. Carousels (1 & 2) have 'A' & 'B' moving skus with computer program potential for floating slot concept & carousel (3) has 'B' & 'C' moving skus. With family group, pairs & kit skus are profiled by their volume to 1 carousel. Features are reduces non-productive picker waiting time due carousels 1 & 2 rotate as a picker completes sku pick/sort transactions from carousel 3 basket that is at a pick/sort station and (4) to access elevated positions with stationary ladder to permits a picker access to 1 – 3 carousel elevated pick positions,

WITH AN OPEN MASTER CARTON/TOTE OR BASKET USE A REMOVABLE FRONT BARRIER
IMPROVE PICKER PRODUCTIVITY & MINIMIZE SKU DAMAGE

A front barrier is used in a small item manual or mechanized pick concept on a vendor opened master carton or pick position front to retain skus in a shelf, decked rack, carton flow rack or horizontal carousel basket pick position that improves picker productivity and minimized sku damage. After a vendor master carton is prepared for pick position presentation, loose skus in a open front carton/tote or loose skus in a pick position, sometimes there is potential for skus to fall from a pick position or from a carton/tote open front. If skus fall from a pick position, there is non-productive picker time to return skus to a pick position or a sku falling to the floor damages a sku that creates need for special sku inventory adjustment or shortage. Some pick position barrier options are (1) with a smiley face master carton to insert a master carton removed top in a carton open front, (2) with a captive tote to insert a master carton removed top in a tote open front and (3) with skus stacked loose in a pick position or horizontal basket to use a Velcro attached plastic or fabric barrier. As a sku becomes depleted in a pick position, a cardboard barrier is save for reuse or thrown in the trash and a Velcro barrier is retain on a pick position/basket front.

SMALL ITEM AUTOMATIC PICK MACHINES
IMPROVE PICKER PRODUCTIVITY & INCREASE COMPLETED CUSTOMER ORDER NUMBER

Automatic pick small items is a computer controlled pick machine that picks a single CO skus. Skus are transferred from a pick machine onto a cleated belt conveyor or into a CO carton/tote. When you profile an automatic pick machine, you allocate heavy and high cube skus at a pick machine pick pattern front/start and small or light weight skus at the patter end. To assure good pick rates and no stock outs, fast moving skus have two pick positions. Replenishments are made from a separate aisle and behind a replenishment aisle are skus ready reverse positions.

Various automatic small item pick machines are (1) S. I. Itematic that from a pick device release skus onto belt conveyor for transport to a pack station slide. (2) ROBO Pick that from a cleated belt conveyor transfers/water falls a sku into a captive tote and (3) A or H frame that from a pick sleeve releases a sku between two cleats on a belt conveyor for transport to water fall into a tote/carton.

AUTOMATIC PICK MACHINE GATHERING BELT IS A CLEATED BELT
ASSURE PICKED SKU SEPARATION

Cleated belt is used in a small item automatic pick machine as a picked sku gathering belt that transports a separated CO to a transfer station. A cleated belt is a belt conveyor with ¼ to ½ in high cleats that are attached full belt width and on 1 ft or pre-determined centers. After an automatic pick machine releases a sku, on a belt conveyor surface a sku is secured between two cleats. Cleats restricts a sku movement and becoming mixed with another CO skus. When using a cleated belt, attention is given to cleat clearance at a water fall transfer station

AN AUTOMATIC PICK MACHINE GATHERING BELT CONVEYOR TRANSFER IN A CAPTIVE PICK TOTE WITH A CUSHION & SPRING LOADED BUTTON
MINIMZE SKU DAMAGE

An automatic pick machine gathering belt conveyor transfer into a captive pick tote with a cushion & spring loaded bottom is a small item automatic pick machine concept that is used to minimize sku damage as skus are transferred from a belt conveyor end for waterfall into a captive tote. With a standard waterfall/dump concept, an elevation change between a conveyor belt and container bottom is high and has potential to create sku damage or sku package edge damage. A captive pick tote with a spring loaded cushion bottom at a sku transfer location, an elevation change between a conveyor belt and container bottom is minimal and minimizes potential to create sku damage or sku package edge damage. As skus accumulate on a tote spring loaded bottom, skus collective weight depresses a tote bottom that creates additional space for skus.

FOR AUTOMATIC PICK MACHINE GATHERING BELT TRANSFER TILT YOUR PICK CARTON/TOTE
MINIMZE SKU DAMAGE

For automatic pick machine gathering belt transfer tilt your pick carton/tote concept is used in a small item automatic pick concept that has picked skus transferred from an automatic pick machine onto a belt conveyor travel path. At a belt conveyor discharge end, skus are waterfalled/dumped from a belt conveyor into a CO container. With a standard waterfall/dump concept, an elevation change between a conveyor belt and container bottom is high and has potential to create sku damage or sku package edge damage. With a tilted container at a sku transfer location, an elevation change between a conveyor belt and container bottom is lowered and minimizes potential to create sku damage or sku package edge damage.

AUTOMATIC PICK MACHINE PICK PATTERN
MINIMZE SKU DAMAGE

Automatic pick machine pick pattern is a small item or GOH sku automatic pick machine release pattern that is from a pick position onto a powered conveyor travel path to complete a CO and minimize sku damage. With a GOH automatic pick machine concept, skus are released from pick lanes onto a powered conveyor travel for transport to a pack station or direct into a delivery truck for transfer to rope hooks. With a small item automatic pick machine, your sku release pattern is determined by your pick machine model. With a S.I. Itematic pick machine, sku pick positions are along a pick machine one side and skus are released from a pick lane onto a pick head for transfer onto a belt conveyor. To minimize sku damage on your belt conveyor and at your pack transfer station, your heavy skus are released first and light weight/fragile sku are released last. With a ROBO Pick machine, skus are transferred/waterfalled from a pick belt conveyor into a container. To minimize sku damage, heavy skus are released first & light weight/fragile sku are released last. With an 'A' or 'H' frame automatic pick machine, sku release pattern is from a pick machine front, down 1 side, from a machine rear & down the other side to the front. Picked sku release pattern is onto a belt conveyor & control at a transfer/pack station is designed to minimize sku damage that is achieve by your heavy skus are released first & light weight/fragile sku are released last.

MECHANIZED PICK SMALL ITEMS
IMPROVE PICKER PRODUCTIVITY & INCREASE COMPLETED CUSTOMER ORDER NUMBER

Mechanized pick small items has your pick concept move pick positions to a pick station. At a pick station with paper document, RF device or pick to light pick instruction, a picker transfers/picks skus from a mechanized pick position into a CO container. A standard horizontal carousel has nominal 50 basket stacks with 5 baskets per stack. A separated basket increases a basket sku capacity to 5 per basket and a rear sloped basket bottom with Velcro removable front reduces skus falling from a basket to the floor. At a pick station a stationary step ladder is used for an employee access to elevated positions. Pick concept options are (1) single COs, (2) bulk pick, sort and final pick and (3) bulk pick & sort. Your mechanized pick concept options are (1) pick from single horizontal or vertical carousel to CO cartons/totes. Features are (a) cost, (b) low picker productivity due to waiting time for carousel rotation and (c) minimal computer program cost, (2) pick from multiple horizontal carousel in a horse shaped layout to CO cartons/totes. Features are (a) higher cost, (b) higher picker productivity with a three carousel layout, carousel B & C rotate as a picker picks from carousel A, (c) for fast moving or large skus double pick positions and (d) additional computer program cost and (3) pick to a horizontal carousel CO cartons/totes from a sku on a cart/conveyor. Features are (a) cost, (b) additional computer program cost and (c) carousel position matches your largest customer order carton/tote.

MANUAL PICK GOH
IMPROVE PICKER PRODUCTIVITY & INCREASE COMPLETED CUSTOMER ORDER NUMBER

Manual pick GOH has your picker push a 4-wheel cart or trolley through storage/pick aisles. Manual pick GOH requires an employee to have a printed document or RF device that shows a picker each CO sku. Each pick document shows pick position, pick quantity and sku description. A manual pick concept is used to pick single COs, bulk or 'en masse' picked skus for later sort and bulk pick and sort skus. Features are (1) easy to implement, (2) used with various pick concepts and (3) low equipment cost.

PICK GOH AS A SINGLE PIECE OR 3 PIECE BUNDLE
IMPROVE PICKER PRODUCTIVITY

Pick GOH as a single piece or 3 piece bundle pick concept is used in a GOH warehouse that has a bulk or 'en masse' pick sku concept increases CO number and improves picker productivity. If GOH is bulk picked for retail store orders or for a pick, sort and final assembly concept, a 3 piece bundle pick concept has your computer program print pick instructions to show GOH bundle picks and single piece picks to complete a bulk pick transaction or retail CO. The approach improves picker productivity due to one GOH pick transaction has 3 GOH pieces instead of 1 GOH CO has one pick transaction that requires an employee to complete 3 pick transactions.

GOH AUTOMATIC PICK MACHINES
IMPROVE PICKER PRODUCTIVITY & INCREASE COMPLETED CUSTOMER ORDER NUMBER

GOH automatic pick machine is a computer controlled concept that has a device that releases CO GOH skus onto a GOH take-away travel for travel to your pack area. If your operation has multi-line/multi-sku COs, your GOH concept has capability to transfer multi-line/multi-sku CO skus direct to a pack station or to a special consolidation area. For maximum efficiency GOH hangers are standard, match your manufacturer's specifications, each GOH has a unique identification and a sku overflow storage area. Your automatic pick machine concepts are (1) MTS, (2) 200 G and (3) Promech. Features are no employee activity means high productivity, high cost and to handle multi-line/multi-sku additional computer program costs or employee activity.

GOH SCAP
IMPROVE PICKER PRODUCTIVITY & INCREASE COMPLETED CUSTOMER ORDER NUMBER

GOH SCAP concept means GOH sort, count and pick concept or is called a GOH GOLDEN highway. A GOH SCAP has one pick lane section or 2 pick lane sections. A GOH SCAP concept has 4-wheel carts or trolley rails that has each lane charge end face your receiving dock and discharge end permits travel to your pack area. A one pick lane section that allows skus transfer from your receiving dock to your GOH SCAP area and after your CO pick activity to transfer completed CO transfer to your pack stations and residual skus are transferred to your storage area. A two GOH SCAP concept has 2 pick lane sections for maximum flexibility and to handle a large GOH number. Prior to unloading a GOH delivery truck, your company purchase order indicates your sku number and quantity & sales date. Per your GOH SCAP design and GOH volume & GOH sales forecast and sales date, each GOH cart or trolley lane has 3 to 4 capacity. If your GOH quantity exceeds 1 SCAP design, you allocate overflow GOH skus to multiple cart/trolley lanes, to your other SCAP section or to warehouse storage positions. A GOH SCAP concept improves put-away productivity and picker productivity due to short travel distances and high sku hit concentration and density.

TRASH MASTER CARTONS HAVE NO (CUT) FLAPS
IMPROVE PICKER PRODUCTIVITY & IMPROVES TRASH HANDLING

Trash master cartons have no flaps is a small item warehouse that has a replenishment or picker remove or fold-in a master carton flaps as it sets in a pick position. No master carton flaps features are (1) improves picker productivity due to unobstructed sku removal, (2) means easier employee trash handling to remove an empty carton from a pick position, (3) at a manual trash baler less time to prep a carton for a baler, (4) less complex transport or carton movement on a conveyor with fewer jams/hang-ups & (5) greater capacity in a trash container/conveyor travel path.

TRASH REMOVAL CONVEYOR
IMPROVE PICKER PRODUCTIVITY

Trash removal conveyor is a method to transport empty master carton and filler material trash from a 'A'/fast moving pick area to a trash disposal area baler or container that assures good picker productivity and efficient trash handling. With a carton flow rack concept, your trash conveyor elevation is set at an elevation for easy picker (reach) transfer onto your trash conveyor belt. With a pick/pass concept, your trash conveyor starts at your first pick position ('A' fasting moving skus) and continues past all pick line pick positions (slow moving skus). The high to low pick volume approach assures that your 'A'/fast moving pick zone has an empty belt surface. Your trash conveyor picker (near) side guard rail is angled for easy picker transfer and far side guard rail is extra high to assure your tallest thrown trash cartons remain on a conveyor travel path. If require additional guard rail protection, you add fish netting above the far side guard rail to retain cartons on a conveyor travel path. Your trash conveyor width is designed for your widest carton, under side has a solid guard and you have an 'E' pull cord full length. To assure minimal carton hang-up and maximum carton capacity on a conveyor travel path, your replenishment employee removes a master carton top flaps. To extend a trash conveyor length your options are (1) between two belt conveyor sections add a gap plate or roller that has the same surface elevation or (2) water fall a front conveyor onto another conveyor. With both conveyor transfer options, at conveyor transfer locations your have angled photo eyes across the travel path that senses jams and sends a message to conveyor computer to stop conveyor belt.

CHAPTER 6
PICKED SKU CHECK & PACK ACTIVITY & SHIP SUPPLY ITEM

EXPENSE REDUCTION IDEAS

ONE CUSTOMER ORDER OR MULTIPLE CUSTOMER ORDERS PER PICK TOTE
  IMPACTS YOUR PACKER PRODUCTIVITY & COMPLETED CUSTOMER ORDER NUMBER & COMPUTER PROGRAM CUBE PROCESS

One CO or multiple COs per pick tote are your manual pick by paper, label or pick to light options that impact your packer productivity, completed CO number and computer program cube process. With one CO per pick tote, you have potential for lower picker productivity, increased CO containers on a travel path, good packer productivity and minimal WMS computer program CO process time. With two or more COs per pick tote has potential for you to increase picker productivity, reduce CO containers on a travel path, low packer productivity, increase your WMS computer cube program process time and cost and additional computer program cost for COs printed at your pack station. With a pick to light concept, additional and costly computer programming time and cost to have multiple COs into warehouse ID pick tote.

WHEN DOES YOUR OPERATION NEED A CUSTOMER ORDER CHECK ACTIVITY
    ASSURE ACCURATE ORDERS & CONTROL YOUR CUSTOMER RETURNS EXPENSES

When does your operation need a CO check activity is a question that is ask many operation managers and the answer to the question is the bases for your check activity design and implementation. Your check activity objective is to have minimal COs with accurate picked and packed skus and no damaged skus. With accurate CO picked skus and excellent package appearance with sufficient filler material, you increase your satisfied customers and minimize customer returns with its associate returns process expense. If your customer returns have a high rate for (1) damaged sku, you consider a post-pack check activity, increase your packer training and review your filler material and container and (2) shorts, over-picks or wrong sku, your check activity is pre-pack check activity and you review your pick instruction concept, assure that your replenishment activity is accurate and on-time and assure that your sku description match a sku.

GET YOUR BAD APPLES
  CONTROL YOUR CUSTOMER RETURN EXPENSES

Get your bad apples is a computer program CO screen process to identify repeat customers with repeated returns & to suggest that your company have a supervisor manual check a CO or to suggest that your company cancel a CO. Get a bad apple is designed to minimize repeat CO returns that require (1) for you to complete a CO, to incur pick, pack & ship expenses that are not off-set with a sale, (2) additional labor & computer expenses to handle a customer order return & (3) to eliminate potential sku damage from your sku return process & activity. With your customer return history & associated customer return expense and pick/pack/ship expense, your management has data for a decision to accept or cancel a CO for a customer who has repeat returns & minimize your future handling expenses.

WHAT GOES OUT BAD COMES BACK
  IMPROVE YOUR CUSTOMER ORDER PACKAGE PRESENTATION & CUSTOMER SATISFACTION

What goes out bad comes back is a pack activity term that refers to a CO pack quality to minimize damage skus. To improve your customer service and reduce customer returns to reduce costs you assure your CO package has sufficient filler material, properly sealed bottom and top flaps and clear customer delivery address.

LIST YOUR CUSTOMER CHECK PROBLEMS
  ASSURE ACCURATE ORDERS

In addition to assuring an accurate CO completion, your check activity lists the reasons that created a problem CO that reduces future CO problems. At your problem CO station, your supervisor identifies (1) each CO ID that identifies a specific pick line or section, (2) identifies CO problem such as (a) over pick, (b) shortage, (c) damage sku 7 (e) wrong sku that IDs potential picker problems. replenishment problems or vendor sku problems & (3) IDs package appearance & packer such as (a) label orientation, (b) tape strand number, (c) tape strand length, (d) filler material that creates package bow & (e) under filler material or not proper filler material that helps identify packer problems. If repeat employee errors occur, you have additional training or re-assign an employee to another activity.

WHAT ARE YOUR CUSTOMER RETURNS REASONS
ASSURE ACCURATE ORDERS & CONTROL YOUR CUSTOMER RETURNS EXPENSES

Your customer returns reasons are a result from your pick and pack activity performance that do not match your CO service standards. Your customer return reasons are (1) Shortage means that a customer did receive an order on-time but a CO picked, packed and delivered sku quantity was less than a CO pack slip/invoice sku quantity. A CO sku shortage means that a customer is dissatisfied with your pick & pack operation performance due to the fact a CO sku was not delivered on-time in a package. A shortage pick has your staff focus on your picker activity quality, (2) Overage means that a CO was received at a delivery address but a CO picked, packed and delivered sku quantity was more than a CO pack slip/invoice quantity. A CO overage means that a honest customer is dissatisfied with your pick & pack operation due to the fact a customer has to take time & expense for a sku return quantity to your pick & pack operation. An overage pick has your staff focus on your picker activity quality, (3) Sku Damage occurs when a CO is received at a delivery address & when a CO picked, packed & delivered sku quality is compared to a CO pack slip/invoice that an actual CO ID, picked, packed and delivered sku quality indicates that a sku is broken or not functioning sku. A CO sku damage means that a customer is dissatisfied with your pick/pack operation performance due to the fact a customer has to take time & expense and return a damage sku to your pick/pack operation and due to the fact that a customer did not received a CO good quality sku on-time. A damaged sku has your staff review your receiving/quality control, pack activity & filler material type, package seal type & quantity & vendor ready to ship carton quality & (4) Incorrect Sku or\mis-pick occurs when a CO is received at a delivery address and when a CO picked, packed & delivered sku quality is compared to a CO pack slip/invoice that an actual CO picked, packed & delivered sku is not a CO sku. A CO incorrect sku means that a customer is dissatisfied with your pick/pack operation performance due to the fact a customer takes time & expense and return an incorrect picked and delivered sku to your pick/pack operation and a customer did not received a correct sku on-time. With an incorrect sku or pick error has your staff focus on your picker activity quality that includes your replenishment activity.

COMPUTER SUGGESTED (PROBLEM) CUSTOMER ORDER CHECK
ASSURE ACCURATE ORDERS & CONTROL YOUR CUSTOMER RETURNS EXPENSES

Computer suggested (problem) CO check concept has your CO process computer program to identify customers who are repeat return customers. Your CO process computer program identifies a repeat return customer and suggests that your pick/pack staff verify your CO pick and pack accuracy and sku quality. Per your pick and pack concept, each repeat CO is manual or mechanically transferred to a special check and pack station. At a special check and pack station, a staff member verifies a completed CO sku quantity accuracy and sku quality. After a check and pack activity, a completed CO package is transferred onto a take-away transport concept. Your additional check expenses are off-set by reducing your CO return number and associated return process and sku return to stock expenses and potential sku damage.

HIGH VALUE SKU CHECK
ASSURE ACCURATE ORDERS & CONTROL YOUR CUSTOMER RETURNS EXPENSES

High value sku check is a computer suggested CO check concept that has your CO process computer program to identify CO with a high value sku. Your CO order process computer program identifies a CO with a high value sku and suggests that your pick/pack staff verify your CO pick and pack accuracy and sku quality. Per your pick and pack concept, each CO with a high value sku is manual or mechanically transferred to a special check and pack station. At a special check and pack station, a staff member verifies a completed CO accuracy and sku quality. After a check and pack activity, a completed CO package is transferred onto a take-away transport concept. Your additional check expenses are off-set by reducing your customer return number and assures a satisfied customer.

100% CHECK ACTIVITY
ASSURE ACCURATE ORDERS & CONTROL YOUR CUSTOMER RETURNS EXPENSES

100% check activity is a check employee or automatic check machine concept that has each CO quantity or quantity/quality checked. Per your pick and pack concept, each CO is manual or mechanically checked a special check station or pack station. At a special check or pack station, a staff member or automatic check machine verifies a completed CO accuracy and sku quality. After a check and pack activity, a completed CO package is transferred onto a take-away transport concept. Features are high check labor expense and requires additional check station number. Your additional check expenses are off-set by reducing your CO return number and assures a satisfied customer.

RANDOM CHECK ACTIVTY
ASSURE ACCURATE ORDERS

A random check activity concept is designed to have your checker randomly select CO containers to verify that picked sku quantity and quality match your CO pack slip/invoice sku quantity and quality. With a random concept, as picked CO containers leave your pick area, an employee or machine checker completes a check activity. Good COs are sent to your pack area and poor quality COs are transferred to a problem CO station. If you have a post pack random check activity, at a separate check station an employee verifies a CO container appearance match your company standard and picked/packed sku quantity and quality match your CO pack slip/invoice. Features are improves picker accuracy, assures accurate order and assures good checker productivity.

SEPARATE CHECK OR CHECK/PACK STATION
ASSURE ACCURATE ORDERS & CONTROL YOUR CUSTOMER RETURNS EXPENSES

Separate check station or check/pack station are two CO check options for your pick/pack operation. With a separate check station concept, after your pick activity, your completed COs are sent to a check station. At a separate check station, an employee or mechanized concept assures that a CO picked skus quantity and quality are per your company standard. Per your check station results, OK or all good COs are sent to a pack station and poor quality/not accurate COs are sent to a problem order station. Features are (1) additional labor cost, (2) additional equipment, (3) completes a high CO number and (4) creates high packer productivity. A checker/packer concept has at a pack station, a packer verify a sku quantity and quality. If a check is OK, a packer completes a CO. If a CO has a problem, a packer transfers a problem CO pack slip/invoice and skus and ship carton/tote to a problem order station. Features are requires additional queue prior to check/pack station, requires sufficient work table surface to complete a check activity, lower packer productivity and lower completed CO number/or you add work stations.

PACKAGE APPEARANCE IS IMPORTANT
ASSURE SAFISTIED CUSTOMERS AND REDUCE CUSTOMER RETURNS

Your package appearance is important in a warehouse to assure that a CO delivery address is in the proper location and that a package exterior appearance is per your company standard. A package with good exterior appearance is the first step to satisfy a customer. A good package appearance factors are (1) customer delivery address label in the correct location, (2) no package bow or bulge, (3) no loose tape strands, (4) carton top and bottom flaps sealed and (5) no extra tape strands.

PRE-PACK CHECK OR POST-PACK CHECK
ASSURE ACCURATE ORDERS

Pre-pack check or post-pack check activity are your two CO check options. A pre-pack check activity is completed after your pick area and prior to your pack area and verifies your CO picked sku quantity and quality match your CO pack slip/invoice sku quantity and description. A post-pack check activity completed after your pack activity and prior to your manifest area. Your post-pack check activity options are (1) a package quality or appearance check that verifies your packer has sufficient tape strand (s) to secure a ship carton top flaps and sufficient filler material to protect skus with no carton top bow or (2) a picked sku quantity and quality check & package quality or appearance check. To maintain your CO package appearance standard, a post-pack check activity that opens a CO carton, requires a new ship carton & a new delivery label. The aspect requires a label printer at a post-pack check station.

MANUAL QUANTITY CHECK
   IMPROVE CHECKER PRODUCTIVITY & ASSURE ACCURATE ORDERS

A manual quantity check activity has an employee compare a picked sku quantity to a CO pack slip quantity. For a manual sku quantity check concept have your CO process computer print a total sku on a CO pack slip/invoice. During your manual sku quantity check activity a total sku quantity is used by a checker as instruction. With the concept, your computer prints a CO total sku quantity in a clear and easy to recognize location on each CO pack slip/invoice. At a check or pack station, in a CO carton/tote a checker or packer counts an actual picked sku quantity and easily compares the actual count to sku total on a CO pack slip/invoice. Features are reduces an employee non-productive count time for skus on a CO pack slip/invoice.

SIMILAR SKUS WITH DIFFERENT COLORED CAPS
   ASSURE ACCURATE ORDERS & IMPROVE CHECKER PRODUCTIVITY

Similar size skus with different colored caps is used in a manual sku quantity check activity to improve manual checker productivity. When you have mixed skus in a CO container, your checker uses a colored cap to assure that an actual sku matches a CO pack slip/invoice sku quantity due to the fact that your CO pack slip/invoice has a colored cap in a sku description. Feature minimizes your checker reading requirement, improves checker productivity and accuracy and has simple instructions.

MANUAL CHECK (TOTAL SKU QUANTITY ON A PACK SLIP/INVOICE) (See Manual Check Activity)

MANUAL QUANTITY & QUALITY CHECK
   IMPROVE CHECKER PRODUCTIVITY & ASSURE ACCURATE ORDERS

A manual quantity and quality check activity is completed prior to your pack area. A check activity has an employee compare a picked sku quantity to a CO pack slip quantity & a picked sku quality to a CO pack slip/invoice sku description. A sku quantity check options are have a (1) checker count each picked sku quantity in a CO carton/tote and compare each sku picked quantity to a CO pack slip/invoice quantity or (2) checker count a total sku quantity and compare an actual total sku quantity to a CO pack slip/invoice total sku quantity. An alternative to a count check concept is to have your checker bar code scan a CO ID and scan each sku WMS ID and sku quantity that are sent to your check computer program. Since your WMS computer has transferred your CO ID and sku ID to your check computer, your check computer program compares each sku scan and quantity transaction to your computer CO sku quantity. To improve your check scan productivity your hand held scanners are elevated for easy sku scan transaction and default a scan transaction for one sku.

DEFAULT YOUR HAND HELD SCANNER TO ONE (See Customer Returns Chapter)

FIXED POSITION YOUR HAND HELD SCANNER (See Customer Returns Chapter)

HAND HELD SCANNER MULTIPLE LIGHT BEAMS OR WIDE LIGHT BEAM (See Customer Returns Chapter)

RF TAG CHECK
   IMPROVE CHECKER PRODUCTIVITY & ASSURE ACCURATE ORDERS

A RF tag check activity is a machine check activity that completes a sku quality and quantity check. With a RF tag check concept your WMS computer has transferred your CO ID and sku ID to your check computer. As a CO container with an RF tag ID and each sku with a RF tag ID arrives at your check station, a RF tag receiver receives a CO ID and each sku ID that is sent your check computer. Your check computer program compares each sku scan & quantity to your computer CO sku quantity. A RF tag check concept is a high tech 'check on-the-fly' check concept.

STATIONARY SCALE CHECK
  ASSURE ACCURATE ORDERS

A stationary scale check concept is a sku quantity check concept that requires your staff to establish a weight variance between your actual and computer projected weight. This is very important with small size, liquid or powered skus, (2) assures each carton/tote size weight is entered into your computer program, (3) assure each sku actual weight is entered in your computer program and (4) per your CO process computer that your CO is cubed for a container. Your conveyor/scale computer has received each CO ID and weight for your CO wave. As your CO containers (cartons/totes) arrive at your scale station, an employee transfers onto a scale & cans a container CO ID that is sent to your scale computer. Also, your scale obtains a CO actual weight that is sent your scale computer. Your scale computer compares your actual CO ID (container) weight to your computer estimated CO ID weight. If your actual and computer projected CO weight variance is within your company allowance, your CO container is returned to the conveyor for travel onto a pack station. If your actual an computer projected order weight variance is out of variance, your employee transfers a CO container onto your problem order conveyor travel path. Features are (1) handles a medium volume, (2) requires computer program cost, (3) requires a actual to computer weight variance and (4) accurate sku and container weight in your computer program.

CHECK ON-THE-FLY OR MECHANIZED CHECK (See RF Tag Check)
  ASSURE ACCURATE ORDERS

Check on-the-fly or mechanized check activity is considered a 100% customer order picked sku quantity check concept. With a check on-the-fly concept, your staff (1) establishes a weight variance between your actual and computer projected weight. This is very important with small size, liquid or powered skus, (2) assures each carton/tote size weight is entered into your computer program, (3) assure each sku actual weight is entered in your computer program & (4) per your CO process computer that your CO is cubed for a container. Your conveyor/scale computer has received each CO ID and weight for your CO wave. As your CO cartons/totes leave your pick area on a conveyor travel path, a scanner reads a container CO ID that is sent to your conveyor/scale computer. With singulated container travel on a conveyor constant travel speed, a CO travels over an in-line scale that obtains a CO actual weight that is sent your conveyor/scale computer. Your conveyor/scale computer compares your actual CO ID (container) weight to your computer estimated CO ID weight. If your actual and computer projected CO weight variance is within your company allowance, your CO travels onto a pack station. If your actual an computer projected order weight variance is out of variance, your conveyor/scale computer has your conveyor travel path divert a CO container onto a problem CO conveyor. Features are (1) handles a high volume, (2) requires computer program cost, (3) additional conveyor cost, (4) requires a actual to computer weight variance and (5) accurate sku and container weight in your computer program.

PASS THE PROBLEM ORDER (See Problem Customer Order Or Poor Quality Sku Station)

PROBLEM CUSTOMER ORDER OR POOR QUALITY SKU STATION
  IMPROVE CHECKER PRODUCTIVITY & INCREASE CUSTOMER ORDER CHECK NUMBER

A problem CO or poor quality sku station is shelf that is located in a check or pack area and is a very short walk distance for a checker or packer to transfer a problem CO. If your check or pack activity determines when compared to a CO pack slip/invoice that a CO container has a poor quality sku or sku quantity error, your company policy requires corrective action taken to assure an accurate CO. To maintain a checker or packer at a work station, when a problem CO occurs, a checker or packer transfers a problem CO (skus, container and CO pack slip/invoice) to a problem CO shelf. The approach has a checker or packer remain at a work station and not have non-productive walk time to a pick area to correct a problem CO. A check or pack area supervisor corrects a problem CO and re-introduces a corrected CO to a check or pack station. Feature is increase check or packer productivity and increased completed CO check or pack number.

CHECK, PACK CUSTOMER ORDER RETURN PROCESS STATION LIGHT FIXTURE LOCATION
  ASSURE GOOD CHECK & PACKER PRODUCTIVITY AND ASSURE ACCURATE ORDERS

A check, pack and customer return process activity light fixture location improves check, packer and process employee productivity. At a manual activity station, a light fixture location is above a CO container on a work station table and at an elevation that allows an employee to read all CO container ID and sku descriptions. With a check weigh station, your light fixture lumens or brightness allows an employee to easily read a scales digital display.

PACK ACTIVITY WARM START
  IMPACTS YOUR PACKER PRODUCTIVITY & COMPLETED CUSTOMER ORDER NUMBER
Pack activity warm start improves your packer productivity and completed CO number. A pack activity warm start means that your pick activity queues picked COs prior to each pack station. To assure a pack activity warm start, your pick and sort activity starts prior to your pack activity. Your pick activity early start time is based on the time required to create a picked CO pack station quantity/queue. The time is based on your required completed CO number that is determined by your picker and sorter productivity and picker and sorter number. In most manual bulk pick and sort operations, your pre-start time is 1 hr to 1 hr 30 min and in a manual bulk pick and mechanized sort operation, your pre-start time is 2 hr to 2 hr 30 mins.

SORT ACTIVITY WARM START (See Pack Activity Warm Start)

PACK ACTIVITY COLD START
  IMPACTS YOUR PACKER PRODUCTIVITY & COMPLETED CUSTOMER ORDER NUMBER
Pack activity cold start lowers your packer productivity and completed CO number. A pack activity cold start means that your pick activity has no queued picked COs prior to each pack station. A pack activity cold start has your pick and sort activity start at the same time as your pack activity. Your pick activity same start time has no time to create a picked CO pack station quantity/queue. With no picked COs, your sort or pack employees are assigned to pick activity or other activity, features are non-productive employee reassignment and walk time between from another activity location to your sort or pack station.

SORT ACTIVITY COLD START (See Pack Activity Cold Start)

KNOW AND BALANCE YOUR PICK, SORT & PACK ACTIVITY PRODUCTIVITY RATES & EMPLOYEE NUMBER
  ASSURE CONTINUOUS CUSTOMER ORDER FLOW & HIGH COMPLETED CUSTOMER ORDER NUMBER
Know and balance your pick, sort and pack productivity rates and employee number is an operation plan that has a direct impact to assure your continuous CO flow and high completed CO number. Your pick, sort and pack activity rates are your budgeted productivity rate that were based on a projected sku volume and used to project your annual expense budget. With CO wave volume and activity productivity rates you determine your required employee work stations. From your day employee work schedule, you know your picker, sorter and packer number that is compared to your projected employee picker, sorter and packer number. For an on-budget operation, you assure your actual projected picker, sorter and packer number matches your budgeted picker, sorter and packer. If one operation activity has an employee number that exceeds your required employee number, there is potential for your CO flow to have uncontrolled queue or low completed CO number. With a CO wave plan, your operation has an opportunity to provide on-time customer service at the lowest cost.

EMPLOYEE OR COMPUTER SUGGESTED CARTON/BAG SIZE
   IMPACTS YOUR PACKER PRODUCTIVITY, FILLER MATERIAL USAGE & TRACKS CARTON/BAG USAGE
Employee or computer suggested carton/bag size are your packer ship carton/bag selection process that has an impact on your packer productivity, filler material usage and ability to track carton/bag usage. An employee suggested ship carton/bag has your packer look at a customer order sku size & quantity and from their experience determine a ship carton/bag. Features are potential for extra filler material placed into a package and if a wrong is made-up and not used, low packer productivity. With a computer suggested carton/bag your computer program requires a package utilization factor, accurate sku exterior cube data and carton/bag interior cube data. From a CO sku quantity, a cube program determines the best carton size to match your CO cube and filler utilization factor. After a computer CO process, your computer prints a suggested carton/bag size on a CO pack slip/invoice or ship label. Features are higher packer productivity, lower filler material usage, requires sku and carton/bag dimension collection, cube program cost, some additional computer CO processing time and from computer program files ability to track each ship carton/bag size usage.

FOLD OR DO NOT FOLD CUSTOMER ORDER PACK SLIP/INVOICE INTO PACKAGE
IMPROVE PACKER PRODUCTIVITY & CUSTOMER SATISIFCATION

When your packer includes a CO pack slip/invoice in a carton, your CO pack slip/invoice options are to have a packer (1) fold option has a packer fold and place a CO pack slip/invoice inside a carton. The fold activity is a non-productive packer time and (2) do not fold has a packer place a CO pack slip/invoice inside a carton that does not require non-productive packer time.

LEGEND ON PACK SLIP/INVOICE TO INDICATE INSERT SALES LITERATURE
ASSURE GOOD PACKER & MANIFEST PRODUCTIVITY

A legend or symbol on each CO pack slip/invoice is a concept that is a packer instruction for a packer to add sales literature to a CO container. After your company merchandising department completes a customer survey that customer after receiving one CO with a specific sku or month sales literature and with a second CO within the same time period do not desire to receive a second specific sku or mother sale literature, you have an opportunity to lower your company sales literature print expense and improve your packer productivity. With modifications made to your CO processing computer program and determination of your CO number that has two or more COs and customer acceptance you can implement the concept.

INSERT SPECIAL GIFT OR SALES LITERATURE INTO A CUSTOMER ORDER PACKAGE
IMPACTS YOUR PACKER PRODUCTIVITY & CUSTOMER SATISFICATION

Insert a special gift or sales literature into a CO package are activities that impact your picker or packer activity. Your special gift handling options are (1) to create a separate CO wave with a special gift sku in a pick position that has a picker complete a pick transaction. Features are sku appears on a CO pack slip/invoice with no charge, simple inventory control, track by your WMS computer program and allows a check activity to verify a special gift in a CO or (2) to have all special gift WMS or warehouse CO IDs entered into your sort computer and each WMS or warehouse ID CO carton or tote is diverted to a specific pack station. At a pack station, a packer automatically transfers a special gift into a CO container. Features are (1) requires a mechanized sort concept, (2) your sort computer receives all CO IDs that require a gift and (3) assures smooth CO flow and your picker productivity. After you have completed a customer survey and conclude your repeat customers do not desire to receive a second or same sku or sales period sale literature, your CO process computer has a mark on a CO pack slip/invoice or delivery label that is in a easily recognized location and serves as a signal for a packer to include sales literature in a CO package. Features are (1) completed a customer survey, (2) computer program cost and additional process time, (3) additional packer training, (4) mark location on CO pack slip/invoice or delivery label and (5) lower sales literature usage means a lower advertising expense.

WORK STATION ADJUSTABLE LEGS OR WORK PLATFORM
IMPROVE EMPLOYEE PRODUCTIVITY

Adjustable legs or work platform are your work station options to improve your check, packer or returns employee productivity by assuring that a work station elevation matches an employee height. An employee work station height design factors are CO in-feed height, CO out-feed, empty tote out-feed height, work station height and employee height. Factors available for adjustment are your (1) work station height that adjusted by adjusting each work station height or legs to match an employee height but a work station height. Features are (a) improve employee productivity due to work station top allows employee to easily complete tasks and (b) low employee productivity die to potential difficulty for an employee to transfer a CO in-feed or out-feed and empty tote between a conveyor and work station surface and (2) raise your employee elevation by adding a wood platform under an employee work station stand area. With a wood platform, it raises your short employee to a height that allows an employee to transfer a CO in-feed or out-feed and empty tote between a conveyor and work station surface. Features are (a) platform height is variable and set to match each short employee height and provides a work station surface that reduces employee fatigue and cold feeling from standing on a cement floor.

PACK TABLE SURFACE
PACKER PRODUCTIVITY

Your pack table surface has sufficient are for your packer to complete a packer's activity. A pack table assures access to picked COs, packed CO take-away concept, trash container, cartons/bags and problem order station. A table surface has space for handling a CO pack slip/invoice from a stack or printer, scan transactions, check picked skus with a 2 to 3 sku average, taper and carton make-up, fill material space and sale literature space. With a sort/pack activity, space includes sort activity.

PASS A PROBLEM CUSTOMER ORDER TO A PROBLEM STATION (See Problem Order Station)

LIGHT FIXTURE LOCATION
CHECKER & PACKER PRODUCTIVITY & ACCURATE CHECK ACTIVITY

Light fixture location at your check or pack station assures your checker or packer productivity improvement and accuracy. At a check or pack station with a paper document, your light fixture location assure proper light lumens/level for a checker or packer to read a CO pack slip/invoice sku ID and quantity and compare a sku actual description and quantity. At most check and pack stations operations, a light fixture is directly over a pack table surface that is a checker or packer front/over a package. With a scan and display screen check or pack activity, your light fixture is in the same location but with a checker or packer reading a display screen you match your light lumens/level to assure easy checker or packer read.

RUBBER MAT OR WOOD FLOOR (See Pick Chapter)

PACK STATION SHELVES
PACKER PRODUCTIVITY & IMPROVE PACK STATION SPACE UTILIZATION

Pack station shelves are a pack station idea that improves pack productivity and pack station space utilization. For best packer productivity, you set your first shelf elevation for your most frequent carton height with flaps up. From an elevated shelf a packer has a simple task to pull and transfer sheet filler material and sales literature into a CO. Features are shelf with structural straight to support paper and sales literature weight, shelf storage space for other ship supplies, used with a regular pack table and provides space for a large paper quantity.

COMPUTER SUGGESTED SHIP CARTON SIZE
IMPROVE PACKER PRODUCTIVITY AND MINIMIZE FILLER MATERIAL EXPENSE

A computer suggested CO ship carton has your WMS computer cube program suggest a ship carton size that improves packer productivity and reduces your filler material usage. A computer suggested ship carton size is based on your CO sku cube, your desired utilization rate and available ship carton sizes. After your CO sku cube is calculated, your WMS computer cube program matches your CO sku cube to your available carton size that allows skus to fit into a carton. Your suggested ship carton computer program requires accurate sku external cube dimensions and ship carton internal dimensions.

HOW TO COLLECT YOUR SKU CUBE DIMENSIONS
IMPROVE PACKER PRODUCTIVITY AND MINIMIZE FILLER MATERIAL EXPENSE

To collect your sku cube dimensions is an important activity that is completed by your receiving or QA department and sent to your WMS computer program. Based on your CO sku cube and available ship carton cube, your WMS computer program suggests a ship carton that improves packer productivity and reduces your filler material usage. Your sku cube dimension collection options are (1) vendor cube data. Features are sometimes does not match your needs, low cost and requires clerk entry, (2) cube platform that is a three side platform with colored lines on each side. Each colored lines represent a ship carton interior cube. After your place a sku onto a platform its physical size is within a specific colored line group and it is preferred ship carton size for a sku. Features are low cost, easy to use, employee activity, requires entry into your cube program and best used for single line/single sku COs and for multiple line CO requires your computer program to add two carton sizes together for preferred carton size that has additional computer programming and cost and (3) automatic cube device that has an employee place a sku onto a surface that moves a sku through a device tunnel. In the tunnel, a device obtains a sku external dimensions and weight that for computer entry are sent to your computer cube program. Features are accurate sku dimensions with weight, on-line computer program entry, does not require an employee and has a higher cost.

PEAL-OFF LABEL
   INCREASE PACKER PRODUCTIVITY & USE PICK LABEL FOR PACK LABEL
A peel-off label is a pick and pack activity idea that improves packer productivity and when your CO ID on a pick carton does not match your CO ID/delivery label on a ship carton location, it allows you to place your CO ID on in carton pick location and at your pack station to transfer a CO ID from a pick carton location to a ship carton location. A peel-off label has two self-adhesive labels. The first self-adhesive label is large and has a second (CO ID) self-adhesive label on its face and is applied to a carton pick location. A packer removes a CO ID label from the carton self-adhesive label and places a CO ID in a ship carton location. The first or large self-adhesive label remains on your CO carton or is removed and thrown in the trash. Features are satisfies both pick and ship label location requirements, slightly higher label cost, requires a packer activity and used with a separate CO pack slip/invoice and delivery label print concept.

ZERO SCAN YOUR CAPTIVE WAREHOUSE IDENTIFIED PICK TOTE
   ASSURE ACCURATE CUSTOMER ORDER HANDLING
Zero scan your captive warehouse ID pick tote at your pack station is a packer activity that has a packer to complete a tote warehouse ID zero scan transaction and send it your warehouse and WMS computer program. After your computer program receives a captive tote warehouse ID zero scan transaction, your warehouse and WMS computer programs breaks a CO WMS ID to a captive tote warehouse ID that permits you to use your captive tote warehouse ID to become related to another WMS CO ID. If a packer does not complete a captive tote warehouse ID zero scan transaction and for another WMS CO a picker completes another WMS CO ID and captive tote warehouse ID scan transaction that is sent to your warehouse and WMS computer programs and associates a both transactions and a WMS CO ID to a captive tote warehouse ID. On pick line and pack area, you have two another WMS CO IDs that are associated to one captive tote warehouse ID and creates potential pick errors.

PACK STATION ZERO SCAN YOUR PERMANENT PICK TOTE IDENTIFICATION (See Zero Scan)

SHIP CARTON SECURE TYPES AND SELECTION FACTORS
   IMPACTS YOUR CUSTOMER ORDER PACKAGE PRESENTATION & CUSTOMER SATISFACTION
Ship carton secure types and selection factors determines your CO package presentation and customer satisfaction. Carton secure material assures that your carton bottom and top flaps are sealed and provide sku security. Various secure types are (1) gummed tape to activate the glue a tape strand pass over a moist brush and a packer applies a tape strand to a carton flaps. Gummed tape machine options are manual operated, electric operated and heated water. Features are requires water supply, potential for packer to cut fingers on tape edge, potential sku damage for a packer to transfer glue from fingers onto a sku, down-time to replenish roll and requires flat work surface, (2) self-adhesive tape has an employee or machine apply a plastic tape strand to a carton bottom or top flaps. Options are (a) manual concept that is best with spare tapers and tape rolls at a pack station, has good packer productivity, handles a wide carton size mix and multiple strands are easily applied to a carton, (b) total random machine taper has a higher cost, applies one tape strand, handles a small carton size range, requires floor space and electric supply, down-time to change a depleted roll and difficult with a narrow pre-delivery labeled carton, (c) fixed machine with manual adjustability has a highest cost, applies one tape strand, handles a small carton size range, requires floor space and electric supply, down-time to change a depleted roll and difficult with a narrow pre-delivery labeled carton, (3) machine applied plastic bands that has one or two bands in one direction or different directions that has some potential hang-up problems with a shoe sorter and down-time to replace depleted bands, (4) shrink wrap requires an electric supply and down-time to replace depleted bands, (5) pop-out carton that interlocks a bottom carton flaps that lowers your tape expense and (6) one piece solid bottom carton that requires no packer activity but a carton form machine. Ship carton secure selection factors are (1) economics, (2) lead time, delivery and storage, (3) required space at a floor area and pack station, (4) employee or machine productivity rate, (5) ability to secure package, (6) customer acceptance and (7) time required to replenish depleted secure material.

HAND TAPER OR MACHINE TAPER
PACKER PRODUCTIVITY, INCREASE CUSTOMER ORDER FLOW & ACCURATE PACKAGE SECURE

Hand tape or machine tape a CO package are options that impact your packer productivity, CO flow and secured packages with self-adhesive tape strand. Machine tape option has a pick line or packer transfer a CO sku transfer to a bottom sealed container and transfer a completed CO container onto a conveyor travel path. As a CO container travels on a conveyor travel path, prior to a tape machine a gap is pulled between 2 containers for tape machine entry. A carton under a tape machine control has one tape strand applied to a carton top flaps. Tape machines are available as (1) fixed position or manual adjustable machine that handles a narrow carton height range and has a higher tape carton rate and (2) random machine that places one tapes strand on a carton top flaps and handles a wide carton size range with a slight lower tape carton rate. With both machine tape machine types, your picker or packer CO delivery label placement on a carton top flaps and tape on a carton does not cover a label that creates potential CO ID read problems. Other features are one tape strand on each package, onetime cost, requires an electric and/or air supply, down-time to replace an empty roll with a full tape roll and requires space to complete tape replacement and maintenance. A hand tape concept has a packer with a self-adhesive dispenser apply one or multiple tape strands per carton. At a pick line end or pack station, an employee applies a tape strand that does not cover a CO delivery label or after a tape strand placed onto a carton places a CO delivery label. Features are handles a wide carton size range, allows one or multiple tape strands per package, no warehouse space and at each tape station for maximum tape employee productivity spare tape dispensers.

GUMMED OR SELF-ADHESIVE TAPE
ASSURE SKU PROTECTION, PACKER PRODUCTIVITY, PACKAGE APPEARANCE & LOW COST

Gummed or self-adhesive tape are a CO container manual seal/tape options that secure a carton top & bottom flaps. Gummed tape requires a water brush to activate tape. A gummed tape machine occupies a pack table surface and at each pack station requires a reserve bottle water supply. As a packer handles a moist gummed tape strand, there is potential for a gum adhesive on an employee hands to be transferred onto a sku and tape strand side to cut an employee fingers. If an electric tape machine is used an electric outlet is required at each pack station. As a gummed tape roll becomes smaller, a gummed tape strand becomes more difficult to handle and apply to a carton. Self-adhesive tape is used with a hand held tape dispenser. To tape a carton, a packer secures a tape strand end to a carton and moves a dispenser over a carton flaps. For maximum packer efficiency each pack station has spare tape dispensers and extra tape rolls. Features are used at any location, easier to handle a wide carton size mix and less potential employee finger cuts and glue damage to skus.

WHAT IS THE BEST TAPE STRAND WIDTH AND LENGTH
CONTROL YOUR TAPE EXPENSE & ASSURE CUSTOMER CONTAINER SECURITY

How many tape strands and a tape strand length (extension over a carton two edges) is policy that is established by your company to assure secured carton surfaces. With a machine formed carton and top sealed carton there is one strand on bottom flaps and one strand on the top flaps. An employee formed carton has typically one tape strand on the bottom and top surfaces. For a heavy sku, most operations allow a packer to add 2 to 3 bottom and top flaps. Tape strand extension over a carton top or bottom edges assures that a tape strand is secured onto a carton. A CO carton with minimal and sufficient tape strands maintains your tape expense and assures that your best package presentation to customer for increase customer satisfaction.

HAND SCANNER WITH BATTERY OR DC ELECTRIC LINE
PACKER PRODUCTIVITY & ACCURATE TRANSACTION TRANSFER

A hand scanner battery or direct electric line refers to a pack station hand held scanner power supply options. A battery powered scanner device has a battery that powers a scanner light. During a work day over 1 or 2 shifts, a packer scan transactions draw power from a battery. On some occasions, a scanner has low power that creates a no read transaction that is low employee productivity and requires a packer to have non-productive time to replace a low battery with a full charge battery. At a work day or shift end, to assure full charge batteries, packers have non-productive time to bring scanners to a charge station. At a charge station, an employee assures each battery is attached to a charger & prior to a pack activity start-up requires each pack station set-up with a full charge scanner. Features are requires spare batteries, requires a charge station with electric outlets & potential low employee productivity. A direct electric line powered scanner has an electric outlet at each pack station that allows an employee to activate a scanner. Features are a pack station electric outlet requires a one-time cost, maximum packer scan productivity due to no low battery problems, no battery charge & scanner set-up time.

FIXED POSITION HAND HELD SCANNER AT A PRE-DETERMINED ELEVATION
PACKER PRODUCTIVITY & ACCURATE TRANSACTION

Fixed position hand held scanner at an employee check, pack station or customer returns process station is an option that improve employee productivity and accurate scan transaction. A fixed position hand held scanner allows an employee to complete a CO ID and sku ID scan transaction without moving a hand held scanner. After a CO container arrives at a work station, an employee simply moves a CO pack slip/invoice and sku IDs under a scanner and transfer the skus into a CO container. A fixed position scanner with a default of one for each good read that is in an elevated position for your most frequent sku height allows an employee two hands to move a sku and complete a scan transaction without reaching or picking up scanner that is non-productive employee time. If required to scan a tall sku a scanner is removed from a stand and an employee completes a scan transaction. Features are improved employee productivity with no hand movement to locate and pick-up a scanner and return a scanner to a pack table and moving a sku with two free hand lowers potential sku drop/damage.

PRINT PACK SLIP WITH DELIVERY LABEL OR PACK SLIP & LABEL PRINTED SEPARATE
IMPACTS YOUR PACKER PRODUCTIVITY & CUSTOMER ORDER DOCUMENT CONTROL

Print on one printer your CO pack slip/invoice with a delivery label or customer order pack slip and label printed separately on two printers. A CO pack slip/invoice important data includes customer name, customer delivery address, sku description and quantity, price, other company information and is placed inside a CO container. A delivery label has your CO delivery address and your company return address and is applied to a CO package exterior. Your print options are (1) both printed on one paper sheet has one printer complete a CO pack slip/invoice and delivery label on one sheet. Features are (1) some slight additional print time, (2) reduces risk of separation, (3) easier to control pack slip/invoice grouping by sku digit and (4) self-adhesive label makes the paper thicker and (2) printed on separate paper and printers that has one printer print your CO pack slip/invoice and another printer print your delivery label. Features are (1) additional paper supply items, (2) used in a bulk pick, transport & sort concept or pick & sort or pick into a CO container, (3) requires two print devices in a central office or pack station table and (4) used to print multiple page CO pack slip/invoice.

PRE-PRINT OR PRINT-ON-DEMAND CUSTOMER ORDER PACK SLIPS/INVOICES
ASSURES CUSTOMER ORDER DOCUMENTS ARE AVAILABLE

Pre-print or print-on-demand CO pack slips/invoices and delivery labels are your options that assure CO documents are available for your pack activity. Pre-printed CO pack slips/invoices are printed and batched/grouped by each pack station in an office and distributed to each assigned sort/pack station. Pre-printed documents require your staff to create a CO wave/work day CO number and based on your active pack station (sort/pack station) number to batch or group COs for each pack station. To assure packer productivity and assure proper distribution, each pack station batch/group have a pack station ID. Features are requires one large capacity printer, print paper in an environmental controlled room, per your CO number requires a computer program to determine each pack station CO number and method to verify correct pack station distribution. Print-on-demand occurs at a pack station and each pack station has a CO pack slip/invoice printer that is activated by a hand held scanner. A packer with a hand held scanner or fixed position scanner scans a captive tote warehouse ID or ship carton WMS CO ID that is sent to your warehouse printer computer. After a computer program activates a printer, a printer prints a CO pack slip/invoice and delivery label. Features are requires a scanner at each pack station, at each pack station and potential wait for print completion and if CO IDs are downloaded to a warehouse printer computer program, there is minimal print wait time.

ONE PRINTER WITH BACK-UP MAINTENANCE OR TWO PRINTERS
IMPACTS YOUR CUSTOMER SERVICE & MAINTAIN EMPLOYEE PRODUCTIVITY

One printer with a vendor back-up maintenance contract or two printers are operations central location (office) print options to print CO pick, pack & ship documents for on-time customer service and good employee productivity.

One printer with a vendor back-up maintenance concept prints your CO pack slips/invoices & delivery labels. If you have a printer problem, your staff telephones your printer vendor for support/repair. Features are your past printer problem frequency and down-time length of time. Features are potential for a very cold pick or pack activity start, for past problems at other customer locations, vendor estimated travel and repair time, low printer cost and customer service below your standard. With two printers a problem with one printer you have a second printer to complete your print requirement and vendor repairs the disable printer. Also, if your delivery label requires special label such as a carbon copy, you require a paper document printer for CO pack slip/invoice and a separate printer for a delivery label. Features are continued customer service standard, maintains your picker and packer productivity, higher cost with additional office space and determined by your print requirement.

MANUAL OR MECHANICAL CUSTOMER ORDER PACK SLIP/INVOICE INSERT
   IMPROVE EMPLOYEE PRODUCTIVITY & ASSURE PACK SLIP/INVOICE IS ENCLOSED IN A PACKAGE
Manual or mechanical CO pack slip/invoice insert activity are your options to assure that each CO container has a CO pack slip/invoice inserted in a package. Your CO pack slip/invoice insert location options are (1) at entry to your pick activity. Pick activity entry options are (a) conventional pick one CO per container or bulk pick/CO sort concept that has your picker or picker/sorter transfer a CO pack slip/invoice into a CO container and (b) pick/pass concept that has an employee picker or machine transfer a CO pack slip/invoice into a package. Features are potential for CO pack slip/invoice to become lost, CO pack slip/invoice is a package bottom, high packer productivity and pre-printed pack slips/invoices, (2) at your sort location that has a sort employee place a CO pack slip/invoice into a CO assigned sort slide/chute, carton or tote. Features are less potential for CO pack slip/invoice becoming lost, pre-printed pack slips/invoices, with slide/chute sort position in a CO package pack slip/invoice is on sku top and packer uses CO pack slip/invoice to check picked skus & (3) at your pack station that has a packer transfer skus into a CO package & placed a pre-printed or printed on-demand pack slip/invoice on sku top. Features are pre-printed or print on-demand pack slips/invoices, less potential for CO pack slip/invoice becoming lost & lower packer productivity.

IDENTIFY YOUR PRINTER PROBLEMS
   IMPROVE PRINTER EFFICIENCY AND MINIMIZE DOWN-TIME
Identify your printer problems has your staff list each printer problem, frequency and length of time that provides data for your to improve your printer efficiency and minimize future printer down-time. If your are experiencing central office printer problems, your staff registers day of week printer problems, problem frequency, vendor repair time and parts, CO and line number that includes both pick and pack documents and paper quality. The information helps you to identify specific events or items that are repeaters.

BAG OR CARTON SHIPPER
   ASSURE SKU PROTECTION & LOW SHIPPER COST
Bag or carton are your small item (s) shipper options that assures a low cost shipper, properly protects a sku, present a delivery label to employees or scanners and encloses a sku in a shipper as your freight company delivers a CO. Your ship bag or carton selection factors are (1) sku protection, (2) pack employee productivity. When required to add sales literature and customer order pack slip/invoice, a pop-out carton has good productivity, (3) container quantity storage at a pack station, (4) security to blend with other small size cartons/packages. A small size carton or pop-out carton matches your other ship cartons, (5) handled by your freight company such as conveyable and able to support other packages. Most freight companies have bags on one conveyor sort concept and cartons on another conveyor sort concept, (6) exterior surface holds your CO delivery label, (7) purchase cost. When compared to a bag, it is possible that a pop-out carton for light weight skus has a lower cost and reduces security and sku protection problems, (8) with void space in a carton, required labor and filler material, (9) customer acceptance and ability to use container for a return and (10) accept by your returns trash recycle program. A carton with filler material is easier to use as a return container. After your analysis and weight given to each factor, you determine the preferred small item shipper.

DELIVERY LABEL WINDOW
IMPROVE PACKER PRODUCTITY & YOUR CUSTOMER ORDER PACKAGE PRESENTATION
Pre-printed label window with your return address on a ship container improves your packer productivity, reduces your customer delivery label print time, scan efficiency and enhances your CO package presentation. A label window is a preferred location for a CO ship label placement that assures maximum employee or bar code scanner/RF tag good read number. For easy employee instruction and to assure maximum area for a carton seal tape, a postage stamp label location on carton side wall or top exterior flap is preferred. The concept has an employee place a CO delivery address label in a pre-printed area on a carton upper right hand top or side surface. Part of a pre-printed label window includes your operation's return delivery address for non-deliverable packages or customer refused packages. With your operation's return delivery address on a carton, it means that a CO delivery label requires less ink & paper space. Less CO delivery label paper space increases a combined CO pack slip/invoice print format flexibility & space for other items such carton size or include sales literature.

SHIP CARTON TYPES
ASSURE GOOD PACKER
Two piece, regular, pop-out, chipboard, creased/slotted and notched cartons are your operation ship carton options. Each carton with tape assures a secured CO container and for manifest activity a CO delivery label is in the proper location. Your options are (1) two piece carton is a CO container that has a bottom and matched top/cover. Each two piece carton size requires a from machine and cardboard sheet. Features are requires a packer to have both pieces, requires a strap secure method and during your transport activity, a lower transfer elevation and travel path window and requires top and bottom form machines, (2) regular carton is a 1 piece carton with bottom & top flaps. Prior to your pick or pack activity, an employee or machine forms & secures a regular carton bottom flaps with a tape strand. After a completed CO package, a packer or machine secures each carton top flaps. Features are requires a top and bottom tape labor and expense, with flaps up tall transport travel path window & a high elevation for sku transfer into a carton and available in a wide carton size mix, (3) pop-out carton is a one piece carton with a performed bottom flap section. When a picker or packer presses a pop-out carton sides together, bottom flaps become interlocked to from a secured bottom. Features are minimal labor and tape expense, handles a light weight sku, assures high carton make-up employee productivity & with some cartons potential powered conveyor transport difficulties. (4) chipboard carton/box is a two piece carton that is employee assembled and secured with tape or plastic bands. The chipboard handles light weight skus such as flatwear and has a low cost, (5) creased/slotted carton is regular carton with pre-determined/vendor creases on the 4 side walls. If a CO skus create a void space inside a carton, with a knife a packer slides each side wall joint to the preferred crease that creates longer flaps. The flaps are folded and sealed to create a solid top. The creased carton increases carton flexibility, higher cost and reduces filler material usage/expense and (6) notched carton with a notched member at each side wall joint. If a CO skus create a void space inside a carton, with a lid with extensions at each corner a packer pushes a lid downward inside a carton until a lid secures skus and each lid extension is locked into a notch. With tape packer seals a carton top flaps. A notch carton increases carton flexibility, higher cost, lower productivity and reduces filler material usage/expense.

PRE-MADE CARTONS
IMPROVE PACKER PRODUCTIVITY & INCREASE COMPLETED CUSTOMER ORDER NUMBER
Pre-made customer order ship cartons is a manual pack station activity that is used with a regular (one piece) top and bottom flap carton. For a carton make-up employee pre-made carton activity is a repetitive activity that means high carton make-up employee productivity. If your pack activity uses a pop-out carton, a pre-made carton concept is difficult to justify. If your operation has a wide carton size mix, at a pack station it is difficult to have sufficient space for pre-made carton staging area. If your operation has a few carton sizes (4 to 5), at each pack station there is sufficient space for pre-made carton staging area.

SHIP BAG TYPES AND SELECTION FACTORS
IMPACTS YOUR CUSTOMER ORDER PACKAGE PRESENTATION & CUSTOMER SATISFACTION
Ship bag types and selection factors determines your CO package presentation and customer satisfaction. Bag material assures that your bag mouth is sealed and as a CO is shipped to a delivery address, it provides very small

sku security. Various bag secure types are (1) plain corrugated/jiffy bag is available in a wide size range and has some water proof feature. Options are no padding, bubble sheet padding or rigid insert to protect a sku. A bag mouth is tape or staple sealed or self-sealed. Features are low cost, provide sku protection and customer can reuse for returns, (2) plastic bag has water proof feature and a self-seal mouth. Features are high cost, water proof protection, difficult to reuse for customer return & difficult to store a pack station & (3) sandwich bag is mechanized pack concept. The concept consists of two kraft paper sections that engulf and complete a 4 side seal of a sku with a CO pack slip/invoice and applies a CO delivery label. Features are handles a high concept, high cost and additional computer programming, requires floor area, high productivity with few employees.

Ship bag selection factors are (1) economics, (2) lead time, delivery and storage, (3) required space at a pack station, (4) employee or machine productivity rate, (5) time to secure bag, (6) space for customer delivery label & (7) customer acceptance.

PLAIN OR COLORED PAPER FILLER SHEETS
PROTECT SKUS & SATISFIED CUSTOMERS

Plain or colored paper filler sheets are an operation options that use paper to fill voids in a CO container and protect skus and satisfy customers. Plain paper has a gray or white color that can have customers feel less satisfied with paper filler material. A light green or blue colored paper have customers feel more satisfied with paper filler material.

FILLER MATERIAL TYPES & SELECTION FACTORS
ASSURE SKU PROTECTION & LOW COST

Filler material fills a CO container voids to protect skus as a container is transported to a CO delivery location. In most operations, at a pack station an employee adds filler material to a container. In some operations, a machine adds filler material to a container. For filler material re-use/re-cycle at a customer returns station an employee removes filler material from a container and transfers to transport concept. Your filler material options are (1) crushed paper from a paper roll, paper sheets or machine, (2) manual or funnel transferred peanuts or peanuts in a bag, (3) cardboard chips, (4) air bubbles or bubble sheets, (5) cardboard cubes, (6) foam in a plastic bag or manual or machine foam in place, (7) meshed cardboard, (8) notched carton with lip insert and (9) sku enclosed on plastic on a cardboard sheet. Filler material selections factors are (1) economics, (2) lead time, delivery and storage, (3) required space at a pack station, (4) transfer into a container requirements, (5) ability to protect sku and fill voids, (6) customer acceptance and (7) re-cycle as filler material or trash.

DO NOT OVER FILL
IMPACTS YOUR PACKER PRODUCTIVITY & FILLER MATERIAL USAGE & CUSTOMER SATISFICATION

Do not over fill is your packer standard to assure that your packers complete a CO package with proper presentation. Proper presentation characteristics are that filler material fills all void spaces to protect skus from damage and there is no convex bow to a package top surface. Features are good packer productivity, low filler material usage and improve customer satisfaction.

PAPER SHEET OR PEANUTS
ASSURE PACKER PRODUCTIVITY & PROTECT SKUS

Paper sheet or peanuts are the most popular package filler material that is used to fill voids in a CO container. Peanuts are formed material that are employee hand or gravity/air blown through a funnel into a CO container. To complete a gravity/air blown fill activity, a packer positions a CO container for filler material transfer by lower a carton flap and assures a funnel is located over a container. With a tall carton, there is some difficulty to position a funnel inside a container. During filler material transfer, an employee spreads the filler material inside a container. If there is extra filler material in a container, your packer re-cycles extra filler material into the next CO container. A packer hand transfer option has a low packer productivity due a packer uses a scope to transfer peanuts from a container into a carton. Features are (1) at most pack stations, over-flow peanuts on the floor require clean-up that is non-productive employee time, (2) gravity/air blown concept has a higher cost and (3) requires large storage bag. Paper sheets are pre-cut sheets (full size and half size sheet) or packer cut from a roll and transferred as crushed paper into a container. For best customer acceptance use light green or blue colored paper. To assure maximum packer productivity, rubber fingers and paper sheets are located on pack table shelves. Features are (1) requires small storage area, (2) less messy and (3) requires a packer to crush the paper.

PAPER ROLL OR PAPER SHEETS
ASSURE SKU PROTECTION & LOW COST

Paper roll or paper sheets are your paper filler material options for a packer to transfer a manual crushed paper sheet into a package. A paper roll concept has a paper roll that is horizontal or vertical to your fill station or pack table. With a roll, a packer pulls a paper from a roll and cuts a paper sheet from a roll. At a pack/fill with a horizontal paper roll concept, a paper roll has a cutter blade and a packer can easily reach a paper end. Features are assure paper roll length & width & weight is easily handled by your replenishment employee and to complete a replenishment and rod insert into a paper roll some fill/pack station down-time. A vertical roll paper concept has a paper roll that is located along a conveyor travel path or pack station in a location that allows a packer to easily reach a paper end, cut a paper sheet and crush/transfer into a package. Features are some cut/ripped paper sheets have jagged ends, after cutting a sheet some paper ends are difficult to reach assure paper roll length & width & weight is easily handled by your replenishment employee and to complete a replenishment and rod insert into a paper roll some fill/pack station down-time. Paper sheets are vendor delivery full size and half size sheets that are placed at a fill/pack station on a shelf or table surface. As requires a packer picks-up a sheet (s) and crushes/transfers a paper sheet into a package. Features are no jagged edges, replenishments have minimal downtime, two sheet sizes means maximum fill and replenishments are easily completed to a pack station.

RE-SUPPLY YOUR PACK STATION SHIP SUPPLIES BY SHIP SUPPLY REPLENISHMENT EMPLOYEE
IMPROVE PACKER PRODUCTIVITY & INCREASE COMPLETED CUSTOMER ORDER NUMBER

Re-supply your pack station ship supplies by a supply replenishment employee has a ship supply replenishment employee assure each pack station has sufficient ship supply quantity for your CO wave CO number. Ship supply items are tape, special labels, filler material such as paper sheets, paper roll, bubble sheet or bubble glove. Your ship supply replenishment activity occurs during prior to start-up. breaks, lunch or other pack station down times. When compared to a pack non-productive walk time to get ship item re-supply, a replenishment employee activity means higher packer productivity and increase completed CO number.

WHERE TO STORE YOUR SHIP SUPPLIES SAFETY STOCK
ASSURE SHIP SUPPLY QUANTITY

Where to store your ship supplies safety stock is an idea that has your ship supply safety stock (from your historical data, you determine each ship supply most frequent or peak day usage & vendor lead time) in a non-vital area in your warehouse. A non-vital storage area is not adjacent to your pack area or pick area. Your non-vital storage options are (1) in your main warehouse remote dense storage locations that does not require over-the road shuttle costs but requires sq ft & (2) in your off-site storage facility that requires shuttle cost & use dense storage concepts.

PACK STATION SHIP SUPPLY RESERVE LOCATIONS
ASSURE PACKER PRODUCTIVITY & SUPPLY ITEM INVENTORY CONTROL

Pack station ship supply reserve locations is a concept that maintains packer productivity and assures a constant ship supply flow to your pack stations. Whenever possible there are sufficient floor level positions for each ship supply item that permits an employee quick access to a ship supply item for transport to a pack station. Between your two pack station rows, your ship supply reserve locations are (1) single rack row that is two forklift truck aisle and one side protection netting on elevated positions. Feature is lowest space utilization due to two wide forklift truck aisles, (2) back to back rack rows that have two wide forklift truck aisles. Feature is poor space due to two wide forklift truck aisles and (3) single off-set rack row that has one wide forklift truck aisle and one personnel aisle. A personnel aisle is adjacent to one pack station row and elevated positions have protective netting. Feature is best space utilization with one wide forklift truck aisle.

KNOW YOUR SHIPPING SUPPLY USAGE & LEAD TIME (See Where To Store Your Ship Supplies)

PARTIAL PRE-PACK
INCREASE COMPLETED CUSTOMER ORDER NUMBER & IMPROVE PACKER PRODUCTIVITY

Partial pre-pack is a sku bulk pick and pack activity that improves employee productivity, provides a smooth CO volume and increases completed CO number. Partial pre-pack is a pack activity that uses a pack line layout and philosophy as a fast pack line. From your historical sales and merchandise sales plan, a few days prior to a sku sales promotion and during a low volume CO day, a partial pre-pack activity has a WMS ID sku placed from a master carton into a CO ship container that has sealed bottom flaps and as required bottom filler material and non-sealed top flaps. At a pre-pack line end, non-sealed cartons are stacked onto a pallet. Per your inventory policy and practice, a full pallet receives a new WMS ID and sku quantity count and for single line/single sku COs your WMS computer CO process program recognizes a pre-pack sku first. After your pre-pack sku quantity depletion, for single line/single sku COs your WMS computer CO process program recognizes a standard non-pre-pack skus. When your operation receives a high CO volume for your CO final pack activity, your operation uses a fast pack line to complete COs. Prior to your CO pack line activities, at a scan station an employee pre scans a sku ID to each WMS CO ID, bulk picked partial pre-packed sku and pre-scanned CO pack slips/invoices are delivered to a pack line. On a pack line your activity stations are (1) transfer a partial pre-pack sku onto a conveyor, (2) as required add top filler material, (3) insert a CO pack slip/invoice and sales literature into a container and (4) add a CO delivery label onto a container, seal a container top flaps and transfer a completed CO container onto a take-away conveyor for transport to your manifest station. As an option at your pre-scan station each CO pack slip/invoice and sales literature are placed into a slapper envelop. A slapper envelop is attached directly onto a container sealed top flaps. When compared to a regular pick and pack activity concept, a pre-pack concept smoothes your CO work activity over days that maintains your employee productivity and CPU and handles a high CO number.

COMPLETE PRE-PACK
INCREASE COMPLETED CUSTOMER ORDER NUMBER & IMPROVE PACKER PRODUCTIVITY

Complete pre-pack is a sku bulk pick and pack activity that improves employee productivity, provides a smooth CO volume and increases completed CO number. Complete pre-pack is a pack activity that uses a pack line layout and philosophy as a fast pack line. From your historical sales and merchandise sales plan, a few days prior to a sku sales promotion and during a low volume CO day, a partial pre-pack activity has a WMS ID sku placed from a master carton into a CO ship container that has sealed bottom flaps and as required bottom filler material and sealed top flaps. At a pre-pack line end, sealed cartons are stacked onto a pallet. Per your inventory policy and practice, a full pallet receives a new WMS ID and sku quantity count and for single line/single sku COs your WMS computer CO process program recognizes a pre-pack sku first. After your pre-pack sku quantity depletion, for single line/single sku COs your WMS computer CO process program recognizes a standard non-pre-pack skus. When your operation receives a high CO volume for your CO final pack activity, your operation uses a fast pack line to complete COs. Prior to your CO pack line activities, at a scan station an employee pre scans a sku ID to each WMS CO ID, each CO pack slip/invoice with your sales literature are placed inside a slapper envelop and bulk picked partial pre-packed sku and slapper envelops (pre-scanned CO pack slips/invoices) are delivered to a pack line. On a pack line your activity stations are (1) transfer a completed pre-pack sku onto a conveyor and (2) transfer a completed CO container onto a take-away conveyor for transport to your manifest station. When compared to a regular pick and pack activity concept, a pre-pack concept smoothes your CO work activity over days that maintains your employee productivity and CPU and handles a high CO number.

VENDOR READY TO SHIP OR SLAPPER LABEL
IMPROVE PACKER PRODUCTIVITY, INCREASE COMPLETED CUSTOMER ORDER NUMBER & DECREASE SHIP SUPPLY EXPENSE

Vendor ready to ship or slapper label is a pack concept that improves your packer productivity, increase completed CO number and decrease ship supply expense. A vendor ready to ship or slapper label concept components are (1) ship carton that has exterior structural wall strength, sealed flaps and exterior package markings assure sku protection and ship label/slapper label attachment and (2) slapper label that is an envelope with a self-adhesive backing, enclosed CO pack slip/invoice & sales literature and several windows for your (a) CO ID line of sight and delivery address, (b) sku ID and (c) sku pick position and your delivery company assures that their scanner reads a slapper label and label is not removed as it moves over the sort concept. For maximum use in an operation, your slapper label length and width and thickness that permits attachment to your maximum sku number. Your sku pick and slapper label options are (1) for high volume sku to bulk pick and have a sample sku ID pre-scanned to each CO ID and stuffed into an envelope. All completed envelops are delivered with the bulk picked sku to a fast pack line for slapper envelop to a sku and (2) for low volume sku at a pick position, with a slapper envelop a picker scans a sku ID and CO ID and a slapper envelop is attached to a sku.

CUSTOMER ORDER PACK SLIP/INVOICE AS A SLAPPER ENVELOP, TAPE OR WRAP
INCREASE PACKER PRODUCTIVITY & INCREASE COMPLETED CUSTOMER ORDER NUMBER

CO pack slip/invoice as a slapper envelop, tape or wrap are two fast pack activity options to secure a CO pack slip/invoice onto a CO carton that increases your packer productivity and increases your completed CO number. A fast pack activity has a clerk pre-scan skus to a CO ID and CO pack slips/invoices are delivered to your fast pack line. Your secure options are based on your CO type, sku size, sku volume, customer acceptance, economics and freight company acceptance. A slapper envelop has a customer order pack slip/invoice & sales literature that are placed into an envelope with a self-adhesive back and is placed onto a carton exterior. Features are additional envelop cost, with windows is used a pick instruction, envelop block some CO pack slip/invoice data and employee or machine applied to carton. Tape concept uses clear/transparent self-adhesive tape and has your pre-scanned CO pack slips/invoice folded and sent to a fast pack line. After a CO pack slip/invoice is placed onto a carton, tape is employee or machine applied to secure a CO pack slip/invoice onto a carton surface. Features are with CO pack slips/invoices on a carton surface have potential difficulty to assure accurate and high productive tape activity and CO pack slip/invoice folded face to have no important customer information. Wrap concept uses clear/transparent plastic sheet and has your pre-scanned CO pack slips/invoice folded and sent to a fast pack line. After a CO pack slip/invoice and sheet are placed onto a carton, an employee or conveyor directs each carton through a shrink wrap (heat) tunnel that has a plastic sheet secure a CO pack slip/invoice onto a carton surface. Features are with CO order pack slips/invoices on a carton surface have potential difficulty to assure accurate activity, requires an electric heat tunnel and electric expense and CO pack slip/invoice folded face to have no important customer information.

SLAPPER LABEL (See Vendor Ready To Ship Carton)

FAST PACK BY SKU
IMPROVE FAST PACK PRODUCTIVITY & INCREASE COMPLETED CUSTOMER ORDER NUMBER

Fast pack by sku is fast pack idea to improve your bulk/'en masse' pick and fast pack productivity and increase your completed CO number. A fast pack line sequential stations are (1) carton make-up and as required bottom fill station, (2) master carton open and sku and sales literature transfer station and (3) CO pack slip/invoice insert, carton top flap seal and delivery label attachment station and transfer to a take-away conveyor. An option is to use a slapper envelop that contains a CO pack slip/invoice and sales literature. With a fast pack by sku concept, you sku determines your carton size and you have potential to change carton size for each sku. The approach has potential to have some non-productive for carton size change. When compared to a regular CO pick/pack activity, a fast pack concept improves picker and pack productivity and increases your completed CO number.

FAST PACK BY CARTON SIZE
IMPROVE FAST PACK PRODUCTIVITY & INCREASE COMPLETED CUSTOMER ORDER NUMBER

Fast pack by carton size is fast pack idea to improve your bulk/'en masse' pick and fast pack productivity and increase your completed CO number. A fast pack line sequential stations are (1) carton make-up and as required bottom fill station, (2) master carton open and sku and sales literature transfer station and (3) CO pack slip/invoice insert, carton top flap seal and delivery label attachment station and transfer to a take-away conveyor. An option is to use a slapper envelop that contains a CO pack slip/invoice and sales literature. With a fast pack by carton size concept, you carton size is constantly replenished to your fast pack line and you change sku. With the concept there is less non-productive time for carton change. When compared to a regular CO pick and pack activity, a fast pack concept improves picker and pack productivity and increases your completed CO number.

DIVERT CUSTOMER ORDER CARTON/TOTE TO PACK STATION
SORT LANE MAXIMUM EFFICIENCY & CONSTANT CUSTOMER ORDER FLOW

Divert a CO carton or tote to a pack station has a conveyor travel path divert a CO pick tote/carton onto non-powered or powered conveyor travel path for transport to a pack table. From your pick area, your completed CO containers travel on a sort conveyor travel path that moves containers through your pack area and did not sort containers are re-circulated on a conveyor travel path. Each pack table conveyor travel path has a full lane photo-eye that sends a block message to your conveyor computer to stop/start container divert onto a lane. At each pack station, a pack table conveyor travel path discharges containers with packer assistance onto a pack table. Features are no packer physical effort, high cost, re-circulation assures constant CO container flow.

PACKER PULLS-OFF TOTE/CARTON TO PACK TABLE
SORT LANE MINIMAL COST & CONSTANT CUSTOMER ORDER FLOW

Packer pulls-off CO pick tote/carton onto a pack table has your completed CO containers travel on a powered zero pressure conveyor travel path from your pick area through your pack area. With a re-circulation conveyor travel path, your conveyor travel path is past each pack station and as a CO container travels past a pack station, a packer pulls-off a container from a conveyor travel onto a pack table. At each pack station, your conveyor travel path (top of roller) and guard rail elevation permits a packer to easily transfer a container to a pack table. If no re-circulation, an employee or mechanical divert device transfers completed CO containers onto a dead end conveyor travel path that services pack stations on both sides of a conveyor travel path. With a mechanical divert concept, each lane has a full lane photo-eye that sends a block message to your conveyor computer to stop/start container divert onto a lane. Features are some physical effort, low cost, re-circulation assures constant CO container flow and dead end conveyor concept to have maximum container available to pack stations, your pack station occupancy is started at the container lane end and pack stations are occupied to the divert location as the last pack station.

CUSTOMER ORDER CARTON OR TOTE DECLINE TO PACK TABLE
SORT LANE MAXIMUM EFFICIENCY & CONSTANT CUSTOMER ORDER FLOW

Divert a CO carton or tote to a pack station is used with your CO container is on highest elevation. The concept has a conveyor travel path divert a CO pick tote/carton onto a non-powered or powered decline belt conveyor travel path for transfer onto a powered roller conveyor travel path for transfer onto a pack table roller queue conveyor. With a right angle transfer device concept, prior to each right angle transfer is pop-up stop device to assure container transfer onto a pack table queue conveyor. With a curve conveyor travel path concept, each pack table queue roller conveyor travel path has a full lane photo-eye that sends a block message to your conveyor computer to stop/start container divert onto a lane. At each pack station, a CO container ID faces a packer and a pack table conveyor travel path discharges containers with packer assistance onto a pack table. Features are no packer physical effort, high cost, requires small sq ft area and re-circulation assures constant CO container flow.

CUSTOMER ORDER CARTON OR TOTE INCLINE TO PACK TABLE
SORT LANE MAXIMUM EFFICIENCY & CONSTANT CUSTOMER ORDER FLOW

Divert a CO carton or tote to a pack station is used with your CO container is on lowest elevation. The concept has a conveyor travel path divert a CO pick tote/carton onto powered incline belt conveyor travel path for transfer onto a powered roller conveyor travel path for right angle transfer onto a pack table roller queue conveyor. Prior to each right angle transfer is pop-up stop device to assure container transfer onto a pack table queue conveyor. Each pack table queue roller conveyor travel path has a full lane photo-eye that sends a block message to your conveyor computer to stop/start container divert onto a lane. At each pack station, a CO container ID faces a packer and a pack table conveyor travel path discharges containers with packer assistance onto a pack table. Features are no packer physical effort, highest cost, requires small sq ft area and re-circulation assures constant CO container flow.

COMPLETE CUSTOMER ORDER TAKE-AWAY CONVEYOR
ASSURE GOOD PACKER & MANIFEST PRODUCTIVITY

A pack station completed CO take-away concept is your cart or conveyor that is used to transport a completed CO package from your pack area to your manifest station. A completed CO take-away concept assures a constant CO flow to your manifest station that assures good employee productivity and maximum completed CO number. Your options are (1) 4-wheel cart take-away concept has one or several load carrying surfaces and is located adjacent to a pack station. After a cart becomes full, an employee replaces a full cart with an empty cart and moves a full cart to your manifest station. Features are low cost, handles a low volume and creates surges at your manifest station, (2) one package conveyor travel path is a declined non-powered or powered skate-wheel or roller conveyor is used to move packages from your pack stations to your manifest station. Features are low cost, constant CO flow, handles a low volume and services few pack station number and (3) powered zero pressure conveyor that travels past all pack stations and has a top or roller that is set at an elevation to permit packer to easily transfer completed CO packages onto a conveyor travel path. Photo-eyes communicate conveyor travel path status to a conveyor computer that controls CO package flow from your pack area to your manifest station. Features are designed to handle a high volume, travels past all your pack stations, high cost and permits controllable queue.

EMPTY TOTE TAKE-AWAY CONVEYOR OR FLOOR STACK
ASSURE PACKER PRODUCTIVITY & CONSTANT CUSTOMER ORDER FLOW

A pack station empty tote take-away conveyor or floor stack assure are your concept options that a packer moves empty totes from a pack table. With a powered conveyor take-away concept, your empty conveyor travel path is placed in a stack with your picked CO container and completed packed CO container travel paths. Empty travel path considerations are at the highest elevation it requires an employee to transfer totes at a high elevation and at the lowest elevation, it requires an employee to bend for tote transfer. Your empty tote final design is determined by your inbound/picked CO container travel path and completed CO container travel path windows (heights). Features are additional conveyor cost, constant empty tote flow and minimal employee effort. With an empty tote floor stack concept, a packer transfers empty totes to a tote stack that is located at a pack table end. When a tote stack obtains a pre-determined height an additional tote stack is started and an employee moves tote stacks from a pack area to a pick area. Features are low cost, requires an additional packer effort, does not have a constant empty tote flow and requires another employee activity.

PROMOTIONAL SKUS TO ONE PACK STATION
IMPROVE PACKER PRODUCTIVITY

Promotional skus transferred to one pack station is a concept that has a bulk picked sku (s) transferred one or selected adjacent pack stations. The approach permits your operation at a scan station, to pre-scan a sku ID to CO pack slips/invoices and deliver scanned CO pack slips/invoices to pack stations. Since your pack station are pre-determined and your know a computer suggested carton size, you can pre-make cartons that are delivered to pack stations. The exception is a pop-out carton that is formed by a packer. Features are high packer productivity and high completed CO number.

MANUAL BULK OR 'EN MASSE' PICK
INCREASE PICKER PRODUCTIVITY & COMPLETED CUSTOMER ORDER NUMBER

Manual bulk or 'en masse' pick is a small item or GOH pick concept that is used to improve your picker productivity and completed CO number. After you establish your pick concept work day or CO wave CO number, your computer printer prints a manual bulk pick instruction. Your pick instruction options are (1) paper document or (2) pick labels. For each sku your bulk pick instruction directs a picker to pick a CO wave total sku quantity. A bulk pick concept, increases a picker's hit concentration and density with at one pick position multiple sku quantity and minimal walk distance between two pick positions.

BULK OR EN MASSE PICKED SKU SORT OR BATCHED PICK SORT
HIGH PICKER & SORTER PRODUCTIVITY & HIGH COMPLETED CUSTOMER ORDER NUMBER

Bulk pick or 'en masse' is a small item or GOH bulk pick and sort concept, bulk pick, transport, sort and final pick concept or bulk pick, transport, sort, final sort and pack concept that is used to improve picker and sort productivity and high completed CO number. After you establish your pick concept CO wave or CO number, your computer program prints a bulk or 'en masse' that is your picker instruction. For each sku, a bulk pick instruction directs a picker to pick a grouped CO sku total quantity from a pick position that increases a high hit concentration and density and minimal walk distance between 2 picks to improve picker productivity. With a pick and sort concept, your bulk pick sku quantity is for grouped CO number that is 9 to 12 manual sort positions. With a bulk pick, transport, sort and final pick concept, your bulk pick sku quantity is for a grouped CO number that is determined by your CO wave quantity and by your sku sort position capacity. With a bulk pick, transport, sort and pack concept, your bulk pick sku quantity is based on your manual sort CO sort positions. With a bulk pick, transport, sort, final sort and pack concept, your bulk pick sku quantity is based on 50 pieces per CO sort position that is 16 to 25 COs and your CO sort position number

YOUR MANUAL SORT TYPES AND CONCEPT SELECTION FACTORS
  HIGH PICKER & SORTER PRODUCTIVITY & HIGH COMPLETED CUSTOMER ORDER NUMBER
Your bulk pick sku and sort concept types and selection factors determine your sort concept for your best bulk pick and sort concept cost and handling volume. Your manual bulk pick sku sort concept options are (1) bulk pick and sort to a cart/tote temporary CO sort/hold position. As a picker/sorter moves through pick aisles, a picker/sorter completes each sku bulk pick and sort activity. Features are (a) with some computer programming low cost, (b) picker picks an entire pick area, (c) difficult to handle a large volume, (d) maximum CO sort locations are 9 to 12 and (e) sort is completed to a slide/chute, carton or tote, (2 bulk pick skus and sort by sku digit to a sort/hold position and with a CO pack slip/invoice final pick customer order skus from sort hold position. Features are (a) low cost with some computer programming cost to create a bulk pick document and separate CO pack slips/invoices by a sku digit, (b) increase picker productivity, (c) handle all CO sizes and (d) individual COs are delivered to a check or pack station and (3) bulk pick sku and each sku is labeled with CO ID that are placed into a tote and sent to sort lane for sku sort to a CO ID sort position. Features are (a) some cost for computer program to create and print CO ID labels, (b) sort area determines your CO sort position number per batch, (c) difficult to handle large CO and (c) skus are sorted into a slide/chute, carton and tote for delivery to a pack station.

MANUAL BULK PICK AND SORT
  INCREASE COMPLETED CUSTOMER ORDER NUMBER
Manual bulk pick & sort concept has your computer batches/groups your COs to match your pick cart sort position number, for each batch/group prints a special bulk pick & sort document and CO pack slips/invoices for each batch/group. After a picker arranges cartons/totes into each sort location and IDs each sort location, a picker travels to a pick position. At a pick position, per a bulk pick & sort document, a picker bulk picks a sku quantity. Per each CO sku quantity that is printed on bulk pick document, a picker sorts a CO sku quantity to each position. A pick & sort document lists each batch sku pick position and quantity and a CO sku quantity is listed under each CO ID. Features are (1) low cost, (2) some computer program cost, (3) cart with sort positions, (4) easy to train & (5) picker picks entire area.

MANUAL SORT BY SKU INSTRUCTIONS
  HIGH SORTER PRODUCTIVITY & INCREASE COMPLETED CUSTOMER ORDER NUMBER
Manual bulk pick & sort small items has your employee picker push a 4-wheel cart through pick aisles. Manual bulk pick & sort small items requires an employee to have a printed bulk pick document. Each bulk pick document shows pick position, bulk pick quantity, and sku description. At each sku pick position, a picker bulk picks a sku quantity and transfers a sku onto a cart hold position. In a sku sort area, you identify each sort position by a position ID that corresponds to your sku inventory ID number. For a sku sort activity, it appears on a sku ID label and for final CO pick activity, it appears on a CO pack slip/invoice document. Your sort locations are shelves and deck standard pallet rack positions. To have all possible sort and final pick locations, your sort area has 5 levels per shelf bay that provides 0 - 9 digits and two shelf bays per digit that provides 0 – 9. Possible sort location sequences are (1) MANUAL BULK PICK, SORT AND FINAL PICK BY SKU LAST TWO DIGITS that has a sku first digit is a shelf bay with and last sku digit is a shelf level, (2) MANUAL BULK PICK, SORT AND FINAL PICK BY SKU FIRST & SECOND DIGIT that a sku first digit is a shelf bay and sku second digit is a shelf level & (3) MANUAL BULK PICK, SORT AND FINAL PICK BY SKU FIRST AND LAST DIGITS that has a sku last digit as a

shelf digit and next to last digit is a shelf level. A manual bulk pick, sort and final pick concept with CO pack slip/invoice improves your total employee productivity & higher CO completion number. Features are (1) requires a computer program to print bulk pick documents, (2) CO pack slip/invoice document is used in your final pick activity & (3) easy to complete a pick check.

MANUAL SORT BY SKU
    INCREASE COMPLETED CUSTOMER ORDER NUMBER
Manual sort by sku concept has a numeric/digit ID on each sku and a computer prints a bulk pick document and CO pack slips/invoices. After pickers bulk pick skus arrive in a sort area, each bulk picked sku is transferred to a sort/temporary hold position. For maximum sku sort productivity, each sort location has numeric or digits that is related to a sku inventory numeric digits. Each sort location has two shelf bays with a total of 10 levels and each level has a numeric or digit ID. After all sku are sorted to the sort locations, a clerk verifies all bulk pick documents are returned to the control desk and CO final pick activity is able to start. Final pick activity occurs with a CO pack slip/invoice and into a CO carton/tote. For maximum final pick productivity, your computer arranges and prints your CO pack slips/invoice in a numeric/digit sequence. The sequence matches a specific CO pack slip/invoice first sku numeric/digit concept that permits your CO pack slips/invoices grouped & distributed to a sort position. The concept has a CO pack slip/invoice first pick in a sort position. A completed CO is transferred to a pack station or sent to a check station. Features are low cost with shelves/racks, easy to implement & train employees & low computer cost.

SORT INSTRUCTION AS PAPER OR LABEL INSTRUCTION
    ASSURE ACCURATE SORT, HIGH SORTER PRODUCTIVITY & HIGH COMPLETED CUSTOMER ORDER
    NUMBER
Sort instruction as a paper document or label instruction is required to assure an accurate sort activity, high sorter productivity and increase completed CO number. A sort instruction is a human/machine readable symbology that directs an employee or machine sort concept to transfer a sku from a sku group/travel path into a temporary sort/hold position. A sort document is computer controlled printed that shows a sku bulk pick quantity and each CO sku quantity & is used in a pick & sort concept. A sku or CO ID/label allows a picker and sorter to complete pick & sort activities. Per your sort concept, a sku ID is vendor applied to each sku and a CO ID is picker applied to each sku. Both sku ID concepts allow bulk picked skus & an employee/mechanical sorter to complete a sort transaction.

MANUAL SORT & FINAL CUSTOMER ORDER PICK BY SKU DIGIT DESIGNS WITH SHELF, DECKED RACKS
    & PALLET RACKS
    IMPROVE SORTER/FINAL PICKER PRODUCTIVITY & INCREASE COMPLETED CUSTOMER ORDER
NUMBER
Manual sort and final CO pick by sku digit designs with shelves, decked racks and pallet racks has sufficient positions for 0 – 9 digits that improve sorter/final picker productivity and increase completed CO number. The approach allows you to sort bulk picked skus by a sku ID label and with a CO pack slip/invoice sku ID to final pick COs. Per your sku size, for very small skus you have 10 shelf bays to provide 1 shelf bay for each digit 0 – 9 and for regular size skus you have 20 shelf bays to provide 2 shelf bays for each digit 0 – 9. To provide picker direction, each two bays has one digit and has numeric IDs that extend outward into the aisle from a first bay first post and a second bay last position and an ID is flat against a top shelf. In a typical layout your shelf bay is 4 ft wide with 2 posts that are I in wide. With regular skus, you have promotional and large size skus that have few skus, your design has a decked standard pallet rack bay opposite each 2 shelf bays and has a floor level and decked level. Ten shelf levels per two bays allows shelves for 0 – 9 digits. To provide picker direction, each shelf has one digit numeric ID that is in a shelf middle and on a first bay first post and a second bay last position. To match a 2 shelf bay span, your rack bay span is 8 ft 2 in C/C that equals distance between a rack bay two posts center lines. Deck your bottom hand stacked/decked standard pallet rack level has your bottom (floor) level skus hand stacked onto a deck instead of two pallets. To provide picker direction, each rack bay has one digit numeric ID that faces the aisle and the bay both posts and an ID is flat against the top load beam. A deck is a solid wood, harden plastic or metal member with 1 in high bottom full depth runners evenly spaced to assure minimal deck bow. When compared to hand stack onto 2 pallets, a deck concept increases vertical open space by a nominal 4 ins and allows a rack bay

entire area used for skus that increases the usable space by 8 to 12 ins or one standard master carton width. Deck and runner cost is equal to 2 pallets cost. Standard pallet rack bays are located at your back to back deck rack rows and are positions for promotional skus that are very few skus. Per your picker height, your rack bay design height & load beam arrangement has floor level for a 1 sku on a double stacked pallet or 2 levels for 2 skus.

MANUAL SORT INSTRUCTIONS
IMPACTS YOUR SORTER PRODUCTIVITY & ACCURATE SORTATION

Manual sort instruction indicates to picker/sorter or sorter a customer order picked sku temporary hold/sort position. A manual sort instruction assures good sorter productivity and accurate sort activity. With a manual pick and sort concept, a paper document shows a bulk pick sku quantity and each CO sku quantity. Features are (1) limited to a cart/tote company temporary hold/sort position, (2) requires a computer program to batch COs per your sort positions, (3) difficult to handle a large CO quantity, (4) requires additional pickers who have potential to walk your entire pick area & (5) requires cart queue at your pick and pack stations. A manual applied self-adhesive label from a sheet or roll label is applied to a picked sku. Each label has a CO ID with other company required information and the pick labels are printed in pick position sequence. All picked and labeled skus are placed into a tote on conveyor travel path or directly onto a belt conveyor travel path that transports skus to a sort lane. In a sort lane each sku CO ID is matched to a CO ID sort position. With a match a sku is transferred to a CO ID sort position. Features are (1) each sku requires a CO ID, (2) per batch, your CO batch number matches your sort position number, (3) requires a batch computer program, (4) potential for sku to lose a CO ID and each label must fit onto all skus and (5) requires label print time & (3) pre-labeled/ID skus with a bulk pick document and CO pack slip/invoice concept has your vendor place a sku ID on each sku. CO skus are bulk picked with a paper document & sent to a sort area. In a sort area by sort ID digit, skus are sorted to sort/hold positions. After sku sort, a final picker with a CO pack slip/invoice that list each sku ID digits picks a CO. Features are (1) requires a bulk pick document, (2) requires a CO pack slip/invoice with each sku ID digits, (3) handles a large CO number and wide sku mix & (4) final pick into CO carton.

MANUAL SORT BY SKU DIGIT POSITION DESIGN AS HORSE SHOE, TWO AISLE OR ONE AISLE
IMPROVE SORTER/FINAL PICKER PRODUCTIVITY & INCREASE COMPLETED CUSTOMER ORDER NUMBER

Your sort by sku digit design assures that you have sufficient sort positions and cube capacity to handle your CO wave and permits a sorter/final picker pattern. To provide sufficient sort positions and cube your design has single or mix of standard shelves, deck racks or standard pallet racks. Your design options are (1) horse-shoe has only shelves and is used for very small skus. Shelves are arranged in a horse shoe shape with one shelf bay per each digit (0 – 9). As a sorter/final picker enters a horse-shoe, start is at a right side with four shelf bays (0 – 3), base with two shelf bays (4 & 5) and left side with four shelf bays (6 – 9), (2) one aisle or tunnel that has shelf bays with two per digit (0 – 9) on a right side and for each digit (0 – 9) a decked pallet rack bay with a C/C dimension to equal two shelf bays. A sorter/picker starts at a first shelf/rack bay and progressively moves to exit end and (3) two aisles has the first aisle shelf bays on an aisle left side with two per digit (0 – 4) on an aisle right side and for each digit (0 – 4) a decked pallet rack bay with a C/C dimension to equal two shelf bays and a second aisle shelf bays with two digit (5 – 9) and for each digit (5 – 9) a deck pallet rack with a C/C dimension to equal two shelf bays. For maximum space utilization and improve sorter/picker productivity, the shelf bays are on the exterior and rack bays are on the interior. Options are (a) to create large cube or high volume sku positions, on a back to back decked pallet rack rows is to have standard pallet racks and (b) to allow an employee early exit to have a middle turn aisle in a decked pallet rack row that requires two additional shelf bays.

PICK BY SKU DIGIT YOUR CUSTOMER ORDER FINAL PICK INSTRUCTIONS
IMPROVE FINAL PICKER PRODUCTIVITY & INCREASE COMPLETED CUSTOMER ORDER NUMBER

Pick by sku digit your CO final pick instructions improve final picker productivity and increase CO number. Your final pick instructions are (1) pick by light for each CO requires a pick position progression through all pick positions. Feature with multiple pickers difficult to provide picker progression, high cost and additional computer programming, (2) separate paper CO pick document that lists each sku and quantity. Features additional ink and paper print expense and computer programming and (3) CO order pack slip/invoice that lists each sku and quantity. Features no additional ink or paper print expense and no additional computer programming.

PICK BY SKU DIGIT YOUR CUSTOMER ORDER PACK SLIPS/INVOICES PREPARATION
IMPROVE FINAL PICKER PRODUCTIVITY & INCREASE COMPLETED CUSTOMER ORDER NUMBER

Pick by sku digit your CO pack slips/invoices preparation that has an impact on your final picker productivity and increased completed CO number. Your CO pack slip/invoice group options are (1) random sku digit sequence that has your computer program print CO pack slips/invoices on a random bases. The approach has potential for your CO pack slip/invoice first/last sku digits mixed as CO pack slips/invoices are given to your final CO picker. Features are (a) low final picker productivity due to additional walk to the first pick position, (b) simple computer printer program and (c) low completed CO number or (2) group by your CO pack slip first or last sku digit sequence that has your computer program print your CO pack slips/invoices and each first or last sku digit CO pack slip/invoice group is placed into match shelf bay digit. Features are (a) high final picker productivity due to no walk distance or time for pick transaction completion, (b) additional computer printer program and (c) high completed CO number.

MANUAL BATCHED PICK
INCREASE PICKER PRODUCTIVITY & COMPLETED CUSTOMER ORDER NUMBER

Manual batched pick is a small item or GOH pick concept that is used to improve your picker productivity and completed CO number. Batched pick concept has your computer to separate a work day or CO wave CO number into pre-determined batches/groups. A CO number per batch is based on your picker and pacer productivity rates and employee number. In a batched CO pick concept, each sku within a CO group are in pick position sequence. With multiple picks for one sku there is increase in your hit concentration and density that increases your picker productivity with minimal walk distance between two picks.

MANUAL BATCHED PICK, TRANSPORT & SORT/PACK
IMPROVE PICKER PRODUCTIVITY & INCREASE CUSTOMER ORDER NUMBER

Manual batched pick, transport & sort/pack concept is designed to handle a large sku volume and large CO number. During your pick activity, skus are bulk picked into totes/cartons or onto a belt conveyor. In most operations, your sku physical, fragile, crushable and potential edge damage characteristics determine your tote/carton or belt conveyor transport concept. With a tote transport concept, your induction station is designed to handle and move full and empty totes. With a belt conveyor transport concept, your induction station has a decline slide for manual or automatic induction. Your pick, transport and sort/pack concept, your manual or mechanized concept design is based your projected work day sku volume, customer order number, labor cost, available building space and sort/computer equipment/program cost.

YOUR CUSTOMER ORDER MANUAL SORT POSTION NUMBER SEQUENCE
IMPROVE SORTER PRODUCTIVITY & REDUCE SORT ERRORS

Your CO manual sort position number sequence has an impact on your sorter productivity and reduce your sort errors and improve accuracy. Your manual customer order sort position number sequence has your lowest number at a sort lane entry, through a sort lane progressively increases and has your highest number at a sort lane exit. If your sort lane has sort positions on an aisle one side, your arithmetic progression is by odd number for sort positions on an aisle left side and by even numbers for sort positions on an aisle right side. If your sort lane has sort positions on an aisle both sides, your arithmetic progression has odd number sort positions on an aisle left side and has even number sort positions on an aisle right side. Features are for maximum positions, sort positions have numeric digits, large as possible digits on a white or yellow background and in a constant sort position location.

MANUAL SORT BY CUSTOMER ORDER IDENTIFICATION
INCREASE COMPLETED CUSTOMER ORDER NUMBER

Manual sort by a CO ID sku concept has a alpha character or numeric/digit ID on each sku. For each sku, your CO process computer prints a pick/sort label and for a CO, pack slip/invoice with CO ID, sku & quantity and other company required information. On each pick label is your pick position and CO ID in largest possible print and black alpha characters or digits onto a white label face. If possible a large bold and clear printed CO ID is in the right hand and upper label corner. In your sort area, your assure that a large bold and clear printed CO ID is on each sort position front and per your company CO pack slips/invoices are distributed to each sort position or to a packer. In your pick area, a picker goes to a pick position places a label onto a sku. A labeled sku is placed into tote or onto a belt conveyor surface and transported from your pick area to your sort area. In your sort area totes or skus are moved past all sort positions. Your sort positions are (a) slide/chute, (2) tote or (3) ship carton. Your sort area transport options are (1) an employee carriers a tote, pushes a tote on a non-powered conveyor or tote is moved over a powered conveyor surface and (2) a belt conveyor. A sorter removes a sku from a tote or belt conveyor surface, reads a sku CO ID and matches a sku CO ID to a sort position ID. With a match, a sku is transferred to a sort position. Sort lane options are (1) one sorter moves a tote or with a belt conveyor over an entire travel path that difficult to obtain good sort productivity due to increased walk distance or (2) multiple sort zones, after zone completion in a sort zone, a sorter moves a tote or belt conveyor skus to a next sort zone that is easier to obtain sorter productivity. When we compare tote & belt conveyor sort transport concepts, (1) both require re-circulation or decline to the floor or dump into a larger tote, (2) tote minimizes sku damage & zone control, (3) tote travels over a skate-wheel or roller conveyor surface & (5) belt conveyor has greater potential sku ID removal & damage.

MANUAL SORT LANE DESIGN
  INCREASE SORTER PRODUCTIVITY & COMPLETED CUSTOMER ORDER NUMBER
Manual sort lane design has an impact on your sorter productivity and completed CO number. Based on your CO wave sort batch number, your sort area design has one sort lane or multiple sort lanes. One sort lane features are all batched pick totes are sent through one sort lane, difficult to handle a high volume due to wait time for packers to transfer sorted COs from sort positions to pack and less complex transport concept. Multiple sort lanes has at least three sort lanes. One sort lane is used for your active sort batch. Second sort lane has sort positions full of completed/sorted COs. Third sort lane is available for next batch sort activity. Features are additional sq ft area, additional computer programming cost to process batches, conveyor or transport concept requires a manual or fixed/adjustable divert device and improved sorter and packer productivity.

MANUAL SORT FOR ENTIRE SORT LANE OR A SORT LANE SEPARATED INTO SORT ZONES
  INCREASE SORTER PRODUCTIVITY & IMPROVE PICKED SKU FLOW
Manual sort for an entire sort lane or sort lane separated into sort zones are manual sort lane sorter length design options that assure good sorter productivity and improves picked sku flow. Sort an entire sort lane has a sorter employee with a tote start at a sort lane entrance, walk through a sort lane aisle and with a partial full or empty tote exit at a sort lane end. If at the last sort position, a tote has non-sorted skus, your tote is returned to a sort lane entrance for another sort lane pass. Features are with multiple sorters per aisle, potential sorter congestion and potential low sorter productivity due longer walk distances for a sort transaction. A separate sort lane into short sorter zones has a pre-determined sort position that are allocated to each sort zone. A sort zone is assigned to one sorter employee. A separated sort lane into short sort zones, has your sort zone front employee receive a tote and review/complete all sku sort transactions & pass tote to next sort zone. Colored or sort zone number banners/flags on each sort zone start & end positions and 50% full tote help improve sort zone employee productivity. Features are higher sort employee productivity due to short walk distance & required multiple sort employees.

MANUAL SORT POSITIONS ACROSS OVER A CONVEYOR OR BEHIND A SORTER AISLE
  INCREASE SORT POSITION NUMBER & SORTER PRODUCTIVITY
Manual sort positions across/over a conveyor or behind a sorter aisle are your manual sort position options. Sort across/over a conveyor travel path has an employee sorter aisle that is adjacent to a sort conveyor. On the conveyor travel path far side are CO sort positions. As a sort employee moves a tote over a conveyor travel path, a sorter employee transfers skus from a tote to a CO ID sort position. CO sort positions are 2 to 3 high above a sort conveyor travel path and as required to access a sort position a sorter moves a tote on a conveyor. Features are limited sort position number, sort positions have a number sequence, to complete a sort transaction makes a difficult reach across a conveyor and to access all sort positions, a sorter moves a tote. Sort positions behind a sorter aisle or on an aisle open side concept has a sorter aisle between a conveyor and CO sort positions. If a sorter moves a tote through an entire sort lane, totes on a conveyor travel path are moved by a sorter employee

through a sort lane. With a sorter zone concept, a sorter employee walks perpendicular between a tote on a conveyor travel path and CO sort positions. After reading a sku CO sort number, a sorter matches a sku CO number to a sort position CO number and transfers a sku into a sort position. CO sort positions are 3 to 4 high sort positions and allows a sorter employee easy and quick access to all sort positions. Features are sort positions have a number sequence, increased CO sort position number per aisle and easy sorter access to all sort positions, minimal sorter reach effort. Hybrid sort lane design combines CO sort positions across/over a sort conveyor and behind a sorter aisle. Features are sort positions have a number sequence with odd number positions on an aisle on side and even number positions on an aisle other side and maximum sort position number per aisle.

MANUAL OR MECHANIZED SORT LOCATIONS AS A CHUTE, CARTON OR TOTE
IMPROVE PACKER PRODUCTIVITY & INCREASE COMPLETED CUSTOMER ORDER NUMBER

Manual or mechanized sort location options are slide/chute, carton or tote that improve packer productivity, increase completed CO number, retain skus in a sort position and assure sorter/packer access to sort positions. Your rectangle shaped CO sort position has the narrow width face as your sort position open/front. This means that your slope, tote or carton long dimension is a sort position depth that creates maximum CO sort positions per inch ft. Each sort position has sufficient space on a structural member for CO ID, structural members are designed for maximum CO sku weight and sufficient clearance for a sorter to complete a sku sort transaction. A sloped slide/chute sort position has a solid bottom and side walls and a lockable solid/window door on a discharge end. With a 5 to 20 degree slope, a slide/chute bottom surface a smooth bottom surface with a low co-efficient of friction to assure sku flow. Your interior cube at ½ of a position height matches your largest CO cube that has a sort position slide/chute depth is an important dimension. Features are higher cost, packer uses a carton or tote for sku transfer from a slide/chute position to a pack table, requires a lockable discharge end door and packer makes-up a ship carton. A tote sort position has a solid or angle bottom side runners as a bottom surface & has meshed between two runners. Meshed side walls assure that skus are retained in a sort position. A tote internal dimension (cube) is designed for your largest cube CO and requires a replenishment employee to place empty totes into sort positions. Features sort position set-up employee, improve packer productivity due to easy transfer a CO to a pack station and handles a wide carton mix and CO size. A carton in a CO sort position to minimize potential carton bottom bow, it requires a solid bottom surface and solid or meshed side walls. For maximum sort position space utilization you have your carton side walls that are secured with rubber bands. Your sort position width, length and height allows your largest carton size in a sort position with sufficient clearance for a sorter to complete a sku sort transaction. Features are sort position set-up employee, additional employee activity to secure carton flaps, improve packer productivity due to no carton make-up activity & easy to transfer a CO to a pack station, handles a wide carton mix and CO size.

WHAT IS YOUR MANUAL OR MECHANZIED SORTER TRAVEL PATH HEIGHT
IMPACTS YOUR SORTER PRODUCTIVITY

Your manual or mechanized sorter travel path height is a key factor that determines your sort station design/elevation and clear space between your ground floor and ceiling bottom structural support member, sort position number and sort productivity. With a manual sort concept, from a tote on a conveyor travel path, your conveyor elevation minimizes a sorter reach/transfer sku to a sort position. Your conveyor travel path is determined by your average sorter employee height and tote side wall height. A lower conveyor travel path provides additional height for your sort positions. To provide a sorter easier access to a tote interior, an option is to tilt your sort conveyor travel path that has your tote travel on a 'V' shaped conveyor travel path. A tote side and tote bottom rides on a standard non-powered roller sections. Features are potential lower tote utilization, used with a tote transport concept, additional conveyor cost and requires employee to adjust totes. Your mechanized sorter conveyor travel path elevation is determined by your selected sort manufacturer standard height to complete a sku induction on an elevated platform and your sort position slide/chute, tote or carton elevation. Your induction platform height has sufficient clearance for your sku in-bound transport concept, an employee to complete an induction activity and your sorter scanner to complete a top scan transaction.

ACCOUNT FOR YOUR BATCH LAST PICKED SKU
ASSURE ACCURATE PACK ACTIVITY & MAINTAIN PACKER PRODUCTIVITY

Account for your last pick in a batch/group CO pick & pack activities assure accurate pack per batch and maintain packer productivity. In your pick activity, your picker attaches a last batch picked sku ID to a sku that signals to a packer that a batched COs skus have been picked and sent to a sort/pack area. After a pack area supervisor recognizes a batch last picked sku, a signal is sent to a pick area to start picking a next batched skus. Batch last picked sku options are (1) sku color coded label with human/machine readable symbology that is applied by a printer or picker, (2) tote color coded label with human/machine readable symbology that is applied by a picker and (3) batch last picked sku or tote symbology is read by a scanner.

SORT & PACK STATION
IMPROVE PACKER PRODUCTIVITY

Sort and pack station is a sort chute platform and pack table surface has area for a small item warehouse with a mechanized sort concept that allows your final sorter and packer to complete a CO final check and pack activities. Your sort chute platform and pack table combined surface has sufficient space for a sorter/packer to complete a final sort for an estimated 25 COs with 50 to 75 pieces. To complete a customer order final sort & pack activity, a final sorter/packer with a CO pack slip/invoice completes a final sku sort and to complete a CO pack activity.

BATCHED PICK, TRANSPORT AND SORT
REDUCE SKU DAMAGE & MINIMIZE SORTER DAMAGE

A batched pick skus are placed onto a transport and sorter travel path. A mechanized sort conveyor travel path that directs picked & inducted sku past all sort locations. A sort travel path with no re-circulation is a straight line with a sort travel path all did not sort skus decline.

MANUAL OR AUTOMATIC INDUCTION STATION
IMPACTS YOUR SORTER PRODUCTIVITY & SORTER UTILIZATION

Manual or automatic sku induction are your sku transfer onto a mechanized sorter travel path options. With both concepts, prior to a sort conveyor scanner and divert position a sku is placed with a sku or CO ID/symbology facing upward (correct direction) for a bar code scanner to read the symbology and cause an inducted sku to divert onto a customer order sort position. Both induction concepts have skus delivered to an induction station as loose skus on a belt conveyor and slide/chute or skus in totes on a low/zero pressure roller conveyor. At a manual induction station an employee physically transfers a sku from a chute/slide or tote direct onto an empty sorter carrier. Features potential for low carrier utilization, in-feed belt and tote conveyor controlled by a chute/slide full & partial photo-eyes and on a platform multiple induction lanes requires a large sq ft area. An automatic induction station has an induction employee physically transfers a sku from a chute/slide or tote direct onto first short belt conveyor of a 4 short belt conveyor lane. Four short belt conveyors pull a gap between two skus. The fourth/last belt conveyor transfers a sku onto an sort empty carrier. Features are requires additional computer program/cost, assures high sorter carrier utilization and on a platform multiple induction lanes requires a small sq ft area.

TOTE DELIVERY TO MANUAL OR AUTOMATIC SKU INDUCTION STATION
INCREASE SORTER CAPACITY & IMPROVE SORTER UTILIZATION

Tote delivery to a manual or automatic sku induction onto a mechanized sorter impact your sort capacity and sorter utilization. Manual or automatic induction has an employee transfer a picked sku from your transport concept (slide/chute or tote) onto an empty sorter carrier or onto the first belt conveyor of an automatic induction concept. With a powered conveyor belt and slide/chute concept, a slide/chute end is at a height for an induction employee to easily complete a sku transfer onto a sorter travel path. Features are (1) potential sku damage or label lose, (2) lower cost, (3) less sq ft space, (4) less employee physical effort and (5) no transport device return travel path. With a powered low or zero pressure conveyor and tote concept, your skus are delivered to an induction station. Your tote presentation or conveyor travel path options are (a) flat that has an employee reach over a tote side wall, into a tote and transfer a sku. Features are (1) increased employee effort, (2) tote side wall top that allows an employee access to a tote and (3) empty totes are stacked or placed onto powered transport concept (b) tote tilted that has an employee reach into slanted tote and transfer a sku. Features are (1) less employee effort, (2) tilted tote side wall top that allows an employee easy access to a tote, (3) additional conveyor cost to control tote travel to and from a tilt position and (4) mechanical device to tilt a tote and (5) empty totes are stacked or placed onto powered transport concept.

HOW MANY READS
IMPROVE SORTER CAPACITY & CARRIER UTILIZATION
How many reads is a mechanized sorter concept that is designed to maximize your sort concept sort rat e. Since your sort conveyor travel speed is at the fastest speed and from a top labeled package your scanner reads a package height with a wide mix and requires your scanner to obtain a good read. The maximum good read assures a sort conveyor has maximum utilization. An over-squared label (black bar height equals total black bars and white spaces width) and good quiet zones (white spaces between first/last black bar and white paper) are two options with minimal cost to improve your good reads. If your scanner reads the same bar code that is sent to your sort conveyor and there is no packer sort, after X good read number you have a your sort computer program to have a repeated bar code package diverted onto a problem order lane. Feature improves your sorter capacity and carrier utilization.

AUTOMATIC INDUCTION SIDE BY SIDE
IMPROVE SORTER CAPACITY & CARRIER UTILIZATION & INDUCTION PLATFORM UTILIZATION
To assure sorter capacity, carrier utilization and induction platform utilization has your induction station that is located on a 13 ft elevated platform that is above your floor. An automatic induction concept has a series of short belt conveyor lanes for sku singulation and transfer onto sorter conveyor travel path. To achieve sku induction, an induction platform is on a mezzanine. Since a mezzanine has additional cost and with possible sprinklers and light fixtures under a mezzanine, a mezzanine has a high cost per sq ft. To minimize a mezzanine sq ft requirement, you place your multiple automatic induction conveyor lanes as side by side conveyor lanes. With this arrangement your assure that your conveyor travel path have maintenance access to conveyor travel paths.

SINGLE OR DUAL INDUCTION
IMPACTS YOUR SORTER PRODUCTIVITY & SORTER UTILIZATION
Single or dual induction are a powered sort conveyor travel path sku induction design options. Sku induction on a sort conveyor travel path has a sku CO ID or sku ID machine readable symbology that is read by a bar code scanner. A scanner sends each CO ID or sku ID to your sorter computer program that activates a divert device that moves a sku from a sorter travel path onto a CO divert/hold station. A single induction concept has one clean-out position, carrier re-set station, induction platform and bar code scanner that inducts and scans all skus. After scanning, a sorter computer program has all skus diverted to sort positions. Features are low cost, simple computer program/cost, sort conveyor travel is designed as a single/straight line or endless loop travel path and does not maximize your sort conveyor travel path. Dual induction is used on an elliptical endless loop or rectangle shaped sorter travel path. Each short or rectangle shaped sorter travel path end has a clean-out position, carrier re-set station, induction platform and bar code scanner. This means you have induction platform A and induction platform B. After scanning skus at induction platform A, a sorter computer program has skus diverted to sort positions between induction platform A and clean-out & carrier re-set prior to induction platform B and after scanning skus at induction platform B, a sorter computer program has skus diverted to sort positions between induction platform B and clean-out & carrier re-set prior to induction platform A. Features are higher cost, more complex computer program/cost, sort conveyor travel is designed as a endless loop travel path and maximizes your sort conveyor travel path and increases your sort capacity by 85%.

SINGLE SCANNER WITH REPLACEMENT PARTS OR DUAL SCANNERS
IMPACTS YOUR SORTER UTILIZATION AND MINIMAL DOWN-TIME
A single scanner on your sorter travel path with on-site replacement parts or dual scanners on a sorter travel path are options to resolve your scanner problems with minimal down-time and maintain your sorter capacity. A single scanner with on-site replacement parts has your operation purchase and maintain key and long lead time scanner spare parts on-site. When you have a scanner problem, your scanner spare parts are available to resolve your

scanner problem in the shortest time. Features are shortest travel path to first sort position, lower cost, minimal sorter computer programming and cost and some down-time. Dual scanners on your sorter travel path has two scanner that are adjacent to each other on a sorter travel path. If your front/first scanner has a problem, you switch your scanner activity to a second/back scanner and your sorter computer program automatically adjusts for the new sorter travel scan and travel to the first sort position distance. Features are added scanner cost, longer sorter travel path to first sort position and minimal sorter down-time.

SORTER TRAVEL PATH
 SORTER TRAVEL PATH COST AND LOW SKU HANDLING COST
Your sorter travel path is a mechanized sort conveyor travel path that directs picked and inducted sku past all sort locations. A sort travel path with no re-circulation is a straight line that at a sort travel path all did not sort skus decline to the floor and are manually returned to your induction station. If your sort travel path has did not sort sku re-circulation, your sort travel path has did not sku return on a conveyor travel path to your induction station.

EMPLOYEE PROTECTION & NOISE COVERS
  EMPLOYEE SAFETY
Employee protection and noise covers are plastic formed section along both sorter travel path sides that improve employee safety and reduces noise level. After a sort travel path is installed, plastic covers and sides are attached to a sorter travel path support members.

NETTING
  EMPLOYEE SAFETY & REDUCE PACKAGE DAMAGE
Netting is a power conveyor sorter travel path safety option that reduces employee injury and sku damage. Netting is more commonly referred to as fish net or fabric/plastic meshed net with openings between strands. With faster sorter conveyor travel path speeds, wide sku characteristic mix, some 90 degree curves and diverters to move sku from a sorter travel path, there is potential for a light weight, tall or smooth surface sku to slide from a sorter carrier onto the floor.

SINGLE/STRAIGHT LINE OR RE-CIRCULATION SORTER CONVEYOR TRAVEL PATH
  IMPROVE SPACE UTILIZATIN & ASSURE SKU FLOW
Single/straight line or re-circulation sorter conveyor travel path are your sorter conveyor travel path options that assure good space utilization and sku flow. With a single line sort travel path, your picked skus travel past your induction station and sort stations and did not sort skus are accumulated at your sorter travel path run-out. The run-out declines to floor level, at a pre-determined times or full & partial full line controls have an employee physically re-introduce or physically sort the skus. Features are low cost, handles a low sku volume and small CO number and in a building with limited space. A re-circulation sorter conveyor concept has did not sort skus by a conveyor travel path that are automatically re-introduce to the induction/scanner. Features are higher sorter conveyor & controls cost, larger building space & designed to handle a large sku volume & CO number.

MECHANIZED SORT TO ONE DIRECTION OR TWO DIRECTIONS
  IMPROVE SPACE UTILIZATION & CAPACITY
For improved space utilization, a mechanized sort concept sort from sorter travel path options are sort to one direction or two directions. One direction sort options are (1) down direction that are Bombay Drop and Flap Sorter and (2) side direction that are sliding shoe, brush sorter, ring sorter, moving vertical or horizontal belt or tilt tray. Both side directions include tilt tray.

FULL AND PARTIAL SORT LANE CONTROLS
 REDUCE SKU DAMAGE & MINIMIZE SORTER DAMAGE
Full and partial sort lane controls are a mechanized sort travel sort lane devices that assure constant sku flow, minimizes potential sku/equipment damage. A partial sort lane control device is located in a sort lane middle (sides or bottom) and when blocked by accumulated skus, the device sends a message to a computer that activates an alarm (noise or light) that signals an employee to remove accumulated skus. A full sort lane control device is a sort

line start section (sides) and when blocked by accumulated skus, the device sends a message to a computer that activates a sort conveyor travel path not to divert a sku onto a sort lane and travel on a re-circulation conveyor.

SORT LANE DOOR WITH PLASTIC WINDOW OR MESHED WINDOW
IMPACTS YOUR SORTER PRODUCTIVITY & MINIMAL SKU DAMAGE

Sort lane door with a plastic window or meshed window is used on a manual or mechanized sort lane discharge door that improves packer productivity and minimizes sku damage. As your manual or mechanized sorter transfers a CO sku into a slide/chute sort lane, skus queue against a sort lane discharge door. A solid discharge door restricts a packer sort lane vision. A plastic or meshed window discharge door allows a packer sort lane vision and determines how a packer opens a door.

MECHANIZED TILT TRAY SORT LANE HAS 3 SORT LANES
ASSURE CONTINUOUS CUSTOMER ORDER FLOW & ASSURE ACCURATE SORT ACTIVITY

Mechanized tilt tray sort lane has 3 sort lanes to assure continuous CO flow and accurate sort activity (batched/group sku mix). Sort lane design options are (1) 3 sort lane allows 1 sort lane for your present/active batch sort, second sort lane for next sort batch and third sort lane for a safety factor and (2) 3 sort lane has two flippers that creates 3 sort lanes and each flipper is open or closed per the batch. Features are requires additional sorter program, wider sort lane and with a flipper has long sort lane.

CHAPTER 7
MANIFEST, SHIP SORT, STAGE & LOAD ACTIVITY EXPENSE REDUCTION IDEAS

WHEN DOES YOUR CUSTOMER ORDER DELIVERY CLOCK START
  ASSURES CUSTOMER SATISFACTION
When does your CO delivery clock start is an operation factor that improves customer satisfaction. When does your CO delivery clock start is the number of days that a customer expects to receive a CO delivery. Your CO delivery varies per industry and company. Various clock time starts are (1) after CO receipt by your host computer, (2) after your pick/pack WMS or host computer receives an approved CO and (3) after your pick/pack activity receives a CO.

CUBE YOUR DELIVERY TRUCK
  ASSURES GOOD LOAD EMPLOYEE PRODUCTIVITY & GOOD DELIVERY TRUCK UTILIZATION
Cube your delivery truck is a delivery truck load idea that improves direct load employee productivity and good delivery truck utilization. A direct load activity has CO packages travel from a sort conveyor into a delivery truck. In a delivery truck, a load employee off-loads packages onto a delivery truck floor. With a WMS computer cube program that suggests a CO carton size your WMS computer program has data to determine a package number per delivery truck. To cube a delivery truck your WMS computer program requires a delivery truck internal cube & your desire utilization and program to total your CO package cubes. After your sort/manifest computer obtains a desire package number, your sort conveyor does not transfer CO packages to a delivery truck, Features are minimizes load employee non-productive time to squeeze cartons into a delivery truck & accurate manifest list for each truck.

ZONE SKIP
  ASSURE LOW COST DELIVERY & IMPROVE CUSTOMER SERVICE
Zone skip is an operation with a freight company that has several terminals (spoke and wheel) and allows you to unitize CO packages for a specific zone onto a full delivery truck, cart or pallet. A full delivery truck, cart or pallet CO packages by-passes your operations freight company terminal sorter concept & driven to your CO local freight company terminal or carts/pallets are transferred onto your CO local freight company terminal delivery truck. With a delivery truck strategy you have medium volume, with your freight company approval for 20 ft long delivery trucks are loaded for a zone skip strategy. Features are: low delivery cost & shorten CO order delivery time or customer service.

SHIP LABEL ON TOP, SIDE OR FRONT
  ASSURES MAXIMUM & ACCURATE SCAN TRANSACTIONS
A package CO ID ship label placement options are carton top, side or front. A package CO ID location assures employee or bar code scanner line of sight for maximum good read and accurate scan transactions. If your warehouse operation uses a RF tag, to complete a package WMS CO ID good read, a RF tag sends a signal that is received by a receiver and does not require line of sight. Most catalog, direct mail and TV marketing operations, the most frequent location is on a package top or side that satisfies your operational and delivery company employee or bar code scanner requirements.

MECHANIZED SORT (See Check & Pack Chapter)

MECHANICAL SORT CONCEPT TYPES & SELECTION FACTORS
  ASSURES PACKAGE SORT
Mechanical sort concept types and selection factors assures that your CO package is diverted from a sorter travel path onto an assigned sort lane. Various sort concepts are (1) active sorter with a powered induction station, conveyor travel path and mechanical device that pushes/pulls a CO package onto a sort lane. Various active sorters are (a) cross-horizontal or vertical moving belt that handles both bags and cartons, (b) pusher diverter that handles carton CO packages, (c) powered belt diverter, pop-up wheel, chain, roller, belt that handles carton CO

packages, (d) ring sorter that handles bag CO packages & (e) rotating paddle, (2) active-passive sorter with a manual induction station, powered sorter travel path that tips or plows a CO package onto a sort lane. Various active/passive sorters are (a) tilt tray that handles both bag and carton CO packages, (b) nova sort that handles both bag and carton CO packages, (c) tilt slat that handles carton CO packages, (d) gull wing that handles both bag and carton CO packages, (e) sliding shoe that handles carton CO packages, (f) flap sorter that handles bag CO packages or low profile carton CO packages, (g) plow diverter that handles carton CO packages, (h) brush sorter that handles bag or carton CO packages. The sorters and (3) passive sorter with a manual induction station with a powered sorter travel path that uses gravity to move a CO package into a sort station. Sorter type is (a) Bombay drop that handles a bag package.

Sorter selection factors are (1) economics, (2) available building area and height, (3) bar code presentation, (4) CO physical characteristics and volume, (4) required sort lanes and sort lane design, (5) required electric power and other utilities & (6) direct load or unitize station.

SIDE OR OVERHEAD BAR CODE SCAN CUSTOMER ORDER PACKAGES
ASSURE MAXIMUM BAR CODE GOOD READS & SCAN MAXIMUM PACKAGE NUMBER

Side or overhead bar code scan CO packages are options for your CO package ID location as a customer order package travels on your sorter travel path past your scan station that assure maximum bar code good reads and scan maximum package number. On a sort conveyor travel path a package CO ID assures a scanner line of sight to a CO ID and on a load conveyor an employee light of sight to a CO ID. A package with a side CO ID on a sorter conveyor has a side scanner complete a scan transaction and package orientation on a load conveyor requires a package CO ID face your load/unitize employee. Features are shorter scanner depth of field, potential fixed scanner device that has a lower cost, potential lower picker/packer productivity due to it requires a CO ID that is placed on a package in a specific location and on some occasions low load/unitize employee productivity, due to a package with a CO ID not facing in the proper direction requires an employee to turn a package. A package with a top CO ID on a sorter conveyor has an overhead scanner complete a scan transaction and all packages orientation on a load conveyor has each package CO ID face your loading/unitize employee. Features are longer scanner depth of field, potential moving beam scanner device that has a higher cost, higher picker/packer productivity due to it a CO ID is placed on a package top in any location and assures good load/unitize employee productivity, due to a package with a CO ID facing in the proper direction.

EMPLOYEE OR MECHANCIAL INDUCT (See Check & Pack Chapter)

MANUAL OR AUTOMATIC INDUCTION (See Check & Pack Chapter)

STRAIGHT LINE OR ENDLESS LOOP (See Check & Pack Chapter)

SINGLE OR DUAL INDUCTION (See Check & Pack Chapter)

DUAL INDUCTION FOR SEPARATE SORT/LOAD LANES
INCREASE YOUR SORT VOLUME & INCREASE SORTER CARRIER UTILIZATION

Dual induction for separate sort/load lanes is a sorter design concept that permits sorter flexibility. With a top labeled CO ID package dual induction allows your sorter to handle both bags and cartons, side by side sort/unitize lanes, increased sort lane number. With dual induction, after your first induction station (A) CO packages are sorted to lanes and travel past a clean-out sort lane to assure each all CO packages are sorted and past a carrier re-set station that prepares a carrier for the next induction station (B). After your first induction station (B) CO packages are sorted to lanes and travel past a clean-out sort lane to assure each all CO packages are sorted & past a carrier re-set station that prepares a carrier for the next induction station (A). Features are requires top label packages, improves space utilization, maximizes sort utilization, permits zone skip and additional sorter & computer cost.

SEPARATE MECHANIZED SORT FOR BAGS OR CARTONS
ASSURE MAXIMUM SORTATION & MINIMIZE PACKAGE DAMAGE

Separate mechanized sort for bags or cartons has an operation use separate sort concept or dual induction for bags and carton that assure maximum sort and minimize package damage. With bags or cartons on sorter conveyor travel path, there is a wide CO package size, height, shape and weight difference. If bags and cartons are placed on the same sorter conveyor travel path, potential problems are with some sort concepts, low profile packages are not sorted by the sort device, difficult to assure a scanner light of site to all packages CO IDs, some bag and small size packages are difficult to convey and some carton packages are heavy weight and bags packages are low weight. If you have separate sorter concepts for bags and cartons, each sort concept is designed to convey and sort each package type. Features are additional sorter and conveyor costs and additional floor space. A hybrid (dual induction and separate sort location concept) sort concept sorts both bags and cartons. With a dual induction and separate sort locations has bags inducted on one scan/induction station (A), sorter completes all bag sorts prior to clean-out and re-set station and sorter carriers are ready to receive cartons and cartons are inducted on another scan/induction station (B), sorter completes all carton sorts prior to clean-out and re-set station and sorter carriers are ready to received bags.

MANIFEST BY HAND HELD SCANNER
ASSURES ACCURATE MANIFEST RECORD AND DATA

Manifest by hand held scanner is manifest activity that has an employee bar code scan each package WMS CO ID. A manifest activity registers each package WMS CO ID as it leaves your operation. Per your freight company requirement your manifest scan transactions are transferred by a paper document, diskette or on-line from your operation to your freight company terminal. A manual bar code scanner manifest concept has at a separate manifest station or at a freight truck door an employee with a hand held scanner read each package WMS CO ID on-line or delayed to your freight company. Features are good employee productivity, minimal errors, accurate/on-line/delayed data transfer and low cost.

MANIFEST AT A SCANNER OR AT DELIVERY TRUCK DOOR
ASSURES MAXIMUM & ACCURATE SCAN TRANSACTIONS

Manifest at your scanner or at delivery truck door (delivery truck entrance) are locations to accept a package WMS CO ID scan transaction. Many operations sort and manifest read a CO ID bar code at a sort conveyor scanner location due to sort conveyor divert onto a travel path that transports CO package into a delivery truck. Features are (1) requires one scanner, (2) minimal employees and (3) accurate scan transactions. To identify a package CO ID read/manifest & load problem, you compare your WMS computer CO IDs and number to your scanner (actual) WMS CO IDs & number. If your travel path has packages fall from a travel path, a manifest option is to have an employee hand scan each package CO ID as a package enters a freight delivery truck. Features are (1) requires a second hand held scanner & additional manifest transfer time, (2) additional employee & (3) accurate scan transactions.

MANIFEST TRANSACTION ON-LINE OR DELAYED UPDATE TRANSFER
ASSURES ACCURATE MANIFEST

Manifest transaction on-line or delayed update transfer to your WMS computer and freight company are your manifest list transfer options that assures an accurate manifest for a freight company truck. After each CO WMS ID passes a manifest bar code scanner, each CO WMS ID is sent to your WMS computer and is considered physically shipped from your facility. In-house on-line CO WMS ID scan transaction has your manifest scanner transfer direct to your WMS computer. Features are on-line ship data and requires your WMS computer with capacity to accept all transactions. Second on-line CO WMS ID has your manifest scanner transfer direct to your WMS computer and your freight company computer. Features are on-line ship data, requires your WMS computer with the capacity to accept all transactions, requires communication to your freight company and allows your freight company to improve delivery truck plans. Delayed CO WMS ID scan transactions are sent to a warehouse computer that holds/accumulates scan transactions in a file. At a pre-determined time or per WMS computer capacity, accumulated scan transactions are released to a WMS computer. Features are less complex WMS computer program, fewer transfer messages and lower WMS computer cost.

FREIGHT DELIVERY TRUCK OR DAY MANIFEST SENT TO YOUR FREIGHT COMPANY
　ASSURES ACCURATE MANIFEST & IMPROVE SCURITY

Freight delivery truck or work day manifest that is sent to your freight company are company manifest list options. Manifest by delivery truck has your sort/manifest computer receive and keep separate for each delivery truck. After a delivery truck is considered full, you have your sort conveyor discontinue sorts to a delivery truck and you have your computer complete a manifest list that is sent your freight company, Features are requires good co-ordination between your loading employees and sort/manifest computer, possible for manifested/sorted conveyor remain on a divert lane, assures security to compare your company manifest list to a freight company scan transactions and additional computer program and costs. At a work day end, manifest by work day delivery has your sort/manifest computer compile a manifest list for one work day at a work day end that is sent to your freight company. Features are if partial full trucks remain at your dock, at a freight terminal difficult to assure accurate manifest. But can be resolved by your work day ends with your last full delivery truck that is entered into your manifest computer, assures security to compare your company manifest list to a freight company scan transactions and simple computer program with standard cost.

OFF-LOAD A MANIFESTED & LOADED WMS IDENTIFIED CUSTOMER ORDER PACKAGE
　ASURES ACCURATE MANIFEST

Off-load a manifested and loaded WMS CO ID package is a ship dock activity that assures an accurate manifest for loaded WMS CO ID packages on a delivery truck. After a manifested WMS CO ID package is physically placed into a delivery truck, a WMS CO ID package is considered shipped to a customer. With a full delivery truck at your dock and your warehouse staff requires to place other WMS CO ID packages onto a delivery truck, your warehouse staff removes manifested and loaded WMSCO ID packages. To assure an accurate manifest of WMS CO ID packages, your staff off-loads and hand scans each off-loaded WMS CO ID package. Each WMS CO ID package scan transactions is transferred to your WMS computer that removes each CO WMS ID from a manifest list. To track off-loaded WMS CO ID packages, each WMS CO ID package is scanned and physically transferred to a WMS ID temporary hold position that is updated in a WMS computer file.

NO READ OR NO DATA
　IMPROVES SECURITY

No read or no data is a manifest scanner activity that improves your operation security to have only packages with an actual CO ID entered into your manifest file and do not ship from your operation. A no read means that your manifest scanner did not get a good read and a no date situation occurs as a package CO ID is read by a scanner. A scanner sends each CO ID to a sort computer that compares a scanned CO ID to a WMS computer CO IDs that are in the files. If a manifest scanner does not get a good read, your warehouse sort computer does not add a CO ID to its manifest files and the package with a no read is divert to a special divert location and is not shipped from your facility. When a sort/manifest computer does not obtain a match, your sort computer diverts a package with no data is diverted to a special divert location.

NO CUSTOMER ORDER IDENTIFICATION (See No Data)

CANCELED CUSTOMER ORDER
　IMPROVES SECURITY

Canceled CO is a manifest activity that improves your security to assure valid CO packages are send from your operation. After your WMS computer transfers a canceled CO WMS ID to your sort/manifest computer, your warehouse manifest computer file creates a canceled CO message for a specific CO WMS ID. After your sort conveyor or hand held scanner completes a CO WMS ID that is sent to your sort/manifest computer, your computer sends a cancel order message to a hand held scanner or sort/manifest computer to transfer a WMS CO ID package onto a cancel customer order sort lane that restricts a package from being shipped from your facility. Your warehouse staff assures that a canceled CO skus are transferred to a WMS ID pick-able position.

DATE DELIVERY SORT
IMPROVE CUSTOMER SERVICE

Date delivery sort is a sort activity that has your sort conveyor computer program receive CO package with a specific delivery date and to have a CO package diverted to sort lane and assure on a specific date that a CO package is transferred onto a ship conveyor. The strategy improves your customer service. After a sort computer program receives a date delivery CO ID and receives a scanner induction message (CO ID), a sort computer program has a date delivery CO ID/package diverted from a sorter onto a specific sort lane. At a sort lane, an employee physically and scans a CO ID onto a WMS ID temporary hold position that is sent and update in your WMS computer program. On the required delivery date, your WMS computer program lists all CO IDs for shipment. On a hand held scanner display screen or paper document, an employee transfers each date delivery CO ID/package onto your re-circulation conveyor for travel to your induction station that manifests and ships a date CO ID/package.

DID NOT SORT OR TO MANY TIMES AROUND A MECHANICAL SORTER (See Check & Pack Chapter)
IMPROVES SORT CONVEYOR UTILIZATION

A did not sort occurs on a mechanized sort conveyor with a CO package that is scanned, not sorted at an assigned location and is re-scanned. A did not sort package occurs due to a sort lane full condition or problem and creates re-circulation that lowers your sort conveyor utilization or completed sort numbers. An option to remove a did not sort package from a sort conveyor is to have sort conveyor computer program to register a package WMS CO ID X number times (did not sort) and to have your sort conveyor computer to activate a sort device for package sort/transfer onto a did not sort lane. Your package is manual manifest scanned and transferred to a delivery truck.

HOW TO GET GOOD SCANNER READS
INCREASE SORT UTILIZATION

How to get good scanner reads is a mechanized sorter concept that is designed to increase your sorter utilization or sort rate. Since your sort conveyor travel speed is set at the fastest travel speed and your scanner reads a top labeled package height with a wide mix and direction of travel, your bar code scanner is required to obtain maximum reads. Your maximum good reads result from over-squared label (bar code height equals total bar bars & white spaces width), good quiet zones (white space between a label first and last black bars and label paper edges and assures your package heights are within your scanner depth of field.

CONTROL YOUR CARTON TRAVEL ON YOUR SORT LANE DECLINE CONVEYOR
ASSURE CONTROLLED CARTON TRAVEL & MINIMIZE DAMAGE

Control your carton travel on your sort lane decline conveyor assures controlled carton travel and minimizes damage. After your carton divert onto a sort lane, there is potential for fast carton travel over a decline conveyor travel path and to have a heavy carton crash and push a light weight carton onto a queued carton. Your carton control options are (1) tilt your roller conveyor travel path that has carton slide against the low side guard. A carton side rubbing against a side guard slows your carton travel speed. Features are low cost and slows heavy and light weight cartons, (2) on your decline roller conveyor travel path restrict pre-determined rollers turning that momentarily restricts or slows carton travel. Features are low cost and slows heavy and light weight cartons and (3) plastic stripes above a decline roller conveyor travel path and extend downward to a pre-determined height to come in contact with a specific carton height and slow carton travel. Features are low cost and slow tall carton travel.

OVER AND UNDER SORT CONVEYOR TRAVEL PATH
PROVIDE SORTER TRAVEL PATH IN A SMALL AREA & GOOD SPACE UTILIZATION

Over and under sort conveyor travel path is used with an endless loop sorter travel and in a building dock area with limited space. An over & under sorter conveyor travel path has after an induction station, a sorter travel path travel at a pre-determined elevation past all sort lanes, completes a 360 degree turn, makes an elevation (higher or lower) change to return travel to an induction station & makes an elevation change prior to an induction station. Features are elevation is per sorter manufacturer, fits into a building & sort lanes are unitize stations & direct load concept.

SIDE BY SIDE SORT/UNITIZE LANES
PROVIDE MAXIMUM UNITIZE POSITIONS, GOOD SORTER PRODUCTIVITY, GOOD SPACE UTILIZATION & MAXIMUM SORTER UTILIZATION

Side by side sort/unitize lanes are used in a unitized onto a cart concept that provides maximum unitize positions, good sorter productivity, good space utilization and maximum sorter utilization. A side by side sort concept is a closed loop sorter travel path that on the travel outward from an induction platform a sorter diverts top labeled CO packages onto one sort lane and after a sorter travel path 360 turn/second induction station that on the return travel to the first or induction station a sorter diverts top labeled cartons onto another sort lane. A second sort lane directs cartons over a sort lane curve and onto a sort lane that is adjacent to the first sort lane. Each sort lane has photo-eyes that stop/start a sorter divert device. Features are some additional conveyor cost, extra unitize stations and top labeled CO package.

UNITIZE ONTO A CART AT A CONVEYOR END OR SIDE
ASSURE PACKAGE FLOW & GOOD LOADER PRODUCTIVITY

Unitize onto a cart at a conveyor end or side are your unitize options that assure package flow and good unitize productivity. Your conveyor travel path between your sort conveyor and unitize conveyor has photo eyes that start/stop sort conveyor divert devices. If your operation has few delivery locations or ship sort locations or sorted at your freight company terminal, unitize at your conveyor end assures good employee productivity and space utilization. Features are requires less sq ft area, requires sufficient space between dock door and conveyor end for employee work station, cart (s) & travel aisle, maximum sort/conveyor lanes per inch ft. If your operation has multiple sort or ship sort locations or your freight company zone skips by your freight local terminal sending a full cart direct to a another freight company terminal that improves your customer service and lowers cost. Features are provides a greater sort locations along a unitize conveyor, provides fewer sort lanes, additional cost, requires two employee work stations, carts and aisles space between two unitize conveyor lanes, requires on-time empty transfer to a unitize conveyor lane.

LOAD CONVEYOR QUEUE OR WHERE IS YOUR SORT CONVEYOR TRAVEL PATH
ASSURE PACKAGE FLOW & GOOD LOADER PRODUCTIVITY

Load conveyor queue or where is your sort conveyor travel path is design idea that is used to assure good loader employee productivity and package flow. Load conveyor queue is low or zero pressure conveyor travel path that is located prior to your direct load conveyor or unitize station. If your loading or unitize activity does not match your loading/unit activity, a queue conveyor section provides temporary hold area for scanned and sorted CO packages and with a surge to one sort lane reduces potential did not sort/re-circulation. In most operations, your sort conveyor travel path speed (250 to 300 ft pr hr) is faster than your direct load conveyor travel speed (65 to 80 ft pr hr), there is potential for CO package queue. Load/unitize conveyor queue travel path options are (1) sort conveyor travel path above your load doors, divert lanes extend toward your dock area rear wall, make a 360 degree turn onto a decline & queue conveyor section for travel onto a direct load conveyor or unitize station. Features are provides maximum queue, additional cost and ceiling structural designed for conveyor load support and (2) sort conveyor travel path is along your dock area rear wall, divert lanes extend toward your loading doors and decline to a load conveyor and unitize station. Features are minimal queue, lower cost and ceiling structural designed for conveyor load support.

UNITIZE OR DIRECT LOAD
ASSURE PACKAGE FLOW & GOOD LOADER PRODUCTIVITY

Unitize or direct load are an operations CO package load/ship options to assure package flow and good loader productivity. After your manifest and sort activities, your unitize or direct load activity is determined by your freight company requirements and assures each CO package is transferred onto a freight company delivery truck. A unitize activity occurs on your dock area with empty carts or pallets are located along a sort lane and has an employee transfer CO packages onto a cart or pallet. Your dock space design allows empty carts/pallet placed at a unitize station and full carts/pallets transferred onto a freight company truck. Features are permits CO package sort by a freight company criteria that permits a low volume operation to utilize zone skip, additional space for unitize stations and cart/pallet storage area or use a freight company truck that uses a dock position, each dock position requires a dock device to bridge a gap between dock and delivery truck and a dock light and matches your freight company delivery requirement. A direct load activity has CO package travel on your sort lane onto a fixed position or mobile conveyor travel path that extends into a freight company truck. In a freight company truck, an employee transfers CO packages onto a freight company truck floor or onto another package. Direct conveyor travel path concepts are belt, roller or skate-wheel conveyors. Features are permits CO package sort by a freight company criteria that permits a high volume operation to utilize zone skip, space for extendable or fixed position direct load conveyor that means less required dock space, electric outlet and a dock light.

LIGHT YOUR DELIVERY TRUCK (See Receiving Activity Chapter)

LOAD ON THE FLOOR, 4-WHEEL CART OR PALLET
    ASSURE FULL DELIVERY TRUCKS, MINIMIZE DAMAGE & GOOD LOADER PRODUCTIVITY
Load your customer order packages onto a delivery truck floor, in 4-wheel carts or on pallets are delivery truck loading options that assures full delivery trucks, maximum load productivity and minimal package damage. Floor load concept uses an extendable conveyor travel path for an employee to transfer CO packages from a conveyor travel path onto a delivery truck floor or another package top. CO packages are stacked to your load employees' highest reach. Features are maximum delivery truck utilization, difficult to ship bags, requires longest load time, to load and unload requires an extendible conveyor with a cost, bottom package of stack has potential damage and requires a high volume for zone skip with 20 ft trucks offer an opportunity. 4-wheel cart concept has an unitize employee place CO cartons/bags from a unitize station into a cart cavity. Full carts at a unitize station are employee pushed into a delivery truck and an empty cart is transferred to a unitized station. Features are packages secured into a cart cavity, empty carts require a staging area or are pushed from a delivery truck onto an unitize area, added cart cost, lower delivery truck utilization due to wheel and truck door clearance space requirements, each dock requires dock leveler/board and requires an employee to load/unload carts. Pallet concept cart concept has an unitize employee place CO cartons/bags from a unitize station onto a pallet. Full pallets at a unitize station are employee with a pallet truck or forklift truck are transferred into a delivery truck and empty pallets are transferred to a unitized station, Features packages are some pallets are secured into a cart cavity, empty pallets require a staging area or are transferred from a delivery truck onto an unitize area, very low cost, lower delivery truck utilization due to low pallet height that does occupy the entire space, each dock requires dock leveler/board and requires an employee with a pallet truck or forklift truck to load/unload carts.

UNITIZE ONTO CART OR PALLET
    ASSURE SECURED PACKAGES, MATCH FREIGHT COMPANY REQUIREMENTS & GOOD LOADER
    PRODUCTIVITY
Unitize onto a cart or pallet are an options to unitize CO packages for transfer onto a freight company delivery truck. Unitize allows your company to have secured packages, match your freight requirements, good loader productivity and participate into a zone skip program for customer service improvement and potential lower sort rate. A zone skip program with your freight company to unitize CO packages for your freight company delivery zones (other freight company regional terminals instead of your own freight company terminal). When you unitize CO packages onto a cart/pallet your freight company receives a cart/pallet that is transferred from your freight delivery onto another freight company zone delivery truck that has your unitize packages by-pass your freight company terminal sort concept. Your freight company requirements determine whether your operation unitize onto carts or pallets. When you unitize onto carts, your open cart side faces your unitize station, requires a dock leveler/board, employee to load/unload carts, empty/full carts are staged on your dock area that requires sq ft area or in a freight company delivery truck that occupies a dock and packages are secured with less potential damage. When you unitize onto pallets, your pallet side with a fork opening face your unitize station, requires a dock leveler/board, pallet truck or forklift truck used to load/unload carts, empty/full pallets are staged on your dock area that requires sq ft area or in a freight company delivery truck that occupies a dock and packages have increased potential damage.

CAPTIVE FREIGHT COMPANY TRUCKS
GOOD LOADER PRODUCTIVITY & MINIMAL EXTENDIBLE CONVEYOR COST

Captive freight company trucks means your freight company has dedicated delivery trucks to transfer your company packages from your operation to their terminal and used to bring customer returns or empty trucks to your operation. A captive truck strategy with your freight company approval, you install roller or skate-wheel conveyor travel path along each delivery truck left side as a truck is at a dock. With a level non-powered roller conveyor travel path allows packages loaded/unloaded between a delivery truck and dock area conveyor. With a level non-powered skate-wheel conveyor travel path allows packages loaded onto a delivery truck from your dock area conveyor. If skate-wheel conveyor is used to unload a delivery truck, there is potential skate-wheel damage from carton placement onto a conveyor. Features are some additional cost, improved loader/unloader productivity and less extendable dock conveyor length and cost.

DIRECT OR FLUID LOAD OPTIONS
ASSURES SORTED PACKAGE LOAD

Direct or fluid load options assure that your CO package is transported from a divert lane into a delivery truck. Inside a delivery truck, an employee transfers a CO package from a conveyor travel path onto a delivery truck floor or another package. Various direct load concepts are (1) non-powered manual nesting or retractable and extendible skate-wheel straight or flexible conveyor travel path. The concept is with lockable/unlockable rear wheels mobile between docks, handles carton CO packages and has a low cost, (2) non-powered manual nesting or retractable and extendible roller conveyor travel path. The concept is with lockable/unlockable rear wheels mobile between docks handles carton CO packages and has a low cost, (3) manual & electric powered nesting or retractable and extendible skate-wheel conveyor travel path, (4) manual & electric powered nesting or retractable and extendible skate-wheel conveyor travel path, (5) mobile position & electric powered nesting or retractable and extendible powered belt conveyor travel path. The concept services multiple/2 docks, handles bag and carton CO packages and has a high cost, (6) fixed position & electric powered nesting or retractable powered belt conveyor travel path. The concept services one dock, handles bag and carton CO packages and has a high cost & (7) electric powered extendible or retractable belt conveyor with a fixed support for the belt conveyor travel path. The concept services one dock, handles bag and carton CO packages and has a high cost

WITH MIXED DIRECT AND PALLET TRUCK LOADING SET CONVEYOR TO THE SIDE
PERMITS LOADING FLEXIBILITY & IMPROVES LOADER PRODUCTIVITY

With mixed direct and pallet truck load activity, you set your direct load conveyor to a delivery truck side that permits loading flexibility and improves loader productivity. With a mix CO package load concept, your dock area direct load conveyor location permits a conveyor to extend into a delivery truck and allows a pallet to travel over a dock leveler into a delivery truck. For maximum dock flexibility, your direct load conveyor is set on your dock in a location that allows your extendible conveyor to run along a delivery truck right side as you face a delivery truck at your dock.

FLOOR STAGE OR STAGE IN A RACK
PROVIDES TEMPORARY PACKAGE HOLDING AREA & SUPPLY ITEM STORAGE POSTIONS

Floor stage or stage in racks along a dock area walls are your dock area options to provide temporary unitized pallets in positions and carts on the floor level and supply item storage positions. If a delivery truck is not available at a dock, staging allows your operation to continue and hold manifest packages for a delivery truck arrival. Floor storage requires floor area, no cost and requires a pallet truck or forklift truck. Racks along dock area walls and above dock doors provide positions that are accessed by a forklift truck. Features are improved space utilization, requires a forklift truck to access positions and first load beam elevation height allows cart storage.

CHAPTER 8
CUSTOMER RETURNS ACTIVITY EXPENSE REDUCTION IDEAS

ONE RETURN ADDRESS OR SEVERAL RETURN ADDRESSES
ASSURE GOOD UNLOAD EMPLOYEE PRODUCTIVITY & CUSTOMER RETURNS FLOW

One return address or several return addresses are your printed customer return address label on your CO pack slip/invoice options. With 1 return address, your freight company sort concept has all your customer return packages that are sorted and delivered onto 1 delivery truck. At your unload dock, all return packages (GOH, jewelry, BIG/UGLY food and hard goods) flow to your first process station or over your sort concept to process stations. Your one return address returns flow has each process station handle high value and other skus. With some sku classifications such as jewelry or GOH your process employee requires additional skills and you mix high value skus with low value skus. If you have your WMS computer creates a separate return address label for each single CO sku classification or for a high value sku classification in a combination CO. With separate return label for each sku classification, your customer returns are separated by your (1) freight company onto separate carts, pallets or delivery truck or (2) your return sort conveyor, sorts each sku classification to specific sort lanes/process stations. Features are (1) less complex and improves process employee productivity & (2) skus flow as group for increase transport and sku sort activities.

CUSTOMER RETURNS LABEL ON YOUR CUSTOMER ORDER PACK SLIP/INVOICE
ASSURES CUSTOMER RETURNS ARRIVE AT YOUR PREFERRED LOCATION

Customer returns label on your CO pack slip/invoice assures smooth customer returns arrive at your preferred warehouse dock position and provides a customer with a return label with an accurate human readable address/bar coded face. Your pre-printed customer returns label provides you or freight company with ability to pre-sort customer returns to your preferred process section that is achieve by your returns label has your CO most important sku to your operation. Examples are combination CO with jewelry, GOH or specific sku. Feature assures a sku flows to your process section that is designed to handle the sku and minimizes in-house transport costs.

FREIGHT COMPANY PRE-SORT
IMPROVES RETURNS EMPLOYEE PRODUCTIVITY & ASSURES GOOD SKU FLOW

Freight company pre-sort concept has your freight company per each customer returns label to sort packages onto one sort lane for load onto a delivery truck, carton or pallet that is delivered to your company assigned dock. Per your pre-printed returns label, a freight company pre-sort activity separates returns by GOH, jewelry/high value, Big/ugly and regular cartons. When your freight company sorts specific returns onto a delivery truck, carts or pallets, there is high potential for improved returns flow. Since your GOH and jewelry returns requires special quality control skills, it improves your returns process employee productivity. Since Big/ugly sku physical characteristics do match your regular customer returns transport concept, big/ugly skus require a special transport concept. Features are improves returns employee productivity and assure good sku flow.

YOUR RETURNS DOCK ARRANGEMENT
IMPROVE UNLOAD PRODUCTIVITY, ASSURE GOOD RETURNS FLOW & INCREASE SPACE UTILIZATION

Dock door arrangement has your freight company returns trucks spotted/parked at a specific dock door to improve your unload employee productivity, assure good returns flow and increase space utilization. If your returns are floor stacked and unloaded onto a mobile belt conveyor or skate-wheel or roller extendible/retractable conveyor for maximum dock door flexibility your unload conveyors traverses between 2 or 3 dock doors. If your operation has three dock doors and your returns are delivered on 4-wheel carts, pallets or containers, you use a three dock door arrangement. A three dock door arrangement has one dock door used for active unload activity, second dock door is scheduled for your next returns truck and third dock door is used for empty cart, pallet or container loading activity.

AFTER UNLOAD YOU HAVE QUEUE
ASSURE GOOD UNLOAD EMPLOYEE PRODUCTIVITY & CUSTOMER RETURNS FLOW

After your customer returns packages are unloaded from your delivery truck you have a queue section that is prior to your first returns process work station. The queue section assures good unload employee productivity, customer returns flow and truck dock turn. With a conveyor unload concept, you have zero or low pressure accumulation conveyor between the unload conveyor and first work station. With a cart, pallet or container unload concept, you have floor staging area between your dock area and first returns work station. To assure proper cart, pallet or container control you have painted parallel lines on your floor to indicate a staging lane.

BETWEEN YOUR UNLOAD AREA & NEXT WORK STATION PROVIDE QUEUE
ASSURES SKU FLOW & GOOD EMPLOYEE PRODUCTIVITY

Between your unload area and next work station (open/dump or returns process station) provide queue for your customer return packages that assures sku flow and good employee productivity. If your carton unload and in-house transport concept is a powered conveyor travel path, you provide low/zero pressure roller conveyor travel path between your dock conveyor and your open/dump or returns process station. If your carton unload and in-house transport concept is 4-wheel carts and pallets, you provide dock staging floor area, pallet racks along your walls or back to back racks in your floor staging area. The pallet rack bottom load height is set at an elevation to allow full carts/pallets through a rack bay and your protect your rack upright posts. All queue concepts provide queue for an imbalance between a slow returns process stations and your unload productivity rate.

KNOW YOUR CUSTOMER ORDER (MOST IMPORTANT YOUR PROMOTIONAL SKUS) RETURN LIFE CYCLE
IMPROVE SPACE UTILIZATION, EMPLOYEE PRODUCTIVITY AND RETURNS FLOW

Know your customer return life cycle or time improves your space utilization, employee productivity and returns flow. Your returns quantity varies from medium volume to high volume. In a returns process area, return to stock and return to vendor temporary or final sort area requires a WMS ID position for each sku. To assure good space utilization and good employee put-away productivity, good warehouse sku location strategy is to associate a sku volume with a sku position. To assist a returns process manager sku location strategy, a manager uses each sku return history or sales as the location criteria. From the sales history, important factors are (1) promotional skus that are allocated to a large sort position and is close to your process station and (2) after a sku sales the day number such as 30, 60 or 90 days and associated sku return volume or percentage that are allocated to a regular sort position. Feature assures a position has capacity to handle a large sku quantity

AGE CUSTOMER ORDER RETURNS IN YOUR STAGING AREA
ASSURE CUSTOMER SATISFCATION

Age customer returns in your returns process staging area assures a FIFO (first-in first-out) customer returns rotation or flow through your process area. Proper customer returns rotation maintains company customer returns policy and assures customer satisfaction. FIFO customer returns concept has your oldest or dated customer returns processed first. If your returns operation receives bulk or floor loaded on a delivery truck, your delivery company, yard control or dock supervisor tracks the oldest delivery truck and schedules the oldest truck at the next vacate dock. If returns are on carts, on pallets or in containers, each cart, pallet or container receives a human readable and color coded date tag with a color for each week day. To assure FIFO returns rotation, dated carts, pallets or containers are grouped together with a first-in first-out flow to a vacate process station.

RACKS IN YOUR RETURNS STAGING AREA
IMPROVE SPACE UTILIZATION

Racks in your returns area is an idea to improve space utilization. Since a returns process area is in a building area with a normal ceiling height, there is an opportunity to place racks along walls and above conveyor travel paths. The positions are considered return supplies, return paper document and returned sku temporary hold storage positions. If your customer returns are delivered on carts or pallets and you do not use powered equipment to move carts or pallets, back to back racks in a staging area provides additional storage positions. To optimize space utilization, a first load beam permits an employee to move a full cart or pallet under rack bays. In most applications, a first load beam has 6 ft 6 in to 7 ft clear space from the floor surface. To protect rack posts, post protectors are place in each rack post front.

SEPARATE YOUR CUSTOMER RETURNS BY BIG/UGLY, CARTON OR SMALL CARTON
IMPROVES RETURNS EMPLOYEE PRODUCTIVITY & ASSURES GOOD SKU FLOW

Separate your customer returns by big/ugly, carton or small carton has your freight company or sort concept (after unload) to separate your customer returns by a sku physical characteristics that improves your employee productivity and assures good sku flow. Sku separation concept matches a sku to your customer returns process section that is designed to handle a sku volume, sku size or returns process employee is skilled to check a sku quality and assures a cost effective and efficient process.

SEPARATE BIG/UGLY SKUS FROM OTHER SKUS
IMPROVE PROCESS EMPLOYEE PRODUCTIVITY AND SKU FLOW

Separate big/ugly skus from other skus is customer returns process activity that has your returns unload or open employee separate your big/ugly skus from other skus that improves process employee productivity and sku flow. Your returns activity handles a wide sku mix, your process options are (1) all skus or sku mix is processed through any process station. When all skus or sku mix is sent to one process station, a process employee has potential to handle a big/ugly sku at a process station that is designed to handle medium size skus. With a large sku at a process station, a process employee has low productivity due to handle and process a large sku that requires a process employee to walk around and move a large and disposed sku and (2) separate your big/ugly skus from your other skus flow to other process stations that handle small and medium size skus. When you design a process station with a sku in-flow and out-flow layout to handle large skus, there is smooth returns flow due to your process station work area and equipment are designed to match your sku size.

HIGH VALUE SKU SEPARATION
IMPROVES EMPLOYEE PRODUCTIVITY, ASSURE GOOD SKU FLOW & IMPROVES SECURITY

High value sku separation is a customer returns idea that improves your returns process productivity, assures good sku flow and improves security. If your operation handles expensive items such as jewelry and your customer orders are sent with a pre-printed customer returns label with a separate address, it separates your high value customer returns from customer returns with other skus. During your freight company customer returns sort and flow to your operation, your high value sku customer returns are delivered to your jewelry operation.

CUSTOMER NON-DELIVERABLE SEPARATED TO ONE PROCESS STATION
ASSURE GOOD UNLOAD EMPLOYEE PRODUCTIVITY & CUSTOMER RETURNS FLOW

Customer non-deliverable separated to one process station has your freight company or your returns sort concept separate/sort CO non-deliverable packages to one process station that improves process employee productivity due to quality is good and constant customer return flow due to no credit issues. A non-deliverable CO is a CO package that was not accepted by a customer and by your company return delivery label return address is sent back to your returns operation. Also, your company package seal is not broken. Features means that in most occurrences skus are in return to stock or have good quality. If your delivery/freight company sorts the non-deliverable that are delivered to your operation in bulk or in a separate container, on a pallet or cart or your returns sort conveyor diverts a non-deliverable package to one process station. Feature allows on process station to improve productivity and processed customer returns due to minimal inspection time.

TRACK AND KNOW YOUR CUSTOMER RETURNS REASONS (See Check Chapter)
MINIMIZE FUTURE RETURNS

Track and know your customer returns reasons are important factors that assist you to reduce your future return package number. Customer return reasons help your determine where your operation needs improvement. Customer return reasons are (1) to some degree within your staff control such as (a) wrong sku was received that is a pick error, (b) CO package was received late due to operational problems, (c) sku was received damaged that has potential pack problems, (d) sku was out-of-date that has inventory control problems and (e) received to many skus that is a pick error and (2) customer order problem such as (a) customer ordered several colors or sizes, (b) sku does not match the catalog or television picture or stated dimensions, (c) recalled by a vendor, (d) customer was not home, (e) package was not accepted by a customer, (f) package was delivered to the wrong address and (g) customer did not like the sku. If you list the customers repeat problems, there is potential justification to refuse another order from a customer who repeats returns and adds to your expenses.

TRANSPORT YOUR CUSTOMER ORDER RETURN PACKAGE TO YOUR FIRST PROCESS STATION
IMPROVES RETURNS EMPLOYEE PRODUCTIVITY & REDUCES SKU DAMAGE & ASSURES SKU FLOW

Transport your customer return package to your first process station improves returns employee productivity, reduces sku damage and assures returns sku flow. Your customer returns transport concept is determined by your customer return package open location. Your options are (1) open at your returns process/sku disposition station that has your customer return carton or bag package travel direct from a delivery truck to a process station. With closed customer returns packages, your transport options are (a) powered belt or roller conveyor travel path that assure a constant one-way flow and additional cost with stop/start controls and (b) 4-wheel with shelves that has an employee move carts, move empty carts to unload dock and requires floor space and (2) if you open/slice your packages at an open station for transport to returns process station, your transport options have controlled sku travel and provide queue at each return process station. Options are (a) powered roller conveyor travel path that have medium size carton and small size carton on a tray to assure good travel and customer order pack slip/invoice inside a package, (b) 4-wheel carton with shelves/netting that has an employee move carts, move empty carts to unload dock and requires floor space.

YOU PROCESS RETURNS (OPEN & DISPOSE) COMPLETED AT ONE STATION
HIGH COST CUSTOMER RETURNS PROCESS

When you process returns (open & dispose) at one process station all your customer returns activities (open, dump filler material, credit process & dispose) are completed at one work station. The return process has return packages delivered to your process stations. At each process station, a highly trained and high wage rate employee completes skilled activities that include credit process and sku quality inspection and unskilled activities that include package open and filler material dump. The one station concept has a high unit cost and under productive employee who completes both skilled and unskilled activities.

RETURN PACKAGE OPEN & DUMP FILLER MATERIAL OR PROCESS EMPLOYEE COMPLETES ALL ACTIVITIES
IMPROVES RETURNS EMPLOYEE PRODUCTIVITY & ASSURES GOOD SKU FLOW

Return package open and dump filler material at a separate work station or at a return process station are your options that improves and assures good sku flow. If your returns process concept has a return process employee open a return container and dump filler material into a trash transport concept, a returns process station employee to completes all customer return activities. Features are (1) multiple returns process employee tasks at one work table that has an employee use a cutting knife to open a package/empty container transport concept and from a package to dump filler material into a trash concept and to assure customer credit approval/sku disposition that make a complex work station, (2) potential employee cutting injuries, (3) a skilled and trained employee completing simple, repetitive and non-skill activity, (4) possible separate trash handling concept & (5) possible separate filler material handling concept. If your returns process concept has a separate package open and filler material dump station and separate returns process station for customer credit approval/sku disposition, it is a more production line design operation. With the concept, each station completes repetitive activities such as open/dump and credit approval/sku disposition. At a package open and dump station an employee works with safety gloves and cutting knife to open each package, dump filler material into a transport concept and transfers skus/CO pack slip/invoice In a return container that is placed onto a transport concept. At a returns process station, an employee completes customer credit approval/sku disposition and a return container is transferred onto a transport concept and disposed sku is transferred onto a transport concept. Features are (1) improves employee safety and productivity, (2) at each open/dump station, separate filler material and at each process station, empty return container and disposed sku transport concepts that a less complex work station, (3) open/dump station completes repetitive and non-highly skilled activity, (4) at a process station employee completes highly skilled activities of credit approval and sku quality check that improves employee productivity and accurate transactions & (5) assure a constant customer returns and disposed sku flows.

YOU PROCESS RETURNS FLOW THROUGH SEVERAL (OPEN, TRANSPORT & DISPOSE) STATIONS
LOW COST CUSTOMER RETURNS PROCESS

When you process returns with skus flow through open/dump station, over a transport path and disposed (credit and sku disposition) station has your return activities separated at unskilled and skilled employees. With (open & dispose) at one process station all your customer returns activities (open, dump filler material, credit process & dispose) are completed at 1 work station. Your first return station has an unskilled employee open packages and dump filler material and transfer open packages onto a cart or conveyor travel path for transport to your process station. At each process station, a highly trained and high wage rate employee completes skilled activities that include credit process, sku quality inspection and sku pre-sort/transfer onto a transport concept or unskilled activities that include package open and filler material dump. The returns process has a continuous return and sku flow.

WHERE TO HOLD YOUR CUSTOMER ORDER LOOK-UP TABLE
IMPROVE RETURNS PROCESS EMPLOYEE PRODUCTIVITY

Where to hold your CO look-up table assures a returns process employee good productivity. To complete a customer return, a process employee requires quick and accurate access to your CO detail information that includes CO ID number, sku description, sku quantity, manufacture lot number and date. Your CO look-up table location options are in your (1) host computer that is not preferred due to difficult to have on-time access from a host computer completing other department activities and security issues. But is used to access old COs, (2) WMS computer is a preferred computer after you complete a survey for time period that determines your returns life cycle or day number after a CO manifest for a customer return received at your returns process station. Life cycle determines a day number for COs that are retained in your WMS computer and reduces your WMS computer look-up time. If an old customer return is received at a process station, your returns process employee accesses your host computer. Features are good returns process productivity & host computer has fewer transactions or (3) warehouse computer that is not preferred due to security issues.

AT A RETURNS PROCESS STATION, RETURNS EMPLOYEE SITS OR STANDS
ASSURE GOOD EMPLOYEE PRODUCTIVITY

At a returns process station do your returns employee sit or stand are your employee option that assure an employee complete all return process activities and good productivity. If your employee sit on a stool your stool options are to use a (1) low level chair that has your returns process employee have increased non-productive time to get-up from a chair, reach a returns package from a conveyor, sit in a chair and complete a sku disposition, get-up front a chair and transfer a disposed sku onto a take-away concept and (2) high level chair that has your returns process employee have minimal non-productive time to reach a returns package from a conveyor, lean against/sit on top of chair and complete a sku disposition and transfer a disposed sku onto a take-away concept.

WHAT IS PRINTED ON YOUR SORT OR DISPOSITION LABELS
IMPROVES RETURNS EMPLOYEE PRODUCTIVITY & ASSURES ACCURATE SKU SORT & INVENTORY CONTROL

What is printed on your RTS, RTV and other sku sort or disposition labels serves as an instruction for employee or mechanical presort or final sort activity that improves returns employee productivity, assures accurate sku sort and inventory control. The returned sku disposition label options are (1) return-to-stock/pick position options are (a) "RTS", (b) QA inspection or (c) sku with an existing sku ID. If a label is blank it is easily ID by a returns process employee. if an sku with a blank label or a QA inspection label is sent to a customer, there is less customer concern, (2) return to vendor with "RTV", (3) damaged sku with a "D", (4) outlet store ("OS") or company store ("CS"), (5) retail or jobber with a "J", (6) charity with a "C", (7) rework with "RW" and (8) spare parts with "SP".

HAND HELD SCANNER DEFAULT TO ONE
  IMPROVE PROCESS EMPLOYEE PRODUCTIVITY AND SKU FLOW
Hand held scanner default to one is a returns process concept that has a RF device with wireless or wire communications to a PC or to a WMS computer for your CO original sku quantity and sku description. To improve checker productivity and returns sku flow consider a hand scanner with a de-fault as 1 for each sku scan transaction due to the fact a checker does not have to search for a 1 button & press a send button & return a hand held scanner to a table. At a returns process station, a return process employee hand scans a CO ID that is sent to your PC or WMS computer that verifies to a process employee that a CO is valid & shows each sku on a WMS computer CO. For each customer returned sku, a process employee uses a hand scanner for each sku scan transaction that has a process employee press an enter button. Features are accurate check transaction, WMS computer verifies CO & sku quantity, minimizes checker reading and button press requirement,

HAND HELD SCANNER MULTIPLE LIGHT BEAMS OR WIDE LIGHT BEAM
  IMPROVE PROCESS EMPLOYEE PRODUCTIVITY AND SKU FLOW
Hand held scanner with multiple light beams or wide light beam improves return process employee productivity and sku flow. When compared to a single fixed light beam scanner, a preferred hand scanner has at least several fixed light beams to improve a good read number that means good employee scanning productivity.

FIXED POSITION YOUR HAND HELD SCANNER
  IMPROVE PROCESS EMPLOYEE PRODUCTIVITY AND SKU FLOW
Fixed Position hand held scanner/reader is a return process concept that as a RF device with wireless communications to a PC or WMS computer with CO data that improves your employee productivity, sku flow and reduces sku damage. A hand held scanner is attached to a fixed position holder with sufficient height above a table surface for a return process employee to move and easily scan a returns document & each sku symbology. With a fixed position scanner in a ready position to complete scan transactions, a return process employee has a sku symbology face a return process employee that reduces a return process employee moving a sku & scanner for each CO sku scan transaction. The approach assures that a customer returns document or sku bar code is properly directed toward a scanner. As required a hand held scanner is removed from a holder to become a mobile scanner. The approach improves employee productivity due to a return process employee does not reach for a scanner.

HAND HELD SCANNER WITH A DIRECT ELECTRIC CONNECTION NOT A BATTERY (See Check & Pack Chapter)

CUSTOMER RETURN PROBLEM STATION
  IMPROVE RETURN PROCESSER PRODUCTIVITY & INCREASE CUSTOMER RETURNS PROCESS NUMBER
A problem customer return sku station is shelf that is located in a returns process area and is a very short walk distance for a process employee to transfer a problem customer return. If your return process activities are (1) a matches a CO WMS ID to your WMS computer CO ID, (2) assures each sku quantity matches a WMS ID CO quantity sku error and (3) determines a sku quality and disposition status. If a process employee has a problem with a customer return, your company policy requires additional action taken to process a customer return. To maintain a process employee at a process station, when a problem customer return occurs a process employee transfers a problem customer return (skus, container and CO pack slip/invoice) to a problem station shelf. The approach has a process employee remain at a process station and not have non-productive wait or walk time to a supervisor to review a problem customer return. A return process area supervisor resolves a problem customer return and re-introduces a corrected customer return to a process station. Feature is increase returns process employee productivity and increased completed customer return number.

LIGHT FIXTURE LOCATION (See Check & Pack Chapter)

HANDLE YOUR RE-CYCLE TRASH
ASSURES TRASH FLOW & GOOD EMPLOYEE PRODUCTIVITY

Handle your re-cycle trash is handling/transport concept that collects and transports re-cycle trash from each open/dump or returns process station to your trash re-cycle concept. When designing an open/dump or returns process station, you assure a collection and constant trash removal concept or your activity station will become clogged that lowers your employee productivity and slow customer returns flow. Your re-cycle trash concept options are determined by your re-cycle trash volume and type. Your options are (1) cartons that includes (a) overhead belt conveyor that is set at an elevation for an employee to easily transfer a carton onto a conveyor travel path and is adjacent to your work stations. At each work station, a side guard is angled type with a high far side guard or has a saw-tooth design between two work stations. If a higher far side guard requires additional height (handle extra tall cartons or double stack cartons) you add fish or meshed netting between a side guard and ceiling/overhead support member. At conveyor merge locations, you have stop/start photo-eyes to minimize jam problems. Features are handles high volume, assure constant flow, travel path is available to all process stations, requires minimal employee effort and high cost that is set at an elevation for an employee to easily transfer a carton onto a conveyor travel path and is adjacent to your work stations, (b) overhead conveyor with flat tray at a pendant end that is set at an elevation for an employee to easily transfer a carton onto a flat tray and travel path is adjacent to your work stations. Features handles medium volume, assure constant flow but an empty carrier/tray is not available to every work station, travel path is past all process stations, requires an employee effort and high cost and (c) overhead conveyor with hooks/clasps on a pendant that is set at an elevation for an employee to easily transfer a carton onto a hook/clasp and travel path is adjacent to your work stations. Features handles medium volume, assure constant flow but an empty hook/clasp is not available to every work station, travel path is past all process stations, requires an employee effort and high cost (2) loose peanut filler material the includes (a) air blower/vacuum and tunnel/tube that is set at an elevation for an employee to easily transfer a peanuts into access opening and tube/tunnel travel path is adjacent to your work stations. Blowers or vacuum concept assures peanuts flow into a container bag for transfer to pack stations. Features handles high volume, assure constant flow is available at every work station, travel path is past all process stations, requires little employee effort, potential maintenance problems and high cost (b) solid or small meshed opening 4-wall container has a meshed opening top and the container sets on a pallet or has fork openings for pallet truck or forklift truck handling. An option has a plastic bag that inserted into the interior. After an open employee opens a package and dumps the sku and peanuts onto the meshed top that allows peanuts to full through meshed openings into a container. Features separate package open activity, handles small volume, moved by a pallet truck or forklift truck, requires floor or rack storage positions and requires an employee to transfer peanuts into a peanut re-cycle concept & (4) crushed paper, meshed cardboard & bagged filler material that has an open employee remove bags from a return package and transfer the bags into a container and has a size handled by an employee or has fork openings for pallet truck or forklift truck handling. Features separate or combined package open activity, handles small volume, moved by an employee, pallet truck or forklift truck, requires floor or rack storage positions and requires an employee to transfer peanuts into a peanut re-cycle concept.

HANDLE YOUR NON-RECYCLE TRASH
ASSURES TRASH FLOW & GOOD EMPLOYEE PRODUCTIVITY

Handle your non-re-cycle trash is handling/transport concept that transports re-cycle trash from each open/dump or returns process station to your trash non-re-cycle concept. When designing an open/dump or returns process station, you assure a collection & constant trash removal concept or your activity station will become clogged that lowers your employee productivity & slow customer returns flow. Your non-re-cycle trash concept options are determined by your non-re-cycle trash volume (usually very low) and type. For damaged filler material or non-standard package material your option is a four wall container or plastic bag that is strategically located at an open/dump or returns process station.

HOW TO HANDLE LEAKERS AND SHARPE EDGE SKUS (See Scrap At Your Process Station)

DAMAGE SKU SCRAP AT YOUR PROCESS STATION
  REDUCE SKU DAMAGE, ASSURE INVENTORY CONTROL AND IMPROVE EMPLOYEE PRODUCTIVITY
Damage sku scrap at your process station is a customer returns activity idea to reduce sku damage, assure inventory control and improve employee productivity. In your customer returns sku flow, a damaged sku (sharp edge or leaker) moves beyond your process station, there is potential for additional/other sku damage, additional employee sku handling and employee injury. To minimize potential damage sku problems and assure accurate inventory, each process station has a scrap sheet for a process employee to place each damage sku printed disposition WMS ID. At a work day end each scrap sheet with a sku disposition label is sent to an office for WMS inventory update. To reduce sku damage and employee injury, each process station has a solid container for leakers and a second solid container sharp edge skus.

TRANSPORT YOUR DISPOSED SKUS TO A TEMPORARY SORT & HOLD POSITION
    IMPROVES RETURNS EMPLOYEE PRODUCTIVITY & REDUCES SKU DAMAGE & ASSURES SKU FLOW
Transport your customer return package from your process stations to a temporary sort and hold position improves returns employee productivity, reduces sku damage and assures returns sku flow. Your customer returns transport concept is determined by your customer return disposed sku volume and sku type. Your options are at your returns process/sku disposition station that has your skus are transferred as (1) loose skus onto a powered belt conveyor travel path that has skus travel from each process station at a slow travel speed past your temporary sort positions. To assure continuous sku flow your 'did not sort' skus are transferred from your sort belt conveyor into a large tote or onto a belt conveyor re-circulation travel path. Features are does not allow pre-sort sku travel, potential sku damage/hang-up, difficult to handle a wide sku mix or label removal, additional stop/start controls and additional employee handling or additional floor space and (2) skus that are (a) pre-sort into a tote or (2) non-sorted/mixed skus into a tote. Both concepts have a zero/low pressure roller or skate-wheel conveyor travel path or on 4-wheel shelf carts from your process stations to your temporary sort location. Features are additional tote cost, handles a wide sku mix, minimizes sku damage & tote has handles and empty totes/carts are returned to process station.

BIG/UGLY DISPOSED SKU PRE-SORT RACK LAYOUT
      IMPROVES RETURNS EMPLOYEE PRODUCTIVITY & ASSURES ACCURATE SKU SORT & INVENTORY
      CONTROL
BIG/UGLY disposed sku pre-sort layout that is designed to handle your RTS & RTV disposed BIG/UGLY sku for improved returns employee productivity, assures accurate sku sort and inventory control. For maximum efficiency & cost effectiveness, you have a separate RTS and RTV sections that allows each position with greater capacity and minimal in-house transport to a final sort location. Your pre-sort rack layout is determined by your final sort concept design and sort instruction. Your pre-sort layout has your inbound/non-disposed return skus arrive on 4-wheel carts/pallets at returns process station side and disposed skus are transferred onto a 4-wheel cart for transfer to a pre-sort position. Your pre-sort position options are 4-wheel carts or pallets that are arranged in a horse pattern that has a short travel distance or straight line that sort position progression is easy to follow. Your pre-sort instruction options are (1) by sku inventory code with your skus sorted to each pre-sort position by sku first digit or last digit that has allows faster final sku sort activity and requires your final sort section to have same sort instruction, (2) mixed skus that decreases your final sku sort productivity or (3) vendor name as individual vendor that allows fast final sku sort and a vendor with multiple skus that requires additional time for consolidation has mixed vendor names that are group by specific alpha characters A - E, F - J, K - O, P - S & T – Z that minimizes your final sku sort travel distance and has lower final sku sort productivity.

SMALL SKU PRE-SORT SHELF & RACK LAYOUT (See Check, Sort & Pack Chapter)

VERY SMALL SKU PRE-SORT SHELF LAYOUT (See Check, Sort & Pack Chapter)

PRE-SORT DISPOSED SKUS INTO A TEMPORARY PICK POSITION BY SKU OR MIXED INTO TOTE
    ASSURE EMPLOYEE PRODUCTIVITY, SPACE UTILIZATION & GOOD SKU FLOW
Pre-sort disposed skus into a temporary pick position by sku or mixed skus into tote are your options that impacts your employee productivity, space utilization and assures disposed skus in a pick position. Sort by sku has one sku

in one pick position that is scanned to your WMS computer program and becomes available for sale/COs. Features are large pick position number and sq ft area, additional time to complete a deposit transaction due to sorter travel past skus in other pick positions that is minimized with a narrow and deep pick position container, slow transfer time to potential multiple trips to same pick positions and good picker productivity, Mixed skus in a tote has multiple skus in one pick position that has each sku WMS ID & pick position WMS ID scanned and sent to your WMS computer program for skus to become available for sale/Cos. Features are requires small pick position number and sq ft area, minimal to complete a deposit and scan transaction, lower picker productivity due to increase search time to find sku that is reduced with sku separation in a tote.

MANUAL OR MECHANIZED PRE-SORT DISPOSED CUSTOMER RETURN SKUS
ASSURES ACCURATE SKU SORT & GOOD SKU FLOW

Manual or mechanized sku pre-sort disposed customer return skus are your options to assure accurate sku sort and good sku flow. Both sort concepts require that each sku has a sku ID and each sort position has an ID. A sort concept design parameters and selection factors are (1) returns sku volume, (2) sku physical characteristics such as crushable, fragile, sharp edges, heavy or light weight, cube or length, width and height, (3) most frequent, average or peak sku number, (4) available building sq ft, (5) cost includes computer programming, (6) labor requirements, (7) final sort labor and cost and (8) time require for sku to become available for sale.

A manual sort concept has disposed skus loose on a belt conveyor or in totes on roller conveyor travel through a sort lane. After a sorter matches a sku ID to a sort position ID, a sku is transferred to a sort position. Per your sort concept, the sort position is a non-pick-able position or pick-able position. If sorted to a pick-able position, a scan transaction is sent to your WMS computer program for sku and pick position up date and sku becomes available for sale/COs. Also, if your WMS computer program receives a sku scan transaction and a sku was previously scanned to a WMS ID position, a hand held scanner display screen shows a sku previous WMS ID position. Features are (1) low cost, (2) employee activity, (3) sort to a pick position or non-pick-able position, (4) handles a wide sku mix, (5) additional computer programming and cost & (6) completed for all sku types.

A mechanized sort concept has disposed skus travel under a scanner and each sku ID is sent to your sort computer. Your sort computer assures that a sku is diverted to a sort position that has other ID skus (mixed skus in on sort position). After sort completion, skus are sent to pick area as skus sorted to an individual pick position or as mixed skus in a tote in a pick position that requires a sku ID and pick position ID scan transactions sent to your WMS computer for sku and pick position update and available for sale/Cos. Features are (1) independent sort concept that is a standalone sort concept with a high cost, requires space and utilities, available any time, handles a large volume and some skus (crushable/fragile/heavy/sharp edge) are restricted or (2) combined picked sku and customer returns sort concept that has your customer returns skus sorted when your picked skus are not sorted or when not available for CO sku sort activity. Features are requires available time that is difficult during peck activity periods, potential double sku handling and added sort computer programming.

RETURNED TO STOCK (RTS) DISPOSED SKU SENT TO A NON-PICKABLE OR PICKABLE POSITION
IMPROVES RETURNS EMPLOYEE PRODUCTIVITY & ASSURES GOOD SKU FLOW

Customer returned disposed RTS sku sent to a non-pick-able or pick-able position are your options to have skus in a WMS ID position. When a disposed sku is placed into a non-pick-able position, it means that a sku is not entered into a WMS ID pick position and a sku is not available for sale/CO. In most returns operations as a disposed sku is placed into a WMS ID pick-able position, a sku ID & pick position ID & quantity are sent to a WMS computer program that updates a sku status as available for sale/CO and are potential to reduce CO back orders or out-of-stock sku.

RETURN TO VENDOR (RTV) SKU PER-SORT BY SKU INVENTORY CODE OR VENDOR NAME
IMPROVES RETURNS EMPLOYEE PRODUCTIVITY & ASSURES GOOD SKU FLOW & TRACKING

Return to vendor (RTV) sku pre-sort options are designed to improve returns employee productivity, assure good sku flow and inventory tracking. Your options are (1) sort by (a) inventory code that has your sorter employee use a sku inventory digit as a sort instruction to a position. Inventory code options are (*) sku first digit as a shelf bay and last digit as shelf level, (*) sku first digit as a shelf bay and second digit as shelf level (*) sku last digit as a shelf bay and next to last digit as shelf level. For additional information & features, we refer a reader to Pick Chapter or (b) vendor name that has each vendor name assigned to a pre-scanned WMS ID position that after a sorter employee scans a sku ID a WMS program communicates on hand held scanner a sku WMS ID position. Features are same a mixed sku tote concept due one vendor has potential to multiple skus in your inventory. If multiple skus in one tote, a reader is referred to mixed skus in one tote in this section (2) single sku to a position that has each RTV sku or has one tote for one vendor. As a sort employee enters a vendor return aisle & scans an sku bar code/RF tag with a RF device & if a RTV sku was previously scanned to WMS ID position, a hand held scanner shows that previous a sku. Features are each sku has a position, large final sort area, low put-away employee productivity, vendor return sku easier and quicker consolidation & accurate inventory & (3) mixed skus by inventory code or vendors in 1 tote that has RTV skus presorted return vendor mixed skus in a tote. As a sort employee transfers the tote to a storage position & per a WMS program, a final sort employee completes position and tote or each RTV sku scan transactions that are sent to a WMS computer. Features are minimal position number, smaller final sort area, improved put-away employee productivity, slower & more difficult sku consolidation for a vendor shipment & potential sku inventory control problems.

PRE-SORT DISPOSED SKUS AT YOUR PROCESS STATION OR SEPARATE TEMPORARY HOLD POSITION
   ASSURE GOOD FINAL RETURNS EMPLOYEE PRODUCTIVITY & ASSURE GOOD SKU FLOW

Pre-sort disposed skus at your process station or separate temporary hold position is a customer returns activity to improve good returns employee productivity and assure good sku flow. After a process returns employee disposes a customer returned sku, a disposed sku flow options are move to a final sort area as (1) wide mixed skus a in tote that requires sort employee to travel through all aisles. Features are low final sort employee productivity due to skus are randomly available to a sort employee, if mixed skus are placed into a WMS ID position, there is good employee put-away productivity and low pick employee productivity or (2) pre-sorted skus in a tote have a returns process employee pre-sort disposed skus by a pre-determined criteria. If a process employee pre-sorts skus, a sku WMS ID digits are a sku sort instruction. A process station has sufficient sort containers for your sort criteria. All full pre-sort containers are sent to a final sort area with pick-able positions that is used with a low volume operation. If a process employee sends loose mixed over a belt conveyor travel path or in totes to a pre-sort station, at a pre-sort station there are sufficient containers to handle your sort criteria & full pre-sort containers are to final sort area with pick-able positions. Features are handles a high volume, requires a pre-sort area and final sort area & additional employee activity.

MANUAL OR MECHANICAL PRE-SORT RETURN TO STOCK & RETURN TO VENDOR SKUS
   IMPROVE PROCESS EMPLOYEE PRODUCTIVITY AND SKU FLOW

Manual or mechanical pre-sort return to stock and return to vendor skus are options to complete separate skus into smaller and more manageable groups for your final sort activity has a constant sku flow and high employee productivity. Your pre-sort concept requires a human/machine readable WMS sku ID, sku travel path from a process station to a pre-sort area and pre-sort sku positions. With a mechanical sort concept all disposed skus travel from your process stations to an induction station, under a scanner device continue travel on a sort conveyor and to divert onto a sku assigned sort position. After a full sort location or at pre-determined times a final sort employee transfers skus from a pre-sort position to a final sort area. Features are (1) one time high cost, fewer sort but some induction employees, difficult to handle a wide sku mix that includes heavy, crushable, fragile or edge skus and requires a high volume. A manual pre-sort concept at your process station all disposed skus are pre-sort in separate containers by return to stock and return to vendor skus and containers are transported to a pre-sort area. In a pre-sort area, employees at pre-sort station sort skus into return to stock positions and return to vendor positions/containers. From each container, pre-sort employee uses a sku WMS ID or disposed label as a pre-sort instruction. Features are (1) designed to handle any volume, requires some additional sort employees, low one-time cost, handles a wide sku mix with minimal sku damage and reduces sort employee walk distance and time.

MANUAL DISPOSED SKU PRE-SORT BY SKU FIRST & SECOND DIGITS (See Check, Sort & Pack Chapter)

MANUAL DISPOSED SKU PRE-SORT BY SKU FIRST AND LAST DIGITS (See Check, Sort & Pack Chapter)

MANUAL DISPOSED SKU PRE-SORT BY SKU LAST TWO DIGITS (See Check, Sort & Pack Chapter)

MANUAL TEMPORARY SORT DESIGN WITH SHELF, DECKED RACKS, RACKS (See Check, Sort & Pack Chapter)

MANUAL TEMPORARY SORT DESIGN AS HORSE SHOE, TWO AISLE OR ONE AISLE (See Check, Sort & Pack Chapter)

PRE-SORT DISPOSED GOH RAIL LAYOUT
  IMPROVES SORTER PRODUCTIVITY & ASSURES GOOD SKU FLOW
Pre-sort disposed GOH rail layout permits a returns employee at a returns process station or in a pre-sort area to separate disposed GOH skus by a sku inventory digit (first or last) that improves sorter productivity and assures good sku flow and a disposed GOH sku is transferred to a pick-able position. GOH pre-sort layout has a 4-wheel cart with a load bar or on a rail, a trolley with a load bar. The 4-wheel carts or trolley rail layout has four lanes with 3 carts/trolley per lane and 2 aisles between lanes that allows cart/trolley and sorter travel. With a trolley concept sufficient drop switches for trolley travel through each aisle and full trolley transfer onto a main travel rail. Each cart/trolley has a digit (0 – 9) for your sort by sku digit primary digit and on each cart/trolley load bar has identification sliders for (0 – 9). Per your GOH return volume, your layout is expanded to have 2 carts/trolley pre primary digit that has 20 to 24 carts/trolleys and 3 aisles between lanes that allows cart/trolley and sorter travel. With a trolley concept sufficient drop switches for trolley travel through each aisle & full trolley transfer onto a main travel rail. Each cart/trolley has a digit (0 – 9) for your sort by sku digit primary digit & on each cart/trolley load bar has identification sliders for (0 – 9).

GOH TEMPORARY SORT CART & RAIL LAYOUT
  IMPROVE SORTER PRODUCTIVITY, SKU FLOW & INCREASE SORTED RETURNED GOH NUMBER
Manual GOH sku temporary sort cart or rail layout has your employee push a 4-wheel cart with a load bar or trolley through sort cart and rail layout. Manual returned GOH sku sort requires each GOH sku to have a disposed label with a sku inventory ID number. After a sorter picks a sku from a cart or trolley and reads a sku ID and transfers a sku onto a cart or trolley temporary hold position. In a sku sort area, you identify each sort position by a position ID that corresponds to your sku inventory ID. Your sort locations are carts with a load bar and trolley rail lanes. To have all possible sort locations, your sort area has 10 to 20 carts or 10 to 20 trolley capacity that has 1 or 2 carts/trolley per digit. Possible sort location sequences are (1) sku first digit is a cart or trolley and on a load bar last sku digit is arranged in arithmetic sequence from 0 to 9, (2) sku first digit is a cart or trolley and on a load bar sku second digit is arranged in arithmetic sequence from 0 to 9 and (3) sku last digit is a cart or trolley and on a load bar next to last digit is arranged in arithmetic sequence from 0 to 9. A manual returned GOH sort by sku ID number to a cart or trolley improves your total employee productivity, sku flow and increase sorted returned GOH number and higher CO completion number. Features are (1) requires a computer program to print disposed label with sku ID number, (2) floor area for carts and trolleys and (3) transfer full carts or trolleys to final sort/storage area.

PICKABLE OR NON-PICKABLE SKU SORT POSITION
  IMPROVE PUT-AWAY AND PICKER PRODUCTIVITY AND INVENTORY CONTROL
A sku non-pick-able position is a customer return area position that holds returned and processed WMS ID skus that are available for sale (CO pick activity). With a sku quantity in a pick-able position, for your next CO your WMS computer directs a pick transaction from your returns temporary or final sort pick-able position. Features are (1) concept to fill back ordered skus & (2) sku picked from a pick position, it reduces a sku quantity that is transferred to storage position. A non-pick-able position means that a WMS identified sku in a position is not available for sale or COs. Some non-pick-able positions are pre-sort positions that are required for controlled sku flow.

VERY SMALL ITEM FINAL SORT TO SHELF OR HORSE SHOE LAYOUT (See Check, Sort & Pack Chapter)

MEDIUM SIZE SKU FINAL SORT TO SHELF AND RACK LAYOUT (See Check, Sort & Pack Chapter)

TEMPORARY PICK POSITION (See Pickable or Non-Pickable Sku Sort Position)

SORT DISPOSED SKUS IN YOUR TEMPORARY PICK POSITIONS
  ASSURE GOOD RETURNS EMPLOYEE PRODUCTIVITY & PROVIDE INVENTORY TRACKING
Sort disposed skus in your temporary pick positions has your returns disposed sku sort employee transfer and scan a sku to a WMS ID temporary pick position that assures good returns employee productivity and provides inventory tracking. By your sku sort concept (by sku first or last as primary or bay ID and sku second or next to last digit as shelf ID or a separate sku pick position), each sku transferred is updated in your WMS inventory as in a pick-able position. This means that the sku is available for your next CO, back order CO or out-of-stock CO. If picked for a CO from a pick-able position, it means less skus for transfer to a storage/pick position in your pick area and your oldest inventory is picked first.

CUSTOMER ORDER PICK FROM TEMPORARY PICK POSITION (See Sort Disposed Skus In Your Temporary Pick Positions)

FIFO CUSTOMER ORDER RETURNS
  ASSURE INVENTORY CONTROL
FIFO customer order return sku rotation is a customer return process sku concept to assure that your oldest skus are picked first for new COs. In a return to stock sort or temporary hold position, skus with different return processed dates are mixed in a one WMS ID position and it is difficult to assure an accurate FIFO sku rotation. A macro FIFO rotation is to have all returned skus in one WMS ID position transferred to another temporary hold or permanent pick position and sku transfer date becomes a sku received date in your WMS computer inventory control program. New returned skus are accumulated in another WMS ID position and in your WMS computer inventory program are considered the newest skus.

HOW TO RECORD MANUFACTURER LOT NUMBER
  ASSURE GOOD RETURNS EMPLOYEE PRODUCTIVITY & PROVIDE INVENTORY TRACKING
To record a manufacturer lot number in your returns process activity is difficult to track a specific manufacturer lot number. A black box approach assures good returns employee productivity and provides inventory tracking. A manufacturer lot number is a unique sku ID that indicates a manufacturer's specific date & production facility. Since customer returns occur on a random bases & could have numerous manufacturer lot number, it is very difficult to identify specifics. With mixed manufacturer's lot number skus in a returns process flow, it is preferred to associate a manufacturer's lot number to a CO ID at a pack station or as a sku is package for a return to vendor pick activity.

RETURN TO VENDOR (RTV) SKU FINAL-SORT BY SKU INVENTORY CODE OR VENDOR NAME
  IMPROVES RETURNS EMPLOYEE PRODUCTIVITY & ASSURES GOOD SKU FLOW & TRACKING
Return to vendor (RTV) sku final sort options are designed to improve returns employee productivity, assure good sku flow and inventory tracking. Your options are (1) sort instructions that are the same as pre-sort instruction that are (a) inventory code or (b) vendor name, (2) single sku to a position & (3) mixed skus by inventory code or vendors in 1 tote. For additional information, we refer a reader to RTV pre-sort in this Chapter.

SORT RETURN TO VENDOR OR RETAIL DISCOUNT STORE SKUS INTO A SQUARED FRONT CARTON
  IMPROVE EMPLOYEE PRODUCTIVITY & SKU HANDLING
Sort return to vendor or retail discount store skus into a squared front carton that increases your sort employee productivity. With the concept, each WMS ID sku position has a squared front carton. A squared front carton has the front section side cut half way down and folded down to the front and secured with tape. On the front section is attached a WMS ID peel-off label that permits WMS scan transaction completion. With a half open carton front, an employee easily and quickly transfers skus into a carton. With a full carton, the peal-off label is removed front folded down front and placed into a proper location for a sku WMS ID. After a carton has top flaps and side taped, the carton is ready for vendor or retail discount store shipment.

FINAL SORTED SKU REVERSE OR CONSOLIDATE PICK
IMPROVE PICKER PRODUCTIVITY

Final sorted sku reverse or consolidate pick activity is a customer returned, processed and disposed sku activity that has after vendor or company approval for an employee pick skus from WMS ID temporary and permanent positions. Skus are prepared for return to vendor, sent to a company store or third party retailer. For maximum picker productivity, your WMS ID temporary and permanent positions have a numerical sequence.

CARTON, GOH OR BIG/UGLY FINAL-SORT RACK LAYOUT
IMPROVES RETURNS EMPLOYEE PRODUCTIVITY & ASSURES ACCURATE SKU SORT & INVENTORY CONTROL

Carton, GOH or BIG/UGLY sku final sort layout that is designed to handle your RTS & RTV disposed carton, GOH or BIG/UGLY sku for improved returns employee productivity, assures accurate sku sort and inventory control. For maximum efficiency & cost effectiveness, you have a separate RTS and RTV sections that allows each position with greater capacity and minimal in-house transport to a final sort location. Your final sort rack layout uses standard pallet rack positions that are in single deep or back to back rack rows with elevated positions for storage positions. Each rack row has a sort position progression that is easy to follow. Your sort instruction has your (1) sku inventory code as (a) sku first digit as a rack row and last digit as rack bay, (*) sku first digit as a rack row and second digit as rack bay & (*) sku last digit as a rack row and next to last digit as rack bay or (2) vendor name as individual vendor that allows fast final sku sort and a vendor with multiple skus that requires additional time for consolidation has mixed vendor names. Your rack rows has specific alpha characters A - E, F - J, K - O, P - S & T – Z with the final alpha characters per rack row to be determined by your number per alpha character. Example rack row has A – E and each bay within a rack row has each vendor name that progresses from A through E.

HOW TO PACKAGE YOUR RETURN TO VENDOR OR RETAIL DISCOUNT STORE SKUS
REDUCE SKU LOSS AND MINIMIZE COSTS

How to package your return to vendor or retail discount store skus is to assure skus are contained in a package and minimizes your costs. Since your return to vendor or retail discount store package is not sent to a regular customer, your container does not require your company log on its exterior. With the criteria, your company purchases your carton vendor second cartons, bad printed cartons or cartons with a plain exterior.

MOVE-OUT AGED CUSTOMER RETURN PROCESSED & FINAL SORTED SKUS
IMPROVE SPACE UTILIZATION, EMPLOYEE PUT-AWAY PRODUCTIVITY AND INVENTORY CONTROL

Move-out aged customer return processed and final sorted skus is an idea to improve space utilization, employee processed sku put-away productivity and inventory control. From your company sku sales history and returns life cycle, you determine number of days that a sku quantity is returned by customers. The information provides you with number of days after a sku sales for the vast majority is returned to your operation. A WMS program computer indicates WMS ID skus that have a 30, 60 or 90 day life cycle and end date and each WMS ID sku temporary hold position that has not had a put-away transaction for a pre-determined time period. With a computer printed list an employee assures that there are sufficient vacate temporary hold positions and ID each position with no put-away transactions. To assist in the aged process, your sku returns label has a return process date or each position has transaction sheet for your put-away employee to list the last return date. Per your company policy, aged skus or skus with no transactions are placed into sealed and WMS ID containers that are scanned and placed into a remote WMS ID storage position. All transactions are updated in your WMS computer

CHAPTER 9
OFF-SITE STORAGE EXPENSE REDUCTIONS IDEAS

BUILD OR LEASE
   LOWER OPERATION COST & REDUCE CASH FLOW
After your company determines a new warehouse total sq. ft. requirement, next major warehouse decision is to lease or build a building. A leased building option has your company design a warehouse, storage and pick concept to fit into an existing building. Leased options are to (1) lease an existing facility that has a short start-up time & low cost for your warehouse operation & (2) 'build to lease' a new facility that has a leasing company constructs a building to your company specifications. The approach has a longer start-up time with a medium cost. Your company construct a new building has your company purchase a site & with an architect & construction company to obtain local authority approval and build a facility. During & after building construction, your warehouse, storage & pick concept is installed in the facility. The own land & build approach has a longer start-up time & higher cost.

TENT ON A SLAB
   LOW COST STORAGE POSITIONS
Tent on a slab is an outside storage concept that minimizes your building construction costs for low cost storage positions. If a slab is located on your main facility site/property, you have an opportunity to minimize your shuttle costs. A tent on slab concept has a cement slab constructed onto the ground and to have a fabric shell with a door installed on the cement slab. After installation completion, the shell interior cement slab area is ready for rack or floor storage concept. If your local government considers a fabric shell/cement slab as temporary construction, there is potential different code requirements. If employees use your main facility printers, restrooms, break rooms, equipment chargers and other support items, there is a lower building cost and greater storage units per sq. ft. In the future for facility expansion, the cement slab is used for low weight facility support areas such as office, returns process, maintenance and computer area

WHERE TO RECEIVE SKUS
   LOW COST UNIT OF PRODUCT & GOOD INVENTORY CONTROL
Where to receive your off-site storage skus options are you receive at your (1) off-site facility with receiving capabilities at your main and off-site facilities. If your sku is a big/ugly, overstock or speculative purchase sku that you ship from your off-site facility, you receive skus are your off-site operation. If your sku is a fast pack sku and you ship from your off-site facility, cross-dock or replenish to your main facility, and your know your fast pack projected quantity your options are (a) with two vendor delivery trucks to have one vendor delivery truck received at your main facility and one truck at your off-site facility & (b) with one vendor delivery truck your select one facility to receive skus and transfers your estimated sku quantity to your other facility & (2) main facility with receiving capabilities at your main facility, you receive sku vendor delivery at your main facility & transfer to your off-site facility. Features are low CPU & good inventory control.

YOUR DOCK DETERMINES YOUR DOCK EQUIPMENT TO BRIDGE DOCK & UNLOAD/LOAD VEHICLES
   SAFE ACTIVITY, LOW COST UNIT OF PRODUCT & SMOOTH SKU FLOW
Your off-site dock determines your dock equipment to bridge dock edge and unload to assure a safe activity, low cost sku and smooth sku flow. Your dock equipment is a device that bridges your delivery truck end and dock edge and allows a unload/load vehicle to enter and exit a delivery truck. A unload/load vehicle enters and exits a delivery truck with a pallet and transports a pallet to a dock staging area or pallet storage position. Your dock equipment options are based on (1) ground level or no elevated dock with a smooth truck yard and ground level facility entry door that requires (a) dock ramp with a level top that allows a forklift truck to enter and exit a delivery truck. Features are ramp has an additional cost and difficult to use in rainy weather and (b) forklift truck to remove the rear two pallets and a forklift truck to place a human powered pallet truck into a delivery truck for an employee to move a pallet to a delivery truck rear for forklift truck removal and (2) elevated platform dock or dock door that requires (a) with a pallet truck to use a fixed position edge of dock or front of dock device for delivery truck

entry/exit. Features are restricted to a pallet truck use and requires delivery in proper dock position and (b) with a pallet truck or forklift truck to use a portable dock plate, portable dock board or in-floor dock leveler. A pallet truck or forklift truck enters and exits a delivery truck and transfer a pallet to a dock staging area or travel to a storage position for deposit. Features are additional cost, used with platform or dock door concept extends into a dock staging area, employee or forklift truck place a portable device in a delivery truck end and has potential damage to your door frame, requires a dock light or forklift truck mast lights and use with a pallet truck or forklift truck. If you receive side load/unload delivery trucks in a smooth truck yard, a forklift truck with proper counterbalance weight and two long forks are used to unload/load a delivery truck and transfers pallets onto a dock or dropped in a staging area.

OFF-SITE STORAGE CANDIDATES
IMPROVE SPACE UTILIZATION, EMPLOYEE PRODUCTIVITY & OPERATION FLEXIBILITY

Off-site storage candidates is a warehouse process to select skus & sku quantity for relocation from a main storage facility to an off-site storage facility. When a warehouse storage position utilization is at 100%, a warehouse requires additional sku storage positions. To create additional storage positions, a warehouse manager has to determine or select skus & sku quantity for off-site or outside storage. Potential candidate skus are (1) aged or 'C'/'D' moving skus, (2) obsolete equipment, (3) extra large quantity buy-ins such as commodities, (4) with a warehouse, heavy & high cube skus that are picked and sent as single line/single sku COs in vendor carton from an off-site facility to a customer, (5) ship supply safety stock & (6) return to vendor skus.

HOW TO WORK OFF-SITE STORAGE
INCREASE SPACE UTILIZATION & MINIMIZE ANNUAL COST

How to work off-site storage is an objective for an off-site storage activity that combines maximum storage space utilization and lowest annual cost. Most companies use an off-site for seasonal buy-ins with a large pallet number per sku, old/aged skus, damaged/obsolete skus or skus that do not match a main warehouse material handling concept such as high cube/heavy skus that are handled a single sku/single line COs. With the reasons, an off-site storage activity has a dense storage concept and lowest possible operation costs. Most off-site storage buildings has a 20 to 25 ft high ceiling and if your skus are stackable, floor stack (3 to 5 deep and 3 high) provides high storage space utilization, good storage lane flexibility and at a low cost. To optimize an off-site floor stack operation, you have at least a few standard pallet rack rows to handle skus with few pallets. If your skus are non-stackable, standard pallet rack rows or a standard pallet row and floor stack in front storage combination is used for the operation. All off-site storage operations have building columns buried in a floor stack or rack rows. If aisle lighting is problem, lights are attached to a forklift trucks masts.

CAN YOU FAST PACK
LOW COST UNIT OF PRODUCT & HIGH UNITS PER HOUR

Can you fast pack in your off-site facility is an option that transfers some of your main facility to your off-site operation. With an off-site fast pack approach, with a two vendor truck delivery you pre-schedule your sku vendor truck delivery to an off-site facility and second truck delivery to your main facility. With one or less sku vendor delivery truck you receive a sku at one facility and for a pre-determined sku quantity it is transferred to or remains in your off-site facility. After you determine your sku fast pack quantity, you have slapper envelopes prepared at your main facility and delivered to your off-site facility or slapper envelops are prepared at your off-site facility. With a slapper envelop you pack, manifest and ship COs from your off-site facility. Features are with off-site sku quantity easy to control WMS computer allocation, low cost activity and allows main facility controllable volume.

SEND IT DIRECT FROM YOUR OFF-SITE OR CROSS-DOCK AT YOUR MAIN FACILTIY (See Overstock Or Speculative Purchase Sku As An Off-Site Sku Candidate)

OVERSTOCK OR SPECULATIVE PURCHASE SKU AS AN OFF-SITE SKU CANDIDATE
LOW COST STORAGE POSITIONS

Overstock or speculative purchase sku as an off-site sku candidate has a sku with very large sku inventory quantity that allows dense or floor stack storage for low cost per storage position. If overstock or speculative purchase sku is stored in a main facility, it allows few positions for regular skus & additional employee time to complete transactions due to travel past positions with no activity. Per your company policy you ship COs direct from an off-site facility, shuttle skus to your main facility for storage activity or shuttle to your main facility for cross dock activity.

ABC OR D OR OBSOLETE SKUS AS OFF-SITE SKU CANDIDATES
   IMPROVE EMPLOYEE PRODUCTIVITY & LOW COST STORAGE POSITIONS

A,B C or D obsolete skus are off-site candidates is determined by your CO demand to identify sku candidate that improves employee productivity and space utilization. In most operations, A and B moving skus have good CO demand and remain in your main facility storage positions. C and D moving skus or obsolete skus have very low or no CO demand and require a storage position. If your C, D or obsolete skus are in your main facility positions and during a work day your pick employees travel past a C or D moving sku positions that creates low employee productivity. If you maintain a C and D small sku quantity in your main facility storage position that is hand stacked or half high position, you improve your space utilization and remaining sku quantity is placed in an off-site storage position, your increase your C & D moving sku concentration and density and your other positions have A & B moving skus, your improve storage and pick employee productivity. Features are creates additional main facility positions, improves employee productivity and enhances space utilization.

WHAT IS SCRAP & WHERE TO PLACE IT
   IMPROVE SPACE UTILIZATION & IMPROVE SANTIATION

In a warehouse there is a possibility to have obsolete or not used material handling equipment in a warehouse. Non-used equipment occupies positions or space in your warehouse that is considered expensive real estate. If your warehouse has a requirement for storage space, relocate obsolete equipment to another area. Relocation is an opportunity to increase available space for good skus. To create space for good skus, scrap equipment is placed in a storage position with a longest travel distance from a pick & pack area, in off-set storage, under a cover & elevated on pallets that are outside in a truck yard or sold.

ONCE A SKU IS IN OUT-SIDE STORAGE IT REMAINS OUT OR IS A CROSS-DOCK SKU
   REDUCE SKU DAMAGE, LOWER SHUTTLE COSTS & IMPROVE & EMPLOYEE PRODUCTIVITY

Once a sku is in out-side storage it remains out or is a cross-dock sku is a warehouse out-side/off-site sku storage strategy that minimizes over-the-road truck shuttle costs, minimize sku damage & improves employee productivity. With good security, inventory control with random sku counts & off-site facility with capability to print all receiving & ship documents & bar code scan/RF tag read & transfer data to a main warehouse computer, once out stay off-site storage strategy means that after a sku is transferred from your main facility to an off-site facility that a sku remains in an off-site facility. From an off-site facility, a sku is sent direct to a customer or returned direct to a vendor, handled as a palletized single sku, multiple skus as an across-dock CO that is sent from an off-site facility to a main facility or sent as master cartons/small quantities for replenishment to a main facility remote storage position.

SHIP SUPPLY SKU SAFETY INVENTORY
   HIGH STORAGE UTILIZATION & PERMITS DENSE STORAGE

Ship supply sku safety inventory is a storage idea for off-site storage. Ship supply skus (bags, cartons, tape, filler material and other items) safety stock is a sku quantity that is not anticipated to be used in your daily or regular pack operation. Safety stock is not track in your WMS computer program and is intended to have a sku supply on-hand to cover for unexpected or more than schedule CO demand situation. Your safety stock position options are in your (1) main facility to occupy storage positions that creates lower forklift truck productivity and no vacate positions for regular skus or ship supply inventory for your CO demand and (2) off-site storage facility that allows you to use dense storage concepts for best storage utilization and does not require shuttle costs.

SINGLE SKUS AND BIG/UGLY SKUS
   HIGH STORAGE UTILIZATION & IMPROVED EMPLOYEE PRODUCTIVITY

Single skus and big/ugly skus in off-site storage allows high storage utilization with dense storage concept and improves employee productivity. Single skus permit your operation to bulk pick, pack, slapper label and ship activity. A big/ugly sku has few skus per storage position, permits you to use a slapper label and ship activity. If handled in your main facility, a big/ugly sku is not placed on a conveyor sort concept and is handled on your manual concept.

REWORK ACTIVITES
ASSURE INVENTORY CONTROL & CONTROLLED SKU FLOW

Rework activities completed in your off-site warehouse assure inventory control, controlled sku flow and maximum main facility positions and space used for skus that are available for sale. Rework skus are created from (a) returned skus and warehouse quality control or (b) vendor delivered skus rejected by QA. Rework skus have an inventory status of 'not available for sale or Cos' & to meet your company standards some skus require rework labor, material expense and storage positions. With re-work skus in an off-site facility, your main warehouse forklift truck drivers and pickers have higher productivity due to not traveling past positions with rework skus that do not have possible transactions.

SINGLE DEEP OR DENSE STORAGE
INCREASE SKU FACINGS, IMPROVE SPACE UTILIZATION & ACCESS POSITIONS

Single deep or dense storage are a warehouse basic storage concept options. A single deep stationary or mobile storage concept has each WMS identified sku (master carton, pallet or GOH) face an employee, employee controlled forklift truck or AS/RS crane deposit/withdrawal transaction aisle. With a standard WMS computer program and a single deep storage concept, an employee, employee controlled forklift truck or AS/RS crane has direct access to withdraw a WMS computer program suggested WMS ID sku from a WMS ID storage position. A dense storage concept has multiple skus deep per storage lane. Dense storage concepts (floor stack, stacking frames/tier racks, drive-in rack, push back racks, 2 aisle mole & 2 deep racks) have a last sku deposited in a storage lane face a storage vehicle transaction aisle (one aisle for both replenishment and withdrawal transactions). Since dense storage concepts have multiple skus per lane, for an employee, forklift truck or AS/RS crane to access a specific sku there is no-productive employee time or a WMS computer program requires modification such a WMS ID substitution feature. Dense storage concepts (drive-thru, 1 aisle mole & gravity/air flow rack) have the first deposited sku flows from a deposit aisle, flows through a rack storage lane & ends at a withdrawal transaction aisle. With gravity flow through or drive thru racks, for an employee, forklift truck or AS/RS crane to access a WMS program suggested WMS ID sku from a WMS ID storage position there is an operation problem to access a suggested WMS computer program ID sku. In most flow through or drive thru rack applications with a pallet riding on a bottom deck boards, a sku bar code label is on a pallet side or sku front that faces a rack. The situation creates some additional non-productive forklift truck time to complete a sku double handling to have a bar code label in a proper orientation for bar code line of sight. With a RF tag symbology a transmission is received in a general area. In conclusion, a single deep storage concept have a low cost, 85% utilization factor, access to any sku, handles a large sku number with any sku quantity & interfaces with a standard WMS computer program. Dense storage concepts have a high cost, 66% utilization factor, with no WMS computer program modifications difficult to access a specific sku or requires additional non-productive to complete a sku scan transaction, handles few skus with a large sku quantity & requires a standard WMS computer program modification.

FLOOR STACK OR STANDARD PALLET RACK STORAGE
INCREASE SKU FACINGS, IMPROVE SPACE UTILIZATION & ACCESS POSITIONS

Floor stack or standard pallet rack storage are a warehouse storage concept most common options. Floor stack storage concept has 1 sku (master cartons, stacking frames/tier racks or pallets) stacked onto another (3 to 4 high) & multiple skus (2 to 10) deep. A floor stack concept is used in a conventional warehouse with a 20 to 25 ft high ceiling & wide aisle (WA) or narrow aisle (NA) forklift truck and with a dead level. A standard pallet rack storage concept has upright frames & load beams that have 1 pallet deep rack bay or 1 to 3 pallet positions per rack bay & up to 6 to 7 pallets high. In conclusion, a floor stack storage concept has minimal cost, 66% utilization factor, preferred for a small sku quantity with a large sku number & a standard WMS computer program modifications. A standard pallet rack concept has 85% utilization factor, preferred for a large sku & interfaces with a standard WMS computer program.

FLOOR AND RACK STORAGE CONCEPT (6 PALLETS IS BETTER THAN 4 PALLETS)
INCREASE SPACE UTILIZATION

Floor and rack storage concept (6 pallets is better than 4 pallets) is a conventional forklift truck warehouse storage rack and floor stack concept that is used for a sku with at least 6 pallets and a sku that does not have the structural strength to support a 3 high pallet stack. A standard 4 pallet floor storage concept has 2 deep pallets & 2 high pallets. Features are no cost, medium storage density and low space utilization. A hybrid 2 deep pallet storage rack & floor stack concept has (1) rear pallet positions as a 4 pallet high storage rack row & (2) front pallet positions as 2 high floor stack pallet positions. Concept options are (1) in a warehouse (a) single high front pallet or (b) double stacked pallets with top carton within an employee picker's reach. In storage operation, your options are (1) one pallet for each storage rack position that 4 high positions or (2) rack floor position with two high stacked pallets. Features are some rack cost, improves storage density and space utilization & both concepts interface with a wide aisle or narrow aisle forklift truck.

PYRAMID FLOOR STACK
IMPROVE SPACE UTILIZATION & MINIMAL SKU DAMAGE

Pyramid floor stack is a floor stack storage concept that is used for your ship supply items or unstable skus with a dimension that restricts use of a pallet rack storage position & improves space utilization & minimizes sku damage. Most warehouse ship supply items are cardboard cartons, sheet paper or filler material, tape or band material, label paper, sheet paper for printers & envelopes. In most warehouse operations, ship supply skus are not tracked by your WMS or inventory control program, usually has a safety stock & with cardboard cartons have an excessive over-hang on a pallet. Palletized collapsed ship cartons have a bowed or concaved top that creates difficulty to stack 3 pallets high due to a forklift truck has difficulty to have a set of forks enter a top pallet fork opening and a 3 high pallet stack has a tendency for tilting to one side. To improve your cube or space utilization & enhance your storage density per aisle, with a same ship carton/sku a pyramid pallet floor stack concept permits 1 to 2 floor stacked pallets that are side by side & become a pyramid base for another pallet that is placed in the middle of a 2 pallet base. In the middle of a 2 pallet base means that 1/2 of a top pallet is setting on 1 bottom pallet half & top pallet other half is setting on another bottom pallet half. With a pyramid arrangement, a pyramid top pallet is stable & permits a forklift truck set of forks to enter a top pallet fork opening that minimize sku damage and improves employee productivity.

HOW TO HANDLE THE BIG/ULGY SKUS
INCREASE SPACE UTILIZATION & IMPROVE EMPLOYEE PRODUCTIVITY

How to handle the big/ugly skus occurs when a warehouse has to handle over-sized or long skus that can not fit onto a standard pallet or into a standard storage position. To handle an extra long sku in a standard rack storage area, your options are (1) use an extra wide pallet that fits into a standard pallet rack bay. With fork opening widths that matches your standard wide aisle forklift set of forks spread (width) & allows a forklift truck to complete storage transactions or (2) use a extra long fork attachment with an extra long that fits into a 2 deep rack storage position. After all big/ugly sku transaction completion, extra long fork attachment is removed and your WA forklift truck completes normal pallet size transactions. If your WA aisle forklift truck requires a 2 wide set of forks or extra long fork attachment, a 2 wide set of forks matches a pallet openings or extra long fork attachments are tested on your WA aisle forklift truck to assure that an existing counterbalance forklift truck has sufficient counter weight. When a wide pallet is placed into a standard pallet position, a deposit scan transaction is made to a first or right hand side storage position that assure sku and position status in a WMS or inventory control program. Features increases space utilization & improves employee productivity.

TWO HIGH/TALL PALLET ON THE FLOOR
INCREASE SPACE UTILIZATION & IMPROVES FORKLIFT TRUCK PRODUCTIVITY

Two high/tall pallet on the floor is a standard pallet storage rack concept that has a storage bottom (floor level) pallet rack position with height for 2 pallets high (1 pallet stacked on another pallet) & elevated pallet rack positions have an opening for 1 pallet. Two pallets high on a floor rack concept is used in a warehouse with palletized skus that have the structural strength to support another full pallet weight. Two pallets on the floor concept requires 1 less load beam pair and one less forklift truck replenishment transaction. Prior to implementation, your rack manufacturer assures that your upright post design or structural strength supports a two tall pallet opening or your rack position requires a double upright post design that has an additional cost. Features are increases pallet positions in an aisle, increases storage density, access to all skus, increases space or cube utilization, used with a wide aisle or narrow aisle forklift truck, reduces an overall stacking height by a nominal 12 ins and reduces your forklift truck replenishment transaction number.

WIDE AISLE (WA) OR NARROW AISLE (NA) FORKLIFT TRUCK
IMPROVE EMPLOYEE PRODUCTIVITY & IMPROVE EQUIPMENT UTILIZATION

An off-site storage activity forklift truck requirement is to unload, in-house transport and deposit/withdrawal transactions that has a wide aisle or narrow aisle forklift truck complete a sku pick-up at receiving & put-away to a WMS storage position. When you have long travel distances, a WA forklift truck is preferred. If you have narrow aisles, your preferred forklift truck is a NA forklift truck. A warehouse with a small storage area and aisles that face a receiving dock & a low sku volume, do it all the way concept has good equipment utilization & good employee productivity. A warehouse with a wide storage area & aisle that do not face a receiving dock & a high sku volume, do it all the way concept represents poor forklift truck utilization & low employee productivity. To transport a sku with a high wage rate forklift truck driver & a high equipment cost, it represents a high CPU. An option is to give-away. A give-away concept uses a single or double pallet truck as an in-house transport vehicle that has a lower equipment cost, lower wage rate & lower CPU. With a pallet truck in-house transport concept, a storage area requires a wider aisle for a pallet placement at an aisle end & proper pallet placement at an aisle end to have a sku WMS ID face a forklift truck driver.

LIGHT YOUR AISLES OR FORKLIFT TRUCKS
MINIMIZE EXPENSE & ASSURE EMPLOYEE PRODUCTIVITY

Light your aisles or forklift trucks are your off-site facility lighting options. To minimize your off-site expenses, the light fixtures remain in an existing ceiling location and a light fixture lighting allows your forklift truck driver to complete a storage transaction and for transaction instruction to read a paper document or RF device display screen and pallet position ID. Your adjust your storage position depth and aisle width to have light fixtures located in an aisle or in an aisle middle. If your light fixture lighting is low, your options are to add (1) light fixtures that has additional costs and additional light fixture could exceed your existing/provided KVA that could require additional major electric transformer and (2) lights to your forklift truck masts that are operated from your forklift truck battery that are attached by your forklift truck vendor to illuminate a storage position and as required operators area. Forklift truck mast lights illuminate storage positions, aisles and inside a delivery truck. Features are forklift truck lights have a lower cost than additional aisle light fixtures.

USE AN OVERHEAD/HEAD ACKE BAR, HIGHWAY GUARD RAIL/ POST & WHEEL-STOP
MINIMIZE DAMAGE & IMPROVE EMPLOYEE PRODUCTIVITY

Overhead/head ache bar, highway guard rail/post & wheel-stop are manual controlled powered pallet truck & forklift truck options to minimize equipment & building damage and improve driver productivity. An overhead or head ache bar is a ceiling hung chain with a bar that extends downward or rack bay that is located prior to a facility wall passage way or door frame bottom. If a forklift truck with an elevated sku strikes a head ache bar or rack bay, it is noticed that your forklift driver who should stop a vehicle forward movement & lower an elevated sku & avoid door damage. Highway guard rails are floor anchored & used in a powered pallet truck or forklift truck in-house transport concept along walls, stationary equipment or people paths to prevent a moving vehicle from striking & damaging a wall, equipment or employee injury. Per a sku elevation above a floor, a guard rail bottom, middle or top members are set above a floor. The elevation protects guard rail support post from damage & sku hang-up on a guard member. Guard posts are cement filled floor anchor or sunk post that is placed in front of a door frame. A guard post prevent a moving pallet or forklift truck from striking & damaging a door frame. Wheel stop is an inverted and flatten 'V' shaped harden metal members that is floor anchored in front of a forklift truck transfer location for sku transfer to or from a P/D station, flow rack conveyor lane or conveyor travel path. A wheel stop is set at a distance from a material handling equipment to restrict a forklift truck front wheels forward movement that prevents a forklift truck from striking & damaging equipment but permits a forklift truck to complete a sku transfer transaction and assure good employee productivity.

HEADACHE BARS AND GUARDS
REDUCE BUILDING DAMAGE

Headache bars and guards are options that are placed along a passage-way or door frame. A headache bar is a ceiling hung bar with chains that extend downward slightly beyond a door frame top. When a forklift truck carries a pallet that is above a door frame top, a pallet strikes the chains that serves as an alarm to a forklift truck driver. Guards are cement filled and anchored posts that are placed in a door way frame to sides. When a forklift truck travels off-path and strikes a guard, a guard stops a forklift truck movement and prevents door frame damage.

NOTCH YOUR MAN-DOWN FORKLIFT TRUCK MAST
MINIMIZE SKU DAMAGE & IMPROVE EMPLOYEE PRODUCTIVITY

Notch your man-down forklift truck mast is a warehouse concept to place marks on a man-down controlled wide aisle (WA), narrow aisle (NA) or man-down very narrow aisle (VNA) forklift truck mast that improves employee productivity and minimizes sku damage. Each forklift truck mast mark matches an elevated set of forks for a forklift truck to complete an elevated storage rack position transaction. At an elevated position, a forklift truck set of forks are withdrawn or inserted into a pallet opening to complete a storage transaction. Each forklift truck set of forks elevation has a unique color or marks such a one mark or red is for level one & two marks or yellow is for level two. Notched masts concept improves man-down forklift productivity, low cost & minimizes sku & rack damage.

WHAT IS YOUR BEST OFF-SITE FORKLIFT TRUCK (See Wide Aisle Or Narrow Aisle Fork Lift Truck)

CHAPTER 10
VALUE-ADDED & PRE-PACK ACTIVITY EXPENSE REDUCTION IDEAS

PRE-PACK SKUS
 IMPROVE PICKER & PACKER PRODUCTIVITY & INCREASES COMPLETED CUSTOMER ORDER NUMBER
Pre-pack is a small item warehouse bulk pick activity for single line/single sku COs that improves picker/packer productivity and increases your completed CO number. A pre-pack activity is completed for your 'A', promotional or special value sku, occurs several days prior to your anticipated sales and for a sku quantity that is similar to previous sku past percentage as single line/single sku CO. The feature allows you to use part-time labor or regular employee activity to complete an 8 hour day. To complete a pre-pack activity, a sku quantity is bulk picked and delivered to a pre-pack station or pack line start station. To complete a pre-pack activity, your options are to (1) partial pre-pack sku that has your pre-pack activity place as required bottom filler and sku into a carton and do not top seal a ship carton. Partial complete ship cartons are placed onto a WMS ID pallet that are placed/scanned into a WMS ID storage position. Scan transactions and sku quantity are sent to a WMS computer update or (2) if you use a slapper label to complete pre-pack sku that has your pre-pack activity place as required bottom filler and sku into a top sealed ship carton. Complete ship cartons are placed onto a WMS ID pallet that is placed/scanned into a WMS ID storage position. Scan transactions and sku quantity are sent to a WMS computer update. To assure good inventory control your CO computer program recognizes a single line/single sku CO as a pre-pack sku and is your computer first sku allocated and suggested for single line/single sku COs. After you receive single line/single sku COs, your pre-pack skus are picked first and assure good picker/packer productivity, increases your computer CO number and assure good inventory rotation.

PRE-PACK SKU FOR A SLAPPER DELIVERY ENVELOP/LABEL
 IMPROVE PICKER/PACKER PRODUCTIVITY & INCREASE COMPLETED CUSTOMER ORDER NUMBER
Pre-pack sku for a slapper delivery envelop/label as a slapper is reference to a small item or GOH warehouse pick and pack concept for single line/single sku COs to improve picker/packer productivity and increase your completed CO number. Your pre-pack sku number is based on your historical sales for a promotional sku single line/single sku COs. A pre-pack activity has 1 sku that is placed into a sealed ship container. A pre-pack activity starts with a sku bulk picked and delivered to a fast pack line or regular pack station. All completed pre-packed cartons are sealed ship containers and placed onto a pallet with a WMS ID that is placed/scanned to a WMS ID position. Sku quantity and scan data are sent to a WMS computer program for update. After your COs are received, for single line/single sku, your WMS computer program allocates and suggests a pre-pack sku on a pallet for your pick activity. Your CO pack slips/invoices and 1 loose sku are sent to scan station. At a scan station, for each CO pack slip/invoice an employee completes a scan transaction that depletes a sku from inventory and attaches a sku to a CO. A slapper sku components are sku in a sealed ship container and CO pack slip/invoice (a) in an envelope with several windows. An employee places sales literature and a CO pack slip/invoice with a customer delivery address in one window. Other windows have a sku pick position and CO ID. A completed slapper envelop is self-adhesive attached or glued to a ship container or (b) your sales literature and CO pack slip/invoice are place on a sku with a customer delivery address facing-up that is sent through a shrink wrapped tunnel to seal a CO pack slip/invoice to a ship container.

USE A SLAPPER ENVELOP/LABEL
 IMPROVE PICKER PRODUCTIVITY & INCREASE COMPLETED CUSTOMER ORDER NUMBER
Slap me is a small item or GOH warehouse pick concept that improves picker/packer productivity and increases completed CO number. When a sku is received in a vendor ready to ship carton or you pre-pack a sku into a ship carton, your pick/pack operation has an opportunity to use a slapper label on single line/single COs. For 'A' fast moving skus, after an employee with a sku sample and CO pack slips/invoices completes sku completes a sku association to a CO WMS ID and completes a sku pick transaction, an employee places a CO pack slip/invoice into a window envelop. A CO pack slip/invoice customer delivery address appears n an envelope window. Bulk picked skus and sealed slapper envelopes are delivered to a pack station. At a pack station, an employee peels off a

slapper envelop self-adhesive back or sends an envelope through a glue pot and places a slapper envelop with glue on to a ready to ship carton. With low volume skus, an employee places a CO pack slip/invoice into a slapper envelop with 3 windows. One window has a CO WMS ID, second window has a sku WMS ID pick position and third window has a sku WMS ID. At a pick position, a picker completes a sku pick transaction and CO WMS ID scan transaction to attach a WMS identified sku to a CO WMS ID and to complete a pick transaction. After an envelope self-adhesive back is removed and placed onto a vendor ready to ship carton, a labeled carton is placed onto a transport concept. Prior to implementation verify that your freight company can handle a slapper envelope.

WRAP & SLAP YOUR READY TO SHIP CARTON SKUS
IMPROVE PICKER PRODUCTIVITY & INCREASE COMPLETED CUSTOMER ORDER NUMBER

Wrap and slap is a small item ready to ship carton that is bulk picked and pack activity to improve picker/packer productivity and increase completed CO number. After a single line/single sku is bulk picked, a sku quantity is delivered to a wrap & pack station. Next, CO pack slips/invoices are delivered to a wrap & pack station. At a wrap & pack station, an employee pick scans sku WMS ID that completes a pick transaction in a WMS computer and scans a WMS ID sku to a WMS ID CO pack slip/invoice that attaches a sku to a WMS ID CO. Each scanned CO pack slip/invoice with required sales literature is placed onto a sku top. To assure security, a CO pack slip/invoice is printed or folded to show a customer delivery address. After a plastic sheet is place around a carton/CO pack slip/invoice and a sheets two ends overlap that are employee or machine attached with a tape, a completed wrapped carton is sent through a heat tunnel to shrink plastic onto a carton. With a plastic sheet, CO delivery label is secured onto a carton, a carton is sent to a manifest station. Prior to implementation, you test wrap & slap cartons with your freight company.

VALUE-ADDED SKUS
IMPROVED CUSTOMER SATISIFCATION

Value-added skus are skus per a CO has an additional activity that increases a sku value to a customer and satisfies a customer. A satisfied customer means a repeat customer.

MONOGRAM SKU HANDLING
IMPROVED CUSTOMER SATISIFCATION

Mono-gram sku handling is a value added activity for GOH or flat-wear skus. After a CO is received for a mono-gram added to a flat-wear or GOH sku, your WMS computer processes a CO as a single line/single sku CO. A picker completes a sku pick transaction and a picked sku is sent to a mono-gram activity station. At a mono-gram station, an employee verifies that a sku is per a CO and request mono-gram. After a mono-gram is added to a sku, a sku is package and sent to the ship conveyor.

GIFT WRAP SKU HANDLING
IMPROVED CUSTOMER SATISIFCATION

Gift wrap sku handling is a value added activity for any sku. After a CO is received for a gift wrap activity sku your WMS computer processes a CO as a single line/single sku CO. A picker completes a sku pick transaction and a picked sku is sent to a gift wrap activity station. At a gift wrap station, an employee verifies that a sku is per a CO & specific gift wrap type. After a sku is gift wrapped, a gift wrapped sku is packaged & sent to the ship conveyor.

LAY-AWAY
IMPROVED CUSTOMER SATISFCATION

Lay-away is an idea that improves customer satisfaction. Lay-away has a customer pre-order a sku and your operation is not required to ship a lay-away sku for several weeks or months such as Christmas Gifts that are to be reserved by your operation. With your WMS computer inventory program your options are (1) for a sku in WMS ID storage position, to place a sku quantity on hold as not available for sale status and schedule for release on a specific date and (2) to pick and transfer sku to a special temporary hold position and place sku quantity on hold as not available for sale status & (3) to pick and pack a sku and place in a temporary hold position and place sku quantity on hold as not available for sale status. The approaches delete your sku quantity available for sale and on an appropriate date to have skus status changed and complete a CO pick and pack activities.

SPECIFIC DELIVERY DATE
IMPROVED CUSTOMER SATISIFCATION

Specific delivery date is an idea that improves your customer satisfaction by assuring that a sku is delivered to a customer on specific date such as birthday or anniversary. With your WMS computer CO process program and CO pool classifications, your options are (1) to hold a CO in your CO pool and have your staff include a specific delivery date CO as part of a CO wave or (2) to pick and pack a CO and place CO container in a temporary hold position and place skus on hold and not available for sale. On a specific delivery date, your staff changes a sku status to available for sale and completes a CO ID and sku scan transaction and manifest activity.

GLOSSARY OF SELECT ABREVIATIONS AND TERMS USED

AS/RS	Automated Sort and Retrieval System
CO	Customer Order
FIFO	First In First Out
GOH	Goods on Hanger
HROS	high rise order system
ICC	Interstate Commerce Commission
jaggered	A saw-toothed configuration of flooring, conveyor, racking or other storage
JIT	Just In Time – replenishment or inventory strategy with low storage and high turns
P/D Station	Pick-up and Delivery Station
Pick-to-Light	System using light displays to direct operators to specific stock locations
RTV	Return to Vendor
RTS	Return to Stock
RF	Radio Frequency
SCAP	Sort Count And Pick
singulated	The process of arranging items in a one-at-a-time single file configuration also: process of communicating with a single RF tag in the presence of many tags
sku	Shelf Keeping Unit –
Stock-to-Light	System using light displays to direct operators to specific stock locations
UPH	units per hour
VNA	Very Narrow Aisle [forklift]
Walkie	A powered pallet mover with a walking, rather than rider, operator
WMS	Warehouse Management System

INDEX

A' moving skus
    Fixed or remain, 79
    How to identify, 8
    Multiple positions, 80
    Re-organize, 79
    Rotate, 79, 121
ABCD strategy, 100
Across-the-dock, 1
Pro-Active warehouse philosophy, 1
All eggs in one basket, 1
Aisle
    Adequate & width, 17, 46
    Identification, 39
    Staging lanes ends, 23
    Turning dimensions, 46
Automatic pick machines
    Gathering belt, 131
    Pick position, 131
    Pick pattern, 132
    Type, 131
Available for sale, 40
Average sku storage, 56

B

Backhaul, 10
Bag Types & selection factors, 146
Balance your activities, 168
Bar code
    Edges, 41
    Over-squared, 41
    Quiet zone, 41
    Transaction record, 30
Batched
    Customer orders, 127
        Last pick signal, 127, 130, 158
        Pick & sort imbalance plan, 128
        Pack slip/invoice, 128
        Identification, 129
    How to control, 129
    Transport concept, 129
    Pick, transport & sort, 159

Batteries when to change, 18
Belt conveyor, 50
Biggest bang for your buck, 2
Bridge
    Above doors, 25
    Dock gap, 22
Build or lease, 13, 185
Building columns
    Minimum, 11
    Where, 11, 73
Bulk pick
    'A' skus, 126, 153, 156
    By customer orders, 127
    By skus, 127
    Pick & sort, 126
    Pick, sort & final pick, 126
    Pick, sort & final GOH, 127
    Pick, transport & sort, 156
Bumpers, 19

C

Cafeteria size, 16
Call-in list, 6
Camera, 17
Cancel customer order, 2, 166
Caretaker, 1
Carousel
    Horizontal, 130
    Position slope & barrier, 93, 130
Carton or bag, 145
Carton flap, 123
Carton flow lane
    Carton AS/RS replenishment, 94
    Front end, 106
    Guides or no guides, 89, 90
    Impact bar, 90
    Jams & hang-up, 87
    Light displays, 106
    Look for jams, 89
    Mark carton widths, 90
    Rack bay, 106

Replenishment, 92
Three wheels or rollers, 90
Un-jam device, 89
Carton secure
Gummed or self-adhesive tape, 143
Human or machine tape, 143
Pre-made, 146
Tape strand width & length, 143
Types & selection factors, 142, 146
Carton size, 35
Computer or employee suggested, 140, 142
Change best time, 11
Clear height, 17
Cold start, 5, 95, 138
Colored caps, 166
Consignment sku, 79
Consolidate pick, 183
Conveyor shut no orders or skus, 14
Conveyor travel path
Downtime, 51
No queue, 51
Re-circulation, 51
Count by numbers, 27
Customer Order
Batched, 97
Bulk pick, 97
Captive tote identification location, 109
Carry-over, 95
Check activity, 134
Bad apples, 134
Check on the fly, 138
Goes out bad comes back, 134
High value skus, 136
Manual quantity, 137
Manual quantity & quality, 166
100%, 136
Problem orders, 135, 138
RF tag, 166
Random, 136
Return reasons, 135
Separate check or check & pack, 137
Stationary scale, 166
Suggested customer orders, 136
Completed customer order
Gap plate or different conveyor elevations, 123

Push off, 122
Take-away conveyor, 152
Delivery
Clock start, 157, 163
Cube, 163
Pack slips/invoice
Fold or do not fold, 140
Legend or sales literature, 140
Manual or mechanized insert, 144
On the floor, 96
Pre-printed or print on demand, 144
Printed with delivery label, 143
Printer considerations, 144
Slapper envelop, 150
Per tote one or multiple, 134
Pick/ship identification location, 109
Pool, 96
Who is first, 96
Reduce problems, 95
Separated by skus, 116
Sequenced by pick carton size, 115
Single, 97, 98
Types, 97
Wave, 96
Where to start, 113
Cube
Collection, 142
Know, 77
Master carton, 28
Sku, 28, 112
Customer is king, 6
Customer order
Delivery cycle time, 6
Wave pieces, 77
Customer service standard, 95
D
'D' moving sku
Picks, 101
Storage location, 59
Dated delivery sort, 166, 192
Dates
Julian, 26
Random, 26
Damaged sku, 178
Decline transport path, 49

Deck rack, 66
Deck rack floor level, 103
Delivery label window, 145
Delivery truck
  Arrival time, 60
  Back-up lane, 21
  Blind side, 19
  Block lock, 24
  Guide rails, 21
  Hold area, 20
  ICC bar 24
  Off-the road 20
  On-the road 20
  Side unload 22
  Turn, 19
Deposit
  Computer directed, 60
  Employee directed, 60
Detail count
  GOH, 39
  Small count, 39
  Master carton, 50
Did not sort, 167
Disposed sku
  Big/ugly, 178
  GOH rail layout, 181, 183
  Manual or mechanized sort, 179, 180
  Pre-sort, 178
  Pre-sort to temporary hold, 180
  RTS sent to pick position, 179, 182
  RTV by vendor name, 180, 183
  Transport sort & hold, 178
Dividers deck rack or shelf, 87
Dock
  Above staging lane storage, 25
  Blind staging lanes, 30
  Clear staging lane, 26
  Door protectors, 25
  Floor painted lines, 26
  One side, 21
  One truck, 22
  Open, 21
  To the truck yard, 23
  Seals, 24
  Shelter, 24

E
'E' Button, 44
  Cord, 44
  Door, 17
'E' S top line of sight, 44
Edible, 102
Electrical Back-up, 17
Employee reach height pallet. 31, 56
Electricity Sufficient, 12
80/20, 102
Employee Team, 4
  Are the key, 5
Empty tote or pallet, 125, 152
Exchange pallet, 10
Expenses
  Budgeted tie to productivity 8
  Fixed or variable 17

F
Faculty
  Gated, 2-1
  New or Existing, 12
Fans move air, 15
Fast pack
  By Carton size, 151
  By sku, 151
Fence me in, 13
FIFO, 81, 101
Filler material
  Do not over fill, 147
  Paper or peanuts, 147
  Paper roll or sheets, 148
  Plain or colored paper, 147
  Reserve locations, 149
  Re-supply, 148
  Types & selection factors, 147
  Where to store, 148
Fit around or in, 12
Flammable, 105
Floor
  Cracks, 17
  Dead level, 70
  Regular level, 70
  Shot the floor, 70

Flows
   Customer orders, 9
   Skus, 9
Forks
   Two long, 22
   Two wide, 22
Fork truck
   Turning aisle, 23
   Types, 74
Freight company pre-sort, 171
Freight company truck, 169

G
Gift wrap, 192
Glove, 123
GOH
   Aisle dust barrier, 64
   Automatic pick machines, 132
   Count, 39
   Bag bottom cut or tie, 63
   Bundles, 28
   Guards, 48, 76
   Hanger type, 64
   Manual pick, 132
   Rail type, 64
   SCAP concept, 64, 132
   Single or 3 piece pick, 132
   Sku types, 64
   Storage positions
      All are pickable, 66
      All the same height, 65
      Automatic or mechanized concepts, 64
      Convert to carton storage, 63
      Different heights, 65
      GOH hang in a cavity, 62, 63
      Identifications, 64
      One or two deep, 62, 64
      Separate storage & pick, 65
      Slide to rail rear or front, 63
      Tall or short, 62, 66
Golden highway, 102
Golden zone, 102
Good reads, 167
Guards, 188

H
Hand held scanner, 38
Have enough work, 4
How long, 17
How many reads, 160

I
Identification
   Attachment, 41
   Bar code, 36
   Directional arrows & colors, 39
   Directory or substitution, 43
   Floor stack, 43
   Front, 28, 38
   Human readable, 38
   Human/machine readable, 38
   Large or small, 40
   License plate, 121
   Machine readable, 38
   One for all, 26, 37
   One for one, 26, 37
   Plain or coated, 41
   Sequence vertical, 39
   Side, 28
   Special, 26
   Storage position 39
   Type, 36
Incline master carton travel path, 49
Induction
   Side by side, 160
   Single or dual, 160, 165
   Sku delivery, 159
   Types & selection factors, 159
Inventory
   Average, 55
   Small quantity, 59
   Moving average, 55
   Old
      How to identify, 58
      How to scrap, 59
      How to store, 57
      What is it, 57

J

K
Kiss it, 108
Know your
    Promotional sku, 8
    Sku size, 13

L
Labor productivity
    Daily, 7
    Detail, 7
    Man-hours, 7
Lay-away, 192
Light fixture
    On-off, 75
        Activity areas, 14
        Café area, 15
    Docks,
    Location where, 16, 74, 112, 138. 141, 188
Liquid run-off, 75
Listen, watch, work with employees, 4
Load
    Unitize or direct load, 169, 205
Load beam type, 41
Load conveyor queue, 168
Look at
    Today & prepare for tomorrow, 4
    Your numbers & employees, 4

M
Manifest
    At delivery truck door, 165
    Hand held scanner, 165
    Off load & manifest, 166
    Send to freight company, 166
    Transaction on-line or delay, 166
Manufacturer lot number, 102, 183
Master carton
    Do not oversize, 77
Mats, 16, 123
Mechanized sorters
    Bags or cartons, 165
    Types & selection factors, 164
Mechanized pick concepts, 132
Minimize peaks & valleys, 4
Mirrors safety, 48

Missiles stop, 75, 103
Monogram, 192

N
Narrow aisle forklift truck, 51
Nets, 76, 161
No data, 166
No read, 166
No stock, 79
Not available for sale, 40

O
Objectives set & define, 5
Off-site
    Fast pack, 186
    Floor stack or rack, 187
    Floor/rack storage, 187
    Fork truck
        Types & selection factors, 188
        Notch masts, 190
    How to work, 186
    Pyramid floor stack, 188
    Receive where, 185
    Remains out or cross dock, 187
    Rework, 187
    Scrap, 186
    Ship supply storage, 187
    Single deep or dense storage, 187
    Single sku or Big/ugly, 187, 188
    Sku candidates, 186, 186
    Tent on slab, 185
    Two high on the floor, 188
Open carton, 116
Operational factors, 17
Occupancy rate
    Position, 56
    Total, 56
Overtime in morning or afternoon, 4

P
Pack table
    Divert to 151
        Divert & decline, 151
        Divert & incline, 151
        Packer transfers, 151

Shelves, 151
Surface, 141
Package appearance, 137
Pairs, 81, 101, 102
Pallet flow lane guards & stops, 90
Pallet truck
  Backrest, 48
  Pull or push, 46
  Ride in front or rear, 46, 47, 48
  Walk or ride, 48
Pallets
  Damage or wrong, 35, 57
  Do not double stack, 35, 57
  Empty
    How many, 32
    Where to locate, 32
Parallel or perpendicular layout, 103
Pareto's law, 100
Part-time employees use & schedule, 5
Peel-off label, 142
Pebble in a pond, 3
People path, 47
People path colors, 47
Pickable or non-pickable, 182
Pick aisle
  Clear, 112
  Do not liter, 112
  Lights, 112
Pick and sort, 98
Pick area
  Cross aisle, 103
  Layout & philosophy, 99
Pick cart
  Caster/wheels, 110
    All swivel. 110
    Swivel in front, 110
  Match to pick concept, 110
  Multi shelves, 111
  Pick front face, 111
  Rear & side nets, 110
Pick cartons empty, 96, 98
Pick cell, 103, 143, 119
Pick clean, 80
Pick conveyor
  Frame edge & guards, 121

Pick zone control, 122
  Set high or low, 152
  Skate wheel or roller, 121
Pick HROS vehicle
  Aisle end slow down, 112
  Aisle guidance, 112
  Pick cart or cage, 112
Pick into small cartons, 115
Pick instruction
  Components, 104
  Kiss it, 108
  Paper document
    Fast skus at the top, 107
    Sku number, 107
  Paper or paperless, 105
  Pick by light, 105
Pick labels
  Holder, 107
  Rolls or sheets, 107
Pick line
  Congestion, 114
  Cycle pickers, 123
  Mirrored, 119
  1, 2 or 3 lines, 128
  Set-up, 101
Pick position
  All occupied, 79
  Capacity, 79
  Float or fixed, 113
  Height, 103, 114
  Identification location, 108
  Lowest, 104
  Master carton narrow face, 78
  Mixes skus in totes, 98
  One or two skus, 59
  Over & under pick conveyor, 118
  Set-up, 98
  Small skus, 98
Pick their minds, 3
Pick train, 143, 119
Pick transaction communication, 96
Pick zone
  Fixed & variable, 123
  Start & end flags, 123
Picker

Clip, 123
Clip board, 99
Height increase, 115
Routing 113
   Block, 114
   Drawer front to rear, 113
   Evens on right odds on left, 113
   Horizontal or vertical, 143
   Horseshoe or 'U', 113
   HROS, 113
   Loop, 113
   Non-sequential, 113
   Sequential, 113
   Sku identification number, 113
   Stitch, 114
   Z, 114
  Walk in pick line, 125
Pigeon hole, 104
Powered truck controls, 48
Pre-pack, 191
  Complete, 150
  Partial, 149
  Slapper label, 191, 192
  Wrap & slap, 192
Prime real estate, 103
Printer
  Capacity, 106
  Problems, 145
Profile, 82, 96, 100
  ABCD, 100
  80/20, 102
  Golden highway, 102
  Golden zone, 102
  Pairs, 101
  Prime real estate, 103
  Random, 102
Promotional
  Front aisle locations, 56
  One pack station, 152
  Sku storage, 56
Protective noise covers, 161

Q
QA sample size, 31

R
Rain stop. 21
Receiving office, 39
Recycle trash, 177
Repetitive activities, 4
Replenishment
  Automatic pick machine, 85
  Before pick activity, 85
  Carton AS/RS, 94
  Directed
    Computer, 78, 82
    Employee, 78, 82
  Employee reach top position, 91
  Errors, 78
  Extra skus, 86
    Where to place, 86
  Full pallet first, 84
  Human or AS/RS crane, 92
  How much, 85
  How to reach top position, 91
  Identification, 92
  Master carton
    Conveyor travel direction, 92
    Exact, 82
    From pallet, 88
    No master carton flaps, 88
    Round-down, 82
    Round-up, 82
    When to cut master carton, 87
  Pallet AS/RS or VNA forklift truck direct, 93
  Partial pallet first, 84
  Position routing, 83
  Quantity,
    All, 84
    Sections, 84
  Record transactions, 83
  Remove filler material, 88
  Save & reuse to flaps, 87
  Signal, 81, 85
  Smiley face, 87
  To
    Carousel basket, 93
    Pallet, 93
    Shelf, decked rack, peg board, drawer, slide, 93
  Tools, 81

Transaction commands
   Delayed, 80
   On-line, 72
  When & how, 83
  Where to transfer master cartons, 92
Returns
  Address, 171
  Age, 172
   Racks In staging area, 172
Rework, 35
  Disposition label, 176
  Dock arrangement, 172
  Employee sits or stands, 174
  FIFO rotation, 182
  Label, 171
  Look-up table, 174
  Non-deliverable, 173
  One station, 174
  Problem returns, 177
  Production line, 174
  Separate, 172
   Big/ugly, 173
   High value. 173
  Track reasons, 173
  Transport to first station, 174

S

Scale count, 40
Scan do not read, 5
Scanner
  Battery or DC cord, 143
  Cord length, 38
  Default as one, 38, 176
  Depth of field, 38
  Fixed position, 143, 176
  Gun or contact, 40
  Replacement part or space scanner
  Transaction update, 38
  Side or overhead, 164
  Wide Beam, 176
Scrap
  What is it, 18
  Where to place it, 18
Seconds & minutes count, 7
Ship label, 163

Short interval schedule, 3
Single commands, 60
Slapper label, 149, 150
Slip sheet
  Back stop, 29
  Delivery, 29
  How to handle, 59
Sku
  As individual master cartons, 28, 31
  As pallet, 28, 31
  Bagged, loose, bins, 81
  Delivery, 28
  Get to know, 28
  Hit concentration & density
  Hold in staging area, 30
  How to hold, 30
  Life cycle, 55
  Location on pick line, 99
  Mixed or separate, 114
  Small in & old consolidation, 81
  One slot or double slots, 78
  Overhang, 59
  Piece count, 39
  Pre-inspect, 39
  Received where to go, 28
  Rejected skus, 31
  Signal when ready, 30, 36
  Small counted in bags, 40
  Tag, 26
  When to move, 58
  Where to move, 58
Small items
  Manual pick, 104
  Pick and pass, 143
Smaller is sometimes better, 9
Sort 153
  By sku, 154
  Customer order identification, 156
  Instructions, 154, 155
  Number sequence, 156
  Pick & sort, 154
  Sku digits, 155, 188, 165
  Types & selection factors, 153
Sort travel path height, 158, 160
  Straight line or re-circulations, 161

One direction or two directions, 162
Sort lanes
   Controls 162
   Sort lanes, 162
   3 sort lanes, 162
      Side by side, 167
      Over & under, 167
   Window, 162
Stage floor stack or racks, 170
Staging lanes side by side, 23
Stock out, 70
Store & hold, 1
Storage
   Area turning aisles, 73
   Bridges, 69
   Floor level 1 or 2 high, 68
   Highest level
      Gets warm, 67
      Security, 67
   How your sku faces, 67
   Lock your pallet, 67
   Narrow aisle truck up & over, 69
   One, two or three wide, 68
   Philosophy, 57
   Position number sequence, 68
   Remote or ready reserve, 68
   Stack your non-stackables, 68
   Two tall on the floor, 68
Surges know, 9
Symbology
   Human readable, 30
   Human readable on bottom, 30
   Human readable on top, 30
   Human/machine readable, 30
   Pick positions, 108

T

Temperature dock, 24
Tent on slab, 184
Tie vehicles to batteries, 18
Transaction number storage, 62
Transport
   Conveyor, 43
   Design parameters, 51
   Location, 51
   One pallet or two pallets, 45
   Trip time, 51
   Vehicle, 43
Trash cartons no flaps, 133
Trash container or conveyor, 94, 133

Travel distance & productivity, 104
Travel path
   Closed loop, 45
   Elevation change & curve, 44
   Fixed or variable, 46
   One-way or two-way, 47

U

Unload pallets, cartons, GOH, 32
Unload queue, 172
Unitize onto carts, 168, 169
Unitize onto pallets, 169

V

Value added, 192
Vendor ready to ship, 149
   How to convert, 8
   Vendor wraps, 8
Very narrow aisle forklift truck
   Above P/D station, 52
   Do not turn a load in an aisle, 71
   Driver travel direction, 73
   Guided or non-guided, 71
   How to slow down, 72
   Man-up or man-down, 72, 73
   P/D station
      Activity, 70
      Aisle width, 51, 55
      Fork truck deposit, 53
   Paint strip on your
      Forks, 73
      Load beams, 73
   Restrict employee from an aisle, 76
   Rub bar & back stop, 53
   Truck features, 74
   Turn a load in an aisle, 70
   Types, 52, 55

W

Walls minimal, 12
Warehouse management system, 9
Warm start, 6, 95, 168
What has to be done first, 6
What is time critical, 6
Where are your in & out, 13
Where can you have extra time, 2
Where does it count, 2
Who is first
   Receiving or pick/pack, 2
   Warehouse or WMS, 10
Wide aisle forklift truck, 51
Withdrawal transactions, 59
Window

Receiving door, 24
   Travel path, 43
Work station, 141
WMS, 9, 26
WMS & warehouse tie knot, 10

X

Y

Z
Zero scan, 80, 142
Zone skip, 163

About the Authors

David E. Mulcahy

David Mulcahy is a speaker, a consultant, a magazine contributing author and the author or co-author of multiple essential reference books on warehouse management including:

- *Warehouse Distribution & Operations Handbook,*
- *Materials Handling Management,*
- *Order Fulfillment And Across The Dock Operations Concepts, Designs And Operations Handbook,*
- *Eaches And Pieces Order Fulfillment Design And Operations Handbook*
- *A Supply Chain Logistics Program For Warehouse Management.*

While working with the AMWAY Corporation, Mr. Mulcahy participated as a project manager for the design, build, install and start-up for order fulfillment operations in Japan, Korea, Taiwan, New Zealand, Australia, China, UK, Italy and Germany. These include 'pick to light' concepts as well as wire guided VNA storage vehicles with tall racks. He was also involved with the re-model for operations in Spain, Netherlands, Mexico, Canada and European Central Warehouses.

As a QVC project manager Mr. Mulcahy was involved with the remodel of QVC's Germany operation to increase storage capacity, improve picker, sort and packer productivity (UPH) and lower operational expenses (CPU) and in QVC's Japan operation to optimize off-site storage activity, improve space utilization, lower CPU and improve picker, sort and packer productivity (UPH). In the QVC Japan operation, the results of Mr. Mulcahy's efforts helped QVC Japan to achieve a positive cash flow within 3 years of startup. For both QVC Germany and Japan operations, Mr. Mulcahy was a key associate in completing site selection and overall warehouse operation design with a Carton and Pallet AS/RS, GOH trolley-less, tilt tray sorter, pick to light, customer returns conveyor concepts and extensive conveyor network and the WMS program written functional specifications.

For Peter J Schmitt, Buffalo, NY, Mr. Mulcahy consolidated two warehouse operations into one facility, improved the facility maintenance and sanitation rating to the top in the region and improved space utilization.

For A & P Tea Co., Dallas, TX Mr. Mulcahy consolidated a small item warehouse into the main warehouse, improved picker productivity and delivery truck utilization. Improvements resulted in raising the division's operational ranking from number 26th to 6th nationally.

Most recently Mr. Mulcahy has also provided his services for the non-profit community.
Mr. Mulcahy received his MBA from the University Of Dallas, Texas. In 1981 Mr. Mulcahy designed a multi-layer case selection concept that won a 1981 Materials Handling Institute award at that year's Material Handling Show.

Steven D. Ritchey

Steven Ritchey is a Consultant, Entrepreneur and Integrated Marketing Professional.
He holds a Bachelors Degree from Cornell University and an MBA from The Whitman School of Management at Syracuse University. Syracuse University's Whitman School is also home to the Salzberg Memorial Program in Transportation, The Franklin Center for Supply Chain Management and the Brethen Operations Management Institute., This is Mr. Ritchey's first book. Mr. Ritchey's expertise is in Management and Marketing with a particular strength in coordinating the rapid growth associated with successful new product introductions, marketing ventures and Direct Response programs.

While at Marietta Corp., in the 1980's up until his departure as his division's Vice President, Marketing, Mr. Ritchey's division (formerly Marietta Packaging) delivered 7 consecutive years of organic sales growth ranging from 20-40+% annually. After attaining his MBA, Mr. Ritchey worked in the nascent Television Infomercial industry for Quantum Marketing (later merged into National Media). Mr. Ritchey was a co-owner and served as Vice President and Chief Operating Officer of King Media Inc a Direct response Marketing Agency. While with King he oversaw numerous client's product & service introductions and managed programs from business segments as far flung as insurance, financial services, Kitchen products, exercise equipment, cosmetic, household goods, self-help programs, new home sales, supplements, security systems, music, and surgical procedures.

As a consultant, Mr. Ritchey has advised clients on a variety of integrated marketing campaigns, advanced web 2.0 & social media, online marketing programs, and conducted a variety of proprietary brand, market, and business development projects.

Mr. Ritchey serves on the Board of Trustees for the non-profit *Adelphic Cornell Educational Fund.* At the time of this writing he serves as its President. He is active as a Cornell University Class Officer. Mr. Ritchey is also active in his Church where he has served as a Ruling Elder and an Executive Committee advisor.

NOTES

NOTES

CPSIA information can be obtained at www.ICGtesting.com
Printed in the USA
LVOW031203180312

273594LV00003B/11/P